medieval

women

writers

Medieval Women Writers

EDITED BY
KATHARINA M. WILSON

THE UNIVERSITY OF GEORGIA PRESS   ATHENS

Copyright © 1984 by the University of Georgia Press
Athens, Georgia 30602
All rights reserved

Designed by Francisca Vassy
Set in 10 on 12 Sabon
Printed in the United States of America

89   5   4   3

Library of Congress Cataloging in Publication Data

Main entry under title:

Medieval women writers.

Includes bibliographical references.
1. Literature, Medieval. 2. European literature—Women
authors. I. Wilson, Katharina.
PN 667.M43 1984   808.8'99287   82-13380
ISBN 0-8203-0640-1
ISBN 0-8203-0641-X (pbk.)

contents

[handwritten annotation: contrast w/ marie de France]

vi   CONTENTS

Compare

íntroöuctíon

KATHARINA M. WILSON

The observations that during the Middle Ages few women were literate and that the bulk of medieval literature was written by men and for men have so often been reiterated that they have become axiomatic.[1] These assertions, correct by themselves, are reinforced by the phenomenon of what an eminent comparatist appropriately termed "literary provincialism": restrictions imposed on what we read and what we study, frequently prescribing "an arbitrary, unexamined, often unimaginative canon of standard authors."[2] Yet, however much outnumbered by men and however much excluded from the literary canon, women did write in the Middle Ages and did offer their perceptions of reality both secular and religious.

This volume will introduce the reader to some of the outstanding women writers of the Middle Ages.[3] Their works, offered here in fifteen selections, span seven centuries (the ninth through the fifteenth), eight languages (Latin, Italian, French, Spanish, Dutch, Provençal, German, and English), and ten regions or nationalities (Frankish, Saxon, Brabantian, French, English, Spanish, Swedish, Occitanian, German, and Italian).[4]

While some of the writers presented here are little read today, this has not always been the case, nor is it the case everywhere even today.[5] Rather, the patterns of their literary fortunes parallel the periodic fluctuations of literary taste and literary patronage; their fall into oblivion in countries other than their own reflects the growing problem of monolingualism and linguistic nationalism. To illustrate: many of these women enjoyed contemporary patronage and subsequent popularity. Hrotsvit was encouraged in her literary endeavors by her abbess, certain learned men, and the royal family, and for the German humanists of the Renaissance her compositions were brilliant manifestations of the glorious Teutonic past. Marie's lais delighted counts, barons, knights, and ladies during her lifetime and were translated into Old Norse, Middle English, Middle High German, Italian, and Latin during the Middle Ages.[6] Hildegard's works were highly regarded during her lifetime, and popes, emperors, and kings sought her intelligent counsel—the breadth of her international correspondence is reflected in her 145 letters printed in the *Patrologia Latina*. Marguerite's *Mirror* and Bridget's revelations are preserved in a number of manuscripts and translations, attesting to the widespread medieval and Renaissance popularity of the texts.[7] And the works of Christine de Pizan, the lady with "the golden pen," were not only highly acclaimed by her French contemporaries but were translated into English at the request of Henry VII.[8]

Similarly, while some of the writers included in this volume are recognized, taught, and anthologized in their own countries, they are often inaccessible to students elsewhere. Hadewijch, to take the most obvious example, is taught in Flemish and Dutch classrooms, but she is little known to students of literature in the English-speaking countries.[9]

Lack of editions does not account for the general paucity of interest in medieval women writers. In England, for instance, thanks to the efforts of the Early English Text Society, the works of women writers are published in good editions, as are the Latin texts of women from various countries in the extensive collections of the *Patrologia Latina*, the *Corpus Christianorum*, and the *Monumenta Germaniae Historica*. The complete works of Marie, Florencia Pinar, and Mechthild and parts of Christine's and Catherine's works are available in good or at least adequate editions, and further editions are forthcoming.

Literary canonization, however, does not thrive on good editions alone; it thrives on anthologization, translation, inclusion in college or high school curriculums, and critical acclaim, often reflected in the sheer bulk of allotted space in literary histories. Thus, while Julian's and Margery's works are available in good editions and while linguistically they are no less accessible than the texts of their contemporaries, Julian is discussed only in a short paragraph in the fourteen-volume *Cambridge History of English Literature* and Margery is not even mentioned.[10]

The selection process that often excludes women writers from the canon is not necessarily sexist. Regardless of the sex of the author or even the literary quality of the work, editors do not generally consider such viewpoints as orthodox Catholicism (as with Hildegard), monastic or eremitic contemplation (as with Julian), devout reflection and overt didacticism (as with Hrotsvit), and conformist religiosity (even when coupled with a plea for Church reform and chastisement of clerical corruption, as with Mechthild, Bridget, and Catherine) to appeal as much to modern tastes as the more unusual expressions of a rebellious, nonconformist spirit.[11] In fact, in the spheres of mystical and spiritual poetry as well as devotional writings, the literary achievements of women have rarely been questioned on grounds other than orthodoxy. Rather, it is the genres themselves and the spirit that pervades them that seem to have fallen into disfavor.

To some degree, exclusion from the canon results from women writers' being obscured rather than scorned: there is safety in numbers, and undoubtedly there were more men than women writing in the Middle Ages. Thus, for example, Florencia Pinar's poems are almost lost in the many volumes of *cancioneros* written by men, and Hrotsvit's eight legends are but a drop in the vast sea of hagiographic literature.

Who, then, were the women who wrote successfully and well in the Middle Ages? Our sources for their biographies are scarce and often unreliable. Concerning those women who were canonized (or were intended for canonization) by the Church, we have the *Protocolla canonizationis*, transcripts that present evidence in a schematized narrative, often embellished with apocryphal and hagiographic ornaments, thus tending often to obscure rather than illuminate the personality of the woman by mingling legend, fact, and fancy. Concerning women accused of heresy, we possess some inquisitorial records that, however, are frequently a patchwork of stereotyped accusations and even stereotyped testimony. For ladies of high birth, we have occasional *vitae* and court records, but for those writers neither sainted nor persecuted nor royal, biographic evidence usually had to be extracted from their works alone. For a detailed historic and literary background to these works, the reader is referred to the individual introductions; we shall, however, venture upon a few general observations here.

For medieval women as well as men, literary productivity goes hand in hand with the opportunity for education, at least a modicum of scholarly idleness, access to materials needed for her work, some financial independence, patronage in social, religious, or financial form, and (sometimes in lieu of all of the above) religious or political zeal. With women writers, an added prerequisite often entails the freedom from repeated pregnancies and childbearing.[12] This combination of prerequisites was most likely to occur in the convents of the early and central Middle Ages. During the twelfth and thirteenth centuries the locations also included the flourishing courts of princes and the Beguine communities; still later, the secular environment of the rising bourgeoisie was another, less important factor.

Consequently, the distribution of the writers included here reflects shifts across national boundaries and chronological periods. Most of the cultural, religious, and literary movements of the Middle Ages produced at least one representative among women writers, but it is in the religious, didactic, and visionary genres that women writers especially prevail, and it is here that their contributions are generally recognized.

While it is pleonastic to call any particular corpus of medieval European literature religious, since, as Eric Colledge observes, "there is none which does not in some way reflect the all-pervading teachings of the Christian faith," the accidentals (setting, patronage, dissemination) of literary productivity do vary.[13] For women, the religious setting of literary productivity in the early Middle Ages was particularly predominant; it resulted not only from the Church's monopoly on education, its cohesive power as a social, political, and cultural institution, and its patronage of much of medieval art but also, and equally importantly, from the ecclesiastic assessment of the estate of women.[14] Most medieval writers considered women as a separate estate in the ecclesiastical and social models, liable, like the other estates, to hierarchical divisions.[15] Women, unlike men, were often categorized by marital status (wives, widows, virgins), with clearly delineated social and religious differences among the three groups.[16] According to ecclesiastical ideology, the virginal life was placed at the pinnacle of excellence in the hierarchy of values, followed, respectively, by widowhood and marriage;[17] in the social model, on the other hand, the heir-producing marital state was deemed highest, followed by widowhood and spinsterhood.[18] These hierarchical divisions of the estate of women as well as their religious affiliation played a role in determining their possible literary endeavors, for until the late Middle Ages, aside from a small number of aristocratic ladies, women in holy orders (that is, chaste single women) were the only recipients of education and the only women for whom literacy was deemed paramount.[19]

Christianity (as defined by the New Testament) and Christianization (as formulated by the subsequent disseminators of the faith) occasioned some change in the status of women, even though no radical revision in the existing social order was effected. Thus, while the New Testament asserts the spiritual equality of both sexes (1 Pet. 3:7; Gal. 3:28), contemporary social customs are reflected in scriptural injunctions concerning female subservience (1 Tim. 2) and in the Church Fathers' repeated exhortations to women to remain submissive to their husbands.[20] Similarly, while attracting and engaging women in large numbers, Christianity followed the Hebrew precedent by excluding them from the ecclesiastical hierarchy (1 Cor. 14:34–35; 1 Tim. 2:12–15).

What Christianity did introduce, however, was a new moral-religious ideal, that of chastity, which was accessible to both sexes. Thus, a life of virginal consecration became open to women (through which they could become men's equals), providing a respected career opportunity for single women and widows whose aspirations were not exhausted by or directed toward the role of mother and wife.[21] It was Saint Jerome, the most influential of the patristic writers, who formulated this opportunity most succinctly by suggesting that through virginity woman can rise above her native position and become like man.[22] Unfortunately, upholding the bilateral chaste ideal not only denied the inherent necessity of traditional sex roles but also epitomized the virtue of overcoming sex. This, in turn, often resulted in the degradation of women, particularly of secular women, because in the ideology of a male-ruled world at whose pinnacle of excellence chastity was placed, woman then became a dangerous temptress representing lust and carnality.[23]

In the initial centuries of Christianity (first through fourth), especially those preceding the acceptance of Christianity as the state religion of the Roman Empire, women played an important part in the young religion. As a corollary to the proposed religious equality of the sexes, women were allowed to participate in Church activities: they assisted the apostles, spread the new faith, suffered martyrdom in large numbers, and held respected positions in the Church, even though they were excluded from the priesthood.[24] But with the heterodox cults, women could achieve positions of leadership: the Montanist sect, for instance, encouraged prophecies by women, and among Gnostic groups women were allowed to preach and to teach.[25]

During the centuries of Christianization (fifth through ninth), women, again, were given important religious roles. In fact, the conversion of many a Germanic tribe is attributed to a Christian princess.[26] Convents and abbeys of the early Middle Ages (that is, following the periods of conversion) were flourishing centers of culture and learning, and abbesses wielded great influence—frequently they even ruled double monasteries (joint foundations for men and women).[27] From the eighth century on, however, the supervision of nuns was increasingly placed in the hands of men, and double monasteries were gradually abolished.[28]

The first Germanic tribes to become Christian were the Goths in the fourth and the Franks in the sixth century, followed by the Visigoths and the Anglo-Saxons in the seventh. It was not until the eighth century, however, that a Frankish dynasty openly cultivated Christianity as a means of strengthening itself. "It was the pious Carloman," as Henry Lea remarks, "who first saw clearly how necessary was the aid of the church in any attempt to introduce civilization and subordination among his turbulent subjects."[29] It was under Charlemagne, finally, that religion and learning became important organizational and administrative tools of the state. Charlemagne not only brought order to a "semi-barbarous" Europe, but he "revised the late Roman ideal of an Empire that was also a Christian society."[30]

Quite appropriately, then, the first writer presented in this volume is the late Carolingian Frankish Dhuoda. Ensconced in her castle and deserted by her husband, she wrote a religious manual for her son in the fifth decade of the ninth century. Dhuoda's preoccupation with etymologies and with the symbolic values of words and numbers is a typical expression of the Carolingian Renaissance, as is her relentless search for transcendental meaning in everything; but as a lay author in a literary world of clerics, she is also an enigma of her age.

While during the ninth century the Rhinelands and northern France were the political and cultural centers of the West, in 919, with the accession of Henry the Fowler to the throne, the political center shifted to Saxony, and by the close of the reign of Henry's son Otto I, the social and cultural centers were also there. Centralization and political expansion were the chief aims of the Ottos, who viewed themselves as cultural and political heirs to Charlemagne's empire. Intent on fostering a flourishing cultural and religious life in Germany, the Saxon dynasty and the Saxon nobles showed a predilection for establishing and maintaining religious houses (the larger number of which were houses for canonesses and nuns) that were famed for their high standards of learning.[31] One of the foremost of these foundations, Gandersheim, housed the second author presented here, Hrotsvit: poet, dramatist, and historian. Hrotsvit, like Dhuoda, both exemplifies her milieu and shows remarkable originality.[32] As a noble canoness of a Saxon imperial abbey, she shows a marked preoccupation with the Byzantine- and Frankish-oriented tastes and interests of the imperial family as well as with the monastic ideal: Byzantine legends constitute a large part of her hagiographic themes; Otto I and Otto II are the subject of her historic narrative. Her dramas, on the other hand, stand as unique literary accomplishments of the tenth century and precede the rise of Western Church drama by at least one and a half centuries.

While the Carolingian and Ottonian periods were but brief bursts of cultural activity, the Renaissance of the twelfth century witnessed major, sweeping, and widely dispersed changes: the bloom of vernacular literature, the rise of the universities, the continued flourishing of Latin literature, the recovery and assimilation of a large part of Greek and Arabic philosophy and science, and the emergence of the phenomenon of courtly love.[33] It also saw the rise of feudal states, the strengthening of sovereign power, and the flourishing of intellectual and cultural activity at the courts of princes as well as in convents and monasteries. But the twelfth-century Renaissance was not merely a burgeoning of secular activities but also an explosion of ascetic, reforming, and militant zeal: it witnessed the formation of new orders, the rise of dualist heresies, the struggle between Church and state, and the fervor of the crusades. Finally, it was during the twelfth century that the cult of the Virgin Mary blossomed to its full in the adoration of the sublime and transcendental, yet also human, motherhood of the Virgin. Important for the history of the literary activity of women, the twelfth century, as Joan Ferrante observes, was also the period when the production of manuscripts began to flourish in some convents. The arts of copying and illuminating were fervently pursued by nun-scribes, of whom several are known by name from the twelfth century on.[34]

The wealth and variety of literary productivity in the twelfth century are reflected in our selection of women writers who, varied indeed, represent some of the cultural currents of this early Renaissance. The courtly and secular Marie de France exemplifies vernacular romance literature at its best as it flourished at the court of Henry II and Eleanor of Aquitaine at the time when the *trobairitz*, or women troubadours, of Occitania composed vernacular love lyrics in the courtly tradition.[35] The erudite scientist-mystic-dramatist-composer Hildegard of Bingen, writing in Latin, stands as an exponent of Christian philosophy and staunch orthodoxy; she is an important forerunner of the mystic literature that was to thrive in Germany during the thirteenth century. Finally, Heloise, pupil, mistress, wife, and religious disciple (in that order) of one of the foremost scholars of the new intellectual movement in France, exhibits in all her Latin writings a thorough knowledge of the classics and the art of dialectic.[36]

The thirteenth and fourteenth centuries were marked by the renewal of religious fervor, with its attendant heterodox manifestations in contemporary heresies, and the rise of the Beguine movement. It was also the golden age of mysticism. In the secular sphere these centuries produced an avalanche of courtly and romance literature coexisting and sometimes interacting with religious writings. The fourteenth century was also the epoch of the catastrophic sweep of the Black Death through Europe, resulting in a demographic collapse and the economic and political crises in its aftermath.

Renewed religious fervor in both its orthodox and heterodox forms was enthusiastically espoused by women, and representatives of the whole range of ideas can be found among them. This is hardly surprising, for most medieval heresies, as Robert Lerner observes, were not cultural anomalies but "grew out of concern for a life of spiritual perfection" and the desire to follow the apostolic life with great urgency.[37]

The heretical movements of the central and later Middle Ages (especially the Waldenses, Cathars, the adherents of the Free Spirit, and later the Lollards and Hussites), like the heterodox sects of the patristic age, not only attracted many women but granted them important positions in their religious hierarchies.[38] Among the Waldenses and Cathars, for instance, women were allowed to preach and could attain clerical posts; like men they could attain the *consolamentum* (be counted among the perfected).[39] Some sects even assigned women a quintessential role in salvation: the Pseudo-Amalrican women of the thirteenth century, for example, believed (according to their opponents) themselves to be incarnations of the Holy Ghost. As such they considered themselves no longer capable of sin, thus having no need of the sacraments.[40] And, for the Guglielmites (a thirteenth-century sect named for their leader, Guglielma of Milan), women were humanity's only hope of salvation. They maintained that "only with the advent of a female church ruled by a female pope and female cardinals would salvation be possible"[41] and that Guglielma's friend and future pope, Manfreda, would successfully convert the Jews and the Muslims and thus initiate a new epoch.[42]

At first, the Church was lenient toward the sporadic outbursts of heresies,[43] but as they spread and became progressively anticlerical, several ecumenical councils were held to anathematize heretics and to establish tenets of orthodoxy; finally, in 1209, Pope Innocent III proclaimed the Albigensian crusade to eradicate heresy.[44] Among the early apologists of unflinching orthodoxy stands Hildegard of Bingen, one of the writers presented here; unswerving and passionate, she denounced Cathar heresy as the work of the devil.

The thirteenth century was characterized by the demographic imbalance of the sexes, attributed to the large number of men who died in the crusades—the disastrous third crusade (1189–1192) seems to have claimed a particularly great number of lives—as well as the large number of men who were professed in orders or were priests. This imbalance continued to exist and became an acute social and economic problem.[45] Nubile women by far outnumbered men, and society had few provisions for their welfare. Some joined convents, but many could not afford the dowries required for entry; some supported themselves by manual labor as well as they could; some joined heretic sects; and many formed Beguine communities.[46]

The lay religious movement of the Beguines commenced in the thirteenth century in the Low Countries and spread over the Rhinelands and northern and southern France. Beguines and Beghards lived in self-supporting communities, following the apostolic life without, however, professing a common rule or formal monastic vows. In imitation of Christ, they dedicated their lives to chastity, poverty, penance, prayer, and work among the sick and the needy.[47] Since they were not officially sanctioned by the Church, their religious enthusiasm and their prophetic gifts seldom received official approbation from the ecclesiastic hierarchy; they were often mocked for excessive piety and viewed with skepticism.[48] To the great concern of the Church hierarchy, many Beguines are reported to have had visions of an impending third age in which the Holy Ghost would be incarnate in a woman,[49] and the heresy of the Free Spirit appears to have found numerous adherents among them. According to this heresy, men and women could attain perfection on earth—a perfection which was a personal and direct relationship between God and the virtuous soul, thus rendering the mediation of the Church unnecessary.[50] The Church was not alone in distrusting the Beguines; the guilds, too, found them objectionable. For the guilds, Beguines constituted competition—some said unfair competition—since they were exempt from taxes.[51]

The third movement that marked the thirteenth and fourteenth centuries, mysticism, though not invented then, flourished at its fullest in the thirteenth. In their self-oblivious quest for union with God and transcending temporal categories of understanding, mystics experience and intuit the love of God and his divine mysteries. With a penchant for allegory, they relate their revelations in intense, dramatic, and often erotic imagery. In this sphere women writers are represented most profusely, and here their literary accomplishments are generally acclaimed. "It is to women," Peter Dronke observes, "that we owe some of the highest flights of mystical poetry in the Middle Ages."[52]

Women writers thrived in the secular sphere as well. Commencing in the twelfth and extending into the thirteenth century, there flourished in Occitania the *trobairitz*, of whom some twenty are known by name.[53] Almost all were members of the nobility; most were married; all conformed to the poetic conventions of the troubadour lyrics, but many provided different focuses on and insights into the conventional themes.

In our text, these movements are represented by eight women, all composing their works in the vernacular. The heretical and Beguine movements are represented by Marguerite Porete, who was burned at the stake for refusing to recant the tenets of her heterodox ideas, which included a seven-step ascent to divine mercy (the last two steps of which brought one to such perfection as to make the need for the sacraments obsolete). *Trobairitz* poetry is represented by Castelloza, whose sensitive and well-crafted lyrics epitomize the sympathetic view of woman passionately and unrequitedly in love. *Minnemystiek*, that brand of mysticism which fuses courtly conventions with spiritual aspirations, is represented by Hadewijch, who may have been a Beguine and whose spiritual lyrics are among the most sublime in Dutch literature, and by Mechthild of Magdeburg, who was a Beguine in the early years of her religious career and whose verses soar to ecstasy in their analogies of the knowledge of God to that of the union between bride and bridegroom.

The fourteenth-century movements are represented by four women of very different social descent and religiopolitical ambitions. Mysticism is coupled with reformatory zeal in the texts of two politically active visionaries, Saint Bridget of Sweden, member of the upper aristocracy, and Saint Catherine of Siena, youngest of an Italian dyer's twenty-three children. Both had monastic ties: Bridget founded the order of the Brigittines and Catherine was a Dominican tertiary; both advocated the return of the pope to Rome from Avignon; during the schism, they sided with Pope

Urban VI.[54] Anchoritic and lay bourgeois mysticism is represented by
two Englishwomen, Julian of Norwich and Margery Kempe, respectively.
Julian, probably literate and consistently orthodox, displays literary skills
and rhetorical polish in her writing not found in the work of the illiterate
Margery.[55] Margery Kempe, on the other hand, is perhaps the most immediate and certainly the most personal and passionate of the mystics in
this volume. Like Bridget's, Margery's revelations are direct, not speculative (in fact, it has been suggested that Margery modeled her "sight-
ings" on Bridget's revelations),[56] and she is the only mystic represented
here whose visions were accompanied by sensual experiences: sounds,
smells, and other sensations.

The quintessential problem surrounding mystics and visionaries concerns the genuineness of their experiences—a question that most often
aims at ascertaining the orthodoxy or heterodoxy of their religiosity and
their views of the Church as an institution. For a visionary or a mystic
to be regarded as orthodox and genuine, his or her visions and experiences had to be funneled through interpretations confirming Catholic
dogma. They had to support the Church as an institution existing by
divine right, confirm its hierarchy, and affirm its role as mediator between
heaven and earth. Another crucial distinction between orthodox and heterodox mysticism concerns the way in which the human soul achieves its
union with God: if that union occurs as a result of God's grace and is
supported by the Church's sacramental ministry, the experience is considered orthodox; if not, it is heterodox.[57]

The authors themselves were often preoccupied with this question of
authenticity. Margery Kempe, for example, visited the anchoress-mystic
Julian of Norwich not only to "have the holy joy of . . . communing in
the love of our Lord Jesus Christ" but also to ascertain whether or not
her revelations were genuine, and both Bridget and Catherine submitted
their visions to their confessors before making them public. Even so, the
validity of their visions (both canonized by the Church) was occasionally
doubted.[58] Saint Catherine was ordered by Elias of Toulouse (general of
the Dominicans) to appear and vindicate herself to the chapter, and Saint
Bridget was accused of sorcery as well as insanity.[59] Margery Kempe was
repeatedly tried for heresy, from which trials she emerged victorious,[60]
but the Beguine Marguerite Porete was burned as a heretic at Paris in
1310, and in 1332 a whole community of Beguines at Schweidnitz was
tried for heresy because they rejected the sole authority of the Church to
act as mediator between heaven and earth.[61]

Clearly, the distinction between the heretical questioning of the Church's
exclusive authority as mediator between Christ and his people and the
mystic's experience of direct communion with God is sometimes difficult
to ascertain. Thus, especially in light of the many heretical movements

and the rise of lay congregations which existed outside its authority, the Church viewed certain self-proclaimed mystics, particularly those not professed in monastic orders, with skepticism.

Mystics considered orthodox and belonging to a monastic order, however, were respected and highly acclaimed; their gifts of prophecy and clairvoyance were generously acknowledged; and the Church made abundant use of their visions. In prefaces to and reflections on texts of female mysticism, medieval and Renaissance writers invariably emphasized the woman's talents for prophecy, inspiration, Christian devotion, and genuine religiosity, not her acuity, erudition, or literary gifts.[62] She is depicted (and frequently depicts herself) as a vessel of divine inspiration, not as a creative genius,[63] and the scriptural injunction that God often elects the weak to confound the strong is frequently invoked to explain the phenomenon of lay and female mystical inspiration. This critical practice may help illuminate the reasons why, in the spheres of mystical and devotional literature, the achievements and contributions of orthodox women have never been questioned. In fact, the beliefs in women's mystical, prophetic, and oracular powers as well as in the female predilection for religious enthusiasm are as old as the record of human history.[64]

While most of our selection of women writers from the thirteenth and fourteenth centuries presents religious women, this anthology concludes with two secular writers of the fifteenth century: the Spanish Florencia Pinar and the Franco-Italian Christine de Pizan. Both signal the advent of a new, secular age, yet both have their roots firmly in the past. Florencia's apotheosis of the female persona and of female desires is a manifestation of the same spirit that pervades the lyrics of the twelfth-century women troubadours of Occitania; her chosen vehicle of expression is the medieval *cancionero*. Similarly, Christine shares many themes and concerns with her predecessors. Like Dhuoda, she compiled educational treatises, not, like the Frankish writer, for her child but for all women (even though she did write one for her son); like Marie de France, she wrote a romance in which women characters are fully developed;[65] like Hrotsvit, she was concerned with the literary denigration of women and, like Hrotsvit, she undertook to modify it; like the great visionaries of the past, she had her revelations, albeit of a secular, mythical nature.

Where Christine's spirit differs fundamentally from that of her predecessors is in her conception of and proposed resolution for the problems that beset women. While Hrotsvit shared Christine's concern with the literary maligning of women, political, intellectual, or moral freedom for women was not an eminent desideratum for her. The tenth-century Hrotsvit's solution remained on the literary level: in order to counter the Terentian model of lascivious and selfish women frolicking in the pleasures of the flesh, she created literary models of virtuous, chaste, altruistic, and spiritual women within the existing system of monastic-hagiographic ideals who confirmed the ecclesiastical canon of ethics.

Christine, on the other hand, probes into the possible social and political causes of the calumnious view of women and advocates social reform, in particular, education for women. Moreover, in her writings she restricts herself neither to the ecclesiastical model of virginal, otherworldly female excellence nor to the social model of passive, altruistic, and fecund conjugality. Instead, she introduces such paradigmatically feminine virtues as warmth, kindness, and pacifism and such nonstereotypic qualities as erudition, common sense, literacy, and economic, legal, political, and literary talents in her hierarchy of valuable qualities in women. Woman is not always man's inferior, she observes; "there have nevertheless been, are now, and will always be women more valiant, honest, better bred, and even wiser, and through whom more good has come to the world, than has ever come from him. And some are even more versed in the affairs of state and have more virtuous habits, some have been responsible for reconciling their husbands with their enemies."[66] This is indeed a novel depiction of womanhood, one that, unlike late medieval and early Renaissance compilations about good women, deals neither exclusively with the past nor only with "martyrs of love," those women who sacrificed everything for their love or honor.[67] Rather, it deals with secular and universal virtues, and as Natalie Zemon Davis remarks, Christine is doing "some rudimentary thinking about the position of women at different periods."[68] As the first professional woman writer of the West to earn her living by her pen, Christine initiates a new age by reflecting on the past. Her works, then, come at the end of the Middle Ages and at the dawn of the Renaissance; her manual of conduct which concludes our selections closes the circle which began with Dhuoda's manual.

The range of texts presented in this volume also prompts a classification of medieval women writers along linguistic, social, and economic lines. In the early Middle Ages women writers, like their male contemporaries, wrote in Latin, the language of culture, diplomacy, and learning. Between the eighth and twelfth centuries, they were also invariably members of the upper nobility, as only daughters of the aristocracy were admitted to the religious houses where they could receive education and literary patronage; only they had the leisure time to indulge in literary activity.[69] During the twelfth century, Latin and the monastic setting were no longer the exclusive domain of literature; Marie de France and the trobairitz of Occitania wrote in the vernacular, composed secular poetry in a secular setting under secular patronage and for a secular audience. Still, their social status was elevated; not until the thirteenth and four-

teenth centuries did women writers from the middle classes make their
appearance. These centuries also saw the acceptance of women of hum-
bler birth into nunneries (usually into houses established by the newer
orders) and the rise of the Beguine movement that accommodated women
from most social strata.[70] Parallel to this development ran the decline of
the use of Latin in nunneries and the increased use of the vernacular even
for religious tracts.

The most fascinating question about women writers of the past concerns how they differed from their female successors and from their male
contemporaries. In contrast with women writers of the more recent past,
medieval women writers did not use male pseudonyms but identified
themselves by name and by sex.[71] In addition, unlike the works of women
writers of the seventeenth, eighteenth, and even nineteenth centuries, those
of medieval women provide little evidence that they were ridiculed for or
prevented from accomplishing their literary endeavors (when there is
criticism, it usually concerns the authenticity of their mystical experiences, not their right, willingness, or ability to record them). Imputations
that their works were the clever forgeries of men stem from subsequent
centuries.[72] Most of them enjoyed literary patronage and literary success:
Marie de France, for example, was so successful and confident in her
narrative talents as to fear that rival authors would claim her works as
their own; Bridget's and Catherine's prophetic texts were widely propa-
gandized by the Church; and many of Christine's works were written on
commission. Furthermore, unlike the history of women painters and
women composers before the nineteenth century, the literary landscape
of women authors in the Middle Ages is not peopled with female relatives of male artists.[73] Rather, only two of the writers—Florencia Pinar
and Heloise—presented in this volume seem to have been related to literary men.

Stylistically and with regard to the choice of genre, medieval women
exhibit preferences similar to those of their male contemporaries. There
are, however, a few exceptions: women seem to avoid satire and the
genres exclusively associated with bellicose pursuits. It is not, however,
the case that women writers are oblivious of ecclesiastic or social corrup-
tions; rather, the difference lies in their way of treating these problems:
satires by men lampooning the misdeeds of the curia and the princes of
the Church have their equivalent in the didactic but no less violent cas-
tigations of Church corruption in the works of several women visionaries.[74] Similarly, while medieval women writers do occasionally treat of
war, they never glorify it: the *chanson de geste* is not a genre favored by
women. Finally, for reasons noted above, there is a greater concentration
of women than men in the devotional and visionary genres.

Concurrently, there is a pronounced difference between the writings of medieval men and women. Both groups write from their respective but collective experiences: men often write of the physically heroic pursuits of men at war; women write of the spiritually heroic exploits of love and devotion. Moreover, women often depict women characters more frequently, more sympathetically, and more convincingly than do male authors.

The consciousness of being a woman, however, is only one (albeit an important one) of the aspects that affect the workings of the poetic imagination; religious, monastic, courtly, class-conscious, educational, and time-related frames of mind are also significant. For both women and men the choice of subject matter, representational framework, and, to a lesser degree, genre appears to depend on each author's educational, social, and religious frame of mind; their point of view, choice of main characters, thematic focus, and character development seem to depend on their sex. Thus, monastic and other religious writers tend to choose religious subject matter and hagiographic, visionary, or devotional vehicles for their expressions, while secular authors prefer secular forms and secular subject matter. For instance, the canoness Hrotsvit relied in almost all of her works on legendary themes and a hagiographic setting, and the religious visionaries included in this collection concern themselves with God's divine mysteries, and humanity's relationship to God and the Church. The courtly and secular Marie de France, on the other hand, chose the then fashionable courtly lais and depicted the adventures of courtly knights and ladies; Castelloza wrote vernacular love lyrics; the learned Heloise composed erudite texts in the epistolary form; and Christine presented her secular allegorical visions on ethical and pragmatic matters.

Parallel to this polarization along religious and secular lines (regarding subject matter and representational framework) runs a pronounced polarity concerning the nature of poetic creation or, more precisely, each woman's conception of her art. Religious writers often use mechanical metaphors for their acts of composition and, thus, depict themselves as mere transmitters of or instruments played by the divine voice, while secular writers frequently employ organic or psychological metaphors for their creative activities. Concurrently, monastic women writers generally claim that their utterances are not their own but God's (and as such are objective, because they are unaltered transmissions of the divine word), while secular women speak *ea voce* and admittedly subjectively. Both Hildegard and Hrotsvit, for example, insist that they are "trumpets" or "tinkling chords" of God's light, and Julian insists that it is not she but God who speaks through her lines. The secular Marie de France, on the other hand, uses the metaphor of a plant for poetic creation: her art, like a plant, thrives only when watered by kind consideration and nurtured by thoughtful reading and a good reception; subjectivity, as the all-powerful tool of the imagination, finds its remarkable manifestation in her *Yonec*, when the lady's inmost desires materialize in the form of her bird-knight lover. Women writers of erotic poetry, be it *minnemystiek* or songs of earthly love, consciously create their works as a means to and a manifestation of their emotional and intellectual growth, as the subjective forming of their reality.[75]

The sex of the author, on the other hand, is clearly reflected in her narrative attitude, thematic focus, choice of main characters, and character development. For instance, most of Hildegard's and Christine's allegorical personages are women, and Hrotsvit's admirable heroines outnumber her heroes; conversely, her male villains by far outnumber her female villains. Sexual dimorphism is reflected in narrative attitude as well. The conventional (and male) view of female lasciviousness is a case in point: both Hrotsvit and Christine explicitly state that they wish to counteract the prevailing negative view of women, in particular that of the female predilection for lust; they present alternative models of feminine excellence and virtue in their works. Similarly, Hildegard of Bingen, while restating the prevalent view of men's superiority over women, consistently counters the traditional theological and biological view that women are more lustful than men. Rather, she maintains that it is men who are lustful—women cohabit only in hope of children.[76]

Concerning character development, women writers often offer alternative models to the conventional (male-created) themes. While Marie de France wrote her lais in the courtly romance tradition, her works, like those of the twelfth-century *trobairitz*, present alternatives to the courtly model of the lady. The *trobairitz* depict disappointed love from the woman's perspective, and Marie freely inverts and interchanges the roles conventionally assigned to the lover (knight) and the beloved (lady); she depicts disappointed and self-sacrificial love from the woman's perspective and creates narrative situations where the ennobling and invigorating effects of love are seen in women. Like the *trobairitz*, Florencia Pinar exploits the female persona and female sexuality in her poems—an aspect of loving sometimes neglected by the troubadours.[77]

With women mystics the presence of female consciousness is less pronounced, but they, too, tend to emphasize the female aspect of the divinity (that is, Christ's role as a mother) more than do their male contemporaries. Julian of Norwich, for example, is one of the few exponents of the concept of Christ as a "tender and loving Mother," the *natura creatrix*, and therefore the creative force of the Trinity.[78]

This volume will acquaint the student and the general reader with some of the outstanding women writers of the Middle Ages. In order to create a representative anthology, we have opted for making the range of selections as broad and varied as possible.[79] To give the reader a sense of the entirety of each work, we have tried to present complete texts, substantial excerpts, or self-contained selections. We hope that in doing so we will stimulate further research and continued interest in the women writers of the Middle Ages, who, far from being mere copyists of their male contemporaries, produced a wide range of works, thus not only embellishing the rich tapestry of medieval literature but providing new dimensions for viewing it.

NOTES

1. In addition, as Eileen Power, *Medieval Women*, p. 9, observes, the two groups of medieval men writing about women were those least familiar with them—the clergy and the aristocracy: "The ideas about women were formed on the one hand by the clerkly order, usually celibate, and on the other hand by a narrow caste, who could afford to regard its women as an ornamental asset, while strictly subordinating them to the interests of its primary asset, the land."

2. Frank Warnke, "Reassessing Existing Programs in Comparative Literature: Where Do We Begin?" p. 54.

3. While the last decades have produced a revival of interest and a number of scholarly works regarding medieval women writers, women writers are not yet represented in the volumes of major anthologies used in literary survey courses: most editions of the *Norton Anthology of World Literature*, vol. 1, include the poems of only one woman, Sappho; the *Norton Anthology of English Literature*, vol. 1, while depicting Queen Elizabeth on its cover, presents a single woman writer, the late seventeenth-century Anne Finch.

4. It is naturally difficult to designate corresponding linguistic and political boundaries for the Middle Ages, for, at least until the late Middle Ages, they did not tend to merge. In the twelfth century, for instance, it is impossible to identify a single European kingdom by the language of its people. This difficulty accounts for the grouping of regions and nationalities together.

5. Some of these works (Hrotsvit, Hildegard, Marie, Heloise, Julian, Margery, and Christine) are available in English. Others (Dhuoda, Catherine, Bridget, Marguerite, Florencia) are not readily available. For those writers whose works are only partially available, we tried to include examples that have been not translated before or are not readily available. All the translations (with the exception of Marie's *Yonec* and Heloise's letter) are new or first translations.

6. Such is the testimony of Denis Pyramus, Marie's contemporary. See *The Lais of Marie de France*, ed. Joan M. Ferrante and R. W. Hanning, pp. 7–8; for Hrotsvit, see Edwin Zeydel, "The Reception of Hrotsvitha by the German Humanists after 1493," *Journal of English and Germanic Philology* 44 (1945): 239–249.

7. See, for example, Marilyn Dorion, "'The Mirror of Simple Souls,' a Middle English Translation," *Archivio Italiano per la Storia della Pietà* 5 (1968): 241–382. In Italy alone, thirty-six translations of Marguerite's works were circulated in the fifteenth century.

8. Germaine Bree, *Women Writers in France*, p. 10.

9. Twenty of Hadewijch's letters are available in English translation in *Mediaeval Netherlands Religious Literature*, ed. Eric Colledge, pp. 31–88.

10. In contrast, Wycliffe and the Lollards are treated at length. In W. T. H. Jackson's

Medieval Literature: A History and a Guide, the only medieval woman writer discussed at some length is the courtly and secular Marie de France. Christine de Pizan and Heloise are also mentioned, but Hadewijch, Dhuoda, Hildegard, Mechthild, Bridget, Marguerite, Julian, and Margery are either omitted or referred to only in passing. This space distribution occurs in spite of the generally recognized fact that Hadewijch's and Hildegard's poetry is by far superior to that of Marie.

11. What underlies the selection process, then, is clearly not an aesthetic judgment but conformist versus nonconformist, ecclesiastical versus secular, and orthodox versus liberal distinctions. Also, these distinctions often underlie the selection process of medieval works for the canon when male writers are concerned.

12. Almost all the authors presented here were either single women or widows; two of the married women writers (Dhuoda and Heloise) lived in some form of separation from their husbands.

13. Colledge, p. 7.

14. This point must be stressed because the Church sharply defined a woman's alternatives to familial roles. See Virginia Woolf, *A Room of One's Own*, for further reflections on the subject.

15. See Shulamith Shahar, *Die Frau im Mittelalter*.

16. Ibid., p. 17.

17. Saint Jerome, for example, assigns the numerical values 100, 30, and 10 to virginity, widowhood, and marriage, respectively. The Pauline conception of marriage (it is better to marry than to burn, 1 Cor. 7:9) does not assign it any inherent value. The Church was also rather late in assuming jurisdiction over marriage: it was declared a sacrament in the eighth century, and marital cases began to be tried in canonical courts in the eleventh century.

18. For a good general discussion of the history of marriage, see Edward Westermarck, *The History of Human Marriage*. More specifically, for the estate of women in the social model, see Frances Gies and Joseph Gies, *Women in the Middle Ages*; Georges Duby, *Medieval Marriage: Two Models from Twelfth Century France*; and Jean Louis Flandrin, *Families in Former Times*.

19. As Joan M. Ferrante, "The Education of Women in the Middle Ages in Theory, Fact and Fantasy," p. 10, observes, "Among the Christianized Germanic peoples in the early Middle Ages, the women of royal families were usually better educated than the men. In some cases, education was apparently considered effeminate." But Philippe de Novare, *Les quatre âges de l'homme*, pp. 24–25, prohibits literacy to all women except nuns, because the ability to read and write may enable them to receive and answer notes from their lovers. More reasonable writers, including many Churchmen, however, encouraged literacy among noble ladies and religious women. They argued that women of the aristocracy may have to take over administrative duties in their husbands' absence. See Shahar, chap. 5, and Power, *Medieval Women*, pp. 76 ff. Power observes, p. 80, that "it is a curious fact that the serious treatises [that is, on female education] often express doubt whether it is wise to allow any women except nuns to have learning."

20. The pagan institutionalization of women's social, political, and economic dependence on their male relatives was the social reality of the early Christian centuries and is reflected in the Pauline assertion of "natural" male superiority within marriage. Woman is inferior to man, the apostle says, for it was man who was made in the image of God; man was not made for the sake of woman but woman for the sake of man (1 Cor. 11:7–9).

21. On this subject see, for example, *Women and Religion: A Feminist Sourcebook of Christian Thought*, ed. Elizabeth Clark and H. Richardson.

22. Jerome says: "As long as woman is for birth and children, she is different from man as body is from soul. But when she wishes to serve Christ more than the world, then she will cease to be a woman and will be called man" (Comm. in epist. ad Eph. 3:5).

23. See Joan M. Ferrante, *Woman as Image in Medieval Literature*, and Katharine M. Rogers, *The Troublesome Helpmate*.

24. The New Testament attests to the presence of deaconesses (Rom. 16:1), and as late as the fourth century Saint Jerome refers to them (Ep. 11:2). See, for example, Albert Mackinnon, *The Rome of St. Paul*; Elaine Pagels, *The Gnostic Gospels*; and Ray Petry, *Christian Eschatology and Christian Thought*.

25. See, for example, Otto Pfleiderer, *Primitive Christianity*; William E. Phipps, *Was Jesus Married?*; and George H. Tavard, *Women in the Christian Tradition*.

26. The important role of women in the ecclesiastical hierarchy of the early and central Middle Ages is documented by such studies as *The Women of England from Anglo-Saxon Times to the Present*, ed. Barbara Kanner; *Women in Medieval Society*, ed. Susan M. Stuard; *The Role of Women in the Middle Ages*, ed. R. T. Morewedge; and *Medieval Culture and Society*, ed. David Herlihy. See also *Medieval Women*, ed. Derek Baker, and Power, *Medieval Women*.

27. See, for example, Power, *Medieval Women*; *Role of Women in the Middle Ages*, ed. Morewedge; G. H. Cook, *English Monasteries in the Middle Ages*; and Ferrante, "Education," p. 15.

28. Shahar, p. 50. Ferrante, "Education," p. 15, observes that some convents continued to flourish and acquired reputations for learning and for the production of manuscripts.

29. Henry Charles Lea, *Sacerdotal Celibacy in the Christian Church*, p. 131.

30. Marjorie Rowling, *Life in Medieval Times*, p. 13.

31. Karl J. Leyser, *Rule and Conflict in an Early Medieval Society: Ottonian Saxony*, p. 64, proposes a hypothesis for the Saxon nobles' preference for endowing nunneries: "Marriages were costly and the presence of many unbetrothed girls in the houses of Anglo-Saxon, Frankish and Old Saxon nobles threatened their peace. . . . The foundation of religious houses for women shifted the burden of safeguarding and maintaining them within their own caste into another sphere."

32. Hrotsvit's abbey was ruled by Gerberga II, the emperor's niece; Otto II sent his daughter Sophia to be educated in the abbey, and the Empress Theophano, Byzantine wife of Otto II, also may have spent some time there. Playwriting by medieval women was not restricted to Hrotsvit of Gandersheim; she was only the first. Hildegard of Bingen wrote a morality play, and Katherine of Sutton, noble abbess of Barking, rewrote the Eastern dramatic offices between 1363 and 1376 in order to excite devotion among churchgoers. See Nancy Cotton, *Women Playwrights in England*.

33. See, for example, Charles H. Haskins, *The Twelfth Century Renaissance*.

34. Ferrante, "Education," p. 15.

35. The poems of the women troubadours are available in Meg Bogin's *The Women Troubadours*.

36. The authenticity of Heloise's letters, while far from unanimously agreed upon, has been persuasively pleaded by convincing interpreters throughout the ages, with Alexander Pope and Peter Dronke in the forefront.

37. Robert E. Lerner, *The Heresy of the Free Spirit in the Later Middle Ages*, pp. 3, 39. For a discussion of orthodox female piety, see Elizabeth Petroff, *The Consolation of the Blessed*.

38. Steven Runciman, *The Medieval Manichee*, observes that some heresies survived in the Balkans and in Asia Minor throughout the Middle Ages and surfaced with great vigor in France and Italy during the central Middle Ages, when many people were predisposed to accept their tenets and their call for a return to a simpler apostolic life because of a growing dislike of the luxury and political activity of the Church. Furthermore, as Gottfried Koch, *Frauenfrage und Ketzertum im Mittelalter*, points out, the frustration of artisans, especially women, with the exploitative practices of the Church-condoned societal structure also hastened the acceptance of heretical views. It is, however, also clear that orthodox

reforming zeal and evangelical religious fervor lay, at least initially, at the heart of many heretical movements.

39. Alain de Lille's *Attack on Heretics*, printed in Walter L. Wakefield and Austin P. Evans, *Heresies of the High Middle Ages: Selected Sources Translated and Annotated*, p. 219, castigates the Waldenses for allowing women to preach:

> If it is a dangerous thing for wise and holy men to preach it is most dangerous for the uneducated who do not know what should be preached; to whom, how, when, and where there should be preaching. These persons resist the Apostle in that they have women with them and have them preach in the gatherings of the faithful although the Apostle says in the first Epistle to the Corinthians: "Let women keep silence in the Churches, for it is not permitted them to speak, but to be subject, as also the law saith."

40. See Shahar, pp. 214 ff.

41. See, for example, Stephen E. Wessley, "The 13th Century Guglielmites: Salvation through Women."

42. Shahar, pp. 214, 215.

43. See, for example, Malcolm Lambert, *Medieval Heresy: Popular Movements from Bogomil to Huss*. Lambert contrasts eleventh- and twelfth-century heresies and says, p. 37:

> The heretical groups of the eleventh century sought a flight from the world to practice their austerities. They were generally content with a personal abnegation and a set of idiosyncratic views to be discussed within the closed circle of the chosen. The new breed of heretics (i.e., those of subsequent centuries) are aggressive reformers who insist on changes in the Church that will bring Catholicism into line with their own ideas. . . . There is a new concern for the social implications of the Gospel.

Also consult the varied selections in Wakefield and Evans, *Heresies of the High Middle Ages*.

44. The Albigensian crusade was concentrated in the regions of southern France where heresy was particularly well disseminated and where many noble ladies joined the ranks of the heretics. As Walter L. Wakefield, *Heresy, Crusade and Inquisition in Southern France*, p. 22, remarks, the ideas that the Church considered most dangerous concerned the belief that "holy authority rested less on ordination than on purity."

45. Men in religious orders by far outnumbered women in orders. For a discussion of this demographic imbalance, see Koch, *Frauenfrage*.

46. On the Beguine movement, see the chapters under these headings in Shahar, *Die Frau*; Lambert, *Medieval Heresy*; Bernard Hamilton, *The Medieval Inquisition*; Koch, *Frauenfrage*; Runciman, *Medieval Manichee*; and Gordon Leff, *Heresy in the Later Middle Ages*.

47. In addition, some Beguines also worked as housekeepers. The Goodman of Paris, available in Eileen Power's edition *The Goodman of Paris*, for example, admonishes his young wife to consult with the Beguine in household matters of importance.

48. Lambert, p. 177, observes: "The treatment of the beguines, beghards and mystics in northern Europe was a more subtle case of misunderstanding, in which genuine grounds for disquiet combined with suspicions, conservatism and the persecuting mentality to smear pious unprotected groups." Also see Lerner, pp. 36–67, and Leff, pp. 167–255.

49. Shahar, p. 63, and Lambert, pp. 205 ff.

50. See Hamilton, pp. 85 ff., and Leff, pp. 308–407.

51. Shahar, p. 64.

52. Peter Dronke, *The Medieval Lyric*, p. 81. He mentions, in particular, Hadewijch, Hildegard of Bingen, and Mechthild of Brandenburg.

53. See Bogin, *Women Troubadours*.

54. Both Bridget and Catherine expressed strong support for the visible Church while criticizing its unworthy representatives. On the Church's political use of saints, see M. Goodich, "The Politics of Canonization in the Thirteenth Century: Lay and Mendicant Saints," *Church History* 44 (1975): 294–307.

55. See David Knowles, *The English Mystical Tradition*.

56. *The Book of Margery Kempe*, ed. Sanford Brown Meech and Hope Emily Allen, p. 47.

57. See Lerner, p. 16.

58. Women mystics are not singled out for suspicion. Meister Eckhart's doctrine, for example, was condemned by Pope John XXII in 1329; Jean Gerson, who also accused Saint Bridget of lunacy, accused Jan Ruysbroeck of Averroism. See Etienne Gilson, *Reason and Revelation in the Middle Ages*, p. 90.

59. Sybille Harksen, *Women in the Middle Ages*.

60. The clerical doubts about Margery concerned her open facility with scripture and scriptural exegesis. Anthony Goodman, "The Piety of John Brunham's Daughter, of Lynn," p. 354, observes that clerics' doubts "were often reinforced and their opposition was often provoked by Margery's suspect facility in quoting and glossing holy writ and in telling homilies. She threatened to usurp priestly prerogatives."

61. Harksen, p. 37; Lambert, p. 205; Lerner, pp. 112–119; and Leff, pp. 386–395.

62. The preface to the sixteenth-century vernacular edition of Angela of Foligno's treatises, in *The Book of Divine Consolation of the Blessed Angela of Foligno*, trans. Mary G. Steegman, pp. xli, xlii, exemplifies the tradition:

Although in the Holy Gospel our most loving Lord hath plentifully shown unto us the means and the way whereby we may attain unto the perfection of Christian life, yet hath His consoling spirit (giver of all comforting and spiritual grace) nevertheless not ceased, nor ever will cease, to reveal unto us continually by means of His most worthy instruments—the which are saints and devout persons—diverse ways and conditions of finding the most perfect and consummate union possible unto wayfarers of this life. . . .

For this reason, also, hath God elected the weak to confound the strong, and thus in our own times hath He inspired many women of exalted spirit. . . . Among these is the blessed Angela of Foligno, who, although a woman (and, therefore, of the weaker sex), did, nevertheless, by means of her humble, patient and steadfast despising of the things of this world and by her chosen and beloved poverty, overcome all the strong and the powerful of her time. . . . This book hath already been printed in Latin. . . . But because it was neither elegant nor learned in that language, it was neither read by scholars nor understood by the simple, and for that reason hath it been deemed well to translate it into the vulgar tongue.

63. Hildegard of Bingen, for example, persistently refers to herself as a "trumpet" that simply purveys sound: God himself is the player (*PL* 217d).

64. All ancient and primitive religions made use of prophetesses; most mystery cults employed priestesses and female seers. See, for example, Eric Neumann, *The Great Mother*.

65. *Le livre du Duc des Vrais Amants* presents the conventional love triangle of the married lady, her husband, and the young knight with an unconventionally genuine sympathy for her dilemma and her attempt to resolve it.

66. For a translation of the full passage, see the final chapter of this volume.

67. Compare, for example, Boccaccio's *De claris mulieribus* and Chaucer's "The Legend of Good Women," which include narratives of Alcestis, Cleopatra, Dido, Lucrece, Philomela, and Ariadne, among others.

68. Natalie Zemon Davis, "Gender and Genre: Women as Historical Writers, 1400–1820," p. 160.

69. Suzanne F. Wemple, *Women in Frankish Society: Marriage and the Cloister 500–900*, pp. 158 ff.

70. Initially, most Beguines were of the upper classes and the wealthy bourgeoisie; later, city dwellers of lesser means also joined their ranks.

71. Medieval women writers do use a particular version of the affected modesty topos by adding *fragilitas feminei sexu* to the disclaimers. But Ernst R. Curtius, *European Literature and the Latin Middle Ages*, pp. 407–413, observes that devotional formulas, particularly those presented in the prefaces to a work, are confined to a schema and are standard introductory topoi and conventions of rhetoric.

72. A glance at anthologies from the seventeenth to the nineteenth centuries will bear out this observation. Anne Finch, countess of Winchelsea, for example, refused to show her poetry at court lest she be ridiculed as a "versifying maid of honor." See *Salt and Bitter and Good: Three Centuries of English and American Women Poets*, ed. Cora Kaplan. See also Gisela Bringer-Gabler, *Deutsche Dichterinnen vom 16 ten Jahrhundert bis zur Gegenwart*. The works of Hrotsvit and Heloise, just to mention two, were labeled forgeries in centuries following the Renaissance; this possibility does not seem to have occurred to their medieval audience.

73. For example, Eva Weissweiler, *Komponistinnen aus 500 Jahren*, p. 9, observes that female composers are either not discussed in music histories or are tangentially treated in chapters dealing with their fathers, husbands, or brothers. Similarly, Germaine Greer, *The Obstacle Race*, p. 12, points out that "the most striking fact about women [painters] who made names for themselves before the nineteenth century is that almost all of them were related to better known male painters." She adds, p. 13: "Any student of women painters, therefore, finds that he is actually studying the female relatives of male artists."

74. Hrotsvit's *Gesta*, for example, is sufficiently different in narrative and thematic focus from the chronicles and epics of her contemporaries Liudprand and Widukind to bear out this observation; a comparison of Marie's lais with contemporary romances yields the same results. For treatments of corrupt Church officials, compare, for instance, goliardic poetry with the tirades of Hildegard, Margery, or Catherine.

75. As are all generalizations, these are oversimplifications. There are, naturally, exceptions to these observations among medieval women writers. The general pattern, however, is clearly discernible.

76. *PL* 197. 461, 594.

77. The courtly romances frequently depict the lady as subjecting her potential lover to many trials and tribulations; the poems of Marie and of the *trobairitz* depict women who are men's equals in love—as active, as devoted, and as willing to make sacrifices as their lovers.

78. Rev. 14:59; similar pronouncements are to be found in the *Ancrene Riwle* and in Mechthild of Hackeborn's *Liber specialis gratiae*. In addition, as Petroff, *Consolation of the Blessed*, has successfully demonstrated, in the visions of female mystics, Mary—in her role as genetrix, not as virgin—assumes an all-important and powerful position; as well, the visions of female mystics seem to follow patterns different from those of male mystics.

79. The heterogeneity of medieval women writers is reflected in the heterogeneity of the contributors and their approaches, which range from predominantly historic to almost exclusively literary. In most cases the focus was determined by the writer's prevalent importance: the influence and significance of Marie's and Florencia's works are purely literary, while Catherine of Siena and Bridget of Sweden were political visionaries and wielded remarkable political and religious influence.

BIBLIOGRAPHY

Baker, Derek, ed. *Medieval Women*. Oxford, 1978.

Bogin, Meg. *The Women Troubadours*. New York, 1976.

The Book of Divine Consolation of the Blessed Angela of Foligno. Trans. Mary G. Steegman. New York, 1966.

Bree, Germaine. *Women Writers in France*. New Brunswick, N.J., 1973.

Bringer-Gabler, Gisela. *Deutsche Dichterinnen vom 16 ten Jahrhundert bis zur Gegenwart*. Frankfurt, 1978.

Clark, Elizabeth, and H. Richardson, eds. *Women and Religion: A Feminist Sourcebook of Christian Thought*. New York, 1977.

Colledge, Eric, ed. *Mediaeval Netherlands Religious Literature*. London and New York, 1965.

Cook, G. H. *English Monasteries in the Middle Ages*. London, 1961.

Cotton, Nancy. *Women Playwrights in England*. London and Toronto, 1980.

Curtius, Ernst R. *European Literature and the Latin Middle Ages*. Trans. Willard R. Trask. Bollingen Series 36. Princeton, 1953.

Davis, Natalie Zemon. "Gender and Genre: Women as Historical Writers, 1400–1820." In *Beyond Their Sex: Learned Women of the European Past*, ed. Patricia H. Labalme, pp. 153–183. New York, 1980.

Dorion, Marilyn. "'The Mirror of Simple Souls,' a Middle English Translation." *Archivio Italiano per la Storia della Pietà* 5 (1968): 241–382.

Dronke, Peter. *The Medieval Lyric*. 2nd ed. London and New York, 1977.

Duby, Georges. *Medieval Marriage: Two Models from Twelfth Century France*. Trans. Elborg Forster. Baltimore, 1978.

Ferrante, Joan M. "The Education of Women in the Middle Ages in Theory, Fact and Fantasy." In *Beyond Their Sex: Learned Women of the European Past*, ed. Patricia H. Labalme, pp. 9–43. New York, 1980.

———. *Woman as Image in Medieval Literature*. New York, 1975.

——— and R. W. Hanning, eds. *The Lais of Marie de France*. New York, 1978.

Flandrin, Jean Louis. *Families in Former Times*. Trans. Richard Southern. Cambridge, Eng., 1979.

Gies, Frances, and Joseph Gies. *Women in the Middle Ages*. New York, 1978.

Gilson, Etienne. *Reason and Revelation in the Middle Ages*. New York, 1938.

Goodich, M. "The Politics of Canonization in the Thirteenth Century: Lay and Mendicant Saints." *Church History* 44 (1975): 294–307.

Goodman, Anthony. "The Piety of John Burnham's Daughter, of Lynn." In *Medieval Women*, ed. Derek Baker, pp. 347–358. Oxford, 1978.

Greer, Germaine. *The Obstacle Race*. London, 1981.

Hamilton, Bernard. *The Medieval Inquisition*. New York, 1981.

Harksen, Sybille. *Women in the Middle Ages*. New York, 1975.

Haskins, Charles H. *The Twelfth Century Renaissance*. Cleveland and New York, 1957.

Herlihy, David, ed. *Medieval Culture and Society*. New York, 1968.

Jackson, W. T. H. *Medieval Literature: A History and a Guide*. New York and London, 1966.

Kaplan, Cora, ed. *Salt and Bitter and Good: Three Centuries of English and American Women Poets*. New York, 1975.

Kanner, Barbara, ed. *The Women of England from Anglo-Saxon Times to the Present*. Hamden, Conn., 1979.

Knowles, David. *The English Mystical Tradition*. New York, 1961.

Koch, Gottfried. *Frauenfrage und Ketzertum im Mittelalter*. Berlin, 1962.

Lambert, Malcolm. *Medieval Heresy: Popular Movements from Bogomil to Huss.* New York, 1976.

Lea, Henry Charles. *Sacerdotal Celibacy in the Christian Church.* Philadelphia, 1867.

Leff, Gordon. *Heresy in the Later Middle Ages.* New York, 1967.

Lerner, Robert E. *The Heresy of the Free Spirit in the Later Middle Ages.* Berkeley and Los Angeles, 1972.

Leyser, Karl J. *Rule and Conflict in an Early Medieval Society: Ottonian Saxony.* Bloomington, 1979.

Mackinnon, Albert. *The Rome of St. Paul.* London, 1930.

Meech, Sanford Brown, and Hope Emily Allen, eds. *The Book of Margery Kempe.* 1940. Reprint. London, 1961.

Morewedge, R. T., ed. *The Role of Women in the Middle Ages.* Albany, 1975.

Neumann, Eric. *The Great Mother.* Bollingen Series 47. New York, 1955.

Novare, Philippe de. *Les quatre âges de l'homme.* Ed. M. de Fréville. Paris, 1888.

Pagels, Elaine. *The Gnostic Gospels.* New York, 1979.

Petroff, Elizabeth. *The Consolation of the Blessed.* Millerton, 1982.

Petry, Ray. *Christian Eschatology and Christian Thought.* New York, 1956.

Pfleiderer, Otto. *Primitive Christianity.* Trans. W. Montgomery. Clifton, N.J., 1965.

Phipps, William E. *Was Jesus Married?* New York, 1970.

Power, Eileen. *The Goodman of Paris.* London, 1928.

———. *Medieval Women.* Ed. M. M. Postan. Cambridge, Eng., 1975.

Rogers, Katharine M. *The Troublesome Helpmate.* Seattle, 1966.

Rowling, Marjorie. *Life in Medieval Times.* New York, 1979.

Runciman, Steven. *The Medieval Manichee.* Cambridge, Eng., 1960.

Shahar, Shulamith. *Die Frau im Mittelalter.* Trans. Ruch Achlama. Königstein, 1981.

Stuard, Susan M., ed. *Women in Medieval Society.* Philadelphia, 1976.

Tavard, George H. *Women in the Christian Tradition.* London, 1973.

Wakefield, Walter L. *Heresy, Crusade and Inquisition in Southern France.* London, 1974.

——— and Austin P. Evans. *Heresies of the High Middle Ages: Selected Sources Translated and Annotated.* New York and London, 1969.

Warnke, Frank. "Reassessing Existing Programs in Comparative Literature: Where Do We Begin?" In *Problems in National Literary Identity and the Writer as Social Critic,* ed. Anne Paolucci, pp. 54–58. New York, 1980.

Weissweiler, Eva. *Komponistinnen aus 500 Jahren.* Frankfurt, 1981.

Wemple, Suzanne F. *Women in Frankish Society: Marriage and the Cloister 500–900.* Philadelphia, 1981.

Wessley, Stephen E. "The 13th Century Guglielmites: Salvation through Women." In *Medieval Women,* ed. Derek Baker, pp. 289–305. Oxford, 1978.

Westermarck, Edward. *The History of Human Marriage.* 5th ed. New York, 1922.

Zeydel, Edwin. "The Reception of Hrotsvitha by the German Humanists after 1493." *Journal of English and Germanic Philology* 44 (1945): 239–249.

medieval

women

writers

THE FRANKISH MOTHER

JAMES MARCHAND

When the famous textual critic and editor Jean Mabillon published, in 1677, a partial edition of a copy of a manuscript given to him by his teacher Luc D'Achery, the academic world learned for the first time of the existence of Dhuoda, one of those shadowy figures out of the past about whom we know so little.[1] The little we do know of Dhuoda, or Dhuodana,[2] as she is frequently called, whets our appetite for more and has led to much conjecture. She is in every way a rarity: a female author of the Carolingian age, a learned laywoman when learning among the laity must have been unusual, a lay writer in an age of clerics. Her writings are precious for us in that they offer a view of the intellectual and spiritual life of her age, but they are more precious in that they also offer an insight into the mind and heart of what must have been a remarkable woman. It would have been a pity if the ravages of the centuries had robbed us of her works as they have of so many others.

To be sure, all we know of Dhuoda we know through her *Manual*, which tells us a few facts of her life and leaves us to infer what we can from her known historical situation.[3] The facts she mentions are quickly told. On June 29, 824, she was married in the palace at Aachen to the famous Bernhard of Septimania, son of the equally famous Saint William of Gellone. On November 29, 826, she gave birth to their first son, named William after his paternal grandfather; on March 22, 841, a second son was born, named after his father. Dhuoda spent most of her life after her marriage in semiabandonment in her husband's castle in Uzès in the southern part of France, where she wrote the *Manual*, as she carefully tells us, between November 30, 841, and February 2, 843. In the summer of 841, Bernhard sent their son William as a semihostage to Charles the Bald, and her second son was taken from her upon the orders of his father before baptism, so that two years later she still did not even know his name.

Just these bare facts already enlist our sympathy for Dhuoda, but when we place them in their historical framework they permit us a glimpse of the tragedy which her life must have been. The story of her marriage and life with Bernhard of Septimania, as we piece it together on the basis of the meager information afforded by the annals and biographies of the day, many of them unfortunately written by his avowed enemies, reads like a dimestore novel.[4] By any account, her wedding must have been the event of the year. Bernhard of Septimania, one of the outstanding heroes of the realm, was known for his defense of the Spanish marches against Moor and Goth alike.[5] It has been suspected that he was not overly handsome, but he seems nevertheless to have been quite the ladies' man.[6] His godfather was none other than the emperor himself, and he was obviously on the way up; only a few short years later, he was the imperial *camerarius* or chamberlain, second in command to the emperor. Dhuoda was marrying into the family of William of Gellone, later famed in song and story as the Guillaume d'Orange of the Old French *gestes* and celebrated by none other than Wolfram von Eschenbach as Willehalm, patron saint of knighthood. William of Gellone was Charlemagne's enatic cousin, the son of Charlemagne's Aunt Alda.[7] The family was well established; William was also a great hero, like his son, and his daughter was married to the redoubtable Wala, leader of the unification party. Bernhard was promoted to commander of the Spanish marches sometime after the marriage and, in the summer of 829, to the position of chamberlain in Aachen to Louis the Pious.

But, as one put it so frequently during the Middle Ages, the things of this world have a way of turning awry. Louis the Pious had had three sons by his wife, Irmengard, and he had arranged a division of the empire between them in 817. Irmengard died on October 30, 818, and Louis took a new wife, Judith, in February of the next year. On June 13, 823, she gave birth to a son, later called Charles the Bald. The new mother naturally desired that her son, too, be given a share in the kingdom, and Bernhard was put in charge of carrying out her and the emperor's wishes in this matter. There was already a good deal of envy among the other nobles at Bernhard's rapid rise, and he seems not to have been overly diplomatic at times. At any rate, the performance of his duty in the matter of obtaining a share of the kingdom for Charles the Bald brought him the enmity of Louis the Pious' three older sons. In addition, the so-called unification party, led by his disaffected brother-in-law Wala, liked neither the emperor nor Bernhard, and they especially disliked Judith. Rumors were circulated concerning an affair between Bernhard and Judith. Bernhard was also accused of using magic to bewitch the emperor and of seeking to depose him in favor of Charles. A modern author has summarized the feelings toward Bernhard in the following words:

Bernhard was an accursed wallower in hog pools of filth, a wild boar on a rampage of destruction. He had violated the imperial bedchamber, broken treaties, practiced tyranny. In his revelry and debauchery he turned night into day and day into night. He was a monster—seditious, blind, mad, immoral and shameless. An adulterer and the impious enemy of religion, he exerted his influence by practicing the art of sorcery. Not one good word does this vicious creature receive from Radbertus.[8]

Indeed, it is not only Radbertus who fails to give Bernhard a good word. None of the chroniclers has anything kind to say about him after 829, and, though we do not know what the circumstances were, when we consider what kind of monster might take a newborn child away from its mother and hide even its name from her for two years, we too might find it difficult to say anything kind about him. Bernhard's cruelty, however, seems slight compared to that of some of his contemporaries in the royal family, where torturing, maiming, and beheading a captured enemy, be he a close relative or not, was a common practice. By way of crushing the revolt of 817, Louis the Pious had his nephew, Bernhard of Italy, blinded. When Lothair captured his father, Louis the Pious, in April 830, he had Judith put into a nunnery and forced his father to take a humiliating oath. He had Bernhard of Septimania's brother, Heribert, blinded and placed in a monastery in Italy. Later, when Lothair again captured two members of Bernhard's family, he had them both killed— his brother Gaucelm was decapitated, and his sister, the nun Gariberga, was drowned as a sorceress. Bernhard himself did not cease trying to regain his lost honors; he continued to practice a politics of joining first this, then that party or of trying to remain neutral. In the summer of 841, as we have seen, he remained "loyal" to Pippin while sending his son William to Charles the Bald, to whom he was to swear allegiance if Charles would return the benefices left to him by his uncle, Theodoric.

This is the situation in which Dhuoda finds herself when she commences to write her *Manual* at the cold beginning of Advent, 841. She is facing another Christmas without her husband, her stalwart son William, and her infant son Bernhard. The members of the splendid family into which she was married are scattered, dead, or maimed. The rumors concerning her husband's behavior and his waning fortunes can scarcely have failed to reach her ears. Perhaps he and she discussed all this during his visit to Uzès in 840, for there are many indications in the *Manual*. Certainly she knew the fate of the family members, for she mentions them as defunct. By way of ending the story of Dhuoda's family, it might be interesting for the reader to know that Bernhard was captured and beheaded by Charles the Bald in 844 and that his son William, forgetting the advice of his mother, underwent the same fate in 850. There is even good evidence that their son Bernhard, "only too much the son of the

elder Bernhard in flesh and in habits," as the *Annales Bertiniani* calls
him, was also beheaded for treason, but we are not sure. Our uncertainty
over his fate has called forth one of those typical scholarly debates known
as "the problem of the Bernhards."[9]

One could probably place Dhuoda's *Manual* in the genre of handbook
or moral guidebook, epitomized for the Middle Ages by Saint Augustine's *Enchiridion*, 'manual, handbook,' but, as Becker so rightly remarks, Dhuoda's *Manual* is *sui generis*, and it is difficult to compare it
with other works.[10] Modern authorities have criticized its lack of organization and of a clear plan, but this complaint could be made against
many of the works of her day. In contemporary rhetoric manuals, *inven-
tio*, or the gathering of quotations and allusions suited to the topic at
hand, seems to have been stressed over *dispositio*, 'organization.' In fact,
it has been pointed out by many authorities that Dhuoda's style is so
allusive and packed with quotations that it is difficult to find her sources.
This is, indeed, one of the fine qualities of her *Manual*; its very artlessness
is an earnest of the validity of her writing as a picture of the intellectual
life of her age. Too often intellectual history turns out to be the history
of professional intellectuals; from Dhuoda we learn how a private person
viewed the Carolingian world.[11]

It is not true, however, that the *Manual* has no organization. We can
see that Dhuoda had a basic plan; perhaps the length of time it took her
to finish the work and the necessity to get it done caused her to add
material here and there. The *Manual* has several pieces of preparatory
matter, as was common in her day.[12] In the first, Dhuoda offers a fanciful
etymology of the word *manualis*, or rather three etymologies, and then
reveals the purpose of the book, namely, to offer guidance to her son. She
says that she has followed the Hebrew, Greek, and Latin tongues, the
three sacred languages. This section is found only in the Barcelona manuscript; in the other manuscripts the incipit is an acrostichon, that is, a
poem in which the first letters of each couplet form a word, a trick not
uncommon in her day.[13] The words say: "Dhuoda, to her beloved son
William, greetings. Read!" It is a long prayer to God for the well-being
of her family and a request to the reader to pray for them, also. The next
section, the prologue proper, begins with a humility formula, telling how
Dhuoda, being a woman, cannot write but hopes that God will aid her.
She tells William that he will find in her book, in condensed form, all
that he needs to know, although he may read many other books. She
wishes to tell him how to attain salvation and how to conduct himself
here on earth, but first a word about his family.[14] The final section before
the work proper is a preface in which she offers William the information
about her marriage and his birth we mentioned above. All this is written
in a style at the same time typically Carolingian and Dhuoda's own.

Book 1 is devoted to God and to worshiping him. Dhuoda speaks of the power of God's name by considering the numbers found in it. *Deus*, 'God,' is composed of four letters and two syllables; in Greek, *delta* has the power of 4 (each letter of the alphabet was used as a number in Greek); in Latin, *D* means 500 (as a roman numeral). God is everywhere, above, below, inside, outside; if all the world were parchment and all its people scribes, we could not describe the All-Powerful. Dhuoda ends with an admonition to William to acquire many books but not to cease reading the *Manual*, to persevere in the search for God.

Book 2 follows naturally from Book 1, for here Dhuoda speaks of the Trinity, a subject which must have been particularly important to her, since she lived in proximity to the Goths, many of whom were still anti-Trinitarian Arians even in her day. Again, in typical fashion, the number 3 reminds her of other 3's, and she delivers a disquisition on the "theological" virtues of faith, hope, and charity. Book 2 ends with an admonition on the proper reverence to be used in *oratio*, 'prayer,' which she pauses to etymologize as *oris ratio*, 'reason of the mouth.' She gives several examples of how to pray and which prayers to use, much like a catechism.

Book 3 is first devoted to the respect due to one's father. Dhuoda gives many examples from the Old Testament of sons who respected their fathers. Next comes service to one's lord, in this case Charles the Bald—how he should be obeyed in all things—then advice on following advice and receiving and seeking it. She carefully outlines how William should comport himself vis-à-vis the nobles of the court and the royal family, advising him to accommodate himself to great and small. Finally, she counsels that he should give special honor to priests as the servants of God and our aid in getting to God. The priest is called *pontifex* because he builds a *pons*, 'bridge,' for us to God.

Book 4 deals with the overcoming of bad habits, mainly through the exercise of the eight beatitudes and the seven gifts of the Holy Spirit. As a doctor cures a disease by applying opposites (for example, a fever by applying cold), so one should oppose virtues to vices. She particularly cautions William against pride, the major vice, and counsels patience. Finally, she recommends almsgiving and other aid to the poor.

Book 5 tells William what to do in times of temptation and tribulation, for these are but trials sent by God which must be borne. She cautions him again to render glory to God in all things.

In Book 6, Dhuoda returns to the theme of the seven gifts and the eight beatitudes and gives the fifteen qualities of the perfect man, which she hopes William may become, with the help of God. To this is added a long disquisition on the powers of the various numbers, especially 7, 8, and 15, and the various calculations which can be made with them.

Book 7 tells of the twofold birth and the twofold death, that of the flesh and that of the spirit, with instruction on perseverance in the life of the spirit and avoidance of death of the spirit.

Book 8 admonishes William to be diligent in prayer and reading, suggesting those for whom he should especially pray. This was probably intended to be the last book of the *Manual* in the original plan, for the other material seems to be more like a series of appendixes than an integral part of the work.

Book 9 is devoted to the significance of numbers, to finger counting and the like. Here we learn that the letters in Adam come from east (*anathole*), west (*dysis*), north (*arktos*), and south (*mesembrios*) in Greek. In Greek, adding the numbers associated with these letters yields 46, the number of years necessary for the restoration of the temple in Jerusalem.

Book 10 contains the following headings: 1. On the periods of your life. 2. Verses composed using the letters of your name. 3. Postscript on your public life. 4. Pray for me while I am in this body and for the salvation of my soul after my burial. 5. Names of the defunct (members of Bernhard's family). 6. Concerning the inscription to be placed on my tombstone.

Book 11, following Alcuin's *Book on the Use of the Psalms* almost verbatim, deals with the liturgical division of the Psalms. It is followed by a conclusion, giving the date of the ending of the book and returning to the words of the incipit—*consumatum est*, 'it is finished,' the last words spoken by Jesus on the cross.

From this outline it should be obvious that Dhuoda was indeed following an overall plan, one which is excellent for a handbook designed for the spiritual and moral guidance of a sixteen-year-old son. All this, as far as its intellectual and spiritual content is concerned, might have been written by a pious Catholic mother of today to her son; it is readily understandable by anyone familiar with the catechism. What makes Dhuoda so difficult of access for the modern reader and so important for us as a source for the Carolingian way of viewing the world is her mode of expression and thought.[15] Modern scholars, in seeking to understand and manipulate their universe, are apt to seek a scientific explanation and to draw their metaphors from science, but Dhuoda lived in a world dominated by religion. God had spoken to humanity in two ways: through scripture and through Creation,[16] and, as Saint Irenaeus had pointed out, there was nothing which did not have meaning in God's eyes.[17] Thus, the Carolingian age sought meaning in everything, and it is necessary to know something about these modes of thought in order to understand any medieval writing.

Dhuoda is a child of her age in that she thinks that the etymology of a word offers a key to its understanding.[18] One of the most important things about a person was that person's name (*sine nomine persona non est*), and the most important thing about the name was its etymology. Just as we do, the Carolingians had an etymological dictionary in Isidore of Seville's *Originum seu Etymologiarum*, and Dhuoda's contemporary, Smaragdus, had given etymologies of Germanic names, but these were not like our etymologies. In Isidore one might find that *fenestra*, 'window,' came from FErens NOS exTRA, 'taking us outside,' or that *cadaver* meant CAro DAta VERmibus, 'flesh given to worms,' but one could also make up etymologies on the spur of the moment, as is probably the case for Dhuoda's etymology of *manualis*. One could even mix various languages, as in the common etymology for *avis*, 'bird': *a* (a Greek negative prefix) plus *via*, 'path,' because the bird follows no path. At any rate, we must not poke fun at such etymologies as *caro*, 'flesh,' from *cadendo*, 'falling' (because all flesh must fall), labeling them as "fantaisiste." [19] As Paul Zumthor has rightly insisted, these etymologies represent a medieval mode of thought which we must try to understand rather than laugh at: "L'étymologie, d'abord admise comme l'un des aspects de la figure *descriptio nominis* . . . se chargea d'un sens presque métaphysique. En l'absence de critères linguistiques objectifs, c'est toute une morale, sinon une théologie, qui s'incorporait ainsi à l'oeuvre, par le moyen de cet ornement." [20]

Dhuoda lived in an age when people took seriously the testimony of the Book of Wisdom that "God has arranged all things in number and measure" (Wisd. 11:20). Thus 7 meant the seven gifts of the Holy Spirit, the seven virtues, the seven cardinal sins, the seven cities, and so on. [21] Dhuoda, using the quotation from Ecclesiastes 11:2—"Give a portion to seven, and also to eight"—expounds on the various 7's in the Bible, such as the seven lamps of Revelation 4:5, the seven days of the week, and the seven ages of the world, then shows that 8 plus 7 yields 15, the number of qualities of the perfect man. And 7 times 7 yields 49, the number of complete satisfaction for sins; add 1 and you have 50, the number of the jubilee and the number of the most important of the Psalms, the fiftieth (fifty-first in Protestant Bibles), the Psalm *miserere*.

In Dhuoda's day, it was common to learn calculation on the fingers, in which the joint involved and the placement of the thumb on the joint indicated the number involved. [22] Thus, when Frederick II wished to tell his men how to hold the bowstring, he could simply say, "In the manner of a master of computation forming the number 73," that is, with the thumb inserted between the first and second finger, with the other fingers bent and supporting them. [23] Dhuoda wishes that William may live long enough to reach the right hand, leaving the 99 of the left. This is but an echo of Juvenal's "felix nimirum, qui tot per saecula mortem distulit atque suos iam dextra conputat annos," for to count on the right hand meant to go into the hundreds.[24] For Dhuoda 100 also meant the life of the blessed to come, since for her it was a perfect number.

Because God is perfect and wishes perfection, he must be worshiped in a perfect way. Thus, according to Dhuoda and the Middle Ages, there must originally have been ten choirs of angels worshiping him.[25] The "Celestial Hierarchy" derived by Dionysius the Areopagite from Saint Paul's teachings contained nine orders of angels. Thus developed the notion that Satan and his angels had formed a tenth choir and that God had made humanity to fill the void left when Satan fell. When the number of the blessed filled up the tenth choir, the world would come to an end, and Jews and Christians would be joined together.

As pointed out above, Dhuoda's style is allusive in the extreme. In spite of the number of footnotes in Pierre Riché's edition, he has not succeeded in finding all of her allusions, for her method consisted in weaving (one of her favorite metaphors and a favorite metaphor of the day) strands gathered from others into a text. For the Carolingian author, excellence did not consist so much in novelty as in the skill with which one wove. She tells us (9. 1), "A part of the teaching of this little book is, as you see, woven together from various volumes, but because of my affection for you, I have rather inserted their testimonies according to the measure of your ability, so that you are brought to the height through fifteen (gradual) degrees and held there." This style is both a joy and a frustration: we rejoice in her learning and in the deftness with which she weaves her quotations, but with our present knowledge we often cannot be sure what is Dhuoda and what is a quotation. To her, of course, this would have made no difference, since she set no store by originality.

In grammatical matters she differs little from her contemporaries. Those who are used to Ciceronian Latin will find her *Manual* full of barbarisms and solecisms. She is not always too careful in matters of case; as Riché points out, she uses the accusative often for other cases, but this is common in her day.[26] She uses the adynaton, that is, invokes something impossible or absurd, as when she says, ". . . if the heavens and the earth were spread through the air like a parchment," but her near contemporary, Walahfrid Strabo, goes much farther than that by stringing together an unexcelled group of adynata.[27] She loves to parade her learning by using strange words, some of which we can find in no dictionary, much in the manner of her countryman Virgil of Toulouse.[28] Finally, she loves to mix verse and prose. In fact, she has done this so well that we still are not sure where the verse ends and the prose begins or what form she is following.[29] She loves riddles, particularly word and number riddles.

Until such time as we can determine Dhuoda's sources better than we now can, it is difficult to make a definitive statement on her learning.[30] Suffice it to say that she seems to have known, either directly or through intermediaries, most of the authors known to her contemporaries. She cites freely from the Bible, Donatus, Augustine, Gregory, Virgil, Prudentius, Alcuin, Isidore, and the rule of Saint Benedict.[31] She is familiar with the theology, both moral and spiritual, of her day as well as with such things as etymology and numerical symbolism. Such learning must have been unusual among the laity and quite unusual among women. To be sure, we do occasionally hear of learned women, such as Otfrid's "noble matron, Judith," but they have failed, with the exception of a few letters, to leave anything behind them.

As we read through the *Manual*, we get some idea of Dhuoda's character. I think we can trust its witness, although Dhuoda does expect William to show the *Manual* to others, so that it is not just a handbook addressed by a mother to her son. She comes through as a warm human being, interested in the earthly well-being of her husband and her two sons as well as their eternal salvation. When we hear her words of wisdom on how to bear up under exile and humble existence (4. 1, 59 ff.), we are forced to think of her own situation, which she bears without a word of complaint. While her husband is away involved in his wars, she has had to meet his obligations at home and has had to incur debts (10. 4, 39 ff.), which she has been at pains to pay off. She is concerned particularly about her younger son and tells William to care for him (10. 4, 53 ff.): "Concerning your little brother, what you should do for him, I admonished you above and I admonish you again. I beg you, if he attains the age of manhood, that he also might deign to pray for me. Already, just as if both of you were together, I admonish you to be willing to make the sacrificial offering and the oblation of the Host for me often." A woman of learning and firmness of character, an exemplary mother, a warm person—what more could one ask of Dhuoda?

In making the present translation, I have tried to consult all the authorities. For the most part, I have followed Riché's text, as the most accessible and undoubtedly the most authoritative, but I have not hesitated to depart from it when another seemed better. As in the previous example, I have tried to present Dhuoda's style wherever possible, since this is an important part of her person. In particular, I have not suppressed her anacolutha, since these reveal how she thinks. I hope in this manner not to have falsified my author.

In the early portions of the text, I have tried to render Dhuoda's style as best I could. She loves long sentences, hypotaxis, parenthetical expressions, and unusual turns of phrase, and she does not always avoid anacolutha. In castigating her son, she offers example after example from the Bible and the lives of the Fathers of people who have done as she says and prospered or of people who have not acted properly and have come to a bad end. I usually cite only one or two of her examples. I have not tried to indicate quotations from the Bible in the footnotes, since the whole text is a tissue of quotations and allusions, but I have usually had recourse to the Rheims-Douay Version of the Bible. In order to understand Dhuoda, read her as if it were your own mother giving you advice.

NOTES

1. Several editions or partial editions of Dhuoda's *Manual* are available. Mabillon, just mentioned, is best consulted in the *Patrologia Latina* 106. 109–118, which can be found in most university libraries. The best nineteenth-century edition is that of Edouard Bondurand, *L'éducation carolingienne: Le manuel de Dhuoda*, which follows for the most part the manuscript of Nîmes, supplemented by that of Paris. It has a facing-page translation into French. By far the best and most complete edition is that of Pierre Riché, *Dhuoda: Manuel pour mon fils*, which also contains a translation. A good German translation, based on Bondurand's text, is found in Gabriel Meier, *Ausgewählte Schriften von Columan, Alkuin, Dodana* . . .

2. She seems to have called herself both Dhuoda, the Germanic form of the name, and Dhuodana, the Latin form, for it was not unusual for Carolingians to use both a Frankish and a Latin form of their names. There has been a great deal of speculation as to the meaning of her name and its derivation, most of it not by professional philologists and thus to be rejected; compare Riché, *Dhuoda*, pp. 22 ff.

3. There have been numerous attempts at writing the biography of Dhuoda, not all of them based on a careful reading of the facts. Besides Riché, see especially Joachim Wollasch, "Eine adlige Familie des frühen Mittelalters: Ihr Selbstverständnis und ihre Wirklichkeit," *Archiv für Kulturgeschichte* 39 (1957): 150–188.

4. To understand the story of Dhuoda's marriage, it is probably best to read the historical sources themselves. I recommend particularly *Carolingian Chronicles*, translated by Bernhard W. Scholz with Barbara Rogers, and *Charlemagne's Cousins*, translated, with introduction and notes, by Allen Cabaniss. For those who wish a more thorough knowledge of the period, consult Bernard Simson, *Jahrbücher des fränkischen Reichs unter Ludwig dem Frommen*, and J. F. Böhmer, E. Mühlbacher, and J. Lechner, *Die Regesten des Kaiserreichs unter den Karolingern 751–918*.

5. On Bernhard and his family, see J. Calmette, *De Bernardo Sancti Guillelmi filio*. Calmette is an outspoken proponent of the view that Bernhard was simply calumniated by his enemies and was not such a bad fellow after all. His "La famille de Saint Guilhem," *Annales du Midi* 18 (1906): 145–165, is also worth reading. Although I cannot agree with his main thesis, Arthur J. Zuckerman has an excellent and readable account of Bernhard's life in his *A Jewish Princedom in Feudal France, 768–900*, pp. 260–288.

6. E. Dümmler conjectures that Paschasius Radbertus calls Bernhard "Naso" because of his nose and not as a complimentary reference to Ovid, in the manner in which Charlemagne called Alcuin "Flaccus" (Horace); compare Zuckerman, p. 263. We know that Saint William was called "crooked nose." Although there is much argument on the matter, there seems to be little reason to doubt that Bernhard had some sort of affair with the Empress Judith.

7. On Saint William, see Calmette, "La famille de Saint Guilhem." The best introduction to the problems connected with the historical and the fabulous Saint William is still Joseph Bédier, *Les légendes épiques*, vol. 1.

8. *Charlemagne's Cousins*, trans. Cabaniss, p. 19.

9. For a discussion of this problem, see Wollasch, pp. 185–187.

10. Ph. Aug. Becker, "Duodas Handbuch," *Zeitschrift für Romanische Philologie* 21 (1897): 73–101.

11. Both Becker and Wollasch go to great pains to reveal Dhuoda's world view. It is unfortunate that the desire to use her as a resource, however, has impaired the study of her as a writer. Neither of these two authorities has tried to *understand* her work, for example, her use of etymologies, number symbolism, and the like.

12. Compare, for example, the gospel harmony of her famous near contemporary, Otfrid of Weissenburg, which has at least three prologues: *Otfrids Evangelienbuch*, ed. Oskar Erdmann.

13. The book by Otfrid mentioned above contains two such poems among its prefatory matter. In Otfrid's case both poems are also *teleosticha*, that is, the final letters also spell words.

14. Dhuoda tells William only about the agnatic side of the family, that is, about Bernhard's relatives. This is surprising, since the Germanic and Frankish system of kinship emphasized also the enatic side, that is, the mother's brother or his surrogate was the most important kinsman. Compare Clair Hayden Bell, *The Sister's Son in the Medieval German Epic*, pp. 67–182.

15. For a study of these symbolic methods of expression and knowing, see James Marchand, "*Sagena piscatoris*: An Essay in Medieval Lexicography," pp. 123–138.

16. Compare Dhuoda's contemporary, Johannes Scotus Eriugena (*PL* 122. 289): "Dupliciter ergo lux aeterna se ipsam mundo declarat, per Scripturam videlicet et creaturam" (thus, the Eternal Light declares Himself to the world in two ways: through Scripture, as it were, and through Creation).

17. Irenaeus *Adversus Haereses* 4. 21. 3: "Nihil vacuum et sine signo apud Deum." In dealing with medieval authors, it is important to remember that they believed that God does nothing in vain and that everything is placed here for some reason. It is especially important to remember that everything, along with every word, has a meaning.

18. For a thorough study of the modes of etymologizing in the Middle Ages, see Roswitha Klinck, *Die lateinische Etymologie des Mittelalters*. On etymology as a category of thought, see Ernst R. Curtius, *European Literature and the Latin Middle Ages*, pp. 495–500.

19. Riché, *Dhuoda*, p. 259. Riché has failed to note that this is a common etymology, given also by the contemporary *Abba pater* glossary; compare Klinck, p. 79.

20. Paul Zumthor, *Histoire littéraire de la France médiévale*, p. 6.

21. On number symbolism in general, see Vincent F. Hopper, *Medieval Number Symbolism*. For a fine study of a work contemporary to Dhuoda's, see Robert E. McNally, S.J., "Der irische Liber de numeris."

22. A good introduction to medieval finger reckoning is Karl Menninger, *Number Words and Number Symbols*, pp. 201–219.

23. Frederick II (d. 1250), *De arte venandi cum avibus*, as quoted in ibid., p. 216 f.

24. Juvenal *Satires*, 10. 246, cited in ibid.: "Happy indeed because he has put off death for so many generations and is now counting his years on his right hand."

25. See Paul Salmon, "Der zehnte Engelchor in deutschen Dichtungen und Predigten des Mittelalters," *Euphorion* 57 (1963): 321–330.

26. As Riché points out, Carolingian Latin is poorly studied, partly because of our habit of "correcting" our texts. Before criticizing Dhuoda, we need to look at the latinity of other Carolingians. An excellent guide is Karl Strecker, *Introduction to Medieval Latin*. It is good to look also at C. H. Grandgent, *An Introduction to Vulgar Latin*.

27. Compare Walahfrid Strabo, "Similitudo impossibilium," p. 392. On the adynaton in general, see Ernest Dutoit, *Le thème de l'adynaton dans la poésie antique*.

28. Compare Strecker, p. 56.

29. For a survey of the various attempts, see A. Burger, "Les vers de la Duchesse Dhuoda et son poème *De temporibus tuis*," pp. 85–102.

30. Compare Becker, "Duodas Handbuch," and Pierre Riché, "Les bibliothèques de trois aristocrates laïques carolingiens," *Le Moyen Age* 69 (1963): 87–103.

31. See the list of sources in Riché, *Dhuoda*, pp. 375–385.

Dhuoda's *Manual*

Here Begins the Manual of Dhuoda Which She Sent to Her Son, William[1]

Having noticed that most women in this world are able to live with and enjoy their children, but seeing myself, Dhuoda, living far away from you, my dear son William, filled with anxiety because of this, and with the desire to be of aid to you, I am sending you this little manual, written by me, for your scrutiny and education, rejoicing in the fact that, though I am absent in body, this little book will recall to your mind, as you read it, the things you are required to do for my sake.

Acrostichon of the Following Work[2]

Divine Creator of heaven's light, Author
    Of stars and pole, Eternal King, Holy One,
Help me by grace to finish what I have begun.
    Being ignorant, I ask intelligence of You;
Urge me to learn Your perfect will,
    To make a proper path through present and future.
One and Three through all the ages,
    You enrich those who belong to You.
Duly do You count the merits of each one,
    You give heaven's reward to Your servants.[3]
As much as I am able, on bended knee,
    I offer great thanks to You, the Creator.
. . . .

Reader, if you wish to know the formula,
    Scrutinize the first letters of the verses.
Easily you will be able to find out
    The meaning of what I have written.
As the mother of two of the masculine sex,
    I ask that you pray to the Good Creator:
"Direct the father of these boys to heaven."

May He join me to them in the kingdom.

Begin reading at the letter *D* (*delta*); everything ends with the *M* (*moida*).[4] The verses are finished; with the aid of Christ, I shall approach the work undertaken for my son.

Begins the Prologue

To many people many things are obvious which are nevertheless hidden from me; those like me, with darkened senses, are lacking in intellect; if I say less, I am more.[5] But He "Who opens the mouths of the mute and makes eloquent the tongues of babes" is present. Dhuoda, although fragile in sense, living unworthily among worthy women, nevertheless your mother, William, to you now is my manual's word addressed . . . I hope that, busy as you are with mundane and secular preoccupations, you will not neglect frequently to read in this little book sent by me to you, for the sake of my memory, as if you were looking into a mirror or at a chessboard.

Even if you increase your possessions of books, may it please you to read frequently this my little work, and you will be able to understand useful things with the aid of God. You will find in it all you desire to know, set down briefly; you will also find a mirror in which you undoubtedly will be able to see the salvation of your soul.[6]

I worry a great deal, William, about sending to you words of salvation, but along with that, I am burning with the desire to tell you, with the aid of God, about your birth, as you may have it written down in this little book, as is put forth first in the following.[7]

Preface

In the eleventh year, by the kindness of Christ, of the reign of our former lord, Louis, who ruled in splendor and happily, I became the wife of my lord and your progenitor, on the 29th of June in the palace at Aix.[8] And again in the thirteenth year of his reign, on the 29th of November, by the aid of God, as I believe, your birth in the world, O dearest firstborn son, proceeded from me.

As the misery and calamities of this world grew and continued to grow, amid many vicissitudes and discords of the reign, the aforementioned emperor went the way of all flesh. And after his death, the next year, your brother, on the 22nd of March, by the mercy of God, left my womb as the second after you, in the town of Uzès. Still a babe, before he received the grace of baptism, your lord and parent Bernhard, and his, too, had him taken into Aquitaine by Elefantus, bishop of the aforementioned city.

But after having resided in the aforementioned city for a long time at the order of my lord, with the absence of your presence,[9] rejoicing in his [success in] battle, but with the desire to see both of you, I took care to write and send to you this little book, according to the poverty of my intelligence.

Although I am taken up with many troubles, the hope to see you again someday is the first according to God, if it be the will of the Lord. I should wish, if some power were given me by God, but since salvation is far from me, sinner that I am, I wish, and in this wish my soul languishes.[10]

I have heard that your father, Bernhard, has commended you into the hands of Charles the King; I admonish you to give a perfect goodwill to the accomplishment of your duties. However, as it says in the Scriptures, "Seek first the Kingdom of God in all things and the rest will follow," all that is necessary for the good of your soul and your body.

On Loving God

I ask and humbly suggest to your noble youth, as if I were present, and also to those to whom you show this book that they may read it, that you might not condemn me and reproach me for the fact that I am so bold as to embark upon such a profound and perilous task: to direct to you instruction concerning God. To be sure, I myself do not cease to reproach myself, considering my human fragility, for I am poor, but dust and ashes. And what shall I say? If the patriarchs and prophets and the other saints, from the first man up to now, have not been able to arrive at a full understanding of the doctrine, how much less can I, born of a weak and low race! And if, as the Scriptures say, "The heaven and the heaven of heavens cannot contain Him," because of His magnitude, what am I going to be able to say, inexperienced as I am?

On God

A learned man—oh, how great he is in merit!—said: "As to the name, God (*Deus*), it contains two syllables and four letters." When you find these and read them, what can you say but, *Deus* contains this great, admirable mystery. Now, as one of the dull-witted ones, I shall begin with its first letter, which expressed alone in two words contains a most useful amount of information in its name.

For our *D*, in which the name of *Deus*, 'God,' begins, among the Greeks is called *delta*. Thus expressed, according to their counting system, it contains the number 4, perfection. But according to our roman numerals, *D* arrives at the sum of 500. And this does not fail to indicate a sacred mystery.

1, 2, 3, and 4, although each pertains to itself, when combined in various ways transform themselves into other numbers. All these things are obvious to the learned: 5 times 5 yields 25, and this doubled rises to 50, V L D.[11]

I am thinking now of those whose stories I have heard read and also of some of my relatives, and yours, also, whom I have known; they were powerful in this world and are no more. Perhaps they are with God because of their merits, but they are not present in body on earth. For them and for others I pray on bended knee: *Requiem aeternam*.[12] Within myself also, although insignificant, when I consider these things and that death is to come, I fear the things to come.

Therefore, He is to be feared, loved, and certainly to be believed to be immortal Who without diminution is Ever-Powerful King, commanding and performing whatever He wishes. All things are placed in His will and His power. "There is none who can resist His will, saying, Why hast Thou done thus?"[13] He Himself is the God of the universes; He is the power, the kingdom, and the empire. Concerning His power and rule the most blessed Daniel firmly said, "His power is an everlasting power that shall not be taken away: and His kingdom that shall not be destroyed."

Moral Lesson

And what shall I say, fragile vessel that I am? I shall turn to others as a friend. To be sure, if the heavens and the earth were spread through the air like a parchment, and if all the various gulfs of the sea were transformed into ink, and if all the inhabitants of the earth born into this world from the beginning of humankind up to now were scribes, which is an impossible thing contrary to nature, they would not be able to comprehend (in writing) the greatness, the breadth, the height, the sublimity, the profundity of the Almighty or tell the divinity, wisdom, piety, and clemency of Him Who is called God.[14] Since He is thus and so great that no one can comprehend His essence, I beg you to fear Him and to love Him with all your heart, all your mind, all your understanding, to bless Him in all your ways and deeds and to sing, "For He is good, for His mercy endureth forever!"

And believe Him to be above, below, inside, and outside, for He is superior, inferior, interior, and exterior.

Admonition

I also admonish you, O my handsome and lovable son William, that amid the mundane cares of this world you not neglect the acquisition of many books, in which you may understand and learn something greater and better than is written here concerning God, your Creator, through the teaching of the most blessed doctors. Beseech Him, cherish Him, love Him; if you do so, He will be a Keeper, a Leader, a Companion, and a Fatherland for you, the Way, the Truth, and the Life, granting you generous prosperity in the world, and He will turn your enemies to peace.

What more can I say? Your admonisher, Dhuoda, is always with you, son, and if I be absent because of death, which must come, you will have this little book of moral teaching as a memorial; and in it you will be able to see me as the reflection in a mirror, reading and praying to God in mind and body, and you will find fully set down the duties you must perform for me. Son, you will have teachers who will teach you other documents of greater utility, but not under the same conditions, not with a soul burning in their breasts as I, your mother, have, O firstborn son.

On Reverence in Prayer

Prayer is called *oratio*, 'prayer,' sort of *oris ratio*, 'reason of the mouth.'[15]

But I, Dhuoda, lukewarm and lazy, weak and always tending toward that which is low, neither a long nor a short prayer pleases me. But I place my hope in Him, Who offers to His faithful the freedom to pray. And you, son William, keep watch, ask of Him and pray in a short, firm, and pure speech. Say, not only in the church, but wherever the opportunity presents itself, pray and say, "Mercy-giving and Merciful, Just and Pious, Clement and True, have pity on Your creation, whom You created and redeemed with Your blood; have pity on me, and grant that I may walk in Your paths and Your justice; give me memory and sense that I may understand, believe, love, fear, praise, and thank You and be perfect in every good work through proper faith and goodwill, O Lord, my God. Amen."

On the Respect You Owe to Your Father
as Long as You Live

I do not tire of impressing upon you, as much as I can, how much you ought to fear, love, and remain faithful in all things to Bernhard, your father, both present and absent. For you have a teacher and an author full of wisdom, Solomon, who castigates you, son, and admonishes you, saying, "God has honored the father flourishing in children." And again, "He that honoreth his father shall have joy in his own children, and shall enjoy a long life. He that obeyeth the father shall be comfort to his mother, and he that honoreth his father is as one that layeth up a treasure of many good things." "Support," if by the aid of God you can aid him, "his old age, and grieve him not in his life, and despise him not when thou art in thy strength."

Far be this from you; may the earth cover my body before your father might have that happen to him, which will not happen, I am sure. Nor do I say this because I am afraid that it will happen; I just want to prevent this crime from ever entering your mind, for we have heard that such things have been committed by others, not like you. Do not forget the evils which happened to the sons of Eli, who, spurning the commandments of their father, were disobedient and for this reason underwent bitter death. One ought also not forget the tree of Absalom.

Certainly in the view of men the royal and imperial pomp and power excel in this world, so that among humans their action and names are first venerated. Nevertheless, my son, this is my will, that according to the admonition of my poor intelligence, and according to God, you must first not neglect to render to him who sired you, so long as you live, a particular homage, sure and faithful. It is a certain and fixed condition (of life) that no one, unless he first proceed from his father, can arrive at any high position.

So I admonish you, most beloved son William, that first you love God as you have it written down above; after that love, fear, and cherish your father; know that your status in life comes from him.

Admonition Concerning Conduct toward Your Lord

The lord whom you have, Charles, since God, as I believe, and your father, Bernhard, have chosen him for you to serve, remember this, is the descendant of a great and noble family. Serve him not only so as to be pleasing to his sight, but also with great intensity, as to both body and soul; keep in all things a pure and sure fidelity to him.

Remember the fine servant of the patriarch Abraham, who went into a far country to seek a bride for the son of his lord. Thanks to the faith of the commander and the worthy display of obedience on the part of the servant, the command was fulfilled, and through her numerous progeny the bride obtained great grace and many possessions. How about the obedience of Joab, Abner, and others toward King David?

Therefore, I adjure you, son, to keep what you have faithfully all your life, in body and in mind. Then, as we believe, your career will flourish, and it will be of great use to your servants. Let the madness of infidelity never press from you an evil misdeed; let it never arise in your heart to be unfaithful to your lord in anything. The reputation of those who do so is hard and shameful. I do not believe that this will happen to you or to your knights; this kind of action, as people say, never appeared among your progenitors, never was, is not, never will be.

You, therefore, my son William, born of their lineage, be, as I said before, truthful, watchful, useful, and prompt toward your lord, and in all affairs concerning the royal power, to the extent that God grants you the strength, seek to show yourself prudent both inside and out.

On Receiving Counsel

If God someday leads you to such a point that you will merit being called to the council among the greats, consider prudently what, when, to whom, or how you can show a worthy and fitting eloquence. Act according to the counsel of those who prepare you for faithful action as to the body and the soul. It is written, "Do all things with counsel, and thou shalt not repent when thou hast done." This "all things" does not include bad actions which destroy sane judgment, but rather higher and greater things which can lead without reprehension to the salvation of the soul and the body . . .

Those who work in metals, when they begin to flatten the gold to make leaves, wait for a fitting and proper day, a time, so that it may shine all the brighter with shining metal in the wrapping of ornaments. Thus also in the judgment of the prudent this consideration of reason must always be present. Indeed, the word of the prudent is whiter than snow, sweeter than honey, purer than gold or silver. Why? Because, as the Scriptures say, "From the mouth of the prudent proceeds honey. Good favor as it were is above silver and gold."

I also urge you not to neglect getting together with the young who love God and seek wisdom, not only the elders, for old age derives its strength from youth. A certain one says, "The things that thou hast not gathered in thy youth, how shalt thou find them in thy old age?" You must seek it [wisdom] of God and say, "Lord, teach me from my youth, unto old age and gray hairs do not forsake me, Blessed Father." You will be blessed, son, if you are taught by Him and merit being learned in His law. Certainly, Samuel and Daniel, still boys, flourishing in the strength of their youth, judged, as did their fathers, as old men.[16]

What shall I say about you, son, I, the unworthy, unhappy, and insignificant Dhuoda? I pray that He Who performed such deeds in these and others like them, He Who is called God, may do the same to you in the vigor of your youth, now and forever. As it shall be His will, so be it done unto you forever.

Toward the Family of Your Lord

Toward the famous, illustrious, and noble relatives and favorites of your powerful and royal lord, those deriving both their origin and their worth from the paternal or the maternal lineage, if you come to merit being a man-at-arms with fellow knights in the royal and imperial chamber, or wherever you can be useful, fear, love, venerate, and cherish them, and offer to them a sure, pure, and proper devotion, both of body and of soul, in all business which concerns them, with faithful execution.

Remember how David acted toward Jonathan, the son of King Saul, to the son just as to the father, as also toward their descendants, not only during their lives but also after their deaths; as long as he lived, he stood by them as a faithful and true champion in all things.

That You Must Be Kind to Great and Small

It is not necessary for me to tell you this, that the example of the greatest, oldest, and best leaders must be followed in dealing with inferiors, for, though far from me, you will have noticed it yourself; also do not doubt that the lesser ones may rise to the heights of offering models for prelates. Therefore, I urge you not to be slow in joining yourself to them, in greater and lesser services.

God is the shaper of the good and the bad in heaven and on earth. For the sake of His lesser ones, He deigned to reveal His presence here below, for, as the Fathers say, although He was the Supreme Creator of all, He was willing to take on the form of a slave. He raises the powerful in order to plunge them into the depths, and He exalts the humble, that they may rise to the heights. . . . And if He, great as He is, comports Himself thus toward the lesser ones, what should we, small as we are, do toward those who are worse off? Those who are able ought to help them, and, according to the urgings and words of the Apostle Paul, bear one another's burdens.

Love all that you may be loved by all, cherish that you be cherished; if you love all, all will love you; if you individually, they plurally.[17] It is written in the *Grammar* of the poet Donatus, "I love you and I am loved by you, I kiss you and am kissed by you . . . "[18]

You, therefore, my son William, cherish and befriend those by whom you wish to be befriended; love, venerate, frequent, and honor all, so that you may be worthy to receive of all reciprocal retribution and due honor. For example, a certain learned man, making a comparison with a dumb animal for our edification, offered a great and clear sermon in a few words. He said in elucidating Psalm 41, "As the hart . . .": "Harts have this custom: when several of them wish to cross a sea or a large river of swirling waters, one after the other they place their horned heads on the back of their companions and hold up each other's necks, so that, by taking a little rest, they can make a more rapid crossing. There is in them such intelligence and such wisdom that, when they perceive the first to be tiring, they change places one after the other, and they let the second be first, now upholding and comforting the others. Thus, changing one by one, they each have pass through them the compassion of brotherly love, always taking care that the head with the horns be shown and held up, lest they be submerged in the waters."[19]

What meaning is hidden here is not hidden from the learned. Everything is immediately clear to their eyes. In this upholding, you see, and in this changing of place is shown the love which is to be kept by all in the human race, both to the great and to the small through brotherly love.

In the upholding or the erection of the heads and the horns is shown that the faithful in Christ must always keep their hearts and minds on Him.

The Respect Due to Priests

One must worship priests, my son, for they have been elected for the ministry of God, so that they may be intercessors for our sins, keeping sacred orders.

They are called also *episcopi*, 'bishops, overseers,' and observers, admonishing us to look always upward and to make heaven our goal. *Epi* in Greek is *super*, 'above,' in Latin; *scopon* is likewise Greek; in Latin it means 'intense look' or 'destination.'[20]

A Special Admonition to Correct Various Habits

To attain model behavior for a human being requires a great effort and studious labor. Contrary remedies are to be opposed to contrary illnesses,[21] and not only against the men of this world, burning with envy, must one fight, but also, as Saint Paul says, against spirits of wickedness in high places. There are those who seem to flourish in the world and who are rich in possessions, but, because of some secret malice, do not cease envying and molesting others, as much as they can, and this by dissimulation.

You have and will have books in which you may read, page through, ruminate on, scrutinize, and understand, or even teachers to instruct you, and these will furnish you with models to follow in the performance of both your duties . . . Although we are small and in exile, and we are not able to be accounted among and put together with the number of these great men, because of the demerits of this world which are embedded in us and because we tend more toward low rather than high things, nevertheless, in accord with the admonition of the Old Testament, we have been commanded to bear the names of the twelve patriarchs on our forehead.

To Be Militant in the Seven Gifts

You, son, if you are humble and peaceful, you will certainly receive, at least partly, the seven gifts of the grace of the Holy Spirit from Him of Whom I have frequently made mention above, and the good spirit of the Lord will rest upon you.

On Applying Contraries

If, because of the persuasion of Satan, author of death, fornication or any other thorn in the flesh should touch your heart, oppose chastity to it and remember the continency of the blessed patriarch, Joseph, or of Daniel, or of others, who, pure themselves in body and spirit, while preserving faithfully the honor of their lords and their friends, had the merit of being saved and greatly honored and of being accounted by the Lord among the number of His saints.

On Various Tribulations

Tribulations and sorrows or anxieties of temptation come about in many ways in this world. This is the case in carnal things as well as in spiritual things. Carnal people are saddened by the loss of possessions, spiritual people worry about losing heaven. "The sorrow of the world," as Saint Paul says, "worketh death," while spiritual sorrow brings life and eternal joy.

There are varieties of birds who naturally express their sorrow by song, by modulating their melodies. What does this suggest but that each mortal, in the course of his travel through life, must draw from his soul a twofold lamentation, one for having omitted to do the good which he should have done, the other because he loves evil?

On the Reconciliation of Sin

If it should happen, my son, that you do something bad, or even if you perceive that your soul is afflicted, hasten as soon as you can to make amends in all things. Turn to Him Who sees everything; always bear witness, externally as well as internally, of your guilt and worthlessness until you have given complete satisfaction, saying, "The sins of my youth and my ignorances, do not remember. I beg You, Lord, do not destroy me with my iniquities, and do not keep my faults to the end in Thy wrath. But, in accord with Thy ancient clemency and Thy great goodness, come to my aid, for Thou art merciful."

Remember, my son, the words of the publican: "O God, be merciful to me, a sinner, for I am not worthy, miserable and unclean as I am, to raise my worthless eyes to Thee, the perfect pure One."

How You Can Be Perfect with the Aid of God

For He has said: "1. He who walketh without blemish, 2. who worketh justice, 3. who speaketh the truth, 4. who doth not use deceit in his tongue, 5. who doeth not evil to his neighbor, 6. who sweareth not to his neighbor to deceive him, 7. who putteth not out his money to usury, 8. who taketh not up a reproach against his neighbor, 9. who taketh not bribes against the innocent, 10. who patiently tolerates injuries, 11. who is pure in heart and chaste in body, 12. who is innocent in hands, 13. who is able to transgress and transgresseth not, 14. who can do evil things and doeth them not, 15. who reacheth out his hand to the poor as often as he can." [22]

On the Seven Parts in Counting

The seven gifts of the Holy Spirit and the eight beatitudes are counted through in fifteen steps. The counter says, you have 7, twice 7 is 14. In a similar manner, 4 times 1 is 4, twice 4 is 8, add 7 to this and it yields 15.

In what way all these calculations differ, my son, would take a long time to recount in detail, but so that you will not remain ignorant of such a science, I shall explain briefly. To say 7 times 7 is to invite each of us to give complete satisfaction. Add but 1 and you obtain the total of 50: in fact, the grace of the Holy Spirit, by correcting us through the remission of sins and betterment of satisfaction, assures us the jubilation of Psalm 50, which is fitting for the jubilee year, a word which indicates remission and absolution.[23]

By the number 7 are indicated the gifts of the Creator, by the number 8 the beatitudes; as you go through these 15 degrees one after the other, my son, I urge you to rise gradually to the number 100, by passing from the left hand to the right; thus you can easily pass without damage to the sum of perfection. The calculators count up to 99 on the fingers of the left hand; then the left ceases to operate and they joyously raise the right for the number 100.

On Prayer

As far as your father is concerned, I urge and admonish you to pray frequently and assiduously for him, and to ask all the levels of Churchmen to intercede for him, so that God may grant him peace and concord throughout his life, if that is possible; that He may grant to him strength of soul, tenacity, and patience to triumph in all situations; and that he may get to the kingdom of heaven, if it please Him, at the end of this life, thanks to the fruits of his penance, his generosity, and his almsgiving. Amen.

Pray for the Defunct Relatives of Your Father

Pray for the relatives of your father, who have left him their goods in legitimate inheritance. Who they were and what were their names you will find written down at the end of this little book. Although the Scriptures say, "Another will rejoice in the other's goods," it is not strangers who possess their inheritance but, as I have said, Bernhard, your lord and your father.

On the Former Lord Theodoric

You must not neglect to pray, my son, for him who, taking you from my arms, adopted you as his son in Christ, through the bath of regeneration.[24] During his life he was called Lord Theodoric, now he is called "the former." He would have been for you in all things an educator and a friend, had he been able. He has been taken, as we hope, into the bosom of Abraham. In leaving you in this world as his firstborn, he willed to you all his goods through our common master and lord, so that they might be of use to you in all things. Pray often for his sins, especially in the company of others during nocturns, matins, vespers, and the other hours; this in case he may have committed some wrong and not have done penance for eternal life.

On the Letters of Adam and Their Meanings

Just as 5 times 3 is 15, so 15 times 3 is 45. By adding 1, one obtains 46. It is this total which the letters [of Adam] contain, according to the number system of the Greeks. Indeed, A, 'alfa,' which indicates the east (Greek anathole) is 1; d, 'delta,' which indicates the west, is 4; again a, 'alfa,' which indicates the north, is 1; and m, 'moida,' which indicates the south, is 40.[25]

Adam stretched himself to these four points of the compass through his children. $1 + 4 + 1 + (4 \times 5 \times 2) = 46$. As many digits as that makes, just as many years did it take to restore the House of the Lord in Jerusalem: forty-six years. Our Lord, in fact, wishing that the appointed number of days might be accomplished, said to the Jews, "Destroy this temple, and in three days I will raise it up." And they said to Him, "Six and forty years was this temple in building, and wilt Thou raise it up in three days?" But He was speaking of the temple of His Body.

The Same (Sort of) Subject

We believe that, from the first man up to the last to be saved at the end of the world, all are to be reunited, in order that the tenth order of angels be legitimately restored, as I mentioned above. In this restoration not only the Gentiles but also the Jews will be saved. The Scriptures say it, "When the fullness of the Gentiles will have come in, all Israel shall be saved."[26]

Reciting Psalms

Finally, William, my son, since Psalms possess so many and such virtues, I urge and admonish you to recite them frequently for yourself and your father, as well as for all the living, and also for those who are dear to you, also for all the faithful dead and for those whose memory was consigned to you above, including those whom you may add to the list. Also for the remedy of my soul do not forget to recite the Psalms which you have chosen, so that when the last day of life comes for me, I will have the merit of being placed, not on the left with the sinners, but on the right with the good and faithful, and to be taken up into heaven.

Finis

Have frequent recourse to this little book. Always be, noble child, strong and brave in Christ!

This book was begun during the second year after the death of the former emperor, Louis, the 30th of November, Saint Andrew's Day, at the beginning of Advent. It was finished, by the aid of God, on the 2nd of February, the Feast of the Purification of the blessed ever-virgin Mary, under the propitious reign of Christ, awaiting the king whom God will designate.

Reader, pray for Dhuoda, if you wish to have the merit of seeing Christ in eternal happiness.

Here ends, thanks be to God, the Manual of William, according to the word of the Gospel: "It is finished."

Epitaph for My Tomb, Which I Would Like for You to Write on It

When I have ended my years also, have my name listed among these honored dead. What I desire and what I beg you with all my power, just as if it were this very day, is that in the place where I am buried, on the stone which covers the grave where my body is buried, you must have inscribed lastingly the following verses, so that the people who see this epitaph will pray in a worthy fashion to God for me, so unworthy.

As to those who one day will read this Manual which you are reading, let them also meditate on what follows and pray to God for my pardon, as if I were already buried.

Read, Reader, the Little Verses of This Epitaph

Dhuoda's body, formed of earth,
Lies buried in this tomb.
   Immense King, receive her!
Here the earth has received in its bowels

The all too fragile clay which belonged to it.
   Benign King, grant her pardon!
Under and over her are the opaque depths
Of the grave, bathed in her wounds.
   O King, forgive her sins!
O you of all ages and sexes who come
And go here, I beg you, say this:
   Great Hagios, unlock her chains!
Detained by dire death in the depths
Of the tomb, she has ended her earthly life.
   O King, pardon her sins!
As that dark serpent wishes to capture
Her soul, pray against him this prayer:
   Clement God, come to her aid!
No one should leave her without having read.
I urge all that they may pray, saying this:
   Almus, give her rest!
And command, Benign One, that she be given
Eternal light with the saints in the end.
   And may she receive Amen after her death![27]

NOTES TO THE TRANSLATION

1. There is a great deal of difficulty in defining chapters and chapter headings, because of the variations in our manuscripts. I have adopted the divisions of Riché, who discusses the problem in *Dhuoda*, pp. 53 ff.

2. I have rendered only part of this long poem, which has been the subject of much discussion. In the original, the first letters of the verses spell out, "Dhuoda, to her beloved son William, greetings. Read!" I have rendered only "Dhuoda . . . read!"

3. These attributes of God show the subtlety of Dhuoda's wit, since they reflect the usual medieval etymology of *Deus*, 'God': *Dans eternam vitam suis*, 'Giving eternal life to His [servants].'

4. Here Dhuoda parades her learning a bit, since a knowledge of Greek, even the letter names, was not common in Carolingian times.

5. This enigmatic sentence is typical of Dhuoda. She is, of course, making a play on 2 Corinthians 11:23, where Paul confesses that he speaks foolishly: *ut minus sapiens dico, plus ego* (Dhuoda says, *si minus dicam, plus ego*). In order to understand what she says, one must have the passage from Paul in mind and also know that Paul was the model of modesty in the Middle Ages, because he used the third person in his narrative of being rapt unto the third heaven (2 Cor. 12:2).

6. The metaphor of *speculum*, 'mirror,' for a spiritual handbook is very widespread in the Middle Ages. Compare Sister Ritamary Bradley, "Backgrounds of the Title 'Speculum,'" *Speculum* 29 (1954): 100–115.

7. One of the great problems faced by the medieval author was the transition from one

part of the narrative to the other. Dhuoda likes to end each segment with a sentence pointing to the next.

8. Dhuoda is not always careful in her statements concerning dates, but it is obvious that she considers Louis to have begun ruling in 813, whereas he first became emperor in 814.

9. Dhuoda loves such turns of phrase as "the absence of your presence." This type of rhetoric, in this case the *antimetabole*, was taught in the schools.

10. Again Dhuoda uses a rhetorical device which one can scarcely render in English, based on varying the root *vol*, 'to wish,' in Latin *volueram, volo*, and *voluntate*; this device is frequently called polyptoton.

11. The letters *V L D* are the roman numerals 5, 50, and 500. Dhuoda continues with a long discourse on the value of the various numbers.

12. Eternal rest.

13. This passage shows how Dhuoda uses the Bible. It is a blend of Esther 13:9, ". . . there is none that can resist Thy will," and Daniel 4:32, "And there is none that can resist His hand and say to Him: Why hast Thou done it?"

14. This passage is a topos, a commonplace, and an adynaton, a rhetorical device based on the recitation of something which is clearly impossible. Such adynata were much loved during the Carolingian period, and Walahfrid Strabo, roughly contemporary with Dhuoda, is famous for them. This particular one has been misunderstood by Dhuoda's editors, who, not knowing the adynaton, did not know how to read *intertinctus*, 'stained, made into ink.'

15. This shows the kind of etymologies Dhuoda uses. This one is probably taken from Isidore *Etymologiae* 1. 5, 3.

16. Here Dhuoda makes use of the topos of the *puer senex*; "Though young in age, they were old in judgment." Such topoi are brilliantly discussed in Curtius, *European Literature*. This particular topos is discussed on pp. 98–104.

17. Again Dhuoda makes use of her favorite stylistic device of *antimetabole*, which is difficult to render in a translation.

18. This is a quotation of a grammatical exercise on the Latin deponent and the passive. Dhuoda knows well that it has nothing to do with moral precepts, but it suits her purposes here and so she uses it. Donatus was a fourth-century grammarian, teacher of Saint Jerome, who wrote the standard grammar book of the Middle Ages.

19. I have included this passage to show how Dhuoda uses the *Physiologus*, a collection of fabulous properties of animals common in the Middle Ages. An excellent collection of such stories is found in T. H. White, *The Bestiary*.

20. As mentioned above, Dhuoda was fond of such etymologies. She is, of course, wrong about the meaning of Greek *scopon*, 'one who looks,' but she uses the same meaning elsewhere.

21. In the Middle Ages, one used both sympathetic and contrary remedies. Dittany was good against arrow wounds because its leaf looked like an arrowhead, but dragonwort was good for cold and wet wounds because a dragon was hot and dry.

22. The observant reader will have noticed that this is mostly taken from Psalm 14, "Lord, who shall dwell in Thy tabernacle? Or who shall rest in Thy holy hill?"

23. All these speculations on the significance of 7 were so common in the Middle Ages that it is impossible to give a source. The jubilee year, the fiftieth, was a period, according to Jewish law, when slaves were freed and land reverted to its owners; see Leviticus 25.

24. This is Dhuoda's way of saying that Theodoric, or Thierry, William's uncle, was also his godfather, a very strong link in the Middle Ages.

25. This speculation on the letters of Adam's name, which ultimately goes back to sibylline oracles through Saint Cyprian (about 300), was extremely widespread in the Middle Ages. This later led to such excesses as the attempt by a seventeenth-century Swede, Buraeus, to

prove that Swedish was the original language, based on the fact that the directions in Swedish, with a little help, spell Sven: *Söder*, 'south'; *väster*, 'west'; *euster*, 'east'; and *norr*, 'north.'

26. Many people believed that both Jew and Gentile would be saved, based on Romans 11:25–26, whence Dhuoda fabricated this quotation.

27. Although the epitaph occurs earlier in the book, I have left it for the end. It is typical of mothers, indeed people of all times and places, but so typical of Dhuoda. Note this time that the acrostichon spells her name out in full in the Latin form: Dhuodana. The Carolingians liked to vary the names they gave to God; there are even long poems consisting almost entirely of names of God, such as the *Alma chorus Domini*. Hagios is Greek for 'holy,' Almus means 'the nourishing one,' and Amen is the personified Amen of Revelation 3:14.

BIBLIOGRAPHY

Primary Works

Bondurand, Edouard. *L'éducation carolingienne: Le manuel de Dhuoda*. Paris, 1887.

Erdmann, Oskar, ed. *Otfrids Evangelienbuch*. 6th ed. by Ludwig Wolff. Altdeutsche Textbibliothek 49. Tübingen, 1973.

Meier, Gabriel. *Ausgewählte Schriften von Columan, Alkuin, Dodana* . . . Bibliothek der katholischen Pädagogik 3. Freiburg, 1890.

Riché, Pierre. *Dhuoda: Manuel pour mon fils*. Sources Chrétiennes 225. Paris, 1975.

Related Works

Becker, Ph. Aug. "Duodas Handbuch." *Zeitschrift für Romanische Philologie* 21 (1897): 73–101.

Bédier, Joseph. *Les légendes épiques*. 3rd ed., vol. 1. Paris, 1926.

Bell, Clair Hayden. *The Sister's Son in the Medieval German Epic*. University of California Publications in Modern Philology 10. Berkeley and Los Angeles, 1922.

Böhmer, J. F., E. Mühlbacher, and J. Lechner. *Die Regesten des Kaiserreichs unter den Karolingern 751–918*. Innsbruck, 1908.

Bradley, Sister Ritamary. "Backgrounds of the Title 'Speculum.'" *Speculum* 29 (1954): 100–115.

Burger, A. "Les vers de la Duchesse Dhuoda et son poème *De temporibus tuis*." In *Mélanges de philologie, de littérature, et d'histoire ancienne offerts à J. Marouzeau*, pp. 85–102. Paris, 1948.

Calmette, J. *De Bernardo Sancti Guillelmi filio*. Thesis, Faculté des Lettres, University of Paris. Toulouse, 1902.

————. "La famille de Saint Guilhem." *Annales du Midi* 18 (1906): 145–165.

Carolingian Chronicles. Trans. Bernhard W. Scholz with Barbara Rogers. Ann Arbor, 1970.

Charlemagne's Cousins. Trans. Allen Cabaniss. Syracuse, 1967.

Curtius, Ernst R. *European Literature and the Latin Middle Ages*. Trans. Willard R. Trask. Bollingen Series 36. Princeton, 1953.

Dutoit, Ernest. *Le thème de l'adynaton dans la poésie antique*. Paris, 1936.

Grandgent, C. H. *An Introduction to Vulgar Latin*. 1934. Reprint. New York, 1962.

Hopper, Vincent F. *Medieval Number Symbolism.* Columbia University Studies in English and Comparative Literature 132. New York, 1938.

Klinck, Roswitha. *Die lateinische Etymologie des Mittelalters.* Medium Aevum 17. Munich, 1970.

Marchand, James. *"Sagena piscatoris:* An Essay in Medieval Lexicography." In *Linguistic Method: Essays in Honor of Herbert Penzl,* ed. Irmengard Rausch and Gerald E. Carr, pp. 123–138. The Hague, 1979.

McNally, Robert E., S.J. "Der irische Liber de numeris." Ph.D. dissertation, Munich, 1957.

Menninger, Karl. *Number Words and Number Symbols.* Cambridge, Mass., 1969.

Riché, Pierre. "Les bibliothèques de trois aristocrates laïques carolingiens." *Le Moyen Age* 69 (1963): 87–103.

Salmon, Paul. "Der zehnte Engelchor in deutschen Dichtungen und Predigten des Mittelalters." *Euphorion* 57 (1963): 321–330.

Simson, Bernard. *Jahrbücher des fränkischen Reichs unter Ludwig dem Frommen.* 2 vols. Leipzig, 1874, 1876.

Strabo, Walahfrid. "Similitudo impossibilium." In *Poetae latini aevi Carolini,* ed. E. Dümmler, vol. 2. Berlin, 1883–1886.

Strecker, Karl. *Introduction to Medieval Latin.* Trans. Robert B. Palmer. 3rd ed. Berlin, 1965.

White, T. H. *The Bestiary.* New York, 1953.

Wollasch, Joachim. "Eine adlige Familie des frühen Mittelalters: Ihr Selbstverständnis und ihre Wirklichkeit." *Archiv für Kulturgeschichte* 39 (1957): 150–188.

Zuckerman, Arthur J. *A Jewish Princedom in Feudal France, 768–900.* Columbia University Studies in Jewish History, Culture, and Institutions 2. New York, 1972.

Zumthor, Paul. *Histoire littéraire de la France médiévale.* Paris, 1954.

THE SAXON CANONESS

Hrotsvit of Gandersheim

KATHARINA M. WILSON

At the close of the fifteenth century, the German world of letters was presented with a literary sensation: Conrad Celtis' discovery of the works of the tenth-century Saxon canoness, Hrotsvit of Gandersheim.[1] The reception of Hrotsvit by the German humanists was euphorically enthusiastic—an excitement that was, indeed, well warranted, for aside from her considerable gifts of poetic and dramatic ingenuity, Hrotsvit also lays claim to a catalog of pioneering achievements.[2] She is the first known dramatist of Christianity, the first Saxon poet, and the first woman historian of Germany. Her dramas are the first performable plays of the Middle Ages, her epics are the only extant Latin epics written by a woman, and, finally, she is the first medieval poet to have consciously attempted to remold the image of the literary depictions of women.[3]

As with the majority of medieval writers, we know little of Hrotsvit's life. There are no contemporary references to her, and no *vita Hrotsvithae* exists; since she was not sainted, no *Protocollum canonizationis* records her exploits. Thus, her biography has to be reconstructed from the few details she gives us in her dedicatory epistles and epics. In the history of the Gandersheim abbey (*Primordia Coenobii Gandeshemensis*), she writes that she was born a long time after the death of Duke Otto of Saxony (November 30, 912), but she also tells us that her birth preceded that of her abbess Gerberga II (circa 940), whom she describes as younger in years. Most scholars now assume that Hrotsvit was born in the fourth decade of the tenth century.[4] The date of her death is equally uncertain. Judging by internal evidence, she finished the last of her extant works, the *Primordia*, before 973. The consensus of scholarly opinion now places the date of her death toward the end of the tenth century.[5]

Even Hrotsvit's name has been the source of some discussion. She records the nominative form of her name as being Hrotsvit and the inflected forms as Hrotsvitham and Hrotsvithae.[6] After many fanciful interpretations of her appellation, ranging from "white rose" to "quick wit," Jacob Grimm in the nineteenth century finally recognized that Hrotsvit herself gave us the etymology of her name. In the introduction to her dramas she refers to herself as *clamor validus Gandeshemensis*, the strong voice of Gandersheim. Grimm observed that her Old Saxon name derived from two words, *hruot = clamor =* voice and *suid = validus =* strong.[7]

Nothing is known of Hrotsvit's childhood and ancestry except that, most probably, she was of noble Saxon parentage. She must have been of noble descent because only daughters of the aristocracy were admitted at Gandersheim, a foundation of the Liudolfs in the Harz Mountains.[8] The abbey was founded in 852 by Liudolf and his wife, Oda, ancestors of the Ottos. Five of their daughters took the veil, and three of them became the first abbesses of Gandersheim.[9] By the mid tenth century under the rule of Gerberga II, Gandersheim, a wealthy imperial abbey, was recognized as a center of intellectual and religious activity.[10] In 947 Otto I even freed the abbey from royal rule and gave the abbess the authority to have her own court of law, keep her own army, coin her own money, and have a seat in the imperial diet. As did the other great religious houses, Gandersheim fulfilled the manifold functions of school, library, hospital, and political and religious center. The canonesses followed the Benedictine rule—they were bound by strict regulations and were obliged to observe the canonical hours—but they did not take one of the three monastic vows, that of poverty.[11]

The date of Hrotsvit's entrance into Gandersheim is uncertain, but judging by the traditions of the time, she was probably quite young.[12] According to her own statement in the preface to the legends, her teachers were Rikkardis and Gerberga II. Rikkardis taught Hrotsvit the rudiments of the liberal arts while Gerberga, probably educated in Saint Emmeran, the cultural center of Bavaria, introduced her to the Roman authors as well as to the patristic writers.[13]

Hrotsvit's great learning has often been noted, and her erudition reflects especially favorably on the Gandersheim library, for she says that she had found all her materials in the abbey's library.[14] Judging by her works, she was versed in both medieval and ancient literature, and it is possible that she may have known some Greek. Of the Roman authors, she was acquainted with the works of Horace, Ovid, Statius, Lucan, Boethius, Terence, and Virgil.[15] From the Christian writers her readings included the works of Prudentius, Venantius Fortunatus, Avitus, Arator, Aldhelm, Jerome, Agius, Alcuin, Bede, Notker, and Ekkehard, as well as the Vulgate, liturgical texts, and many legends of the saints and martyrs.[16] In addition, she shows familiarity with grammatical and metrical textbooks and commentaries, such as those of Donatus and Isidore of Seville.[17] Hrotsvit knew and used apocryphal acts and gospels which were venerated in the Greek Church and in popular tradition without, however, the sanction of the Latin Church. Against any charge that she relied on sources which she used in ignorance of their apocryphal nature, Hrotsvit answers with charm and self-assurance that "what may appear to be false today may prove to be true tomorrow."[18]

Encouraged in her studies by her abbess, Hrotsvit tells us that she felt compelled to put to use her God-given talent for writing, however small it may have been. Along with a set of modesty, devotional, and submission topoi, so characteristic of the exordia of medieval legends and *vitae*, Hrotsvit also deprecates her sex in a similarly formulaic manner.[19] In the preface to the legends, she says:

> Even though poetic expression may seem difficult for female frailty, yet always relying on heavenly grace and not on my own powers, I have tried to compose the songs of this little work in the dactylic form, in the hope that my little talent given by God should not lie in the dark recesses of the mind and be destroyed by the rust of neglect; hoping, rather, that through the mallet of devotion, my little talent may sound the little tinkling chord of divine praise. In this way even if no other opportunity for gain be given to my little talent, it might still be transformed into an instrument of utility in the end.[20]

Writing in Latin, the language of Church, culture, education, and diplomacy in the tenth century, Hrotsvit defines her literary aim in hagiographic terms. Strong in her faith, she writes for the faithful, glorifying the ways of God and providing literary models of exemplary conduct for her audience to emulate; firm in her conviction of the superiority of the monastic ideal, she writes for a sympathetic monastic audience familiar with and conforming to the pinnacle of ascetic excellence: the virginal ideal. On a more pragmatic level, Hrotsvit's literary purpose is similar to that of Saint Jerome and Saint Gregory: to give Christian readers something morally good and palatable to read as a substitution for the evil but stylistically beautiful pagan works.[21]

Hrotsvit's works reflect three main interests and preoccupations: first, her royal patrons and, thus, the Liudolf dynasty; second, the history of the Gandersheim abbey; and, third, the glorification of the Christian Church and, more specifically, the exaltation of the chaste ideal. Her third interest is profoundly manifested in her legends and dramas, for they both treat of the glory of the Christian faith, the inevitable triumph of good over evil and Christianity over paganism—themes which are usually couched in the depiction of exemplary lives of chaste Christian saints and martyrs through whom God works his miracles.

Hrotsvit's works consist of eight legends, six plays, two epics, and a short poem.[22] The works are organized chronologically and generically into three books and, in turn, they fall into three clearly marked creative periods, the breaks occurring after the fourth legend and the fourth play.[23]

Book 1, containing the legends, begins with a preface and a dedication to Gerberga II. The first legend, "Maria," is a romantic treatment of the Virgin's life based on an apocryphal source, the *Pseudo-Evangelium* of Mattheus. In the exordium to the poem, Hrotsvit introduces her major theme: the exaltation of the virtue of steadfast, obedient, and, therefore, triumphant and life-giving virginity. "Maria" narrates the miraculous conception and birth of Mary, her childhood, and her stay at the temple, her reluctance to marry, the selection by divine judgment of Joseph as her husband, and, finally, her motherhood. Mary's glorification is entirely Christocentric—her laudable chastity and exemplary conduct are subordinated to her role as *genetrix*, and the poem closes with a prayer to Christ. Hrotsvit's second attempt, the "Ascensio," the shortest of her works, is drawn from a Greek source describing the ascension of Christ. The third legend deals with the eighth-century Frankish knight Gongolf, who lived under Pippin the Short.[24] Gongolf is the meek, courteous, wise, and chaste knight. His magnanimity and virtue, however, are a source of envy for the devil, who uses his favorite weapon, human sexuality, to plot the saintly Gongolf's destruction. Gongolf's wife, crazed with lust for a cleric, not only commits adultery but also instigates her husband's murder. Subsequently, she suffers for the deed (and for her lack of contrition) by means of a scatological miracle when her blasphemy of Gongolf's miracles is punished by an involuntary *obscenus sonus* (a motif popular in folklore) every Friday whenever she opens her mouth.

Hrotsvit's fourth legend is based not on a written source but on an eyewitness report. It describes the martyrdom of the chaste Pelagius, a tenth-century Spanish saint who died persevering against the arduous homoerotic advances of the caliph of Córdoba, Abderrahman III.[25] The fifth and sixth legends are the first literary treatments of the Faust theme in Germany. They deal with the Greek saints Basilius and Theophilus; both concern men who made a pact with the devil and sold their immortal souls for earthly gain. The sinners are saved at the intercession of Bishop Basilius and the Virgin Mary, respectively. In both poems Hrotsvit uses the themes of fall and conversion, sin and salvation; in both she apotheosizes the unlimited power of prayer and contrition that are rewarded by divine forgiveness. The seventh legend describes the martyrdom of Dionysius, the first bishop of Paris, whom Hrotsvit, following her source, confuses with Dionysius the Areopagite. The canoness' last legend glorifies Saint Agnes, martyr for virginity, who rejects the advantageous and honorable suit of Sempronius' son in favor of the heavenly bridegroom and resists, with Christ's help, the ignominious attempts of her adversaries to defile her chastity when she is placed in a brothel for punishment. At the conclusion of her earthly sufferings, Christ awaits his virginal bride in the celestial bridal chamber, which Agnes depicts in glowingly ecstatic passages and unabashedly sensuous language.[26] Several of the legends, probably read in the refectory during meals, conclude with a prayer.

The second book, Hrotsvit's most important (because most original) creation, contains her plays. The book is introduced by a dedication to Gerberga, followed by a prose letter to the learned patrons of the book (sometimes identified as Gerberga's former teachers at Saint Emmeran).[27] *Gallicanus*, the first of Hrotsvit's dramas, deals with the conversion and martyrdom of the pagan Roman general Gallicanus. He has been promised the hand of Constantia, Emperor Constantine's daughter, if he wages a successful war against the Scythians. Constantia, however, has taken the vow of chastity and, therefore, cannot marry him. Through divine intervention and the assistance of Saints Paul and John, Gallicanus becomes a Christian and renounces marriage. Like Constantia, he devotes the rest of his life to religion and dies persevering in his faith. *Dulcitius*, the second play, takes place during the Diocletian persecutions of the Christians and dramatizes the martyrdom of three virgin sisters, Agapes, Chionia, and Hirena, who refuse to forego their faith and their chastity (thereby avoiding idolatry and adultery against the heavenly bridegroom). *Dulcitius* contains elements of an almost mimelike character. The would-be executioner of the sisters, Dulcitius, is depicted as a philandering pagan. He imprisons the girls in a room adjacent to the pantry so that he may visit them undisturbed at night. The girls, very much afraid, spend the hours in prayer. Dulcitius arrives at nightfall, but when he tries to seduce the virgins, a miracle happens: he is deluded and mistakes the pots and pans for the sisters. He embraces and kisses the kitchen utensils until he emerges so smeared and blackened with soot that his soldiers mistake him for the devil and the guards chase him from the palace's doorsteps. This instance of typical medieval kitchen humor is an excellent example of the concretization and visualization of themes; external appearance is a reflection of the internal state—Dulcitius, whose soul is possessed by the devil, appears as the *imago diaboli* in body.[28]

The third play, *Calimachus*, depicts the sin and subsequent conversion of a pagan youth. Calimachus is passionately in love with Drusiana, Andronicus' respectable wife, who has taken the vow of chastity. Upon learning of his violent passion, Drusiana prays for death in order to forego temptation, and she expires immediately. Ablaze with lust, Calimachus bribes Fortunatus, the tomb guard, in a desperate attempt at necrophilia. Before he can profane Drusiana's body, however, he and Fortunatus both die. They are subsequently resurrected by Saint John, and Calimachus is

converted to Christianity. As did Sempronius' son in "Agnes," so Calimachus vividly exemplifies the Christian paradox that in order to live the
Christian has to die to the world first. Because of the tomb scene, some
scholars have pointed out a comparison with Shakespeare's *Romeo and
Juliet*.[29]

In the fourth and fifth dramas, *Paphnutius* and *Abraham*, Hrotsvit
again treats of the themes of fall and conversion. Two harlots, representing the most abominable vice of *luxuria carnis* (joys of the flesh), are
converted by two saintly anchorites and consequently live ascetic lives.
In *Paphnutius* the courtesan Thais is converted by a saintly hermit who
aspires to this task as the result of a vision, while in *Abraham* the hermit
is the courtesan's uncle and former guardian. The recognition scene between the aged Abraham, posing as a lover, and his niece Mary in the
brothel has evoked especial praise for Hrotsvit's talent as a dramatist.[30]
Finally, *Sapientia*, the last of the dramas, deals with the martyrdom of
the three allegorical virgins Fides, Spes, and Karitas (Faith, Hope, and
Charity), who, like the heroines of *Dulcitius*, willingly face death on earth
so that they may earn eternal life in heaven.

Paphnutius and *Sapientia* commence with a dialogue lesson in music
and mathematics, respectively. In *Paphnutius* the saintly hermit is ex-
pounding upon the mysteries of the celestial harmonies to his disciples,
while in *Sapientia* the mother of the three virgins confounds the pagan
emperor with her arithmetical learning or, rather, her Boethian exposition of numerical values.[31] In sum, in almost all of Hrotsvit's plays, women
show true heroism while men are the villians—and what is worse,
the men are almost always pagans. Book 2 concludes with a poem of
thirty-five hexameters on Saint John's *Apocalypse* which is believed to
have been intended for inscription under the twelve murals at Gandersheim.[32]

Book 3 contains the two extant epics, the *Carmen de Gestis Oddonis
Imperatoris* or, in short, the *Gesta* and the *Primordia Coenobii Gandeshemensis*.[33] The *Gesta*, it has been argued, is one of the most successful
tenth-century attempts at a Christian epic.[34] Otto the Great is depicted
as the ideal Christian ruler—a descendant not necessarily of Aeneas but
of David. Otto's heroic excellence, as Dennis Kratz argues, comprises
characteristics derivative of the *figura David*: *sapientia, pietas, clemen-
tia*, and *fortitudo*.[35] He is the earthly replica of the heavenly king, deriving his just power from God. By implication, insurrection against him
(and there were more than a few during Hrotsvit's lifetime) is depicted
as the work of the devil. Among the female characters of the *Gesta*, Otto's queens Edith and Adelheid stand out; both are depicted as paragons
of feminine excellence, described in the superlatives of the hagiographic
tradition and in the consciously court-oriented schemata of values.

Finally, the *Primordia* presents the history of the Gandersheim abbey from its founding until the death of Abbess Christina in 918. The *Primordia* is replete with hagiographic topoi, legendary characters (whose exemplary lives are reminiscent of the heroes and heroines of Hrotsvit's legends and dramas), miracles, and visions. At the same time, the work also manifests a strong political tendency: any part that the Hildesheim bishops played in the foundation of the abbey is conspicuously ignored. Rather, emphasis is placed on the role of the Liudolfs in establishing an autonomous religious house that is to be entirely independent of the jurisdiction and influence of the Hildesheim bishops.[36] This important omission at the height of the Gandersheim-Hildesheim quarrel over the abbey's autonomy cannot be coincidental.[37]

The organization of the three books in this manner shows Hrotsvit to be a master of symmetry and balance. The themes and motifs of the first book are repeated in a different generic form in the second, and there is also a statistical inversion of the predominant sex in the two books: in the legends men predominate; in the dramas women do. The themes of the legends and dramas are transferred to a historic context in the third book.[38] The books are also linked by recurring personal and topological references. Constantia (the heroine of the first drama), for example, is converted to Christianity at the intercession of Saint Agnes (heroine of the last legend) through a vision in which Christ shows her the undefiled bed of his virgin mother (heroine of the first legend).

Hrotsvit's reliance on hagiography in all her works is not manifested only in her choice of Christian saints and martyrs or exemplary virgins as her main characters. More fundamentally, it is reflected in her use of absolute moral opposites for the development of her themes: Christ and the devil are fighting the eternal battle over human souls in her works—good invariably carrying off the palm of victory; the struggles between Christians and pagans and between the sacred and the profane are merely extensions and reflections of the supernatural fight. *Aemulatio* and *imitatio* are Hrotsvit's didactic purpose, and the presenting of exemplary lives is her method.[39]

This didactic intent admits only a few incidentals in its schematized presentation. God's grace and the power of faith constitute Hrotsvit's overriding interest—psychological verisimilitude is not her concern. The miraculously swift conversions in her legends and plays, the triumph of frail Christian virgins over their mighty pagan persecutors, and the exaltation of the many glorious repentants that people her pages are intended to show God's benevolence and grace in overcoming the human proclivity for sin.[40] Thus everything—plot, character development, imagery, and argumentation—is subordinated to the moral idea. The stylized hero or heroine must be shown to be the worthy agent of God, and the equally stylized antagonist must appear as the potent agent of the devil, but all other details are of tangential importance.

The psychomachy in these works is depicted by means of a sophisticated use of moral opposites and developed by the rhetorical use of *e contrario*. The most persistent binary pairs include good versus evil, Christ versus the devil, heaven versus hell, female versus male, wisdom versus fraud, spiritual versus physical, life versus death, good-tempered versus savage, pride versus humility, salvation versus perdition, and chaste versus unchaste. The city of God (*civitas dei*), ruled by the just judge (*iustus iudex*), Christ, is contrasted both in hagiographic and historic contexts with the city of the devil (*civitas diaboli*). The city of God and, by implication, the realm of the just earthly ruler are characterized by peace, harmony, mercy, and compassion, while the devil's city and its earthly satellites are noted for rebellion, discord, pride, and envy. The pairs either denote exactly opposing moral absolutes or contrast God-related good with devil-inspired perversion. Thus, for example, treachery and fraud are the perversions of divine wisdom, magic is the perverse art of the devil, while a miracle is the sign of God.

Characterization, as well as thematic development, thrives on moral opposites. Pagans are characterized by sensuality (*luxuria carnis*), pride (*superbia*), and cruelty (*saevitas*); in contrast, Christians are marked by chasteness (*castitas*), humility (*humilitas*), and gentleness and self-control (*temperantia*).[41] Very frequently, these character delineations occur along sexual lines: the villains are the male pagan persecutors, the heroines frail Christian virgins.

As is generally the case in hagiography, and almost always in early Germanic lore, the saint is also usually of noble blood. In addition, manifesting the conviction that the outside mirrors the inside, all of Hrotsvit's heroines and martyr-saints are beautiful.[42] In her emphasis on the physical beauty of her virtuous characters, Hrotsvit often elaborates on and sometimes departs from her sources by adding grace, charm, good manners, and polite speech to the schemata of her saintly figures' standard characteristics. One important omission of standard hagiographic topoi should be noted: self-imposed poverty and the full distribution of one's wealth among the poor are not emphasized in her legends and plays. As a noble canoness of a wealthy imperial abbey, Hrotsvit clearly reflects her own and her abbey's hierarchy of values.

To us Hrotsvit's plays are of particular interest chiefly because historians of drama often use not only aesthetic but other criteria for excluding works from the literary canon and from anthologies—which not only perpetuate but often designate the canon. Thus, for example, the *Quem Queritis* dialogue is part of any respectable medieval literary anthology not because it has any inherent aesthetic claim but because it is generally recognized as the first manifestation of Church drama. By implication, Hrotsvit's most pressing claim to the canon and to anthologization rests largely with her recognition as the first medieval playwright. Consequently, the most volatile questions regarding her works concern her plays. Why did she use Terence as her literary model? Why did she experiment with the dramatic genre? More specifically, why did she choose the Terentian comedy form to glorify Christian virgins and saintly women? Were her plays known during the Middle Ages, particularly during the period of renewed dramatic interest, or did they, as many have claimed, fall into complete oblivion after her death until Celtis' discovery of her works in 1493?[43] Finally, the most often pondered question of all: were her plays performed during her lifetime?

Hrotsvit herself answers some of these questions. She used Terence, she says, because as people read him for aesthetic pleasure, they become corrupted by the wickedness of his subject matter. She is especially indignant with his female characters, whom she describes as lascivious and shameless. Therefore, she states, she is determined to substitute virtuous women for Terence's courtesans:

> Many Catholics may be found, and we cannot be acquitted of the same charge, who, because of the beauty of their eloquent style, prefer the uselessness of pagan books to the usefulness of sacred Scripture. There are also others who, while devoted to sacred readings, and scorning the works of other pagans, yet read the worldly stories of Terence rather frequently, and as they delight in the sweetness of his style, they are stained by the wickedness of his subject matter. Therefore I, the Strong Voice of Gandersheim, have not found it objectionable to imitate him in composition, whom others study in reading, so that in that very same form of composition through which the shameless acts of lascivious women were depicted, the laudable chastity of sacred virgins may be praised within the limits of my little talent.

Terence was an important school author in the Middle Ages, studied not only because of the elegance of his style and diction but also because of his powers of observation.[44] Saint Jerome, for example, refers to him as an acute observer of human vices. In fact, Jerome was so fond of Terence that, next to Virgil, Terence provided the second main source of pagan quotations for the Sidonian father.[45] Thus, sanctioned by ecclesiastical authority and by the educational tradition, Hrotsvit must have considered the Terentian model safe enough. At the same time, as a woman and a canoness at that, she must have objected to Terence's view of women—perhaps because her assessment of his female characters corresponded closely to medieval sermons, exempla, and satires that depicted women as the daughters of Eve, as personifications of lasciviousness, and, most persistently, as a constant danger to man's salvation.[46] These

treatises were written by Churchmen, assiduously quoting the Bible—
Terence, on the other hand, was a pagan without the protective shield of
scriptural authority. As such, he could be countered and corrected as the
worthless maligner of women.

In her glorification of Christian women, Hrotsvit is entirely orthodox.
Like Saint Jerome, who made the famous pronouncement that through
virginity woman can rise above her position and become like man (Eph.
3:5), Hrotsvit depicts her heroines as deriving their strength from the
chaste ideal; virtue and chastity are almost synonymous to her.[47] Given
the fact that Mary is the first of her heroines and that almost all of her
subsequent female characters live a life in imitation of the Virgin, Hrotsvit's dramatic attempt appears as the conscious effort to substitute the
ideal of Mary for that of Eve. "Mors per Evam, Vita per Mariam," reads
Jerome's famous pronouncement; and Hrotsvit apotheosizes the Virgin
Mary in a similar vein ("Maria" 15, 16): "Quae parens mundo restaur-
asti, pia virgo, Vitam, quam virgo perdiderat vetula" (You, Virgin who
through obedience restored life to the world, which the ancient virgin
destroyed). Mary and, by implication, all adherents of the chaste ideal
restore the hope for salvation and eternal life to the world. Hrotsvit's
saintly women not only earn eternal life for themselves by their exemplary lives, but by inspiring men to the love of God, they become the
catalysts and transmitters of heavenly life. Significantly, in her prologue
Hrotsvit refers only to the disgusting behavior of Terence's female characters, and she shows little indignation for the equally immoral actions
of the Roman poet's male characters. Like Euripides' Medea fourteen
centuries before and Christine de Pizan four centuries later, Hrotsvit is
primarily concerned with correcting the negative picture drawn of women
in literature.

Eve's happiness was in marriage, Mary's in virgin motherhood; Eve
tempted one to sin, Mary inspired one to virtue. Thus, it becomes apparent that for the happy ending achieved by marriage and reconciliation in
Terence's comedies, Hrotsvit could substitute only the happy martyrdom
in defense of virginity and religion or the protagonist's conversion to
Christianity and asceticism. Mary, Agnes, Agapes, Chionia, Hirena, Fides,
Spes, and Karitas all have the strength of religious devotion to overcome
the enticements of the flesh and to become female paradigms of virtue
and endurance, while Constantia and Drusiana act.as the worthy agents
of God in bringing about the conversion of their pagan lovers. To the
Saxon canoness this was the other side of the coin: an aspect of womanhood that she held up to be compared with the Terentian (and ecclesiastical) depictions of women, for as epitomes of the ascetic ideal and catalysts
of men's salvation, Hrotsvit's heroines are the exact antithesis of the
medieval misogynistic stereotype.

Whether or not Hrotsvit's plays were performed during her lifetime is still the subject of fierce debate.[48] That they are eminently performable is no longer doubted, thanks to the efforts of Sister Mary Margaret Butler and the many successful performances of her plays.[49] As well, the popularity and effectiveness of Brecht's epic theater have accustomed modern audiences to didactic and schematized stage presentations, thereby preparing the way for an understanding and appreciation of Hrotsvit's plays in the twentieth century.[50]

However, while Hrotsvit did not lack dramatic ingenuity, it is much more likely that her plays were read aloud than that they were performed.[51] In her preface to her dramas she refers only to the reading of Terence's plays, and, aside from mime performances and perhaps dramatic readings, the Roman theater was unknown in the tenth century. Moreover, Hrotsvit's notion of Terentian comedy owes much to the lexicographers and grammarians of the early Middle Ages. Her conception of comedy is likely to have been based on the definition of Isidore of Seville (or some derivative source), who suggests that in comedies the acts of private people are depicted in speech and action and that comedies are fictitious tales that deal with the defilement of virgins and the love affairs of prostitutes.[52] In other words, comedy is defined more by subject matter than by form. Consequently, Hrotsvit's plays could even be viewed as antiplays.[53] Thus, while a strong case has been made for a possible contemporary performance of her plays (Magnin, Bendixen, Butler, and so on), extant evidence, as has been persuasively argued (Nagel, Homeyer, Sticca, and so on), contradicts the likelihood of their tenth-century performance.[54]

Equally important is the inquiry into her literary fortunes. The question of whether or not her works were known during the Middle Ages is, as Edwin Zeydel suggests, "of more than academic significance, because upon its answer hinges the solution of the further question of Hrotsvitha's position as a possible factor during the 500 years of important literary development."[55]

Until 1900 only a single and incomplete manuscript of the canoness' works was known: the Emmeran codex,[56] discovered in 1493 by the poet laureate and humanist Conrad Celtis.[57] Celtis' excitement over his discovery and the outpouring of enthusiasm by the German humanists over the talents of Hrotsvit were so unprecedented that some were led to doubt the authenticity of the discovery.[58]

The second discovery of a Hrotsvit manuscript occurred in 1902, when Paul von Winterfeld identified the *Gallicanus*; complete with didascalia, it was incorporated in the twelfth-century *Alderspach Passionale* as a work by Hrotsvit.[59] In 1922 Goswin Frenken found an independent twelfth-century copy of the canoness' first four dramas in Cologne, and in 1925 Hermann Menhardt discovered some eleventh-century fragments of "Maria" and *Sapientia* in Klagenfurt.[60] Finally, in 1933 Gerhard Eis demonstrated that Hrotsvit's *Gallicanus* was incorporated into the *Magnum Legendarium Austriacum*.[61] All extant copies of the *Legendarium* which preserve the June volume contain the *Gallicanus*.[62]

Of Hrotsvit's literary echoes, only a few have been found. The connection between her *Gesta* and both Widukind's *Res gestae Saxonicae* and Liudprand's *Antapodosis* has been established, but the question of priority is not solved.[63] Two scholars have pointed to the geographic proximity of the place of genesis of the eleventh-century Hildesheim Saint Nicholas plays and Gandersheim.[64] The presbyter Eberhard may have used Hrotsvit's *Primordia* for his *Reim-Chronicon*, and Thankmar of Hildesheim used the *Primordia* for his biography of Willigis of Mainz.[65] Boris Jarcho has demonstrated Hrotsvit's influence on the *Vita Mathildis reginae II*,[66] and Bruce Hozeski points to a possible connection between Hildegard of Bingen's dramas and Hrotsvit's plays, but further research in this area is sorely needed.[67]

These discoveries make it abundantly clear that Hrotsvit's work did not fall into complete oblivion after her death and that knowledge of her writings was not restricted to Gandersheim and Saint Emmeram. In addition, it may be more than coincidental that several now extant copies of her plays were recognized as dramas and were copied in the twelfth century. Considering the fact that the twelfth is generally acclaimed as the century during which Church drama began to flourish, the renewed copying of Hrotsvit's plays at this time is significant. If her plays were known, read, and copied in the century of renewed dramatic interest, it is difficult to imagine that they were entirely ignored by the authors of saints' plays and moralities, for unlike the *Quem Queritis* dialogue, Hrotsvit's dramas are based on hagiography, not on liturgy; they are at home in the refectory, not in the church. Like the saints' plays and moralities, the canoness' dramas are about Christian saints and martyrs, or they are dramatized sermons about allegorical virtues, psychomachy, and the chaste ideal. As such, they anticipate the mystery and morality plays by at least one and a half centuries.

Hrotsvit is not the foremost stylist of the Ottonian period; neither are her works, as some have ventured to suggest, without literary merit. Her style, clearly saturated with expressions, vocabulary, and images from the liturgy and from sacred texts, yet shows much originality, power of observation, and imagination.[68] Neither are her works without adornment, and she improves both stylistically and conceptually on her sources.

Her legends and epics are composed chiefly in leonine hexameters.[69] The choice of hexameters (that is, the heroic meter) was natural because it was in this form that the admirable deeds of exceptional men were sung. Hrotsvit rhymes one or occasionally two syllables, although in most cases she contents herself with assonance or homoeoteleuton. She also alliterates frequently, particularly for emphatic effect. Her preferred form of poetry is a strong caesura after the fifth half foot. Her works abound in rhetorical embellishments. In her legends and epics she is fond of using hiatus, simple and compound hyperbaton, anaphora, symmetrical and asymmetrical repetition, chiasmus, simile, metaphor, and personification.[70] Her dramas, on the other hand, are written in rhymed rhythmic prose, whereby rhyme and speech pause coincide.[71] Among rhetorical figures, stychomathia, interjection, ellipsis and aposiopesis prevail. In all her works, as Zeydel has shown, she avoids synaloepha.[72] One stylistic characteristic may be attributable to her sex: she is exceedingly fond of using diminutives.[73]

The present translation is based on Helena Homeyer's edition of Hrotsvit's works, which utilizes the textual emendations resulting from recent manuscript finds. As no English translations exist that attempt to reproduce the original poetic form of these works, I have tried to present the legend in leonine hexameters and the drama in rhymed rhythmic prose.[74] In doing so, I hope to give the reader a taste not only of what the Strong Voice of Gandersheim says but also of the form in which her resonant chords are couched.

NOTES

1. Contrary to widespread belief, Hrotsvit was a canoness, not a nun. Bert Nagel, *Hrotsvit von Gandersheim*, pp. 47, 48, for example, says: "A widespread error must be corrected: Gandersheim was not a nunnery but an abbey and Hrotsvit not a nun but a canoness . . . in fact the difference between a canoness and a nun is not insignificant." Also see Kurt Kronenberg, *Roswitha von Gandersheim*, pp. 52 ff.

2. On the Renaissance reception of Hrotsvit, see Edwin Zeydel, "The Reception of Hrotsvitha by the German Humanists after 1493," *Journal of English and Germanic Philology* 44 (1945): 239–249, and his "A Chronological Hrotsvitha Bibliography through 1700, with Annotations," *Journal of English and Germanic Philology* 46 (1947): 290–294.

3. As Dennis M. Kratz, "The Nun's Epic: Hroswitha on Christian Heroism," p. 132, observes, Faltonia Proba's epic (fourth century) on the war of Constantine to which she refers in her Virgilian canto is not extant. Hrotsvit was not the first "Germanic" woman to write Latin legends or *vitae*; around 800, the nun Hugeburg composed a *vita* of the Anglo-Saxon brothers Willibald and Wynnebald.

4. Thus, for example, Nagel, *Hrotsvit*, p. 45; *Hrotsvithae Opera*, ed. Helena Homeyer, p. 7.

5. See also Otto Grashof, "Das Benediktinerinnenstift Gandersheim und Hrotsvitha, die 'Zierde des Benediktinerordens,'" *Studien und Mitteilungen aus dem Benediktiner und dem Cistercienser Orden* 6 (1884): 80, who points out that the *Chronicle* of the bishops of Hildesheim records that Hrotsvit wrote *Lives of the 3 Ottos*, which would necessitate that she lived until 1002. Now the information of the Hildesheim codex is considered to be

incorrect. Thus, she lived during what scholars call the Ottonian Renaissance. As Karl A. Zaenker, "Homage to Roswitha," *Humanities Association of Canada* 29 (1978): 117, remarks, 1973 was probably wrongly commemorated as the millennium of her death.

6. Preface to Book 3; "Maria" 18; "Ascensio" 148; "Gongolf" 3; "Pelagius" 3.

7. Jacob Grimm and A. Schmeller, *Lateinische Gedichte des zehnten und elften Jahrhunderts*, p. 9—compare the more recent claims (see Nagel, *Hrotsvit*, p. 39) that her name actually means 'famous' or 'strong in fame.'

8. So, for example, *Heldenlieder der deutschen Vergangenheit*, ed. Wilhelm Gundlach, vol. 1, p. 225: "But we are in no doubt that she was descended from a noble Saxon family because only they were admitted to the convent of Gandersheim."

9. The reigns of the three Liudolf abbesses (Hathumonda, Gerberga I, and Christina) were followed by those of two women not affiliated with the crown but chosen by the sisters from among themselves. Hrotsvit I was the first of these abbesses; she may have been related to the author, or Hrotsvit may have chosen her name for the abbess. In 965 the rule of royal abbess was reinstated when Bishop Otwin of Hildesheim ordained Gerberga II, niece of Otto I and daughter of Henry, duke of Bavaria.

10. Gerberga II, Gundlach, ed., vol. 1, pp. 23 ff., observes, was one of the most erudite members of the Saxon dynasty; she was educated in Regensburg.

11. See, for example, Nagel, *Hrotsvit*, p. 48.

12. The first abbess of Gandersheim, Hathumonda, for example, entered Herford at the age of six; Sophia, daughter of Otto II and Theophano, was sent to Gandersheim for education at the age of five. However, the suggestion, first voiced by Magnin in his *Théâtre de Hrotsvitha*, that Hrotsvit shows such deep understanding of erotic passion that she must have taken the veil rather late in life enjoyed, for a while at least, some popularity with German Hrotsvit scholars. I question the absolute necessity of this conclusion.

13. Preface to Book 1, p. 38. All references to pagination are to the Homeyer edition.

14. Ibid., pp. 37, 38.

15. See Homeyer, ed., p. 8; Nagel, *Hrotsvit*, p. 43; Gundlach, ed., vol. 1, p. 304.

16. On Ekkehard's influence, see Edwin Zeydel, "Ekkehard's Influence upon Hrotsvitha: A Study in Literary Integrity," *Modern Language Quarterly* 6 (1945): 333–339.

17. Homeyer, ed., p. 8.

18. Preface to Book 1, p. 37.

19. On the submission topos, see Ernst R. Curtius, *European Literature and the Latin Middle Ages*.

20. Preface, Book 1, p. 37. Interestingly, Celtis' friend Charitas Pirckheimer (*Der Briefwechsel des Konrad Celtis*, ed. Hans Rupprich, p. 478) uses Hrotsvit's own formula of *humilitas feminei sexu* when she commends Celtis for not spurning the writings of a frail woman and enthusiastically furthering Hrotsvit's fortunes: "Extollenda atque laudanda vestra humilis diligentia, qua studuistis scripta et carmina mulierculae in lucem producere atque arti impressorae tradere non spernendo fragilem sexum humilemque status sanctimonialis pauperculae."

21. See Jerome's *Vitae Sanctorum* (PL 23. 23 ff.) and E. K. Rand's *Founders of the Middle Ages*, pp. 121–125.

22. The short poem, long believed to have been Hrotsvit's, is now identified as a quotation from Bede. We have no original copy of the *Primordia*; it is not contained in the Emmeram codex, and the copy from which Leuckfeld prepared his edition (and which was also consulted by Leibnitz) is now lost. Hrotsvit may have composed a song on the patron saints of Gandersheim, Popes Anastasius and Innocent, but if she did, no traces of it are left.

23. Homeyer, ed., p. 9.

24. As Ludwig Zoepf, *Das Heiligenleben im Zehnten Jahrhundert*, p. 127, points out,

Hrotsvit uses a ninth-century *vita* for her Gongolf legend which does not designate Gongolf as a martyr. However, she sings of Saint Gongolf, the "famous martyr." She emphasizes his martyrdom because, by the tenth century, the term "martyr" has already undergone a semantic change. As Marianne Schütze-Pflugk, *Herrscher und Märtyrer Auffassung bei Hrotsvit von Gandersheim*, pp. 54, 55, observes, by the tenth century martyrdom denoted either actual persecution and death as a result of persistence in the faith or asceticism. A third meaning occurs with Hrotsvit: as Gongolf's piety inspires the devil's hate, so he becomes the agent of Christ in fighting the eternal battle, dies as a result, and is triumphantly rewarded by Christ.

25. Connections between the courts of Otto and Abderrahman were cultivated during Hrotsvit's lifetime. In 953 Johannes of Gorza was sent at the head of an embassy to Córdoba. It is possible that one of the men in his retinue could have told Hrotsvit about the recently martyred Pelagius. See *Die Sendung des Mönches Johannes von Gorze nach Cordoba*, in Gundlach, ed., vol. 1, pp. 500 ff.

26. Agnes ("Agnes," 226) describes the joys of the heavenly bridegroom's embrace in the sensual terms of earthly love:

Sum . . . luciflua regis caelestis in aula
Virginibus sacris sociata perenniter istis.
Et nunc in caelis illi coniungor amoris
Amplexu dulci, quem semper mente fideli
In terris colui, cupiens sine fine tueri.

27. *Hrotsvithae Opera*, ed. Paul von Winterfeld, p. viii.

28. Sandro Sticca, "Sin and Salvation: The Dramatic Context of Hroswitha's Women," p. 12, observes that the kitchen, the "symbolic abode of the Devil on earth," is a most appropriate place for an attempted seduction, particularly since medieval exegesis attached carnal associations to pots and pans.

29. The similarity was first suggested by Magnin, *Théâtre de Hrotsvitha*; see Nagel, *Hrotsvit*, p. 13.

30. *Abraham* was a favorite with the German humanists; it was the first of Hrotsvit's plays to be translated (Adam Wernher von Themar, 1503) and is still considered one of her masterpieces. See R. Düchting, "Hrotsvitha von Gandersheim, Adam Wernher von Themar und Guarino Veronese," *Ruperto Carola* 33 (1963): 77–89.

31. For a discussion of the two lessons, see P. A. Sturm, "Das Quadrivium in den Dichtungen Roswithas von Gandersheim," *Studien und Mitteilungen zur Geschichte des Benediktiner Ordens und Seiner Zweige* 33 (1912): 331–338.

32. See Nagel, *Hrotsvit*, p. 27.

33. There are two gaps in the *Gesta* (11. 753–1140, 1189–1478); presumably they contained damaging information on the Ottos. See Edwin Zeydel, "The Authenticity of Hrotsvitha's Works," *Modern Language Notes* 61 (1946): 52, 53. Gundlach, ed., vol. 1, p. 30, suggests that Hrotsvit composed the *Gesta* at the request of Bishop Wilhelm of Mainz in 967.

34. Kratz, p. 132, remarks: "In many respects [the *Gesta* is] Hroswitha's finest literary achievement; and the fact that its author is a woman is a far from inconsequential element of its success. For Hroswitha's consciousness of the epic genre as a 'masculine' domain provided her with the justification, if not the inspiration, for a departure from tradition which helps raise her narrative above any other 10th century attempt at a Christian epic." Further, pp. 141–142, he says: "In using the *excusatio* to introduce the subsidiary theme of a woman's aversion to describing battles, she sets the stage for her most striking pivotal departure from epic tradition. In the place of a battle she has the pivotal scene—which includes the use by Otto of David's very words—in the establishment of the Biblical exemplar for Otto's *pietas*."

35. Ibid., pp. 138–139.

36. See Schütze-Pflugk, pp. 5, 6.

37. To break the ties with Hildesheim, Otto II's daughter, Sophia, persuaded Archbishop Willigis of Mainz to claim Gandersheim for his see on the basis of Fulda's rights over Brunshausen (the initial domicile for the canonesses). The struggle was not entirely settled until 1028.

38. On a host of verbal and structural echoes in her works, see Rudolf A. Köpke, *Die älteste deutsche Dichterin.*

39. See, on the Christian legend, Siegfried Ringer, "Zur Gattung Legende, Versuch einer Strukturbestimmung der Christlichen Heiligenlegende des Mittelalters," pp. 255–286; Heinrich Günter, *Die Christliche Legende des Abendlandes*; Hans Ulrich Gumbrecht, "Fascinationstyp Hagiography: Ein historisches Experiment zur Gattungstheorie," pp. 37–84; and the excellent study by František Graus, *Volk, Herrscher und Heiliger im Reich der Merowinger: Studien zur Hagiographie der Merowingerzeit.*

40. Hrotsvit depicts the final glorification of many sinful saints. Her frequency of employing this particular theme has prompted Erhard Dorn, *Der sündige Heilige in der Legende des Mittelalters*, p. 118, to suggest a connection between Hrotsvit's preoccupation with repentance and the reform movement of Cluny, whose Abbot Odo (927–942) fervently espoused the cult of Saint Mary Magdalen, the glorious repentant *par excellence.*

41. See also Schütze-Pflugk, pp. 22 ff.

42. Ibid., p. 26.

43. All the standard histories of drama reiterate the statement of the oblivion of Hrotsvit's works for five hundred years. Thus, for example, see Heinz Kindermann, *Theatergeschichte Europas*; Karl Young, *The Drama of the Medieval Church*; Wilhelm Creizenach, *Geschichte des neueren Dramas*; and O. B. Hardison, *Christian Rite and Christian Dramas in the Middle Ages.*

44. See Curtius, *European Literature and the Latin Middle Ages.*

45. See David S. Wiesen, *St. Jerome as a Satirist*, and Harold Hagendahl, *Latin Fathers and the Classics.*

46. Woman is a dangerous temptress, always inclined to beguile man with sinful passions, says Athanasius (contra Arian 2. 69), and his statement is echoed throughout biblical exegesis. The *Glossa Ordinaria* (ad Heb. 4:12) also emphasizes that man is the *animus*, the higher and nobler soul, and woman the *anima*, the lower and sensible soul. Glosses on Genesis 1, for example, invariably emphasize Eve's bad counsel, which resulted in Adam's fall and the introduction of original sin. See Hrabanus Maurus' Glosses on Gen. *PL* 107. 495 ff.; *Glossa Ordinaria*, Lib. Gen. *PL* 113.

47. Her only negative female characters are unchaste: Gongolf's adulterous wife and Thais and Mary before their conversions.

48. See Nagel, *Hrotsvit*, pp. 68 ff.

49. See Sister Mary Margaret Butler, *Hrotsvitha: The Theatricality of Her Plays*; also, for a list of performances, see Anne L. Haight, *Hrotsvitha of Gandersheim.*

50. See Nagel, *Hrotsvit*, p. 22.

51. Thus, for example, see Homeyer, ed., pp. 20, 21, and Nagel, *Hrotsvit*, p. 79.

52. Isidore *Etymologiae* 18. 46; see Wilhelm Cloetta, *Beiträge zur Literaturgeschichte des Mittelalters und der Renaissance*, vol. 1, p. 20.

53. Not only does Hrotsvit substitute chaste virgins for Terence's prostitutes, but she depicts *veritas* (that is, hagiographic truth) in contrast with his *figmenta.*

54. For a summary of the controversy, see Nagel, *Hrotsvit*, pp. 70–75.

55. Edwin Zeydel, "Knowledge of Hrotsvitha's Works prior to 1500," *Modern Language Notes* 59 (1944): 382. See also my article, "The Old Hungarian Translation of Hrotsvit's *Dulcitius*: History and Analysis," *Tulsa Studies in Women's Literature* 1 (1982): 80–91.

56. The codex is now in the Munich state library (Codex Clm 14485).

57. In order to understand the excitement of the German humanists over the Hrotsvit discovery, one needs to recall the strongly patriotic nature of early German humanism. Celtis, the leading spirit of the early phases of northern humanism, expressed his ideas in his oration at Ingolstadt. He maintained that German men of letters—as political heirs to the Holy Roman Empire—must bear a cultural responsibility also. Thus, he emphasized the importance of the study and conscious awareness of native history, geography, and literature. It was in the light of this emphasis that Celtis held up the Hrotsvit manuscript as an illustrious example of the Teutonic past.

58. Joseph von Aschbach, "Rosvitha und Conrad Celtis," *Sitzungsberichte der Kaiser-lichen Akademie der Wissenschaften* 56 (1867): 3–62, suggests that Celtis and his humanist friends actually forged the manuscript. More recently, Zoltán Haraszti, "The Works of Hrotsvitha," *More Books* 20 (1945): 37–119, 139–173, subscribes to a similar theory. Haraszti's article was countered by Zeydel, "Authenticity of Hrotsvitha's Works."

59. Nagel, *Hrotsvit*, p. 34. Also, in 1903 Karl Strecker found that several manuscripts of the Austrian legendary contained Hrotsvit's *Gallicanus*.

60. Goswin Frenken, "Eine neue Hrotsvithhandschrift," *Gesellschaft für Ältere Deutsche Geschichtskunde* 44 (1922): 101–114, and Hermann Menhardt, "Eine unbekannte Hrotsvitha-handschrift," *Zeitschrift für Deutsches Altertum und Deutsche Literatur* 62 (1925): 233–236.

61. Gerhard Eis, *Die Quellen des Märterbuches*, p. 109.

62. Nagel, *Hrotsvit*, p. 3.

63. See Zeydel, "Knowledge of Hrotsvitha's Works prior to 1500."

64. George R. Coffman, "A New Approach to Medieval Drama," *Modern Philology* 22 (1925): 239–271, and Charles Jones, *The St. Nicholas Liturgy*.

65. Heinrich Böhmer, *Leipziger Studien aus dem Gebiet der Geschichte* 1 (1895): 200.

66. Boris Jarcho, "Zu Hrotsvithas Wirkungskreis," *Speculum* 2 (1927): 343–344.

67. Bruce Hozeski, "The Parallel Patterns in Hrotsvitha of Gandersheim, a Tenth Century German Playwright, and in Hildegard of Bingen, a Twelfth Century German Play-wright," *Annuale Mediaevale* 18 (1977): 42–53.

68. See Homeyer, ed., pp. 20, 29, and Nagel, *Hrotsvit*, p. 66.

69. Leonine hexameters are internally rhymed or assonanced hexameters, named for Pope Leo the Great (440–461), who used them with great facility and frequency. See Karl Langosch, *Lateinisches Mittelalter Einleitung in Sprache und Literatur*, p. 64.

70. See, for example, Homeyer, ed., pp. 12–26. On Hrotsvit's stylistic and linguistic individuality, see Sister Mary Gonsalva Wiegand, "The Non-Dramatic Works of Hrotsvi-tha," pp. xix ff.

71. On rhymed prose, see Karl Polheim, *Die Lateinische Reimprosa*. The first chapter is devoted to Hrotsvit.

72. Edwin Zeydel, "A Note on Hrotsvitha's Aversion to Synalepha," *Philological Quarterly* 23 (1944): 379–381.

73. On Hrotsvit's vocabulary, see Eva May Newnan, "The Latinity of the Works of Hrotsvit of Gandersheim."

74. For a possible performance of the canoness' plays, Larissa Bonfante's recent translation of the dramas, *The Plays of Roswitha*, should be recommended. Bonfante has provided a fine adaptation of Hrotsvit's plays for the stage by including stage directions, often softening and loosening the terseness of the original passages. Rendered into rhymeless but rhythmic prose, her translation does remind the audience that Hrotsvit "was not writing in plain prose" (p. xiii). "No mean sign of scholarship," she adds, "is the fact that [Hrotsvit] apparently realized the plays of Terence were written in meter, and tried to render this poetry in her own 'imitations.'"

Basilius

He who wants to learn   and by sure proof discern
God's mercy and the Lord's   many and great rewards,
With humble heart and meek,   these small verses should read.
Scorn he should not render   at the writer's weaker gender
Who these small lines had sung   with a woman's untutored tongue,
But, rather should he praise   the Lord's celestial grace
Who wants not that due pain   sinners their punishment gain,
But eternal life He grants   to the sinner who repents.
This shall be proven here;   thus, shall he rejoice in cheer
Whoever these verses reads   and the present account heeds.

At the time when Basilius[1]   (famous for his virtues)
Our holy Church guided   and in just rule presided
As Bishop of Caesarea,   elected to that see,
There lived in that place   a man of illustrious race.
Proterius was his name,   he was of noble fame;
Honored by young and old,   he was, too, rich in gold.
A single child he had,   one of the female sex
(No other child was there   to be his riches' heir).
He loved this only child   with devotion tender and mild,
And hoped in love paternal   and in fear of God eternal
For this virtuous goal: that the girl's immortal soul
Forever adorned would be   with gems of perfect virginity,
Rather than that her earthly form   be decked out in worldly pomp.
Therefore, he took good care   that she be with virgins fair,
Who to Jesus consecrated   and with holy veil elated
In the cloister's confines   spend their godly lives.

Yet the author of all evil,   seducer of man primeval,
This just father's laudable vow   detested and planned to disallow.
He caused a servant of the sire   to burn in mad desire
For the daughter's love,   the girl mentioned above.[2]
This miserable swain,   by love's arrows slain,
Pined and pined away,   the more he burned in pain.
He knew himself unworthy   for such an exalted union;
Thus, he dared not reveal   his heart's hurt and zeal;
But after searching around,   a magician at last he found
To whom, hoping for gain,   the secret of his pain
And bitter sadness told.   He promised gifts and gold
If the magician could bind   the daughter's tender heart

To the servant's affection   and in equal passion.
This perverse friend of fraud   then to the youth thus spoke:[3]
"I don't believe I hold   the power so bold
As to join a lady   as consort to her slave;
But if according to my way   you're willing to obey
The prince of eternal dark   to whose commands I hark,
Then he can quickly act   and your desires grant
If only nevermore   Christ's name you will adore."

Blinded by mad craze,   his heart with passion ablaze,
The wretched youth agreed   and to all his consent decreed.
The magician then wrote   to his master this note:
"Prince of infernal hell,   great ruler of the deep,
Your servants are always eager   to seduce and lead to evil
Those who were cleansed by the font   of baptism, and from the flock
Of Christ are departed   and now to you are charted,
So that your fellowship's size   be always on the rise.
Today I send this youth   greatly rejoicing in truth,
For as soon as you conspire   to fulfill his secret desire,
You shall incur for sure   a servant for the future."
Then the magician gave   this note to the poor youth
· ·
At night,   over the tomb of a heathen.
· ·
The young man was all eager   to follow the evil intriguer,
And to the spot he turned   to which the magician referred
So he may ask for aid   from the ancient snake,
Who always tempts his friends   to destruction's ends.
Without any delay   hell's servants came his way
And led the erring boy   gloating with malicious joy
To the cruel seat   of the dark spirits' meet.
There the author of all fraud   and of all crime and feud,
The damnable champion   of the contemptible legion,
Was seated in their group   circled by his dark troop.
There traps he prepares   for wretches unawares,
And forever he compiles   insidious plans and guiles.
There he studies the wrong   committed by all his throng.[4]

When he had carefully read   the note that the magician sent,
Like a lion he roared   and in fury thus deplored
(In his savage rage   he terrified the poor youth):[5]
"Never do you stay   faithful to me, you Christians,
But as soon as I ordain   your desire to obtain,

Then from me you promptly flee   and to Christ take your plea.
Me you despise and scorn   after the gifts I had borne,
And full trust you embrace   in Christ's mercy and grace,
Because He's willing to grant   to those who repent
His forgiveness sublime   regardless of the crime.
Therefore, if you desire   the lawful embrace to acquire
Of your master's child,   then you must deny Christ
And also holy baptism   that Christ gave to His people.
And you must agree   forever to belong to me
And always to remain   in eternal infernal pain.
Give me then a note   that in your own hand you wrote
And I shall quickly act   to show my might's effect."

By these speeches captivated,   the poor servant soon abated
And signed with happy heart   his own damnation's chart.
He gave without fear   his soul to the hellish fiend.
Joyful with the affirmation   of the servant's sure damnation,
The fiend in happy mood   soon sent his hellish brood
So that they could incite   the poor virgin's plight,
And make her burn in sinful passion   for her own servant.

As soon as her fragile heart   by love's charms was beguiled,
This offspring of a noble house   desired to be his spouse.
And she exclaimed aloud   that to him she wished to be bound.
Her father she addressed   with these words of request:
"Sweetest father mild,   have mercy with your daughter
And give me right over   to the youth whom I love
So I may not die   in languishing desire!"
Her plea the father heard   and with bitter tears returned:
"Alas, alas, what's this,   sole hope of your father?
Tell me who caused this pain   and turned your head with flatteries
    vain?
And who had done this wrong   and deceived you with a honeyed
    tongue?
Have I not made a vow   to give you an exalted bough
And pledged you with pride   to be Christ's heavenly bride?
With chaste heart forever,   Him alone you were to honor
And sing His praise in mire   together with the celestial choir,
So when freed from death   you may join the virginal band!
But now you burn in affection   for a lascivious servant's passion.
With voice soft and mild   I beg you, my child,
Please, avoid such craze   and stultitude so base.
Else you will bring us shame   and all your ancestors defame.

But if you insist to retain   this evil wish insane,
Then, sweet daughter, may you perish   and in disgrace soon vanish."

Yet she scorned with spite   the father's good advice
And resisting her father,   she thus complained further:
"If you delay to act   and my wish not quickly grant,
Then soon you shall repent   and your child's death lament."
Forced by her bitter plaint,   not freely, but constrained,
The father joined them both   and his child to the slave betrothed.
He also gave them freely   a substantial dowry.
When they were to part,   he said with embittered heart:
"Daughter forlorn,   of luckless parents born,
Once honor but now shame   to the mother who bore you.
You brought foul disgrace   to our ancestral race.
Go now and rejoice   in your darling servant;
But later you shall grieve   and due punishment receive."

When the marriage vows were taken,   so fraught by the fraud of
    Satan,
Then it pained Christ the King   Who salvation to us did bring,
That those whom He had saved   and with His precious blood
    redeemed
Should in the enemy's chain   as captives still remain.
It pleases Christ to aid   even those renegade.
Soon the servant's wife,   erring in her life,
Was told that her husband   was not a good Christian,
And that he never set   his foot on the Church's step,
That he signed himself over   to the greedy serpent's power,
And the true faith denied   and Christ's name maligned.
When with her own ears   she heard of his atrocious deeds,
The poor wife concluded   that she had been deluded.
She began to tremble   and with lifeless members
She fell to the floor;   her hair anon she tore,
And she beat her breast   with her fists without rest.
With bitter tears and sighs   she addressed the skies;
"Those who do not heed   when dear parents plead
Never shall be saved.   This has been proven here.
Alas, alas, the light   at birth why did I sight,
And why was I not enclosed   in dark sepulchral vaults,
So, thus, I would have missed   falling in death's abyss!"

While she so commented   and sadly lamented,
Suddenly her husband came,   criminal and full of blame.

He quickly swore an oath   that all this was not in troth,
But she responded thus   to his repeated denials:
"If you are, by and large,   innocent of the charge,
Then come with me to Church   tomorrow morn, I urge,
And there the Holy Mass   celebrate with me."
By her sound reason defeated[6]   the husband then conceded
And told her the true cause   of how the deed arose.
Then she did not abide,   but put womanly weakness aside
And summoned manly strength   to her prudent heart.
She hurried to the house   of the saintly Basilius.
At his sacred feet   prostrate she did entreat
And poured forth this moan   from her disturbed soul:
"Saintly man of God,   succor us poor sinners,
And save us from the grasp   of the savage fiend
Who already unfolds   the perish of our souls!"
When she had gotten rid   of this weighty sin,
The bishop of the Lord   the wretched servant implored.
He began to inquire,   in benevolent desire,
Whether after his dissent,   he were willing to repent
And to Christ return.   The servant said he yearned
For his salvation greatly—   yet he despaired of mercy:
"I committed the crime,   of free will I signed
With my hand the letters   that gave me to the fiend in fetters.
With my heart turned blind   Christ's name I denied."
The man of God then said: "You don't need to dread
Your future, or doubt   that divine grace shall abound,
Because God's only Son,   the mildest judge of all,
Has never turned away   a repentant sinner.
If you rue your sins,   He will grant you help.
Relinquish thus the depth   of sin that brings only death,
And flee to the safe haven   of divine mercy and love.
That haven grants its shores   to all who approach."
With these admonitions   and with the servant's permission
The bishop set him right   and had him in a cell confined
So Christ he might implore   and his enormous sins deplore.

After three days went by,   the bishop came to inquire
How the sinner bore   the penance so sore.
The servant, greatly exhausted,   with these words responded:
"I can hardly bear   the punishment of dark spirits,
They beat me and tear me   with continuous strokes,
And besiege me ceaselessly   with hard and heavy stones.
Mostly they oppose me   and bitterly reproach me

Because to them I came   and of free will became
One of theirs. Never   did they force me to surrender."
Then the learned healer   and languishing souls' redeemer
Caused him to be fed   and then away he sped.
Some days later he came   to visit the sinner again,
And ask him how he fared   in the chamber dark.
The servant then said: "Good father I now fared
Much better, for I hear   those voices from afar."
Heartily delighted,   Basilius departed
After refreshing him more   just as he did before.
Forty days then passed,   and the bishop came again;
Awhile the penitent   bewailed his bitter sins.
Basilius found him glad   whom he expected to be sad,
And he greatly wondered   and the happy change so pondered.
Through bitter tears now cleansed   the sinner the bishop addressed
And said that he was sure   divine forgiveness to procure:
"I hope I shall be saved,   and through you redeemed
Because, dreaming, at night   I saw you in a fight
With the savage snake   battling for my sake.
I saw that the fiend retreated   with divine force defeated."

Listening intently,   the bishop heard these words
And sang the loud praise   of Christ's heavenly grace.
He removed the captive   from the chamber dark
To his own small chambers   next to the holy Church
So in the bishop's cell   for the night he would dwell.
Then the bishop ordered   the faithful to assemble,
So with him all night   in prayer they unite
And the good Shepherd implore   to rejoin once more
The lost sheep to the flock   as it is His wont.
When the sun emerged   and the black shadows dispersed,
The bishop firmly grasped   the sinner by his right
And to the Church he led   the servant by the hand.
When they touched the threshold   of the sacred house,
From a hidden spot   the demon darted forth.
Intent on hidden harm,   he snatched the man's left arm
And pulled with curses coarse   the servant with great force.
But Basilius discharged   his office with great might:
"Let go, you thief," he scorned,   "This creature of the Lord!
Conquered now you lay;   so give back your prey!"
The hellish fiend replied,   the enemy to all,
Filling the air with a howl   and with his perverse growl:
"How dare you say   you take my slave away

Who out of free will   submitted to my chains?
The written agreement   that he gave to me
I shall bring to show   on the final day of law."
The saintly bishop spoke   and gave him this reply:
"By Christ's command, I trust,   that equitable judge,
You shall soon relinquish   the letters that you hold."
After he had spoken,   the whole flock of the faithful
Began with pious hearts   to praise the Almighty
And to entreat His aid   for their shepherd's crusade
Against the savage fiend.   Anon the hellish writ
Fell from above and lay   right in the bishop's way.

Then the folk rejoiced   and with their bishop joint
They all began to raise   their voices and so praise
Christ the benign, who showed   His usual compassion
And rescued the captive   from the lion's jaws.
To heaven let us raise   our voices and so praise
And laud the Lord Christ   with our happy hearts,
He has kindly bequeathed us   hope for grace and mercy,
To Him all glory be rend   and honor without end,
All praise and victory   be His eternally, AMEN.

Dulcitius

The martyrdom of the holy virgins Agapes, Chionia, and Hirena
whom, in the silence of night,   Governor Dulcitius secretly visited, desiring that in their embrace he might delight;   but as soon as he entered,   he became demented   and kissed and hugged the pots and the
pans, mistaking them for the girls   until his face and his clothes were
soiled with disgusting black dirt. Afterward the Count Sissinus, acting
on orders,   was given the girls so he may put them to tortures.   He,
too, was deluded by a miraculous bane   but finally ordered that Agapes
and Chionia be burned and Hirena by an arrow be slain.[7]

DIOCLETIAN: The renown of your free and noble descent   and the
brightness of your beauty demand   that to the foremost men of my
court you be wed.   According to our command this will be met   if
Christ you deny   and comply in bringing offerings to our gods.
AGAPES: Be free of care,   don't trouble yourself our wedding to pre-
pare   because we cannot be compelled under any duress   to betray
Christ's name, which we must confess,   or to stain our virginity.
DIOCLETIAN: What madness possesses you? What does this mean?

AGAPES: What signs of our madness do you see?

DIOCLETIAN: An obvious and great display.

AGAPES: In what way?

DIOCLETIAN: Chiefly in that renouncing the practices of ancient religion   you follow the useless newfangled ways of Christian superstition.[8]

AGAPES: Heedlessly you offend the majesty of God omnipotent.   That
is dangerous . . .

DIOCLETIAN: Dangerous to whom?

AGAPES: To you and to the state which you rule.

DIOCLETIAN: She is mad; remove her!

CHIONIA: My sister is not mad,   justly did she your folly reprehend.

DIOCLETIAN: Her rage is even more absurd.   Remove her from our
sight and arraign the third.

HIRENA: You will find the third, too, a rebel   and resisting you forever.

DIOCLETIAN: Hirena, although you are younger in birth,   be greater in
worth!

HIRENA: Show me, I pray you,   how?

DIOCLETIAN: To the gods bow your neck   and an example for your sisters so set   and be the cause for their freedom!

HIRENA: Let those worship idols, sire,   who wish to incur God's ire.
But I won't defile my head, anointed with royal unguent sweet,   by de-
basing myself at the idols' feet.

DIOCLETIAN: The worship of gods brings no dishonor   but great
honor.

HIRENA: And what dishonor is more disgraceful,   what disgrace is any
more shameful,   than when a slave is venerated as a master?

DIOCLETIAN: I don't ask you to worship slaves   but the lord gods of
princes and greats.

HIRENA: Is he not anyone's slave   who, for a price, is up for sale?

DIOCLETIAN: For her speech so brazen,   to the tortures she must be
taken.

HIRENA: That is just what we hope for, that is what we desire,   that
for the love of Christ through tortures we may expire.

DIOCLETIAN: Let these insolent girls   who defy our decrees and words
be put in chains and kept in the squalor of prison   until Governor Dulcitius conducts the interrogation.

DULCITIUS: Bring forth, soldiers, the girls you hold sequestered.

SOLDIERS: Here they are whom you requested.

DULCITIUS: Wonderful, indeed, how beautiful, how graceful, how admirable these little girls are!

SOLDIERS: Yes, they are perfectly lovely.

DULCITIUS: I am captivated by their beauty.
SOLDIERS: That is understandable.
DULCITIUS: To draw them to my love, I am eager.
SOLDIERS: Your success will be meager.
DULCITIUS: Why?
SOLDIERS: Because they are firm in faith.
DULCITIUS: What if I sway them by flattery?
SOLDIERS: They will despise it utterly.
DULCITIUS: What if with tortures I frighten them?
SOLDIERS: Little will it matter to them.
DULCITIUS: Then what should be done?
SOLDIERS: Consider carefully.
DULCITIUS: Under guard they must be held   in the inner room of the
workshop in whose vestibule the servants' pots are kept.
SOLDIERS: Why there?
DULCITIUS: So that I may visit them often at my leisure.
SOLDIERS: At your pleasure.

DULCITIUS: What do the captives do at this time of night?
SOLDIERS: Hymns they recite.
DULCITIUS: Let us go near.
SOLDIERS: From afar we hear their tinkling voices clear.
DULCITIUS: Stand guard before the door with your lantern   but I will
enter   and satisfy myself in their longed-for embrace.
SOLDIERS: Enter. We will guard this place.

AGAPES: What is that noise outside the door?
HIRENA: That wretched Dulcitius is coming to the fore.
CHIONIA: May God protect us!
AGAPES: Amen.
CHIONIA: What is the meaning of this clash   of pots, utensils, and
pans?
HIRENA: I will check.   Come here, please, and look through the crack!
AGAPES: What is going on?
HIRENA: Look, the fool, the madman so base,   he thinks he is enjoying
our embrace.
AGAPES: What is he doing?
HIRENA: Unto his lap he pulls the utensils,   he embraces the pots and
the pans, giving them tender kisses.
CHIONIA: Ridiculous!
HIRENA: His face, his hands, his clothes   are so soiled, so filthy, and so
loath,   that with all the soot that clings to him, he looks like an Ethio-
pian.

AGAPES: It is only right, that he should appear in sight as he is in his mind: possessed by the fiend.

HIRENA: Wait! He prepares to leave. Let us watch how he is greeted, and how he is treated by the soldiers who wait for him.

SOLDIERS: Who is coming out? A demon without doubt. Or rather, the devil himself is he, let us flee![9]

DULCITIUS: Soldiers, where are you taking in flight? Stay! Wait! Escort me home with your light!

SOLDIERS: The voice is our master's tone but the look the devil's own. Let us not stay! Let us run away, the apparition will slay us!

DULCITIUS: I will go to the palace and complain, and reveal to the whole court the insults I had to sustain.

DULCITIUS: Guards, let me into the palace, I must have a private audience.

GUARDS: Who is this monster vile and detestable? Covered in rags torn and despicable? Let us beat him, from the steps let us sweep him; he must not be allowed to enter.

DULCITIUS: Alas, alas, what has happened? Am I not dressed in splendid garments? Don't I look neat and clean? Yet anyone who looks at my mien loathes me as a foul monster. To my wife I shall return, and from her learn what has happened. But there is my spouse, with disheveled hair she leaves the house, and the whole household follows her in tears!

WIFE: Alas, alas, Dulcitius, my lord, what has happened to you? You are not sane; the Christians have made a laughingstock out of you.

DULCITIUS: At last now I know— this mockery to their witchcraft I owe.

WIFE: What upsets me, what makes me sad, is that you were ignorant of all that passed.

DULCITIUS: I command that those insolent girls be led forth, and that they be stripped from all their clothes publicly, so that in retaliation for ours, they experience similar mockery.

SOLDIERS: We labor in vain; we sweat without gain. Behold, their garments remain on their virginal bodies, sticking to them like skin. But he who ordered us to strip them snores in his seat, and cannot be woken from his sleep. Let us go to the emperor's court and make a report.

DIOCLETIAN: It grieves me greatly to hear how Governor Dulcitius fared, that he has been greatly deluded, so greatly insulted, so ut-

terly humiliated.   But these vile young women shall not boast with im-
punity   of having made a mockery   of our gods and those who
worship them. I shall direct Count Sissinus to take due vengeance.

SISSINUS: Soldiers, where are those insolent girls that are to be tor-
tured?
SOLDIERS: They are kept in prison.
SISSINUS: Leave Hirena there,   bring the others here.
SOLDIERS: Why do you except the one?
SISSINUS: Sparing her youth.   Forsooth, she may be converted easier, if
she is not intimidated by her sisters' presence.
SOLDIERS: It makes sense.

SOLDIERS: Here are they whose presence you requested.
SISSINUS: Agapes and Chionia, give heed,   and to my counsel accede!
AGAPES: We will not give heed.
SISSINUS: Bring offerings to the gods.
AGAPES: We bring offerings of praise forever   to the true Father eter-
nal, and to His Son coeternal,   and also to the Holy Spirit.
SISSINUS: This is not what I bid,   but on pain of penalty prohibit.
AGAPES: You cannot prohibit that ever,   never shall we bring sacrifices
to demons.
SISSINUS: Cease this hardness of heart, and make your offerings.   But
if you persist   then I shall insist   that you be killed according to the
emperor's orders.
CHIONIA: It is proper—that you shouldn't delay,   and the orders of
your emperor obey,   whose decrees you know we disdain.   But if you
spare us then—you, too, deserve to be slain.
SISSINUS: Soldiers, don't delay,   but lead these blaspheming girls away,
and throw them alive to the flames.
SOLDIERS: We shall instantly build the pyre you ask,   and into the raging fire these girls we will cast,   thus we will end their insults at last.
AGAPES: O Lord, nothing is impossible for You,   not even that the fire
forget its nature and obey You;   but we are weary of delay,   therefore,
solve the earthly bonds that hold our souls, we pray,   so that as our
earthly bodies perish,   our souls in heaven Your glory may cherish.
SOLDIERS: Oh, marvel, oh, stupendous miracle! Behold their souls no
longer to their bodies are bound,   yet no traces of injury can be found;
neither their hair nor their clothes are burned by the fire,   and their
bodies are not at all harmed by the pyre.
SISSINUS: Bring forth Hirena.
SOLDIERS: Here she is.

SISSINUS: Hirena, at the deaths of your sisters tremble, and fear to perish according to their example.

HIRENA: I hope to follow their example and expire, so with them in heaven eternal joy I may acquire.

SISSINUS: Give in, give in to my persuasion.

HIRENA: I will never give in to evil persuasion.

SISSINUS: If you don't give in, I shall not give you a death quick and easy, but multiply your sufferings daily.

HIRENA: The more cruelly I'll be tortured, the more gloriously I'll be exalted.

SISSINUS: You fear no tortures, no pain? What you abhor, I shall ordain.

HIRENA: Whatever punishment you'll design, I will escape it with help divine.

SISSINUS: To a brothel you'll be conducted, where your body'll be shamefully polluted.

HIRENA: Better that the body be dirtied with any stain, than that the soul be polluted with idolatry vain.

SISSINUS: If you be in the company of harlots—so polluted, among the virginal choir you no longer could be counted.

HIRENA: Lust deserves punishment, but forced compliance the crown; neither is one considered guilty, unless the soul consented freely.

SISSINUS: I pitied her youth in vain; I spared her without gain!

SOLDIERS: We knew this before; she could not be moved our gods to adore, nor can she be broken by terror.

SISSINUS: I spare her no longer.

SOLDIERS: Rightly you ponder.

SISSINUS: Seize her mercilessly, drag her with cruelty, take her in dishonor to the brothel.

HIRENA: They will not succeed!

SISSINUS: Who will intercede?

HIRENA: He Whose foresight rules the world.

SISSINUS: I shall see . . .

HIRENA: Sooner than you wish, it will be.

SISSINUS: Soldiers, be not frightened by the false prophecies of this blaspheming girl.

SOLDIERS: We are not afraid, but are eager to do what you bade.

SISSINUS: Who are those approaching? How similar they are to the men, to whom we gave Hirena just then. They are the same. Why are you returning so fast? Why so out of breath, I ask?

SOLDIERS: You are the one for whom we look.

SISSINUS: Where is she whom you just took?

SOLDIERS: On the peak of mountain high.

SISSINUS: Which one?

SOLDIERS: The one close by.

SISSINUS: O you idiots, dull and blind. You have completely lost your mind!

SOLDIERS: Why do you accuse us, why do you threaten us with voice and face and abuse us?

SISSINUS: May the gods destroy you!

SOLDIERS: What have we committed; what harm have we done; how have we transgressed against your orders?

SISSINUS: Have I not given orders resolute that you take that rebel against the gods to a place of ill repute?

SOLDIERS: Yes, so you did command, and we were eager to fulfill your demand, but two strangers intercepted us, saying that you sent them to us to lead Hirena to the mountain's peak.

SISSINUS: That's new to me.

SOLDIERS: We can see.

SISSINUS: What were they like?

SOLDIERS: Splendidly dressed and an awe-inspiring sight.

SISSINUS: Did you follow?

SOLDIERS: We did so.

SISSINUS: What did they do?

SOLDIERS: They placed themselves on Hirena's left and right, and told us to be forthright and not to hide from you what happened.

SISSINUS: I find a sole recourse, that I mount my horse and seek out those who so freely made sport with us.

SISSINUS: Hm, I don't know what to do. I am bewildered by the witch-craft of these Christians. I keep going around the mountain and keep finding this track, but neither do I know how to proceed or how to find my way back.

SOLDIERS: We are all deluded by some intrigue; we are afflicted with a great fatigue; if you allow this insane person to stay alive, then neither you nor we shall survive.

SISSINUS: Anyone among you, I don't care which, string a bow, and shoot an arrow, and kill that witch!

SOLDIERS: Rightly so.

HIRENA: Wretched Sissinus, blush for shame, and your miserable defeat proclaim, because without the force of arms, you cannot overcome a tender young virgin.

SISSINUS: Whatever shame may come to me, I will bear it more easily, because without a doubt I know that you will die now.

HIRENA: For me this is the greatest joy I can conceive, but for you this is a cause to grieve, because you shall be damned in Tartarus for your cruelty, while I shall receive the martyr's palm and the crown of virginity; thus I will enter the heavenly bridal chamber of the eternal King, Whose is all honor and glory in all eternity.

NOTES TO THE TRANSLATION

1. Basilius was archbishop of Caesarea from 370 to 379; Hrotsvit used the Latin version of the Greek *vita* (translated by Ursus) for her legend. See Homeyer, ed., p. 174.

2. Hrotsvit uses the term *servus* to describe the young man. In the early Middle Ages *servus* and *sclavus* were often used interchangeably, but by the tenth century modifiers such as *saracenus* were added in order to assure the audience that only infidels could be slaves. Hrotsvit's concern here is less with the actual position of the young man than with the inappropriateness of the union between two people of entirely different socioeconomic backgrounds.

3. The magician is described as *perversus amicus*; he receives his magical powers from the devil. Thus, his craft becomes the perversion of the divine power to work miracles.

4. That is, Satan makes his inquiries as to whether the planned evil plots have been executed.

5. The raging lion imagery is almost invariably associated with unjust rulers: pagan princes and the devil.

6. That is, the husband, having made a pact with the devil, naturally cannot take communion—her "sound reason" is the attempt to persuade him to take communion to prove his innocence or expose his guilt.

7. The event depicted in the play is historical: the martyrdom of the three virgins occurred during Diocletian's persecution of the Christians. The names of the three girls signify Love, Purity, and Peace.

8. As Christians accused the pagan Romans of superstition, so did the Romans accuse the Christians of the same.

9. In this passage, Dulcitius' presumably pagan soldiers act as if they were Christians.

BIBLIOGRAPHY

Primary Works

Celtis, Conrad, ed. *Opera*. Nuremberg, 1501.
Homeyer, Helena, ed. *Hrotsvithae Opera*. Munich, 1970.
The Plays of Roswitha. Trans. Larissa Bonfante. New York, 1979.
The Plays of Roswitha. Trans. Christopher St. John. London, 1923.
The Plays of Roswitha. Trans. H. J. W. Tillyard. London, 1923.
Wiegand, Sister Mary Gonsalva. "The Non-Dramatic Works of Hrotsvitha." Ph.D. dissertation, St. Louis University, 1936.
Winterfeld, Paul von, ed. *Hrotsvithae Opera*. Berlin, 1902.

Related Works

Aschbach, Joseph von. "Rosvitha und Conrad Celtis." *Sitzungsberichte der Kaiserlichen Akademie der Wissenschaften* 56 (1867): 3–62.

Bauer, A., and R. Rau, eds. *Quellen zur Geschichte der Sächsischen Kaiserzeit.* Darmstadt, 1971.

Böhmer, Heinrich. *Leipziger Studien aus dem Gebiet der Geschichte* 1 (1895).

Butler, Sister Mary Margaret. *Hrotsvitha: The Theatricality of Her Plays.* New York, 1960.

Cloetta, Wilhelm. *Beiträge zur Literaturgeschichte des Mittelalters und der Renaissance.* Vol. 1. Halle, 1899.

Coffman, George R. "A New Approach to Medieval Drama." *Modern Philology* 22 (1925): 239–271.

Creizenach, Wilhelm. *Geschichte des neueren Dramas.* New York, 1965.

Curtius, Ernst R. *European Literature and the Latin Middle Ages.* Trans. Willard R. Trask. Bollingen Series 36. Princeton, 1953.

Dorn, Erhard. *Der sündige Heilige in der Legende des Mittelalters.* Munich, 1967.

Düchting, R. "Hrotsvitha von Gandersheim, Adam Wernher von Themar und Guarino Veronese." *Ruperto Carola* 33 (1963): 77–89.

Dunn, C., et al. *The Medieval Drama and Its Claudian Revival.* Washington, D.C., 1970.

Eis, Gerhard. *Die Quellen des Märterbuches.* Reichenberg, 1932.

Euringer, Sebastian. "Drei Beiträge zur Roswitha Forschung." *Goerres-Gesellschaft zur Pflege der Wissenschaft im Katholischen Deutschland* 54 (1934): 75–83.

Frenken, Goswin. "Eine neue Hrotsvithhandschrift." *Gesellschaft für Ältere Deutsche Geschichtskunde* 44 (1922): 101–114.

Grashof, Otto. "Das Benediktinerinnenstift Gandersheim und Hrotsvitha, die 'Zierde des Benediktinerordens.'" *Studien und Mitteilungen aus dem Benediktiner und dem Cistercienser Orden* 5 (1883): 92–99, 149–161, 383–390; 6 (1884): 78–96, 114–124, 351–356; 7 (1885): 67–84, 87–109.

Graus, František. *Volk, Herrscher und Heiliger im Reich der Merowinger: Studien zur Hagiographie der Merowingerzeit.* Prague, 1965.

Grimm, Jacob, and A. Schmeller. *Lateinische Gedichte des zehnten und elften Jahrhunderts.* Göttingen, 1838.

Gumbrecht, Hans Ulrich. "Fascinationstyp Hagiography: Ein historisches Experiment zur Gattungstheorie." In *Deutsche Literatur im Mittelalter: Kontakte und Perspectiven,* ed. Christoph Cormeau, pp. 37–84. Stuttgart, 1979.

Gundlach, Wilhelm, ed. *Heldenlieder der deutschen Vergangenheit.* 3 vols. 1896. Reprint. Aalen, 1970.

Günter, Heinrich. *Die Christliche Legende des Abendlandes.* Heidelberg, 1910.

Hagendahl, Harold. *Latin Fathers and the Classics.* Göteborg, 1958.

Haight, Anne L. *Hrotsvitha of Gandersheim.* New York, 1965.

Haraszti, Zoltán. "The Works of Hrotsvitha." *More Books* 20 (1945): 37–119, 139–173.

Hardison, O. B. *Christian Rite and Christian Dramas in the Middle Ages.* Baltimore, 1965.

Hozeski, Bruce. "The Parallel Patterns in Hrotsvitha of Gandersheim, a Tenth Century German Playwright, and in Hildegard of Bingen, a Twelfth Century German Playwright." *Annuale Mediaevale* 18 (1977): 42–53.

Jarcho, Boris. "Stilquellen der Hrotsvitha." *Zeitschrift für Deutsches Altertum und Deutsche Literatur* 62 (1925): 236–240.

———. "Zu Hrotsvithas Wirkungskreis." *Speculum* 2 (1927): 343–344.

Jones, Charles. *The St. Nicholas Liturgy.* Berkeley and Los Angeles, 1963.

Katona, Lajos. "Die altungarische Übersetzung des Dulcitius der Hrotsvitha." *Allgemeine Zeitung* 123 (1900): 6–7.

Kindermann, Heinz. *Theatergeschichte Europas*. Salzburg, 1957.

Köpke, Rudolf A. *Die älteste deutsche Dichterin*. Berlin, 1869.

———. *Hrotsvit von Gandersheim*. Berlin, 1867.

Kratz, Dennis M. "The Nun's Epic: Hroswitha on Christian Heroism." In *Wege der Worte: Festschrift für Wolfgang Fleishhauer*, ed. D. C. Riechel, pp. 132–142. Cologne and Vienna, 1978.

Kronenberg, Kurt. *Roswitha von Gandersheim*. Gandersheim, 1962.

Kuehne, Oswald. "A Study of the Thais Legend with Special Reference to Hrotsvitha's 'Paphnutius.'" Ph.D. dissertation, University of Pennsylvania, 1922.

Langosch, Karl. *Lateinisches Mittelalter Einleitung in Sprache und Literatur*. Darmstadt, 1963.

———. *Profile des lateinischen Mittelalters*. Darmstadt, 1965.

Leyser, Karl J. *Rule and Conflict in an Early Medieval Society: Ottonian Saxony*. Bloomington, 1979.

Loomis, R. "Were There Theatres in the Twelfth and Thirteenth Centuries?" *Speculum* 20 (1945): 92–95.

Menhardt, Hermann. "Eine unbekannte Hrotsvitha-handschrift." *Zeitschrift für Deutsches Altertum und Deutsche Literatur* 62 (1925): 233–236.

Nagel, Bert. "Hrotsvith von Gandersheim." *Ruperto Carola* 33 (1963): 5–40.

———. *Hrotsvit von Gandersheim*. Stuttgart, 1965.

Newnan, Eva May. "The Latinity of the Works of Hrotsvit of Gandersheim." Ph.D. dissertation, University of Chicago, 1939.

Piltz, Otto. *Die Dramen der Hrosvitha von Gandersheim*. Leipzig, 1925.

Plenzat, Karl. "Die Theophiluslegende in den Dichtungen des Mittelalters." *Germanische Studien* 43 (1926): 1–263.

Polheim, Karl. *Die Lateinische Reimprosa*. 2nd ed. Berlin, 1963.

Rand, E. K. *Founders of the Middle Ages*. New York, 1957.

Rigobon, M. *Il teatre e la latinita di Hrotsvitha*. Florence, 1930.

Ringer, Siegfried. "Zur Gattung Legende, Versuch einer Strukturbestimmung der Christlichen Heiligenlegende des Mittelalters." In *Philologische Studien Kurt Ruh zum 60. Geburgstag*, ed. Peter Kesting, pp. 255–286. Munich, 1975.

Rupprich, Hans, ed. *Der Briefwechsel des Konrad Celtis*. Munich, 1934.

Schütze-Pflugk, Marianne. *Herrscher und Märtyrer Auffassung bei Hrotsvit von Gandersheim*. Wiesbaden, 1972.

Spitz, L. *Conrad Celtis the German Archhumanist*. Cambridge, Mass., 1957.

Sprague, R. "Hrotsvitha: Tenth Century Margaret Webster." *Theatre Annual* 13 (1955): 16–31.

Stach, W. "Die Gongolflegende bei Hrotsvit." In *Mittellateinische Dichtung*, ed. Karl Langosch, pp. 219–283. Darmstadt, 1969.

Sticca, Sandro. *The Latin Passion Play*. Albany, 1970.

———. "Sin and Salvation: The Dramatic Context of Hroswitha's Women." In *The Roles and Images of Women in the Middle Ages and Renaissance*, ed. D. Radcliff Umstead. Pittsburgh, 1975.

Sturm, P. A. "Das Quadrivium in den Dichtungen Roswithas von Gandersheim." *Studien und Mitteilungen zur Geschichte des Benediktiner Ordens und Seiner Zweige* 33 (1912): 331–338.

Wiesen, David S. *St. Jerome as a Satirist*. Ithaca, 1965.

Wilson, Katharina M. "*Clamor validus Gandeshemensis*." *Germanic Notes*. Forthcoming, 1983.

————. "The Old Hungarian Translation of Hrotsvit's *Dulcitius*: History and Analysis." *Tulsa Studies in Women's Literature* 1 (1982): 80–91.

Young, Karl. *The Drama of the Medieval Church*. Oxford, 1933.

Zaenker, Karl A. "Homage to Roswitha." *Humanities Association of Canada* 29 (1978): 117–134.

Zeydel, Edwin. "The Authenticity of Hrotsvitha's Works." *Modern Language Notes* 61 (1946): 50–55.

————. "A Chronological Hrotsvitha Bibliography through 1700, with Annotations." *Journal of English and Germanic Philology* 46 (1947): 290–294.

————. "Ego Clamor Validus." *Modern Language Notes* 61 (1946): 281–283.

————. "Ekkehard's Influence upon Hrotsvitha: A Study in Literary Integrity." *Modern Language Quarterly* 6 (1945): 333–339.

————. "Knowledge of Hrotsvitha's Works prior to 1500." *Modern Language Notes* 59 (1944): 382–385.

————. "A Note on Hrotsvitha's Aversion to Synalepha." *Philological Quarterly* 23 (1944): 379–381.

————. "The Reception of Hrotsvitha by the German Humanists after 1493." *Journal of English and Germanic Philology* 44 (1945): 239–249.

————. "Were Hrotsvitha's Dramas Performed during Her Lifetime?" *Speculum* 20 (1945): 443–456.

Zoepf, Ludwig. *Das Heiligenleben im Zehnten Jahrhundert*. Leipzig and Berlin, 1908.

THE FRENCH COURTLY POET

 arie de france

JOAN M. FERRANTE

Marie de France is the first known woman to write narrative poetry in the vernacular in Western Europe. We know little about her beyond her name, three of her works, the period of her literary activity, and her probable setting. We do not know who she actually was, where she was brought up, or how she lived, but we can assume that her work was popular, since her lais were translated or adapted in many languages — Old Norse, Middle English, Middle High German, Italian, and Latin— during the Middle Ages. We can also be certain that she was educated to some extent, since she translated one of her works from Latin. We know her name because she mentions it in each work, at the beginning of the first lai ("Listen my lords to what Marie tells"), at the end of *St. Patrick's Purgatory* ("I, Marie, have recorded the book of Purgatory in Romance"), and more forcefully in the epilogue to the *Fables*:

> Marie is my name,
> I am from France.
> It may be that many clerks
> will take my labor on themselves—
> I don't want any of them to claim it.

This assertion tells us that Marie is confident enough of her accomplishment to fear rival claims and suggests that she may already have had such experiences with her lais.

Marie composed her three known works—the *Lais*, the *Fables*, and *St. Patrick's Purgatory*—somewhere between 1160 and 1215.[1] She was probably connected with the court of Henry II and Eleanor of Aquitaine for a time: her use of English words and allusions, although all her works are in French, suggests that she spent time in French-speaking courts in England and was probably writing for such audiences. The subject matter of the lais and the morals drawn in the fables indicate that she wrote for sophisticated people in positions of power. Furthermore, the number of people who communicate by letter in her lais suggests that literacy and letter writing were not unusual in her milieu. The lovers in "Milun," who send letters for twenty years by a hungry swan, are the most striking example, but there are many others: sisters write to each other in "Milun," the heroine of "Deus Amanz" writes to her aunt, kings summon their nobles by letter in "Yonec" and "Eliduc," Tristan communicates with Isolt by a written message carved on a branch, and the education of Fresne is part of her attraction for the hero. Indeed, Marie makes much of her own education: in the prologue to the *Lais*, she talks about the books of the ancients, of their obscurity and the need for glosses, implying that she has studied all that, and then mentions that she considered translating a good story from Latin to Romance but instead decided to record the lais in rhyme. She has chosen, in other words, to write something more popular, but first she has established her literary credentials. She did, of course, later translate the *Purgatory* from Latin, so this was not a false claim.

Marie has a strong sense not only of her own abilities but also of her moral obligations to her audience. As she says in the prologue to the *Lais*,

> Whoever has received knowledge
> and eloquence in speech from God,
> should not be silent or conceal it,
> but demonstrate it willingly.

Again, in the prologue to the *Fables*, she asserts that those who are literate should turn their attention to the works of philosophers who wrote down moral precepts for the edification of others, and in the lessons she herself draws from the fables, she reveals her own great concern for social justice. At the end of her translation of the *Purgatory*, she says that she has put the work into Romance in order to make it accessible to lay people, and she prays that God will cleanse them and her of their sins; that is, she intends the work to help lead her readers away from sin.

The moral import of the *Fables* and the *Purgatory* is self-evident in the choice of subject. It is less obvious, but not less present, in the *Lais*. In these relatively short narrative poems, ranging from 118 to 1,184 lines, Marie is concerned with the problems of human relations in families, in marriages, between lovers, or between vassal and lord. She examines the constraints of unhappy and imprisoning marriages, of chivalric demands and ambitions; she presents heroes and heroines who are trapped by their circumstances and must find a way to escape from or, better, to improve their situation. She shows how destructive selfishness and possessiveness can be, how much people can suffer even from those who apparently love them, but she also shows how one can free oneself, if only in the mind, from the oppression of life, how much a love that is generous and selfless can do. Her stories differ from most courtly romances of the period in that she treats of the problems of women as well as of men and is concerned less with their social position or responsibility and more with the inner man and woman, with their emotional needs. Possessive love brings sterility, shame, frustration, even death, but generous love heals, brings joy, wealth, and honor in the world and, in some cases, the strength to renounce the world or the objects of desire.

The twelve lais offer different perspectives on love and personal relations. "Guigemar" tells of a young man who does not know how to love until he meets a woman, married to a possessive old man, who is also in need of love; they remain faithful to each other through a long separation and various obstacles, their constancy symbolized by the knots on her belt and his shirt which only they can undo. In "Equitan," the heroine is married to a good man, the seneschal of a king who leaves him to run the country while he makes love to the seneschal's wife; the lovers are both killed in a scalding bath, a trap they had set for the husband. "Fresne" is the story of a girl abandoned by her mother, who was afraid to admit to giving birth to twins; the girl is educated in a convent, falls in love with a nobleman, and remains loyal to him even when he is about to marry her unrecognized twin, but her own identity is discovered in time to reunite her with her family and enable her to marry her lover.

The hero of "Bisclavret" is a good man who periodically becomes a werewolf; betrayed by his wife when she discovers his secret, he is imprisoned in his animal form until his king, recognizing the devotion and gentleness of the beast to all but the wife, forces her to return the beast's clothes so that he can resume his human form. In "Lanval," a knight whose service is not appreciated by Arthur's court despairs until he finds love and wealth with a fairy; he then abandons the chivalric world to follow her. "Deus Amanz" tells of a princess whose father discourages all her suitors by requiring them to carry her up a high mountain; she procures a special potion for her lover to enable him to succeed where all the others failed, but, confident in the power of his love, he refuses to take it and dies in the attempt. The heroine of "Yonec," imprisoned by a possessive and suspicious husband, imagines a lover who then comes to her as a bird but is discovered by the husband and killed, leaving her with a son who later avenges his father by killing the husband.

In "Laustic" the lovers are neighbors, unable to meet, who converse through their walls under the pretense of listening to a nightingale in the garden; when the woman's husband kills the bird, her lover preserves it in an ornate casket as a symbol of their love. The lovers of "Milun" are separated for twenty years while he travels from tourney to tourney and she is married to another man, but they correspond by swan and are finally reunited by their son, who meets his father in battle and brings him home. The heroine of "Chaitivel" is courted by four men, three of whom die fighting to impress her; the fourth is seriously wounded, and the lady nurses him and composes a poem to record the fate of all four and her own loss. "Chevrefoil," the shortest lai, recounts a moment in the story of Tristan and Isolt, when Tristan returns from exile and meets Isolt in the forest for a brief encounter which inspires him to compose a poem. "Eliduc," the last and longest of the lais, tells of a man who leaves his wife and home when his king wrongly exiles him; he goes to a new land, serves a new king, and falls in love with another woman; from this time on, he is torn between the two, until his first wife selflessly retires to a nunnery, leaving him free to marry the second; ultimately, they also renounce the world, the second wife joining the first in her convent, and all three devote their lives to God.

How much Marie's concern with the inner life of the emotions and the mind is caused by her frustration as an intelligent and gifted woman with few outlets for her skills in the secular world is hard to say, but there is no question that she sees literature as a way of controlling or ordering life. In two of her lais, she has the main character, a man in one, a woman in the other, compose a lai about their situation—in "Chevrefoil," the poem captures the joy of the love and serves as a counter to the intense pain of separation; in "Chaitivel," it records the suffering and death of the would-be lovers and offers the bereaved lady a satisfying substitute for their devotion. Marie herself never lets us forget her role as author, noting either at the beginning or at the end of many lais, sometimes in both places, that she is the one who put it in its present form. Although she occasionally claims to have read the story, most often she cites an ancient Breton lai as her source, implying that she has heard it told or sung and is putting it into written form for the first time. At the beginning of "Equitan," she says that the old Bretons of Brittany made lais from the adventures that befell people in order to keep their deeds alive in memory. Whether she heard them in French or in Celtic is not clear; she does give an occasional name in "Bretan," but we cannot be sure that she understood the language. Two of her lais involve characters well known in contemporary romances—Arthur and his court in "Lanval," Tristan and "the queen" in "Chevrefoil"—but the incident Marie relates is not found in any of them. Indeed, she seems to avoid stories which have been fixed in literary form and to keep to those whose oral presentation leaves a good deal of freedom to her treatment.

The *Lais* is the only work for which Marie does not have a direct literary source. The *Purgatory* is a rather close translation, and the *Fables* has a long tradition, although Marie seems to have taken liberties with the morals, if not with the narrative details. In her prologue to the latter, she cites Romulus, under whose name many fables circulated in the Middle Ages, and Aesop, who, she claims, translated fables from Greek to Latin. In the epilogue, she says that she translated her fables from an English version of Aesop which was done by King Alfred. The English source is not extant and in any case would probably have been much later than Alfred.[2] Her tales include fables from the Latin version of Romulus, which goes back ultimately to Aesop, episodes from the *Roman de Renart*, and popular tales with no identified source. There are 102 fables in her collection, the majority using animal characters, some people and animals, some just people, but all reflecting the mores of the society Marie and her audience knew.

The *Purgatory* is a straightforward rendition of a twelfth-century Latin text, which relates the otherworldly journey of the Irish knight Owein.[3] Owein, while still alive, enters a hole which leads him to purgatory, where he experiences or witnesses the pains of the damned in graphic detail, but he never gives in to the devils and finally makes his way to the earthly paradise. He is able to retrace his steps from that scene of joy through purgatory and return to the world, where he leads an exemplary life. Although Marie does not tamper with the original text, one can see certain connections between it and her lais, which may partially explain why she chose to translate it: the very real otherworldly experience which transforms the hero's life when he returns to his own world is curiously reminiscent of the lady's journey to the bird-knight's land in "Yonec," her approach through a deep hole in the earth, a long, dark passage that eventually opens onto a field with a beautiful city. In the *Lais*, as in the *Purgatory*, the heroes or heroines can experience the joy of such a place only briefly in this life, but that vision is often enough to sustain them.

Marie's style in all three works is relatively simple. She writes in octosyllabic couplets, with a fairly small vocabulary and frequent repetition of words. Her texts are filled with unidentified pronouns, for which I have occasionally substituted specific nouns for the reader's comprehension. I have also adopted a consistent use of the past tense where Marie shifts from past to present, a practice which was standard in twelfth-century narrative but which jars in English. The French text on which the translation of "Yonec" was based is found in the edition by Alfred Ewert, *Lais* (1944; reprint ed., Oxford, 1963). The text of the fables is in the selected edition by Alfred Ewert and R. C. Johnston, *Fables* (1942; reprint ed., Oxford, 1966). The complete fables can be found in Karl Warnke, *Die Fabeln der Marie de France* (Halle, 1898). The numbering of the fables in my translation is based on the Ewert-Johnston edition, with the Warnke number given in parentheses. The translation of the fables is new; "Yonec" is reprinted from *The Lais of Marie de France*, edited by Joan M. Ferrante and R. W. Hanning (New York, 1978), pp. 137–152, by permission of the Labyrinth Press.

NOTES

1. For details on the dating of the works and the possible identity of the author, see E. J. Mickel, Jr., *Marie de France*, pp. 16 ff., and *The Lais of Marie de France*, ed. Joan M. Ferrante and R. W. Hanning, pp. 7–8.

2. See Mickel, *Marie de France*, p. 34, and *Fables*, ed. Alfred Ewert and R. C. Johnston, p. xi, on other sources.

3. Marie's translation may be found in *Das Buch vom Espurgatoire S. Patrice der Marie de France und seine Quellen*, ed. Karl Warnke.

Yonec

Yonec begins with what appears to be a conventional literary situation, an old and jealous husband keeping his young wife under close guard. The audience expects a plot to deceive the husband and smuggle in a young lover. A young lover does indeed make his way to the wife, but otherwise, in all the details and in the oeverall tone of the story, the treatment is quite unusual. The lovers do not use their wits to deceive the husband—it is the husband who plots to trap and kill the lover, while the wife uses her imagination to create the kind of love she needs.

The wife is young and lovely, with all the social graces, but these are wasted in the tower in which she is imprisoned; the husband, wanting to keep her charms all to himself, only destroys them. He is too old, a point underlined in the French by the repetition of the word *trespas* (line 16) in *trespassez* (line 17); the river of his city once offered a *trespas*, "passage," to boats, that is, it has since dried up; and the husband is *mult trespassez*, "very far along in years," presumably also dried up. Furthermore, his love is possessive, life-denying—he married supposedly to have heirs, but the marriage is childless—and ultimately evil. He will not allow his wife even to go to church and she accuses her family of committing a grave sin in marrying her to this man; she suspects that he was baptized in the waters of hell. As if to emphasize the husband's evil, the lover's first act when he comes to the lady is to ask for a priest and take the host.

The love, in other words, is not a sin. In fact, it restores the lady's beauty and joy (joy is the dominant theme in the love scenes, the word *joie* is constantly repeated), so that even the husband notices the change.

That is what drives him to search out and destroy the lover who is the source of it. The husband is a hunter—he is always having to go off to the forest—and he sets a particularly vicious trap for his prey, the lover who comes to the lady in the shape of a bird. The bird, a hawk, is at once the only creature who could gain entrance to the tower and a symbol of the lover in lyric poetry. He is also, by nature, a predator, a hunter, but the bird-knight of this story, in another reversal of expectation, is a gentle, tame creature who comes at the lady's call to bring her love and joy.

The lady, forced inward on herself by the lack of love in her marriage and the absence of family or friends to console her, escapes into her imagination. She thinks of adventures, which she associates with blameless love between knights and ladies; she prays for one to come to her, and the bird appears. As she stares at it, it becomes a handsome man. That is, her will brings him, and her look gives him form. But when the reality of her world intrudes on her fantasy, when the husband discovers the existence of the bird, the dream is shattered, destroyed by his envy. The bird, wounded by the husband's trap, withdraws forever. But love has given the lady the power to overcome the problems of her life. She is able to leave her prison (she leaps from a window of the tower without injury), follow her dying lover to his land, and then return to her husband, but she is never again to be imprisoned by him.

The lover's land is a kind of dream world, a city of silver that she reaches by making her way through a long, dark tunnel. When she enters his palace, she goes through room after room of sleeping knights. Her own life is in danger here, as her lover's was in her husband's tower; when her dream is taken from her, she loses the desire to live. But her lover tells her that she will have a son and gives her a sword to keep for him, so that he can one day avenge them and their love. It is the child who gives reality to the love; it is through him that the love can endure.

What Marie seems to be saying in this *lai*, as in several others, is that the world can imprison the body but not the mind, once the mind wills itself free. Love gives the lady the power, by giving her the will, to free herself.

Now that I've begun these lais
the effort will not stop me;
every adventure that I know
I shall relate in rhyme.
My intention and my desire
is to tell you next of Yonec,
how he was born and how his father
first came to his mother.

The man who fathered Yonec
was called Muldumarec.

There once lived in Brittany
a rich man, old and ancient.
At Caerwent, he was acknowledged
and accepted as lord of the land.
The city sits on the Duelas,
which at one time was open to boats.
The man was very far along in years
but because he possessed a large fortune
he took a wife in order to have children,
who would come after him and be his heirs.
The girl who was given to the rich man
came from a good family;
she was wise and gracious[1] and very beautiful—
for her beauty he loved her very much.
Because she was beautiful and noble
he made every effort to guard her.
He locked her inside his tower
in a great paved chamber.
A sister of his,
who was also old and a widow, without her own lord,
he stationed with his lady
to guard her even more closely.
There were other women, I believe,
in another chamber by themselves,
but the lady never spoke to them
unless the old woman gave her permission.
So he kept her more than seven years—
they never had any children;
she never left that tower,
neither for family nor for friends.
When the lord came to sleep there
no chamberlain or porter
dared enter that room,
not even to carry a candle before the lord.
The lady lived in great sorrow,
with tears and sighs and weeping;
she lost her beauty,
as one does who cares nothing for it.
She would have preferred
death to take her quickly.

It was the beginning of April
when the birds begin their songs.
The lord arose in the morning
and made ready to go to the woods.
He had the old woman get up
and close the door behind him—
she followed his command.
The lord went off with his men.
The old woman carried a psalter
from which she intended to read the psalms.
The lady, awake and in tears,
saw the light of the sun.
She noticed that the old woman
had left the chamber.
She grieved and sighed
and wept and raged:
"I should never have been born!
My fate is very harsh.
I'm imprisoned in this tower
and I'll never leave it unless I die.
What is this jealous old man afraid of
that he keeps me so imprisoned?
He's mad, out of his senses;
always afraid of being deceived.
I can't even go to church
or hear God's service.
If I could speak to people
and enjoy myself with them
I'd be very gracious to my lord
even if I didn't want to be.
A curse on my family,
and on all the others
who gave me to this jealous man,
who married me to his body.
It's a rough rope that I pull and draw.
He'll never die—
when he should have been baptized
he was plunged instead in the river of hell;
his sinews are hard, his veins are hard,
filled with living blood.
I've often heard
that one could once find
adventures in this land

that brought relief to the unhappy.
Knights might find young girls
to their desire, noble and lovely;
and ladies find lovers
so handsome, courtly, brave, and valiant
that they could not be blamed,
and no one else would see them.
If that might be or ever was,
if that has ever happened to anyone,
God, who has power over everything,
grant me my wish in this."
When she'd finished her lament,
she saw, through a narrow window,
the shadow of a great bird.
She didn't know what it was.
It flew into the chamber;
its feet were banded; it looked like a hawk
of five or six moultings.
It alighted before the lady.
When it had been there awhile
and she'd stared hard at it,
it became a handsome and noble knight.
The lady was astonished;
her blood went cold, she trembled,
she was frightened—she covered her head.
The knight was very courteous,
he spoke first:
"Lady," he said, "don't be afraid.
The hawk is a noble bird,
although its secrets are unknown to you.
Be reassured
and accept me as your love.
That," he said, "is why I came here.
I have loved you for a long time,
I've desired you in my heart.
Never have I loved any woman but you
nor shall I ever love another,
yet I couldn't have come to you
or left my own land
had you not asked for me.
But now I can be your love."
The lady was reassured;
she uncovered her head and spoke.

She answered the knight,
saying she would take him as her lover
if he believed in God,
and if their love was really possible.
For he was of great beauty.
Never in her life
had she seen so handsome a knight—
nor would she ever.
"My lady," he said, "you are right.
I wouldn't want you to feel
guilt because of me,
or doubt or suspicion.
I do believe in the creator
who freed us from the grief
that Adam, our father, led us into
when he bit into the bitter apple.
He is, will be, and always was
the life and light of sinners.
If you don't believe me
send for your chaplain.
Say that you've suddenly been taken ill
and that you desire the service
that God established in this world
for the healing of sinners.
I shall take on your appearance
to receive the body of our lord God,
and I'll recite my whole credo for you.
You will never doubt my faith again."
She answered that she was satisfied.
He lay beside her on the bed
but he didn't try to touch her,
to embrace her or to kiss her.
Meanwhile, the old woman had returned.
She found the lady awake
and told her it was time to get up,
she would bring her clothes.
The lady said she was ill,
that the old woman should send for the chaplain
and bring him to her quickly—
she very much feared she was dying.
The old woman said, "Be patient,
my lord has gone to the woods.
No one may come in here but me."

The lady was very upset;
she pretended to faint.
When the other saw her, she was frightened;
she unlocked the door of the chamber
and sent for the priest.
He came as quickly as he could,
bringing the *corpus domini*.[2]
The knight received it,
drank the wine from the chalice.
Then the chaplain left
and the old woman closed the doors.
The lady lay beside her love—
there was never a more beautiful couple.
When they had laughed and played
and spoken intimately,
the knight took his leave
to return to his land.
She gently begged him
to come back often.
"Lady," he said, "whenever you please,
I will be here within the hour.
But you must make certain
that we're not discovered.
This old woman will betray us,
night and day she will spy on us.
She will perceive our love,
and tell her lord about it.
If that happens,
if we are betrayed,
I won't be able to escape.
I shall die."
With that the knight departed,
leaving his love in great joy.
In the morning she rose restored;
she was happy all week.
Her body had now become precious to her,
she completely recovered her beauty.
Now she would rather remain here
than look for pleasure elsewhere.
She wanted to see her love all the time
and enjoy herself with him.
As soon as her lord departed,
night or day, early or late,

she had him all to her pleasure.
God, let their joy endure!
Because of the great joy she felt,
because she could see her love so often,
her whole appearance changed.
But her lord was clever.
In his heart he sensed
that she was not what she had been.
He suspected his sister.
He questioned her one day,
saying he was astonished
that the lady now dressed with care.
He asked her what it meant.
The old woman said she didn't know—
no one could have spoken to her,
she had no lover or friend—
it was only that she was now more willing
to be alone than before.
His sister, too, had noticed the change.
Her lord answered:
"By my faith," he said, "I think that's so.
But you must do something for me.
In the morning, when I've gotten up
and you have shut the doors,
pretend you are going out
and leave her lying there alone.
Then hide yourself in a safe place,
watch her and find out
what it is, and where it comes from,
that gives her such great joy."
With that plan they separated.
Alas, how hard it is to protect yourself
from someone who wants to trap you,
to betray and deceive you!

Three days later, as I heard the story,
the lord pretended to go away.
He told his wife the story
that the king had sent for him by letter
but that he would return quickly.
He left the chamber and shut the door.
The old woman got up,
went behind a curtain;

from there she could hear and see
whatever she wanted to know.
The lady lay in bed but did not sleep,
she longed for her love.
He came without delay,
before any time had passed.
They gave each other great joy
with word and look
until it was time to rise—
he had to go.
But the old woman watched him,
saw how he came and went.
She was quite frightened
when she saw him first a man and then a bird.
When the lord returned—
he hadn't gone very far—
she told him and revealed
the truth about the knight
and the lord was troubled by it.
But he was quick to invent
a way to kill the knight.
He had great spikes of iron forged,
their tips sharpened—
no razor on earth could cut better.
When he had them all prepared
and pronged on all sides,
he set them in the window—
close together and firmly placed—
through which the knight passed
when he visited the lady.
God, he doesn't know what treachery
the villains are preparing.
The next day in the morning
the lord rose before dawn
and said he was going hunting.
The old woman saw him to the door
and then went back to bed
for day was not yet visible.
The lady awoke and waited
for the one she loved faithfully;
she said he might well come now
and be with her at leisure.
As soon as she asked,

he came without delay.
He flew into the window,
but the spikes were there.
One wounded him in his breast—
out rushed the red blood.
He knew he was fatally wounded;
he pulled himself free and entered the room.
He alighted on the bed, in front of the lady,
staining the bedclothes with blood.
She saw the blood and the wound
in anguish and horror.
He said, "My sweet love,
I lose my life for love of you.
I told you it would happen,
that your appearance would kill us."
When she heard that, she fainted;
for a short while she lay as if dead.
He comforted her gently,
said that grief would do no good,
but that she was pregnant with his child.
She would have a son, brave and strong,
who would comfort her;
she would call him Yonec.
He would avenge both of them
and kill their enemy.
But he could remain no longer
for his wound was bleeding badly.
He left in great sorrow.
She followed him with loud cries.
She leapt out a window—
it's a wonder that she wasn't killed,
for it was at least twenty feet high
where she made her leap,
naked beneath her gown.
She followed the traces of blood
that flowed from the knight
onto the road.
She followed that road and kept to it
until she came to a hill.
In the hill there was an opening,
red with his blood.
She couldn't see anything beyond it
but she was sure

that her love had gone in there.
She entered quickly.
She found no light
but she kept to the right road
until it emerged from the hill
into a beautiful meadow.
When she found the grass there wet with blood,
she was frightened.
She followed the traces through the meadow
and saw a city not far away.
The city was completely surrounded by walls.
There was no house, no hall or tower,
that didn't seem entirely of silver.
The buildings were very rich.
Going toward the town there were marshes,
forests, and enclosed fields.
On the other side, toward the castle,
a stream flowed all around,
where ships arrived—
there were more than three hundred sails.
The lower gate was open;
the lady entered the city,
still following the fresh blood
through the town to the castle.
No one spoke to her,
she met neither man nor woman.
When she came to the palace courtyard,
she found it covered with blood.
She entered a lovely chamber
where she found a knight sleeping.
She did not know him, so she went on
into another larger chamber.
There she found nothing but a bed
with a knight sleeping on it;
she kept going.
She entered the third chamber
and on that bed she found her love.
The feet of the bed were all of polished gold,
I couldn't guess the value of the bedclothes;
the candles and the chandeliers,
which were lit night and day,
were worth the gold of an entire city.
As soon as she saw him

she recognized the knight.
She approached, frightened,
and fell fainting over him.
He, who greatly loved her, embraced her,
lamenting his misfortune again and again.
When she recovered from her faint
he comforted her gently.
"Sweet friend, for God's sake, I beg you,
go away! Leave this place!
I shall die within³ the day,
there will be great sorrow here,
and if you are found
you will be hurt.
Among my people it will be well known
that they have lost me because of my love for you.
I am disturbed and troubled for you."
The lady answered: "Love,
I would rather die with you
than suffer with my lord.
If I go back to him he'll kill me."
The knight reassured her,
gave her a ring,
and explained to her
that, as long as she kept it,
her lord would not remember
anything that had happened—
he would imprison her no longer.
He gave her his sword
and then made her swear
no man would ever possess it,
that she'd keep it for their son.
When the son had grown and become
a brave and valiant knight,
she would go to a festival,
taking him and her lord with her.
They would come to an abbey.
There, beside a tomb,
they would hear the story of his death,
how he was wrongfully killed.
There she would give her son the sword.
The adventure would be recited to him,
how he was born and who his father was;
then they'd see what he would do.

When he'd told her and shown her everything,
he gave her a precious robe
and told her to put it on.
Then he sent her away.
She left carrying the ring
and the sword—they comforted her.
She had not gone half a mile
from the gate of the city
when she heard the bells ring
and the mourning begin in the castle,
and in her sorrow
she fainted four times.
When she recovered from the faints
she made her way to the hill.
She entered it, passed through it,
and returned to her country.
There with her lord
she lived many days and years.
He never accused her of that deed,
never insulted or abused her.
Her son was born and nourished,
protected and cherished.
They named him Yonec.
In all the kingdom you couldn't find
one so handsome, brave, or strong,
so generous, so munificent.
When he reached the proper age,
he was made a knight.
Hear now what happened
in that very year.
To the feast of St. Aaron,
celebrated in Caerleon
and in many other cities,
the lord had been summoned
to come with his friends,
according to the custom of the land,
and to bring his wife and his son,
all richly attired.
So it was; they went.
But they didn't know the way;
they had a boy with them
who guided them along the right road
until they came to a castle—

none more beautiful in all the world.
Inside, there was an abbey
of very religious people.
The boy who was guiding them to the festival
housed them there.
In the abbot's chamber
they were well served and honored.
Next day they went to hear Mass
before they departed,
but the abbot went to speak to them
to beg them to stay
so he could show them the dormitory,
the chapter house, and the refectory.
And since they were comfortable there,
the lord agreed to stay.
That day, after they had dined,
they went to the workshops.
On their way, they passed the chapter house,
where they found a huge tomb
covered with a cloth of embroidered silk,
a band of precious gold running from one side to the other.
At the head, the feet, and at the sides
burned twenty candles.
The chandeliers were pure gold,
the censers amethyst,
which through the day perfumed
that tomb, to its great honor.
They asked and inquired
of people from that land
whose tomb it was,
what man lay there.
The people began to weep
and, weeping, to recount
that it was the best knight,
the strongest, the most fierce,
the most handsome and the best loved,
that had ever lived.
"He was king of this land;
no one was ever so courtly.
At Caerwent he was discovered
and killed for the love of a lady.
Since then we have had no lord,
but have waited many days,

just as he told and commanded us,
for the son the lady bore him."
When the lady heard that news,
she called aloud to her son.
"Fair son," she said, "you hear
how God has led us to this spot.
Your father, whom this old man murdered,
lies here in this tomb.
Now I give and commend his sword to you.
I have kept it a long time for you."
Then she revealed, for all to hear,
that the man in the tomb was the father and this was his son,
and how he used to come to her,
how her lord had betrayed him—
she told the truth.
Then she fainted over the tomb
and, in her faint, she died.
She never spoke again.
When her son saw that she had died,
he cut off his stepfather's head.
Thus with his father's sword
he avenged his mother's sorrow.
When all this had happened,
when it became known through the city,
they took the lady with great honor
and placed her in the coffin.
Before they departed
they made Yonec their lord.

Long after, those who heard this adventure
composed a lai about it,
about the pain and the grief
that they suffered for love.

Fables

2 (2). Of the Wolf and the Lamb

It is told of the wolf and the lamb
that they were drinking from a brook.
The wolf was drinking at the source

and the lamb downstream;
angrily the wolf spoke—
he was quite cantankerous
and spoke with ill will:
"You are," he said, "annoying me."
The lamb answered:
"How, sire?" "Can't you see?
You've stirred up my water so,
I can't drink my fill.
I must go away, I think,
just as I came, dying of thirst."
Then the lamb answered:
"Sire, you are drinking upstream;
what I drank came from you."
"What!" said the wolf, "are you contradicting me?"
The other replied, "I didn't mean to."
The wolf answered: "I know how it is.
Your father did the same thing to me
at this source, where I was with him
six months ago, I believe."
"Why are you blaming me?" he said,
"I don't think I was even born then."
"What of that?" the wolf replied,
"you were arguing with me now,
something you should not do."
Then the wolf took the little lamb,
and strangled him with his teeth, and killed him.
That is what rich lords do,
viscounts and their judges,
to those who are in their jurisdiction;
they make accusations against them out of greed
and find enough to do them in.
Often they bring them into court
and take their skin and their hide,
just as the wolf did to the lamb.

4 (4). Of the Dog and the Ewe

This tells of a lying dog
with nasty tricks, a deceiver,
who brought suit against a ewe.
He took her to court,
claiming some bread

which he had, so he said, lent her.
The ewe denied it all
and said he had lent her nothing.
The judge asked the dog
whether he had any witnesses.
He answered that he had two,
the kite and the wolf.
They were brought forth
and affirmed, by oath,
that what the dog said was true.
Do you know why they did it?
Because they expected a share
if the ewe lost her life.
The judge then asked
the ewe, whom he cited,
why she had denied the bread
which the dog had given her.
She had lied for a small amount,
now let her pay before it got worse.
The poor thing didn't have enough
so she had to sell her wool.
It was winter and she died of the cold.
The dog came and took her wool,
and the kite as well,
and then the wolf, but it was too late,
for the meat had been torn up by them,
since they were in need of food.
And the ewe did not live—
her lord lost her completely.
This example should show us:
it can be proven of many men
that by lying and deceit
they frequently bring the poor to court;
they often find false witnesses
whom they pay with the belongings of the poor.
They don't care what becomes of the victims
as long as each of them gets his share.

18 (27). Of the Man and His Members

I want to tell now about a man,
to record it as an example,
about his hands and his feet,

and his head that got angry
with his stomach which it carried,
because of their earnings, which he wasted.
They didn't want to work anymore
so they kept him from eating.
But when the stomach fasted,
it quickly weakened
the hands and feet, so they could not
work as they once had;
when they felt their great weakness,
they offered food and drink to the stomach,
but they had made it fast too long
so it could not take anything.
The stomach gave out
and so did the hands and feet.
In this example, one can see,
and every good man should know it:
no man can have honor
who shames his lord,
nor can the lord have it
if he wants to shame his people;
if either one fails the other,
both will be hurt.

29 (56). Of the Peasant and His Crow

This tells of a peasant who had
a crow that he reared;
he cared for her so well that she spoke.
But a neighbor of his killed her.
He took him to court over it
and related just how
that bird used to speak
in the mornings and sing.
The judge said he had been injured;
he summoned the other to the bar.
The accused[4] took a hide of leather
and put it under his cloak,
letting one end hang out
so the judge would understand
that he brought it in payment
for his help in the suit.

He kept opening the cloak
until the judge saw it.
Then the judge called the other peasant
who had come to him with the claim.
He asked him about the crow,
what it was that she sang
and what word she spoke.
The peasant replied that he did not know.
"Since you," the judge said, "know nothing about it—
you don't understand the word
or what the song was—
you should not receive the judgment."
So he went away without his rights,
because of the bribe.
That is why no prince or king
should commit his commands or laws
to the care of the greedy,
for his justice will be destroyed.

33 (63). Of the Horse and the Hedge

A horse saw grass growing
in a meadow, but he didn't see
the hedge that surrounded the meadow.
When he jumped over it, he was impaled.
Many men do the same, as you know well:
they are so anxious for what they want,
they don't see what trouble
follows, harsh and heavy.

38 (81). Of the Priest and the Wolf

Once a priest wanted to teach
a wolf to understand letters.
"A," said the priest. "A," said the wolf,
who was quite evil and clever.
"B," said the priest, "say it with me."
"B," said the wolf, "I agree."
"C," said the priest, "come on."
"C," said the wolf, "is there so much then?"
The priest answered: "Now say it by yourself."

The wolf told him: "I don't know how."
"Say what you think and spell."
The wolf answered and said: "Lamb."[5]
The priest said that he hit the truth:
what is in his thought is on his lips.
One can often see this with men:
what they are thinking about intensely
is known from their mouths
before it is revealed by any other source.
The mouth shows the thought,
although it would speak of other things.

46 (102). Of the Woman and the Hen

A woman was sitting
before her gate, watching
as her hen scratched
and gathered her food.
The hen worked hard all day.
The woman spoke to her with great love:
"Beauty," she said, "let it be,
you don't have to scratch so much.
Each day I'll give you
a full measure of grain to your desire."
The hen replied:
"Why do you say this, lady?
Do you think I like your wheat better
than what I have always had?
Not at all, not at all," said the hen.
"If there were half a bushel before me,
every day, full, I would not stop
nor would I delay
to seek more every day
according to my nature and my custom."
By this example, it is shown
that many people can find
goods and whatever they need,
but they cannot change
their nature or their habits;
every day their courage revives.

NOTES TO THE TRANSLATION

1. The original has *curteise*, 'courtly.'
2. The Body of the Lord, the eucharistic Host.
3. Rychner gives *en mi*, 'in the middle of the day'; Ewert gives *devant*, 'before.'
4. I have identified the other peasant as the accused here in order to distinguish him from the one making the claim.
5. The word he utters is "Aignel"; one is tempted to see in it a play on the letters *a*, *n*, and *l*.

BIBLIOGRAPHY

Primary Works

Ewert, Alfred, ed. *Lais*. 1944. Reprint. Oxford, 1963.
——— and R. C. Johnston, eds. *Fables*. 1942. Reprint. Oxford, 1966.
Ferrante, Joan M., and R. W. Hanning, eds. *The Lais of Marie de France*. New York, 1978.
Jenkins, Thomas Atkinson, ed. *L'Espurgatoire Saint Patriz*. Chicago, 1903.
Rychner, Jean, ed. *Les lais de Marie de France*. Paris, 1969.
Warnke, Karl, ed. *Das Buch vom Espurgatoire S. Patrice der Marie de France und seine Quellen*. Halle, 1938.
———, ed. *Die Fabeln der Marie de France*. Halle, 1898.
———, ed. *Die Lais der Marie de France*. Halle, 1925.

Related Works

Burgess, G. *Marie de France: An Analytical Bibliography*. London, 1977.
Damon, S. F. "Marie de France, Psychologist of Courtly Love." *PMLA* 44 (1929): 968–996.
Ferguson, M. H. "Folklore in the *Lais* of Marie de France." *Romanic Review* 57 (1966): 3–24.
Frey, J. A. "Linguistic and Psychological Couplings in the Lays of Marie de France." *Studies in Philology* 61 (1964): 3–18.
McCulloch, F. "Length, Recitation, and Meaning of the Lais of Marie de France." *Kentucky Romance Quarterly* 25 (1978): 257–268.
Mickel, E. J., Jr. *Marie de France*. New York, 1974.
———. "Marie de France's Use of Irony as a Stylistic and Narrative Device." *Studies in Philology* 71 (1974): 265–290.

THE FRENCH
SCHOLAR-LOVER

 eloise

BETTY RADICE

The name of Heloise is widely known, nearly always in connection with that of Abelard, as one of a pair of lovers whose brief relationship ended in tragedy. Abelard was indeed one of the most powerful and original minds of his day, and his teaching laid the foundations of the medieval university of Paris. His was a strong and dominant personality, well able to overrule Heloise's judgments, which were sometimes wiser than his, though she lacked his experience of the world and was some twenty years younger than he. But she was much more than a gifted girl who fell deeply in love with her teacher. She outlived Abelard by many years, dying in her sixties as the respected abbess of a famous religious house and its daughter foundations, corresponding on equal terms with abbots and prelates.

Nothing at all is known of Heloise's parentage, apart from the name of her mother, which appears in the necrology of the Paraclete as Hersinde. Her father is unknown, and she may have been illegitimate. Thought to have been born in 1100 or 1101, she is known to have been brought up in the convent of Sainte Marie of Argenteuil, some six miles northwest of Paris. At the age of seventeen she came to Paris to live with her uncle Fulbert, one of the canons of Notre Dame. All credit is due to the nuns of Saint Benedict for her early education and to Fulbert for his encouragement of her remarkable intellectual gifts at a time when women were rarely educated at all. During the short time that she worked with Abelard, they probably studied philosophy; hers was certainly a trained logical mind which could counter his arguments.

Peter Abelard was born into the minor Breton nobility in 1079. His career up to the age of about fifty-four is set out in a remarkable piece of autobiographical writing, the *Historia calamitatum* or *Story of His Misfortunes*. With a sense of dedication which never left him, he renounced his rights as eldest son and embarked on a scholar's career, concentrating on dialectic, which we now call logic, the study of the meaning of words and concepts as a basis of rational understanding. After a successful progress through the provincial schools, he came to Paris and, in due course, took over the Cloister School of Notre Dame.

Abelard, then in his midthirties, was at the peak of his powers. All accounts agree that he was a wonderful teacher, with a rare gift for kindling enthusiasm in his pupils and inspiring their devotion. He enjoyed controversy and may well have been bored when he found himself without a rival. He says himself that it was pride and overconfidence in the security of his position that made him yield to the lusts of the flesh; it was then that he noticed the presence of Heloise. His own words in the *Historia calamitatum* tell the story:

> There was in Paris at the time a young girl named Heloise, the niece of Fulbert, one of the canons, and so much loved by him that he had done everything in his power to advance her education in letters. In looks she did not rank lowest, while in the extent of her learning she stood supreme. A gift for letters is so rare in women that it added greatly to her charm and had won her renown throughout the realm. I considered all the usual attractions for a lover and decided she was the one to bring to my bed, confident that I should have an easy success; for at that time I had youth and exceptional good looks as well as my great reputation to recommend me, and feared no rebuff from any woman I might choose to honor with my love.

Luck was with him when Fulbert asked him into his house to be tutor to Heloise. Though he writes coolly in the *Historia* as if he embarked on a calculated seduction, he soon became wholly committed and quite reckless in his behavior. He abandoned any serious teaching of his pupils, ignored gossip, and allowed his love songs to be sung in public; concentration flagged "when my nights were sleepless with lovemaking . . . Our desires left no stage of lovemaking untried, and if love could devise something new, we welcomed it." Inevitably Fulbert found out and tried to separate the lovers, but without success; and when Heloise became pregnant Abelard removed her secretly, disguised as a nun, to his people in Brittany, where her son, Astralabe, was born.[1]

Abelard returned to Paris and offered amends to Fulbert: he would marry Heloise as long as the marriage was kept secret and did not damage his reputation. Fulbert agreed, and Abelard went back to Brittany, only to find Heloise strongly opposed to any form of marriage. She saw clearly, as he did not, that a *secret* marriage would not appease Fulbert for a public scandal and, indeed, that "no satisfaction could ever appease her uncle." (Fulbert's possessiveness has made some suspect that she was his daughter, but it would appear to have a strong sexual element, probably subconscious.) She saw marriage as a disgrace to them both, not so much a bar to Abelard's future career in the Church (the only one open to an educated man at this time) as a betrayal of the ideal which they both admired, that of the philosopher as a man who is set apart from and above human ties. She argued from a classical rather than a Christian standpoint, taking her illustrations from Theophrastus, Cicero, Seneca, and Socrates as recorded by Saint Jerome. She pointed out the distractions and petty hindrances of domestic life which would be inimical to philosophical contemplation, comparing philosophers with such dedicated solitaries as John the Baptist or members of the ascetic Jewish sects. She concluded (Abelard says) that "the name of mistress instead of wife would be dearer to her and more honorable for me"; they would then be free of a permanent legal tie, and Abelard could realize his true self as a philosopher. They should be bound by *gratia*—love freely given in the ideal relationship of Cicero's *De amicitia*, the true friendship of disinterested love, where intention was all-important. This is the "ethic of pure intention" in which they both believed. Heloise returns to it in her letters, and it is the subject of Abelard's great *Ethica* or *Scito te ipsum* (*Know Yourself*).

Abelard did not deny the validity of her arguments, but it was too much to expect that he would be persuaded by them. He admitted in a later letter that "I desired to keep you whom I loved beyond measure for myself alone." In the end Heloise let him have his way, without any reproach for the secrecy of the marriage, which must have seemed to her a further betrayal of the ideal. The baby was left with Abelard's sister, and they returned to Paris, to marry and separate. Furtive meetings were followed by scenes with Fulbert, who broke his promise and spread the news, until Abelard decided to remove his wife from her uncle's house to the convent at Argenteuil where she had spent her childhood. This was near enough to Paris for further meetings, and we know that Abelard could not keep away. He argues in one of his letters that they were more justly punished for their conduct when married than for anything they did before, because of their sacrilege in making love in a corner of the convent refectory, the only place where they could snatch a moment together alone. No one can know why he made her wear a postulant's habit, when she could have stayed with the nuns indefinitely without it, unless it was to give her greater protection from Fulbert, but the effect was disastrous. Fulbert, naturally assuming that Abelard was trying to get rid of her by making her a nun, took horrible revenge: his servants broke into Abelard's room at night and castrated him.

Years later Abelard could write of this as an act of God's mercy which rid him of his personal dilemma along with the torments of the flesh. In the *Historia* he vividly recalls the pain and horror, his desire to escape from the noisy sympathy of the crowds at his door, his disgust at being a eunuch, the unclean beast of Jewish law. He admits that it was no "devout wish for conversion which brought me to seek shelter in a monastery cloister"; but his hurried entry into the abbey of Saint Denis, where the clerks were clamoring for him to resume his teaching, was his salvation.[2] It brought him back into the company of students eager to learn, and there is no reason to doubt that his subsequent conversion was sincere. He was now single-minded in his purpose of challenging beliefs and practices which he judged to fall short of truth and honesty.

The *Historia calamitatum* records Abelard's life with all its tribulations between his entry into Saint Denis in 1119 and his autobiography's circulation sometime after 1132. It details his quarrels with the unreformed monks of Saint Denis, his persecution by old rivals and new enemies, leading to his condemnation by the Council of Soissons in 1121, more trouble at Saint Denis, and his flight to Champagne—where he retired to a hermitage near Troyes, followed by his students, and built the oratory he named the Paraclete.[3] He was certainly helped by the devotion of these young people and the feeling that his gifts as a teacher were unimpaired, though his repeated references to persecution and fears of further prosecution for heresy seem excessive, and his statement that the ecclesiastical authorities forced him to leave the Paraclete is not confirmed by a lament written by his pupil Hilary, who says that the school was closed because of the rowdiness of the large number of students camping there.[4]

In his despair Abelard even contemplated leaving Christendom and taking refuge in Islam, and when in 1126 he accepted the office of abbot of the remote monastery of Saint Gildas de Rhuys on the west coast of Brittany, his exile proved to be the worst time of his life. He suffered from a total lack of self-confidence, knowing that he had failed his students, and he was rejected by the monks, who were idle, dissolute, and even murderous in intent. More than anything he was tormented by the thought that the oratory of the Paraclete was abandoned.

It was not until 1128 that Abelard heard that Adam Suger, who had become abbot of Saint Denis in 1122 and was engaged in necessary reforms, had found documents proving the abbey's claim to the convent at Argenteuil and had expelled the nuns, making no provision for their future.[5] Heloise was already prioress and may have been so as early as 1123, though this is only a supposition based on the obituary roll of the blessed Vital of Savigny, who had died in 1122. It was customary for such parchment rolls to be carried round the monastic houses for each to inscribe its title and promises to pray for the departed. The convent of

Sainte Marie is fortieth in a long list, and beneath its title is a Latin poem in correct elegiacs, written in a well-formed, clear hand.[6] The prioress stood second to the abbess and was responsible for the education of the nuns, novices, and children brought up by the convent, as Heloise had been herself.

This is the first mention of Heloise since she had taken her vows some nine years before—taken them with no sense of vocation and at Abelard's command, as he knew. The *Historia* says that she refused to listen to those trying to dissuade her; she had wept and quoted from Lucan, a stoic Roman poet they both knew, Cornelia's last words before her suicide after the death of her husband, Pompey.[7] She had had about eighteen months with Abelard and was nineteen when she renounced any future life outside the convent walls. Abelard also tells us that she took her vows before he did, but it is only from her letters that we know how much this hurt and offended her, as a sign of mistrust, though she would have followed him to the very flames of hell. Perhaps she guessed that he was prompted by the same possessive jealousy as in their secret marriage. Whatever her feelings during those long years, she must have been saved by her strong character and good brains; she would not have been made prioress if her outward observations had not been correct or retained if her teachings had not been conscientious.

Abelard traveled from Saint Gildas and arranged to hand over the Paraclete and the lands which went with it to Heloise ("now my sister in Christ rather than my wife") and some of the dispossessed nuns who had remained together. It was their first meeting in ten years. Life for the women was very difficult at first, dependent as they were on what they could get out of the fields and the stream, and the buildings could have been only the small stone church, which the students had built to replace Abelard's first chapel, and the primitive huts they had lived in. But the neighborhood was generous with gifts once their plight was known, and in 1131 Pope Innocent II, through the bishop of Troyes, granted them a charter to confirm in perpetuity what they had received.[8] There were further meetings, for Abelard records that at first local opinion criticized him for not doing enough for the nuns, and then there was malicious gossip about his seeming unable to keep away. He must have stayed away from Saint Gildas for some time, for he is known to have been present in the abbey of Morigny, near Etampes, in January 1131, when the pope consecrated the high altar.[9] He had indeed had hopes of finding a haven of peace with the nuns, but the *Historia* ends with him back at Saint Gildas, having narrowly escaped murder by poison and ambush, still feeling himself an outcast with no prospect of a solution to his problems.

The *Historia calamitatum*, written in 1132 or soon afterward, was set out in the form of a letter to an unnamed friend, who was probably imaginary; the genre of consolatory letter was an accepted medieval convention. If it had been a genuinely personal letter to a fellow monk, it is difficult to see how a copy reached Heloise, as she says herself that it did, in her first letter. There may have been several copies intended for circulation at a time when Abelard was trying desperately to be relieved of his office as abbot at Saint Gildas and return to his true vocation of teaching. We know that Abelard did leave eventually, with his bishop's consent and the right to retain his rank as abbot, and that he was teaching in Paris in 1136 when the English scholar John of Salisbury heard him and recorded the date.[10] If his sole purpose was to gain sympathy for his longing to return to Paris, it is at first hard to see why he had to write his entire life story, set out factually, even baldly, and veering between detachment and self-pity to present a self-centered though not an insensitive man. Then it becomes apparent that he is looking back on a life which he believes to have often been misjudged, to recapture the past as part of a pattern continuous with the present.

The *Historia* is more self-revelatory than any writing which exists between the *Confessions* of Saint Augustine and Petrarch's *Secretum*. And it prompted four personal letters between two individuals who would be remarkable in any age in their devotion to their Church, their concern for problems of morality, their admiration for classical learning, and their ability to express themselves fluently in an elegant Latin far removed from the less sophisticated phrasing of many of their contemporaries.

Heloise's reactions in her first letter are dismay at the recital of his misfortunes, the details of which are unlikely to have reached her before, and horror at the idea of his life being in danger at Saint Gildas. She then points out that if he can write a long letter of consolation to a "friend," he can also write and encourage the community at the Paraclete, as is his duty as their founder. He is wasting himself on monks such as he describes, but he would find her nuns receptive. He can also write to *her*, to whom he has a personal obligation. For twelve years or more she has brooded over his apparent indifference in never giving her a word of recognition for the sacrifice she made in entering monastic life. He knows very well that she did it only for love of him, but his neglect has forced her to the conclusion that what he had felt for her was no more than lust and, when physical desire had gone, any warmth of affection had gone with it. She virtually demands a letter of explanation from him as her right.

Abelard defends himself on the charge of negligence: he had not supposed that after their joint conversion Heloise had need of him. Could he really have thought that? No one can be sure, but it cannot be dismissed as simple wishful thinking. Disgust with his mutilated person may have made him want to shut the past out of his mind; he was changed, and knowing that she was prioress and now abbess he may have been all too ready to believe that she was changed too. And his own conversion had, at some point, been sincere and permanent, so that he was now dedicated to God. The tone of his letter is set by the superscription: he writes as abbot to abbess. He does not allow himself to enter imaginatively into Heloise's plight, and this prompts her to be more explicit.

She now writes urgently of her sexual frustration and inability to forget their happiness as lovers. She puts her dilemma clearly: she took vows not for love of God but for love of Abelard. Taking vows meant that she ought to be a nun in the true sense and that her life should be ruled by love of God, but how was that possible when she loved only Abelard? She is perpetually conscious of being a hypocrite, for when the world admires her piety it sees only her outward behavior and this means nothing to her; the intention is all, and her intention is lacking. She looks for reward only from Abelard, and he has denied it to her. She can hope for nothing from God, for she has denied him, and she cannot repent. "How can it be called repentance for sins, however great the mortification of the flesh, if the mind still retains the will to sin and is on fire with its old desires?" She implores Abelard's help in resolving an intolerable situation.

This is a terrible picture of a soul in agony and of total human love which has brought only suffering. It is painful to contemplate how such intensity of feeling has been stoically concealed from the outside world for years of a young woman's life. It is characteristic of Heloise that she never compromises and never wavers from the moral view she shared with Abelard, that of the ethic of intention. Her keen intellect can analyze herself and her problem clearly, but the feeling behind her words is passionate and painful. This letter jolts Abelard out of any suspected complacency. He replies at length, especially on the point of "your old perpetual complaint against God concerning the manner of our entry into religious life and the cruelty of the act of treachery performed on me." The epithets (repeated later) imply that he had heard it before; the only time could have been when they met between his mutilation and her taking the veil.

Abelard sounds irritated by her raking it all up again, but perhaps that is reading too much into his words. He will not recall the past with nostalgia, as she does, but at least he shows that he has not forgotten. He reminds her of certain events—their mockery of God when she dressed as a nun to go to Brittany, their overwhelming desire which led them to make love during the season of the Passion or in the refectory at Argenteuil—but he tries to make her see them as episodes calling for just punishment from God or, rather, for an act of God's mercy to free them both from the flesh which can be only a barrier to divine love. He begs her to make a supreme effort to shake off bitterness and resentment and to think only of the love of Christ. All the time he is trying to make her see the whole story of their relationship, from its start until their entry into religion, from the Christian monastic point of view, knowing that they were at least agreed in believing that chastity was higher than wedlock. The letter ends with a prayer that though parted on earth they may be forever united in heaven.

Heloise replies with great dignity, and the first paragraph of her letter marks the turning point of the correspondence. She will not argue with him or trouble him further with heart searchings; she now asks only for his help in occupying her mind with more constructive thoughts. We can only admire her resolute self-control and, equally, her intellectual and practical ability. She has lived under the Benedictine rule for at least fourteen years, studying it, in a sense, from the outside. She is well equipped to offer criticism of what seems to her unsuitable if the rule is to apply to women. She appreciates that Saint Benedict was willing to temper his rule to meet men's capacity to observe it, and she suggests that women should not have too great demands made upon their physique. She also argues cogently that details of observance are no more than outward "works" which are unimportant in comparison with faith and spiritual intent. Accordingly she asks for guidance on such questions as manual labor, fasting, clothing, and diet, as well as for suitable arrangements for the Divine Office and for the reading of the Gospel at night. Her emphasis is on reasonable demands, avoidance of extremes, and sincerity of intent, for it is better to promise what is within our capacity and then do more than to break down under too rigorous demands. She would like a longer novitiate, a deeper personal commitment, a truly spiritual training, and a poorer and simpler life, different perhaps from the one she had known at the more wealthy and fashionable community at Argenteuil.

Abelard replies with two long treatises, one on the origin of religious communities of women, the other a detailed rule for observance at the Paraclete which provides important information about convent life at a time when very little was written about women's orders. It is in many ways a curious document, starting formally and ending abruptly, combining lengthy sermonizing with a down-to-earth treatment of practical details. The nuns are to be sensibly dressed in underwear and in habits which hang clear of the dust, with a full change of clothing and proper sanitary protection; they should wear stockings and shoes and have adequate bedding. Dirty hands and knives must not be wiped on bread intended for the poor, to save washing of table linen. There are to be no self-imposed fasting, no undue mortification of the flesh, and no reduction of necessary hours of sleep, or the nuns will not be mentally alert for prayer or study. Routine tasks may be left to nuns with no aptitude for letters, but any nun with the ability to learn must be taught to read and write, for as far as possible God should be worshiped with understanding—a statement which Abelard amplifies into an attack on current illiteracy in monasteries. Throughout there is a characteristic emphasis on education.

The letter seems to be the basis for a later set of rules,[11] preserved at the Paraclete, which were evidently intended for the use of a mother foundation and its daughter houses, such as the Paraclete became under Heloise. This rather later rule could be by her, but this cannot be firmly dated. There are minor differences between it and Abelard's rule, as well as two major changes: the nuns are no longer to be strictly cloistered but may go outside on essential business, and instead of a male superior ruling a double monastery, the abbess is to have authority over the monks and lay monks who serve the convent.

This exchange of letters is vital for an understanding of the developing relations between Abelard and Heloise in the only way possible to them. In a sense Heloise won her point by forcing Abelard to face up to her problem and renew contact with her, though not in the way she may have first hoped. Abelard sincerely tried to make her see that the only love which could unite them was the love of God, but in doing so he had to learn something of what human love like hers could mean. Once she had agreed to try to put the past behind her, all his learning and experience were at the service of the Paraclete.

Many of the texts survive which subsequently passed between them. A long letter from Abelard addressed to the nuns stresses the importance of study and even suggested that they learn Hebrew, twice referring to Heloise as knowing Greek and Hebrew as well as Latin. This is very surprising, for Abelard had little or no Greek and no Hebrew beyond an occasional quoted word; Heloise probably had enough Greek for liturgical purposes. She writes a short letter in which she addresses him as "loved by many but most dearly loved by us" to accompany the "Problems of Heloise": forty-two difficulties of interpretation in the Scriptures, to which Abelard writes his answers. Her request for hymns for the use of the nuns is lost, but his reply starts, "At your urgent request, my sister Heloise, once dear to me in the world, now dearest in Christ"; there are 133 extant Latin hymns which he sent to the Paraclete in three batches, as well as some fine verse laments and 34 short sermons, sent to "Heloise my sister whom I love and revere in Christ," and the *Hexameron*, a commentary on the six days of the Creation. As all his writings for the nuns are introduced by letters to Heloise, it looks as though he did not visit the convent again. Apart from the one fact that John of Salisbury heard him lecture in Paris in 1136, nothing is known of his movements after he left Saint Gildas until his confrontation with Saint Bernard of Clairvaux in the cathedral of Sens in June 1140, but as he was attacked mainly for corrupting the young through his theological teaching, he was most probably with his pupils in Paris. Again, we do not know how much Heloise knew at the time of the proceedings at Sens or if she received the moving "Confession of Faith" which he wrote immediately afterward, probably the last personal message he addressed to her.[12]

Abelard refused to make any answer to Bernard's charges and left Sens to appeal to the pope. He may well have been ill and exhausted; the news of his sentence for heresy reached him at Cluny, where he had stopped to rest and stayed on at the invitation of Peter the Venerable, the great Benedictine scholar and abbot. The pope granted Peter's request[13] that Abelard should remain at Cluny in retirement, and the sentence was afterward lifted. Abelard died some eighteen months later, in April 1142. Peter the Venerable's letter to Heloise describes his death in a daughter house of Cluny, the priory of Saint Marcel at Chalon-sur-Saône, and pays tribute to the piety and simplicity of his life and to his devotion to his studies as long as his health permitted.[14]

A further exchange of letters between Heloise and Peter the Venerable took place in 1144.[15] Heloise thanks him for visiting the Paraclete and bringing Abelard's body to rest in the care of the community he had founded. She asks him for a written absolution for Abelard to be hung over his tomb and for help in getting her son a benefice in one of the cathedrals. Peter sends the absolution[16] and a ratification of his verbal promise that Cluny will say thirty masses for Heloise after her death. He promises to do his best for Astralabe, who would have been about twenty-six at this time, but nothing more is known of him. Abelard wrote him a long verse letter of rather platitudinous advice, probably in 1135, but he is never mentioned in his parents' letters. His death is recorded in the necrology of the Paraclete as occurring on October 29 or 30, and he is named as Abelard's son, but no year is given.

Peter the Venerable died in 1156 or 1157, but Heloise outlived Abelard by some twenty-one years; she is recorded in the necrology of the Paraclete as dying on May 16 in 1163 or 1164. The romantically minded have liked to think that she died, like Abelard, at the age of sixty-three. During her lifetime the Paraclete grew to be one of the most distinguished religious houses in France, and six daughter houses were founded to take the increasing number of postulants. The cartulary of the Paraclete in the library of Troyes has no less than twenty-nine documents which confirm privileges and register deeds of gift; eleven of these are papal bulls, and several are royal charters. Wherever Heloise's name is mentioned, it is with affection, admiration, and deference. We find her purchasing tithes and property and engaged in complex negotiations over boundary demarcations. Such things called for exceptional practical competence and

a clear legal mind. At the same time it is clear from Peter the Venerable's
letters that Heloise was revered for her sanctity and learning. She was
indeed one of the Church's great abbesses.[17]

NOTES

1. Heloise probably stayed with his sister Denis at Le Pallet, about twelve miles east of
Nantes; the child's strange name is unexplained. Breton folklore preserves a lingering recollection of her stay: the 1839 *Barzaz-Breiz: Chants populaires de la Bretagne avec une
traduction française* by Th. Hersart de la Villemarque is quoted in French by Marcel Jouhandeau, *Lettres d'Héloïse*, pp. 244–245, and translated by Enid McCleod, *Héloïse*, pp.
55–56. In this Heloise says she followed "mon clerc, mon bien cher Abailard," to Nantes
at the age of twelve and that between them they have magical powers to turn the world
upside down.

2. The Benedictine abbey of Saint Denis, built just north of Paris to house the shrine of
the first bishop, was later to be embellished and have its discipline reformed under Abbot
Suger.

3. He went first to the priory of Saint Ayoul in the lower town of Provins. The site of
the Paraclete can still be seen on the bank of the Ardusson River, four miles southeast of
Nogent-sur-Seine.

4. Text in *PL* 178. 1855–1856; *Petri Abœlardi Opera*, ed. Victor Cousin, vol. 1, p. 708;
and *The Oxford Book of Medieval Verse*, ed. F. J. E. Raby, pp. 243–245.

5. Pope Honorius II and King Louis VI agreed to the transfer in 1129. For a full account, see McCleod, pp. 93 ff.

6. See further ibid., pp. 86 ff., and its frontispiece.

7. Lucan *Pharsalia* 8. 94.

8. The original document is in the library of Châlons-sur-Marne; text in Cousin, ed.,
vol. 1, pp. 719–720.

9. *Chronicle of Morigny* and *PL* 212. 1035.

10. *Metalogicon* 2. 10 and *PL* 199. 867.

11. Text in *PL* 178. 313–326 and Cousin, ed., vol. 1, pp. 213–224.

12. This is preserved only in an open letter by one of Abelard's pupils, Berengar of
Poitiers, which violently attacks Saint Bernard and all Abelard's detractors at the Council
of Sens; see *PL* 178. 375c and Cousin, ed., vol. 1, p. 680.

13. Letter 98 in Giles Constable, *The Letters of Peter the Venerable*.

14. Letter 115 in ibid.

15. Letters 167–168 in ibid.

16. Text in Cousin, ed., vol. 1, p. 717, but it cannot be traced in the records of the
Paraclete.

17. The following translation first appeared in *The Letters of Abelard and Heloise*,
translated with an introduction, notes, and bibliography by Betty Radice.

Heloise to Abelard

*To her master, or rather her father, husband, or rather brother; his handmaid, or
rather his daughter, wife, or rather sister; to Abelard, Heloise.*
Not long ago, my beloved, by chance someone brought me the letter of

consolation you had sent to a friend. I saw at once from the superscription that it was yours, and was all the more eager to read it since the writer is so dear to my heart. I hoped for renewal of strength, at least from the writer's words which would picture for me the reality I have lost. But nearly every line of this letter was filled, I remember, with gall and wormwood, as it told the pitiful story of our entry into religion and the cross of unending suffering which you, my only love, continue to bear.

In that letter you did indeed carry out the promise you made your friend at the beginning, that he would think his own troubles insignificant or nothing, in comparison with your own. First you revealed the persecution you suffered from your teachers, then the supreme treachery of the mutilation of your person, and then described the abominable jealousy and violent attacks of your fellow-students, Alberic of Rheims and Lotulf of Lombardy.[1] You did not gloss over what at their instigation was done to your distinguished theological work or what amounted to a prison sentence passed on yourself. Then you went on to the plotting against you by your abbot and false brethren, the serious slanders from those two pseudo-apostles, spread against you by the same rivals, and the scandal stirred up among many people because you had acted contrary to custom in naming your oratory after the Paraclete. You went on to the incessant, intolerable persecutions which you still endure at the hands of that cruel tyrant and the evil monks you call your sons, and so brought your sad story to an end.

No one, I think, could read or hear it dry-eyed; my own sorrows are renewed by the detail in which you have told it, and redoubled because you say your perils are still increasing. All of us here are driven to despair of your life, and every day we await in fear and trembling the final word of your death. And so in the name of Christ, who is still giving you some protection for his service, we beseech you to write as often as you think fit to us who are his handmaids and yours, with news of the perils in which you are still storm-tossed. We are all that are left you, so at least you should let us share your sorrow or your joy.

It is always some consolation in sorrow to feel that it is shared, and any burden laid on several is carried more lightly or removed. And if this storm has quietened down for a while, you must be all the more prompt to send us a letter which will be the more gladly received. But whatever you write about will bring us no small relief in the mere proof that you have us in mind. Letters from absent friends are welcome indeed, as Seneca himself shows us by his own example when he writes these words in a passage of a letter to his friend Lucilius:[2]

> Thank you for writing to me often, the one way in which you can make your presence felt, for I never have a letter from you without the immediate feeling that we are together. If pictures of absent friends give us pleasure, renewing our memories and relieving the pain of separation even if

they cheat us with empty comfort, how much more welcome is a letter
which comes to us in the very handwriting of an absent friend.

Thank God that here at least is a way of restoring your presence to us
which no malice can prevent, nor any obstacle hinder; then do not, I
beseech you, allow any negligence to hold you back.

You wrote your friend a long letter of consolation, prompted no doubt
by his misfortunes, but really telling of your own. The detailed account
you gave of these may have been intended for his comfort, but it also
greatly increased our own feeling of desolation; in your desire to heal his
wounds you have dealt us fresh wounds of grief as well as re-opening the
old. I beg you, then, as you set about tending the wounds which others
have dealt, heal the wounds you have yourself inflicted. You have done
your duty to a friend and comrade, discharged your debt to friendship
and comradeship, but it is a greater debt which binds you in obligation
to us who can properly be called not friends so much as dearest friends,
not comrades but daughters, or any other conceivable name more tender
and holy. How great the debt by which you have bound yourself to us
needs neither proof nor witness, were it in any doubt; if the whole world
kept silent, the facts themselves would cry out.[3] For you after God are
the sole founder of this place, the sole builder of this oratory, the sole
creator of this community. You have built nothing here upon another
man's foundation.[4] Everything here is your own creation. This was a
wilderness open to wild beasts and brigands, a place which had known
no home nor habitation of men. In the very lairs of wild beasts and lurking-
places of robbers, where the name of God was never heard, you built a
sanctuary to God and dedicated a shrine in the name of the Holy Spirit.
To build it you drew nothing from the riches of kings and princes, though
their wealth was great and could have been yours for the asking: whatever was done, the credit was to be yours alone. Clerks and scholars
came flocking here, eager for your teaching, and ministered to all your
needs; and even those who had lived on the benefices of the Church and
knew only how to receive offerings, not to make them, whose hands were
held out to take but not to give, became pressing in their lavish offers of
assistance.

And so it is yours, truly your own, this new plantation for God's purpose, but it is sown with plants which are still very tender and need
watering if they are to thrive. Through its feminine nature this plantation
would be weak and frail even if it were not new; and so it needs a more
careful and regular cultivation, according to the words of the Apostle: 'I
planted the seed and Apollos watered it; but God made it grow.'[5] The
Apostle through the doctrine that he preached had planted and established in the faith the Corinthians, to whom he was writing. Afterwards

the Apostle's own disciple, Apollos, had watered them with his holy exhortations and so God's grace bestowed on them growth in the virtues. You cultivate a vineyard of another's vines which you did not plant yourself and which has now turned to bitterness against you,[6] so that often your advice brings no result and your holy words are uttered in vain. You devote your care to another's vineyard; think what you owe to your own. You teach and admonish rebels to no purpose, and in vain you throw the pearls of your divine eloquence to the pigs.[7] While you spend so much on the stubborn, consider what you owe to the obedient; you are so generous to your enemies but should reflect on how you are indebted to your daughters. Apart from everything else, consider the close tie by which you have bound yourself to me, and repay the debt you owe a whole community of women dedicated to God by discharging it the more dutifully to her who is yours alone.

Your superior wisdom knows better than our humble learning of the many serious treatises which the holy Fathers compiled for the instruction or exhortation or even the consolation of holy women, and of the care with which these were composed. And so in the precarious early days of our conversion long ago I was not a little surprised and troubled by your forgetfulness, when neither reverence for God nor our mutual love nor the example of the holy Fathers made you think of trying to comfort me, wavering and exhausted as I was by prolonged grief, either by word when I was with you or by letter when we had parted. Yet you must know that you are bound to me by an obligation which is all the greater for the further close tie of the marriage sacrament uniting us, and are the deeper in my debt because of the love I have always borne you, as everyone knows, a love which is beyond all bounds.

You know, beloved, as the whole world knows, how much I have lost in you, how at one wretched stroke of fortune that supreme act of flagrant treachery robbed me of my very self in robbing me of you; and how my sorrow for my loss is nothing compared with what I feel for the manner in which I lost you. Surely the greater the cause for grief the greater the need for the help of consolation, and this no one can bring but you; you are the sole cause of my sorrow, and you alone can grant me the grace of consolation. You alone have the power to make me sad, to bring me happiness or comfort; you alone have so great a debt to repay me, particularly now when I have carried out all your orders so implicitly that when I was powerless to oppose you in anything, I found strength at your command to destroy myself. I did more, strange to say— my love rose to such heights of madness that it robbed itself of what it most desired beyond hope of recovery, when immediately at your bidding I changed my clothing along with my mind, in order to prove you the sole possessor of my body and my will alike. God knows I never sought anything in you except yourself; I wanted simply you, nothing of yours. I looked for no marriage-bond, no marriage portion, and it was not my own pleasures and wishes I sought to gratify, as you well know, but yours. The name of wife may seem more sacred or more binding, but sweeter for me will always be the word mistress, or, if you will permit me, that of concubine or whore. I believed that the more I humbled myself on your account, the more gratitude I should win from you, and also the less damage I should do to the brightness of your reputation.

You yourself on your own account did not altogether forget this in the letter of consolation I have spoken of which you wrote to a friend;[8] there you thought fit to set out some of the reasons I gave in trying to dissuade you from binding us together in an ill-starred marriage. But you kept silent about most of my arguments for preferring love to wedlock and freedom to chains. God is my witness that if Augustus, Emperor of the whole world, thought fit to honour me with marriage and conferred all the earth on me to possess for ever, it would be dearer and more honourable to me to be called not his Empress but your whore.

For a man's worth does not rest on his wealth or power; these depend on fortune, but worth on his merits. And a woman should realize that if she marries a rich man more readily than a poor one, and desires her husband more for his possessions than for himself, she is offering herself for sale. Certainly any woman who comes to marry through desires of this kind deserves wages, not gratitude, for clearly her mind is on the man's property, not himself, and she would be ready to prostitute herself to a richer man, if she could. This is evident from the argument put forward in the dialogue of Aeschines Socraticus[9] by the learned Aspasia to Xenophon and his wife. When she had expounded it in an effort to bring about a reconciliation between them, she ended with these words: 'Unless you come to believe that there is no better man nor worthier woman on earth you will always still be looking for what you judge the best thing of all—to be the husband of the best of wives and the wife of the best of husbands.'

These are saintly words which are more than philosophic; indeed, they deserve the name of wisdom, not philosophy. It is a holy error and a blessed delusion between man and wife, when perfect love can keep the ties of marriage unbroken not so much through bodily continence as chastity of spirit. But what error permitted other women, plain truth permitted me, and what they thought of their husbands, the world in general believed, or rather, knew to be true of yourself; so that my love for you was the more genuine for being further removed from error. What king or philosopher could match your fame? What district, town or village did not long to see you? When you appeared in public, who did not hurry to catch a glimpse of you, or crane his neck and strain his eyes to follow your departure? Every wife, every young girl desired you in absence and was on fire in your presence; queens and great ladies envied me my joys and my bed.

You had besides, I admit, two special gifts whereby to win at once the heart of any woman—your gifts for composing verse and song, in which we know other philosophers have rarely been successful. This was for you no more than a diversion, a recreation from the labours of your philosophic work, but you left many love-songs and verses which won wide popularity for the charm of their words and tunes and kept your name continually on everyone's lips.[10] The beauty of the airs ensured that even the unlettered did not forget you; more than anything this made women sigh for love of you. And as most of these songs told of our love, they soon made me widely known and roused the envy of many women against me. For your manhood was adorned by every grace of mind and body, and among the women who envied me then, could there be one now who does not feel compelled by my misfortune to sympathize with my loss of such joys? Who is there who was once my enemy, whether man or woman, who is not moved now by the compassion which is my due? Wholly guilty though I am, I am also, as you know, wholly innocent. It is not the deed but the intention of the doer which makes the crime, and justice should weigh not what was done but the spirit in which it is done.[11] What my intention towards you has always been, you alone who have known it can judge. I submit all to your scrutiny, yield to your testimony in all things.

Tell me one thing, if you can. Why, after our entry into religion, which was your decision alone, have I been so neglected and forgotten by you that I have neither a word from you when you are here to give me strength nor the consolation of a letter in absence? Tell me, I say, if you can—or I will tell you what I think and indeed the world suspects. It was desire, not affection which bound you to me, the flame of lust rather than love. So when the end came to what you desired, any show of feeling you used to make went with it. This is not merely my own opinion, beloved, it is everyone's. There is nothing personal or private about it; it is the general view which is widely held. I only wish that it *were* mine alone, and that the love you professed could find someone to defend it and so comfort me in my grief for a while. I wish I could think of some explanation which would excuse you and somehow cover up the way you hold me cheap.

I beg you then to listen to what I ask—you will see that it is a small favour which you can easily grant. While I am denied your presence, give me at least through your words—of which you have enough and to spare— some sweet semblance of yourself. It is no use my hoping for generosity in deeds if you are grudging in words. Up to now I had thought I deserved much of you, seeing that I carried out everything for your sake and continue up to the present moment in complete obedience to you. It was not any sense of vocation which brought me as a young girl to accept the austerities of the cloister, but your bidding alone, and if I deserve no gratitude from you, you may judge for yourself how my labours are in vain. I can expect no reward for this from God, for it is certain that I have done nothing as yet for love of him. When you hurried towards God I followed you, indeed, I went first to take the veil—perhaps you were thinking how Lot's wife turned back[12] when you made me put on the religious habit and take my vows before you gave yourself to God. Your lack of trust in me over this one thing, I confess, overwhelmed me with grief and shame. I would have had no hesitation, God knows, in following you or going ahead at your bidding to the flames of Hell.[13] My heart was not in me but with you, and now, even more, if it is not with you it is nowhere; truly, without you it cannot exist. See that it fares well with you, I beg, as it will if it finds you kind, if you give grace in return for grace,[14] small for great, words for deeds. If only your love had less confidence in me, my dear, so that you would be more concerned on my behalf! But as it is, the more I have made you feel secure in me, the more I have to bear with your neglect.

Remember, I implore you, what I have done, and think how much you owe me. While I enjoyed with you the pleasures of the flesh, many were uncertain whether I was prompted by love or lust; but now the end is proof of the beginning. I have finally denied myself every pleasure in obedience to your will, kept nothing for myself except to prove that now, even more, I am yours. Consider then your injustice, if when I deserve more you give me less, or rather, nothing at all, especially when it is a small thing I ask of you and one you could so easily grant. And so, in the name of God to whom you have dedicated yourself, I beg you to restore your presence to me in the way you can—by writing me some word of comfort, so that in this at least I may find increased strength and readiness to serve God. When in the past you sought me out for sinful pleasures your letters came to me thick and fast, and your many songs put your Heloise on everyone's lips, so that every street and house echoed with my name. Is it not far better now to summon me to God than it was then to satisfy our lust? I beg you, think what you owe me, give ear to my pleas, and I will finish a long letter with a brief ending: farewell, my only love.

NOTES TO THE TRANSLATION

1. Two of Anselm's pupils at Laon. They were Abelard's principal accusers at the Council of Soissons in 1121 which ordered his treatise *On the Unity and Trinity of God* to be publicly burned.

2. *Epistulae ad Lucilium* 40. 1.

3. Compare Cicero *In Catalinam* 1. 8.

4. Compare Rom. 15:20.

5. 1 Cor. 3:6.

6. Compare Jer. 2:21.

7. Matt. 7:6.

8. This suggests that Heloise believed the *Historia calamitatum* to be a genuine letter to a real person, not an example of a conventional epistolatory genre, unless she is writing ironically.

9. Aeschines Socraticus, a pupil of Socrates, wrote several dialogues of which fragments survive. This is, however, no proof that Heloise knew Greek, as the passage was well known in the Middle Ages from Cicero's translation of it in *De inventione* 1. 31.

10. None of Abelard's secular poems survives, and there are no love poems in northern France which can be dated as early as this.

11. Compare my introduction for the "ethic of pure intention"; our actions must be judged good or bad solely through the spirit in which they are performed, not by their effects. The deed itself is neither good nor bad.

12. Compare Gen. 19:26.

13. The Latin is *Vulcania loca*, 'Vulcan's regions' or Tartarus, and illustrates how Heloise's natural manner of expressing herself is classical.

14. John 1:16.

BIBLIOGRAPHY

Primary Works

Cousin, Victor, ed. *Petri Abœlardi Opera*. 2 vols. Paris, 1849.

Jouhandeau, Marcel. *Lettres d'Héloïse* (ed. French translation by Octave Gréard, 1875). Paris, 1959.

The Letters of Abelard and Heloise. Trans. Betty Radice. Harmondsworth, 1974.

Monfrin, J. *Historia calamitatum: Texte critique avec introduction*. Paris, 1962.

Morten, H., ed. *The Love Letters of Abelard and Heloise*. 10th ed. London, 1937.

Muckle, J. T., and T. P. McLaughlin, eds. *Historia calamitatum* and Letters 1–7. *Medieval Studies* 12, 15, 17, 18 (1950, 1953, 1955, 1956).

Scott Moncrieff, C. K. *The Letters of Abelard and Heloise*. London, 1925.

The Story of Abelard's Adversities. Trans. J. T. Muckle. Toronto, 1964.

Related Works

Brooke, Christopher. *The Twelfth Century Renaissance*. London, 1969.

Charrier, Charlotte. *Héloïse dans l'histoire et la légende*. Paris, 1933.

Constable, Giles. *The Letters of Peter the Venerable*. 2 vols. Cambridge, Mass., 1967.

Gilson, Etienne. *Heloise and Abelard*. London, 1953.

Grame, Leif. *Peter Abelard*. London, 1970.

Hamilton, Elizabeth. *Héloïse*. London, 1966.

James, Bruno Scott, ed. and trans. *The Letters of St. Bernard of Clairvaux*. London, 1953.

John of Salisbury. *Historia pontificalis*. Ed. and trans. M. Chibnall. Edinburgh. 1956.

Knowles, David. *The Evolution of Medieval Thought.* London, 1962.

———. *From Pachomius to Ignatius.* Oxford, 1966.

Leff, Gordon. *Medieval Thought: St. Augustine to Ockham.* London, 1958.

Luscombe, D. E. *Peter Abelard's "Ethics."* London, 1971.

———. *The School of Peter Abelard.* Cambridge, Eng., 1969.

McCann, Justin, ed. and trans. *The Rule of St. Benedict.* London, 1952.

McCleod, Enid. *Héloïse.* 2nd ed. London, 1971.

McLaughlin, Mary M. "Abelard as Autobiographer: The Motives and Meaning of His *Story of Calamities.*" *Speculum* 42 (1967): 463–488.

Moore, George. *Heloise and Abelard.* London, 1921.

Murray, A. Victor. *Abelard and St. Bernard.* Manchester, 1967.

Panofsky, Erwin. "Abbot Suger of St.-Denis." In his *Meaning in the Visual Arts.* Harmondsworth, 1970.

Pernoud, Régine. *Héloïse et Abélard.* Paris, 1970.

Raby, F. J. E., ed. *The Oxford Book of Medieval Latin Verse.* 2nd ed. Oxford, 1959.

Rashdall, H. *The Universities of Europe in the Middle Ages.* Vol. 1. Oxford, 1895.

Sikes, J. G. *Peter Abailard.* Cambridge, Eng., 1932.

Smalley, Beryl. *The Study of the Bible in the Middle Ages.* 2nd ed. Oxford, 1952.

Southern, Richard W. "The Letters of Abelard and Heloise." In his *Medieval Humanism and Other Studies,* pp. 86–104. Oxford, 1970.

———. *The Making of the Middle Ages.* London, 1967.

———. *Western Society and the Church in the Middle Ages.* London, 1970.

Waddell, Helen. *Mediaeval Latin Lyrics.* 4th ed. London, 1952.

———. *Peter Abélard.* London, 1933.

Wolff, Philippe. *The Awakening of Europe.* London, 1968.

THE GERMAN VISIONARY

Hildegard of Bingen

KENT KRAFT

Although Blake undoubtedly had the seers of the Old Testament in mind when he wrote, in *All Religions Are One*, that "the Religions of all Nations are derived from each Nation's different reception of the Poetic Genius, which is every where call'd the Spirit of Prophecy," it would not be difficult to argue that the quintessential incarnation of the "Spirit of Prophecy" in twelfth-century Europe was a woman. And it would not be unfair to claim, on the testimony of her writings, that she was also a finer embodiment than most of her masculine counterparts of what the term "Poetic Genius" implies even to those of us who are not visionaries—for Hildegard of Bingen, scientist and mystic, poet and dramatist, not only provided her age with an image of history and its divine fulfillment but also created a portrait of the world and a language to describe it that were both fresh and powerful. During later periods she was most frequently characterized as the first of the prophets of the modern age,[1] but contemporary scholarship has discovered in her life and work material for study by methods as diverse as those of the psychologist, the archaeologist, the musicologist, and the iconologist. And for the historian of science and the historian of ideas, she reflects, in her rationalizing Platonism, the brief and brilliant period of transition from the symbolic cosmology of the prescholastic era to the orderly coherence of Aristotelian and Ptolemaic astronomy.

Born in 1098 into a family of the upper nobility in Bermersheim, near Alzey, Hildegard possessed from an early age a gift of prophecy and clairvoyance whose legitimacy was freely acknowledged by her contemporaries. If we can credit the account given by the *Protocollum canonisationis*, an investigation of her life and miracles undertaken in the thirteenth century, she had already demonstrated, by the age of five, a power to see through ordinary appearances by predicting correctly the form and markings of a calf within a pregnant cow.[2] But even if we disregard such witness as an item of apocryphal hagiography, the unquestioned authority of her later visionary pronouncements is substantiated not only by the letters written to her by notables as diverse as Frederick I (Barbarossa) and Bernard of Clairvaux but also by the fact that Pope Eugenius III approvingly read sections of her first major work, the *Scivias* (*Know the Ways*), before the Synod of Trier (1147–1148). Such official sanction of her prophetic abilities, along with her noble rank, gave Hildegard power and freedom far above those of most women of her time and permitted her to express her convictions with little hesitation.

Hildegard was also possessed of another important quality evinced relatively early in life which was to determine the shape of her spiritual career as much as did her noble birth and prophetic powers: a pronounced and decisive ability to lead. As the tenth child of Hildebert von Bermersheim and his wife, Mechthild, Hildegard was dedicated by them to the religious life, entering the hermitage attached to the isolated Benedictine monastery of Disibodenberg at the age of eight. By the time her abbess and teacher Jutta von Spanheim died in 1136, Hildegard had gained such influence among her sisters that she was unanimously elected their new head. For a time her affairs proceeded in a relatively unremarkable fashion. Then, in 1141, she experienced an astonishing series of revelations that caused her to break a self-imposed silence concerning her visionary gifts. Above all, she found herself subject to a divine command to "write what you see and hear!"[3] At first resisting, she found herself assaulted by a severe and painful illness that abated only when she began to set down the visions appearing to her.

Over the next ten years, as Hildegard recorded the material that was to form the *Scivias*, news of her powers spread. Pope Eugenius III, even before the readings at the Synod of Trier, had sent a committee to Disibodenberg to confirm Hildegard's prophetic gifts. At about the same time we have the beginning of what was to become an extensive correspondence not only with respected ecclesiastical and political figures but with the common folk as well, couched chiefly on Hildegard's part in the form of visionary counsel and exhortation. It is during this period of disclosure and development in Hildegard's life that we also see the first evidence of the courage and resourcefulness that will allow her repeatedly to carry through her own plans even against the wishes and the apparently wiser views of her superiors.

In 1148 Hildegard made it known to Kuno, abbot of Disibodenberg, that it was God's will that she establish her own convent on the rather desolate slope of the Rupertsberg, on the Rhine near Bingen. Kuno and his monks, as might have been expected, were reluctant to let their newest claim to spiritual renown depart. In order to encourage them, Hildegard's *Vita* informs us, God struck her down again with a wasting illness. As she lay in her bed "like a block of stone,"[4] Kuno, suspicious, approached and attempted to lift her head. Astonished at his inability to do so, he realized that he was dealing "not with human suffering, but with a divine punishment."[5] After searching his soul, he decided to capitulate:

> Going in to the one lying afflicted, the abbot told her to rise up in the
> name of the Lord and go to the dwelling ordained for her by heaven. At
> the order she then arose so quickly, as if she felt no trace of her prolonged
> period of debility, that stupor and amazement seized all who were pres-
> ent—and not without good reason.[6]

With the aid of her former adversaries, Hildegard was able to procure the necessary landholdings and arrange for construction to begin. In 1150, along with eighteen nuns, she moved into the new quarters. The convent on the Rupertsberg boasted running water in the workrooms, a scriptorium, and a carefully worded document establishing at once its independence from Disibodenberg and the responsibility of that monastery to provide a provost to see to the nuns' spiritual welfare.

The period around 1150 was a time of great turmoil and activity in Hildegard's life for other reasons as well. Not only was she busy completing the *Scivias* and learning to deal with the accompaniments of fame, she also faced what was probably the greatest crisis of both her personal life and her pastoral career. The occasion was a conflict of love and ecclesiastical ambition. One of her secretaries and helpers during the composition of the *Scivias* was Richardis von Stade, sister of Archbishop Hartwig of Bremen. In 1151, encouraged by her mother, her brother, and various churchly dignitaries, Richardis accepted a position as abbess of a convent at Bassum, near Bremen. Hildegard violently opposed the move. A series of letters to the officials involved, and an especially poignant plea written to Richardis herself after she had left for Bassum, reveal not only the depth of Hildegard's love and concern for the young nun but also her sense of helplessness in her affliction:

> I loved the nobility of your ways, your wisdom and chastity, your soul and
> all your life, so that many said: "What are you doing?" Now may all la-
> ment with me, all who have woe like my woe, who in the love of God
> bore such love in their heart and their mind for a person, as I had for
> you—one snatched away from them in an instant, just as you were taken
> from me.[7]

Sometime later Richardis, penitent, decided to return to the Rupertsberg. Before she could act, however, she was suddenly stricken ill and died soon thereafter, on October 29, 1152. In a reply to Hartwig's letter

informing her of his sister's death, Hildegard wrote that while the world
loved Richardis' intelligence and beauty, God loved her even more:
"Therefore he did not want to surrender his Beloved to that inimical
lover, the world. . . . And I too dispel from my heart the pain you have
prepared for me through this daughter of mine." [8]

Over the next decade, despite bouts of illness, Hildegard experienced
the satisfaction of watching the Rupertsberg convent grow increasingly
independent.[9] It was at this time that she wrote her technical works on
medicine and natural philosophy as well as her second visionary treatise,
the *Liber vitae meritorum* (*The Book of Life's Rewards*), completed in
1163. In the latter she depicts the various human vices as allegoric em-
blems that speak and are answered by the corresponding virtues. Thus
Anger, for example, has the mouth of a scorpion and eyes so twisted that
one sees the whites more than the pupils; he asserts, in Marlovian fashion, "I trample and cast down all that brings me injury. . . . I open wounds
with the sword and thrash with cudgels," while Patience replies, "I resound in the heights and touch the earth, and exude from it like bal-
sam." [10] Although there are traces of Hildegard's interest in nature and
the cosmos in the *Liber vitae meritorum*, it basically reflects a deep understanding of the human predicament.[11] She shared this sometimes
painfully acquired knowledge with others by undertaking, between 1158
and 1161, what was for a woman of her time, and indeed of any time, a
singular and extraordinary venture: the first of a series of preaching tours
that would lead her as far away as Bamberg and Zwiefalten.

In 1163 Hildegard began a project that would take ten years to complete. The *Liber divinorum operum* (*Book of the Divine Works*), last of
her visionary writings, incorporates both a complex and sophisticated
portrait of the relationships of the universe to humanity and an elaborate
vision of future history.[12] Recent scholarship suggests that it reflects an
awareness of the microcosmic speculation of the mid twelfth century and
the contemporaneous eschatological innovations of Anselm of Havel-
berg and others.[13] In their ordered complexity, the visions of the *Liber
divinorum operum* embody the concerns of an age of transition and its
quest for the reasons behind appearances, so that the famous miniatures
in the thirteenth-century codex of the work at Lucca, which led Fritz
Saxl to declare that they "show us the exact shape in which pagan
cosmologies made their first reappearance in the Middle Ages," [14] now
seem to represent rather the same Platonic ferment that produced such
works as Bernardus Silvestris' *Cosmographia* and Alain de Lille's *Anti-
claudianus*.

The period in which Hildegard wrote the *Liber divinorum operum* was
filled with other activity also. In 1164 she composed a tract condemning
the Cathars and also sent a letter to her former friend and supporter

Frederick I, reprimanding him for his role in the appointment of Paschal III as antipope. The emperor, who had the year before given the Ruperts-berg a letter of protection,[15] was undoubtedly abashed, for he wrote no reply. Neither did he reply to Hildegard's last message to him. Curt and harsh, it records a revelation that came to her after the installation of Paschal's successor, Calixtus III, in 1168: "He who is, speaks: I through Myself destroy recalcitrance and crush the opposition of those who defy me. Woe, woe upon the evildoing of the unjust who scorn me! Hear this, king, if you would live—else my sword will pierce through you!"[16] Be-sides such literary activism, Hildegard also founded another convent (at the site of the Augustinian monastery of Eibingen, above Rüdesheim, where today the abbey of Saint Hildegard stands), suffered from severe illness for three years, and undertook her fourth and last preaching tour.

Completion of the *Liber divinorum operum* was complicated by the death of her secretary, Volmar, provost of the Rupertsberg, in 1173. Since her method of composition required the assistance of collaborators, some monks from Trier and her nephew Wezelin, provost of the abbey of Sankt Andreas in Cologne, were called to help. Subsequently Godefrid, a monk from Disibodenberg, was appointed the new provost and became Hilde-gard's amanuensis. (The *Vita*, completed by Theodoric of Echternach, together with Hildegard's letters, autobiographical testimony in her works, and the *Protocollum canonisationis*, constitutes the basis for our knowl-edge of her career.) In the autumn of 1175 Guibert of Gembloux wrote to Hildegard, inquiring about the nature of her visions. Her reply (see the translation below) is an important document in the history of mysti-cism and an extraordinary statement about the powers of the mind. When Godefrid died in 1176, Guibert became her new secretary.

One final controversy was to mark the last years of Hildegard's life. In 1178, the prelates of Mainz placed the Rupertsberg under an interdict, and only through exerting considerable influence was she able to arrange for its removal. The circumstances, recorded in her correspondence on the issue, were essentially the product of a misunderstanding. Hildegard had permitted a previously excommunicated nobleman to be buried in the convent cemetery, in the knowledge that he had, prior to his death, been reconciled to the Church and had received the sacraments. The of-ficials at Mainz, however, acting in the absence of their archbishop, Christian, judged the atonement invalid and ordered Hildegard to have the body exhumed. When she refused, they announced censure of the Rupertsberg convent. After obliterating the outlines of the grave and ap-pealing unsuccessfully to the prelates in Mainz, Hildegard wrote an im-passioned appeal to Archbishop Christian in Rome. In the letter she gives vent to the despair of her nuns at being denied communion and insists that God himself in a vision declared to her that the nobleman had been properly restored to the Church. Christian, a cosmopolitan with the good sense not to contest the entreaties of one as revered and respected as Hildegard, assured her that the interdict would be rescinded as soon as adequate testimony concerning the deceased's absolution was received at Mainz. In March of 1179, the nuns of the Rupertsberg were restored to their rights. Not long after, Hildegard became ill again, and on September 17, 1179, as the *Vita* tells us, "she passed over to her heavenly Spouse in a blessed death." [17] According to legend, the very skies celebrated her departure. Two vast arcs illuminated the night, while beneath them a glowing red cross, surrounded by cross-studded circles, waxed to immensity. For a moment, at least, Hildegard's daughters shared her great gift.

Of all of Hildegard's literary efforts, the most remarkable are the *Scivias* and the *Liber divinorum operum*. She offers them to us as the record of actual visionary revelations, perceived in a waking state with open eyes. In each, her customary style of presentation is to describe the vision first and then provide an elaborate exegesis (which she attributes to a divine voice) that comments on each feature of the vision. Thus her famous depiction of the "world-egg" (*Scivias* 1. 3; see the translation below), for example, includes both a verbal rendition of what she actually sees and an allegorical commentary that discloses the underlying theological significance of such cosmic objects as the sun, the moon, and the stars. We are fortunate in having also three manuscripts that contain illustrations to the visions. Of these the most important and striking is a codex that may well have been prepared under Hildegard's supervision at the scriptorium on the Rupertsberg. The original manuscript was sent to Dresden for safekeeping during the Second World War and subsequently disappeared; there do, however, exist both a black-and-white photocopy of the original and an excellent full-color facsimile produced by the nuns of the abbey of Saint Hildegard at Eibingen in 1928. The colored versions published in various editions are a valuable aid to interpreting the text. [18]

In design the *Scivias* is tripartite. The first six visions show how the relationship of God, humanity, and the world evolved. Included are symbolic depictions of the fall of the angels and of Adam, the elemental composition of the universe, the constitution of the soul, the synagogue (embodiment of the Old Testament), and the hierarchic choirs of the angels. As throughout the *Scivias*, the imagery is intense and dynamic, often full of motion and dramatic incident. In the second book, consisting of seven visions, we see the process of redemption: the coming of the Savior and the battle of his church and sacraments against the onslaughts of the devil. The final book centers its thirteen visions about an architectural image of salvation. Here Hildegard describes an elaborate edifice containing the various divine virtues—faith and humility, patience, charity, and the rest—necessary for the welfare of the soul. The drama of the *Scivias* concludes with a revelation of the final days, as the damned and the saved are eternally parted and the universe is purified of everything mean and perishable:

> And presently all the elements gleamed again in the utmost serenity, as if the blackest skin had been pulled off them, so that fire no longer contained any heat, nor air any denseness, nor water its turbulent seething, nor earth its frailty. The sun, too, the moon and the stars, shone with great splendor and beauty, like countless ornaments in the sky; and they stayed fixed without circling motion, so that they no longer distinguished day from night. And so it was not night, but day. And it was finished.[19]

While the *Scivias* sets before us a world in flux from Creation to Apocalypse, the *Liber divinorum operum* presents an ordered disposition of the relations inhering in the universe and a structured account of the divisions of past and future history. The first vision of the book portrays the *ignea vis*, the life-force personified, which courses through all living beings (see the translation below). In the second vision this creative power appears as a mediator between God and the world, rendered here in the form of a wheel rather than as an egg. Other differences from the universe that Hildegard depicts in the *Scivias* include an emphasis on the interconnection of various portions of the cosmos through a system of rays and, most significantly, the central position of humanity in the whole. Bound inextricably by the rays, winds, and other natural powers to the rest of reality, each of us is a microcosm, a "little world," whose bodily operations both depend upon and parallel the activities of the greater totality. M.-D. Chenu notes that there was a surge of interest in microcosmic speculation in Western Europe after 1150, especially in places like Chartres, where Plato's *Timaeus* was important in the curriculum.[20] There are indications of possible Platonic or, more specifically, Timaean influence in the *Liber divinorum operum* also in the sense of orderliness attributed to the cosmos there. The tumultuous universe of the *Scivias*, derived primarily from Stoic models, has been restructured by the imposition of *ratio*, of measuring reason; the world of the *Liber divinorum operum* is at once more delineated, detailed, and static, reflecting an underlying order or harmony in nature that verges on the mathematical.

The third and fourth visions of the *Liber divinorum operum* continue to elaborate humanity's place in the scheme of things; the fourth, by far the longest vision in the book, provides a detailed analysis of the parts of the human body and brings in much of Hildegard's medical learning. A change of theme is sounded by the fifth vision, which transfers our gaze from this world to the next as Hildegard describes otherworldly locales of punishment and purification. After an exegesis of the Creation account in Genesis, Hildegard concludes her work with an outline of history, from Adam and the patriarchs to the Antichrist and time's end.

Although her three visionary works must stand as Hildegard's greatest intellectual accomplishment, she was also responsible for a number of other writings that continue to attract popular attention and scholarly interest. Of these, the most noteworthy are her songs (*Symphonia harmoniae caelestium revelationum*), a play now considered to be the first liturgical drama (*Ordo virtutum*), and a bipartite treatise on natural science and medicine (*Liber subtilitatum diversarum naturarum creaturum*, comprising the *Liber simplicis medicinae* [or *Physica*] and the *Liber compositae medicinae* [or *Causae et curae*]). She has even provided a curiosity for the philologist in the *Lingua ignota* and *Litterae ignotae*, which present a secret language and alphabet of Hildegard's own invention.[21] Marianna Schrader and Adelgundis Führkötter, who attempt to establish the authenticity of the Hildegardian corpus in *Die Echtheit des Schrifttums der heiligen Hildegard von Bingen*, also number a Gospel explication (*Expositio evangeliorum*), two saints' lives, a tract on the Benedictine rule, and her numerous letters among her legitimate productions.[22] Since the appearance of their book, controversy over the authorship of her works has abated considerably; the situation today is certainly a far cry from what it was in 1874, when Wilhelm Preger felt himself able to assert with confidence that the only writing we could attribute to Hildegard with certainty was her letter to Bernard of Clairvaux, and that only in part![23]

Peter Dronke contributed much to awakening the current interest in Hildegard's songs and dramatic poetry by his 1970 essay, "Hildegard of Bingen as Poetess and Dramatist."[24] There he points out her vivid and original use of imagery and her renovation of older forms of the sequence and analyzes the elements contributing to "some of the most unusual, subtle, and exciting poetry of the twelfth century."[25] In a Benedictine house like the Rupertsberg, music was the natural accompaniment of daily living—or, better, music was the essence of that life, since both the Divine Offices and the liturgy of the Eucharist were sung each day. Indeed, one of the reasons why the interdict of 1178 hung so heavy on Hildegard and her sisters was that it forbade them the normal chanting of their prayers and songs. The *Symphony of the Harmony of Heavenly Revelations* (*Symphonia harmoniae caelestium revelationum*), probably completed by 1158, consists of seventy-seven songs with neumatic notations: antiphonies, responsories, hymns, and sequences, some written at the request of other abbeys and cloisters. In melody and design, range and melismatic technique, they are innovative, going beyond the limits of ordinary Gregorian chant.[26] Likewise, a loose, organic interweaving of images marks the poetry of the sequences, which abandon the strict metrical conventions of similar twelfth-century compositions for what we would call free verse. One of the most striking is the sequence for Saint Ursula, commemorating the martyrdom of Ursula and her "11,000 virgins" in a stream of brilliant imagery that fuses the agony of death with a visionary fire that at once overcomes Ursula and her celebrant, Hildegard.[27] Like her other lyrics, this represents the spontaneity of insight that led Hildegard to describe herself not as a maker of songs but as an instrument of revelation, as "the trumpet of God."[28]

Appended to the *Symphonia* in what is known as the "Riesencodex," a manuscript at Wiesbaden weighing in at fifteen kilograms, is Hildegard's dramatic composition, the *Ordo virtutum* (see the translation below). The earliest extant liturgical morality play, it embodies her penchant for allegory, almost all of the characters being personified spiritual qualities. In essence it depicts a psychomachy, a contest between the devil and the virtues for possession of the soul. Anima, the soul, longs for the divine, but her desire is tainted by an element of sensuality. When Diabolus encourages her to seek the honor that the world can offer her, she leaves Queen Humilitas and her entourage of sister Virtutes. Lamenting, they dance, sing, and debate with the devil until Anima returns, penitent. As she attempts to struggle up to where the Virtutes are waiting for her, Diabolus attacks. Queen Humilitas orders the Virtutes into the fray, and they soon capture and restrain their enemy. After a final exchange of theological argument, in which the devil tries to persuade Chastity and her comrades that the virgin birth is unnatural, Anima and the Virtutes invoke the mystery of the Crucifixion; in a chorale that echoes the opening images of the play, they portray the world in the course of redemption.[29]

Hildegard, though justly famed for her poetic talents, has as often drawn attention as "Germany's first woman doctor and scientist."[30] Although the manuscripts of her medical and scientific works date back only to the thirteenth century, Schrader and Führkötter argue their authenticity convincingly.[31] While the visionary works, especially the *Liber divinorum operum*, build a cosmic edifice out of the interaction of divine, natural, and human forces, Hildegard's treatises on medicine and natural philosophy are handbooks of particularities. We find in the *Physica*, for example, descriptions of plants and animals, metals, stones, and minerals, along with their characteristic medicinal properties. It is both a pharmacopoeia and an encyclopedia, informing us of the voracious appetite of the pike and the healing powers of thyme and close to three hundred other herbs. More specific discussion of the origin and treatment of disease appears in the *Causae et curae*. After a description of the constitution of the world, we find chapters on topics ranging from nutrition and metabolism to gynecology and emotional hygiene. Herself the victim of intense onslaughts of pain and illness, Hildegard counsels a regimen based on moderation. Equilibrium and balance in the cycles of daily life, in eating and drinking, waking and sleeping, speaking and silence, help maintain the human body in the same harmony that sustains the motions and exchanges of the cosmos.[32]

Hildegard's writings reflect that vast range of interest in things both symbolic and natural typical of the age of imaginative vigor in which they were created. For a person of the twelfth century, the world was a storehouse of meaning, all its objects and activities referring ultimately to a realm both transcendent and divine. And from the perspective of that period, her works, from essays on alimentation to allegorical drama, are the expression of a robust unity of personality and outlook. For later ages, however, Hildegard was famed not as a writer of songs or a compiler of herbal lore but as a gifted prophet. She influenced Gebeno of Eberbach and was known to millenarians and compilers of prophecies from Henry of Kirkstede to Johannes Wolf.[33] Even Goethe commented on the splendid illuminations of the Wiesbaden *Scivias*.[34]

Though her life and works have been a recurrent source for study and inspiration to her followers in the Benedictine tradition and to those devoted to her memory, the vicissitudes of scholarship and public education have made the past few decades a period of revival, if not the heyday, of Hildegard studies. In part this has been the result of serious scholarly endeavors like those of Schrader and Führkötter and of equally serious researches into her use of symbolism and imagery, such as Christel Meier's outstanding study of the significance of color in Hildegard.[35] But just as much impetus has been provided by an excellent series of German translations of Hildegard's writings published by Otto Müller of Salzburg. These have made her works accessible to an ever-expanding public and have spurred on the production of much-needed critical editions, such as the one of the *Scivias* recently issued in the series *Corpus Christianorum*.[36] At present a number of American scholars are engaged in either translating Hildegard's writings into English or producing studies of topics ranging from her trinitarianism to her humanism.[37]

The most fascinating of Hildegard's writings have been and continue to be her visionary books. Even the songs, the letters, and her drama only reflect the intense imaginative power at play in those longer works. If we are to comprehend the full range of her artistry, some understanding of how her visions operate is necessary. When we consider the visions in themselves, two questions arise immediately: how are they produced, and how do they function? According to Hildegard, the visions appear to her as apparitions on a mirrorlike object constantly in her visual field that she calls "the *Shadow of the living light*."[38] In this she sees people and objects at a distance, future events, and the symbols that constitute the complex allegories of her visionary works (see the letter to Guibert of Gembloux below). A number of scholars have offered explanations for these visions; the most famous etiology is that of Charles Singer, who attributed them to migrainous "scintillating scotoma."[39] Whatever their cause, pathological or divine, they (those in the *Scivias* to a greater degree than those in the *Liber divinorum operum*) follow a pattern similar to that of hallucinations, which can be produced by any number of methods. In general, the visions are a composite of geometric, symbolic, and narrative elements that seem to combine essentially contentless patterns with meaningful material from the memory and the unconscious.[40] To Hildegard these appear to come from without, interpreted by a voice in a Latin that she avers never to have mastered.[41]

What are we to make of such assertions, when we are also faced, for example, with the obvious and carefully articulated difference between the cosmological views of the *Scivias* and the *Liber divinorum operum* and see evidence of her considerable learning in the scientific writings? Although it is tempting to dismiss her self-deprecating disclaimers as instances of the humility topos, it is surely reasonable to assume that, raised in a Benedictine house, Hildegard was well educated in the Bible and the Church Fathers and in the traditional practical lore of her time. Though she cites no secular authors in her works at all, it is likely that she was conversant with a good deal of the learning of her age, perhaps as a result more of her regular contact with educated monks than through her own reading. She claims that her assistants—Volmar, Richardis von Stade, and her later secretaries—had as their sole task the refinement of the Latin dictated to her by God, but as collaborators they were undoubtedly a source of information and ideas as well.[42] Certainly the visions of the *Liber divinorum operum*, at least, with their careful rendering of a subtly interconnected world, seem the product more of rational thought and labor than of feverish inspiration. We may never be able to determine with precision how forms acquired through learning were recombined in Hildegard's mind to create new images. The attempt to understand her visions, however, requires that we make at least some effort to unweave them, whether we treat them as explosions from the unconscious or as meticulously cultivated growths. We may even discover that in Hildegard we have a visionary of various powers, who like the young and the old Wordsworth or the young and the mature Shakespeare exhibited different spiritual blooms in different seasons.

NOTES

1. See, for example, Marjorie Reeves, *The Influence of Prophecy in the Later Middle Ages: A Study in Joachism*, pp. 93, 335, 342, 360, 368, 488 n. 11.

2. *Acta inquisitionis de virtutibus et miraculis Sanctae Hildegardis, PL* 197. 136b. Hildegard herself asserts that the visionary gift was impressed on her soul by God while she was yet in the womb: "In prima formatione mea, cum Deus in utero matris meae spiraculo vitae suscitavit me, visionem istam infixit animae meae" (*Vita* 16; *PL* 197. 102c). Compare also the opening of her letter to the prelates of Mainz (*PL* 197. 218c). The process of canonization was initiated under Pope Gregory IX in 1227 but never completed. Hildegard is, however, listed as a saint in the Roman martyrology. Her feast day is September 17.

3. *Scivias*, preface, ed. Adelgundis Führkötter and Angela Carlevaris, p. 3, 11. 9–10; *PL* 197. 383a.

4. "Tanquam saxea rupes," literally, "like a stony rock" (*Vita* 7; *PL* 197. 96b).

5. *Vita* 7; *PL* 197. 96c.

6. *Vita* 8; *PL* 197. 96d–97a.

7. *Die Echtheit des Schrifttums der heiligen Hildegard von Bingen: Quellenkritische Üntersuchungen*, ed. Marianna Schrader and Adelgundis Führkötter, p. 137.

8. *PL* 197. 163c–d.

9. See Maria Laetitia Brede, "Die Klöster der heiligen Hildegard Rupertsberg und Eibingen," in *Hildegard von Bingen 1179–1979: Festschrift zum 800. Todestag der Heiligen*, ed. Anton Ph. Brück, pp. 79–80.

10. *Liber vitae meritorum* 1. 22–23, ed. Joannes Baptista Pitra, *Analecta Sanctae Hildegardis opera spicilegio Solesmensi parata*, p. 14. I have translated the perfect tenses as present for the sake of consistency and euphony.

11. In an autobiographical fragment, Hildegard recounts that the composition of the *Liber vitae meritorum* was made more difficult when the "spirits of the air" (*aerii spiritus*) conspired to snare her nuns in a net of vanities (*Vita* 30; *PL* 197. 112d). When Hildegard tightened the reins on her daughters, some stood by her, but "certain of them, looking at me with grim eyes, secretly tore at me with their words, saying that they could not bear the insufferable squawking about the regular discipline, by which I wanted to fetter them" (*Vita* 30; *PL* 197. 112d–113a).

12. Also called the *De operatione Dei* (*On the Working of God*), the *Liber divinorum operum* presents one of the most fully articulated statements of the relationship between the macrocosm and the microcosm found in twelfth-century thought, fusing Galenic physiology, astral and meteorological determinism, and rational theology to produce a complex amalgam of medical and cosmological speculation. On the scientific and medical aspects of the work, see Hans Liebeschütz, *Das allegorische Weltbild der heiligen Hildegard von Bingen*, and Charles Singer, "The Scientific Views and Visions of Saint Hildegard (1098–1180 [*sic*])," in *Studies in the History and Method of Science*, pp. 1–55 (an abridged revision of the latter appears as "The Visions of Hildegard of Bingen," in Singer's *From Magic to Science: Essays on the Scientific Twilight*, pp. 199–239). Essential to Hildegard's scheme is a system of metaphorical correspondences between the elemental layers in the universe and the various parts of the human body. These correspondences are in part geometrical, so that the human body can serve as a canon of proportion for the greater world; see Ildefons Herwegen, "Ein mittelalterlicher Kanon des menschlichen Körpers," *Repertorium für Kunstwissenschaft* 32 (1909): 445–446. At the same time, Hildegard perceives the affective and moral correlation of the movements of nature, the circulation of fluids in the body, and the activities of the soul. Health and disease are consequently a result of the balance or imbalance of spiritual, physical, and cosmic forces. For a discussion of physiology and medicine in the *Liber divinorum operum* and Hildegard's other works and for further bibliography, see Heinrich Schipperges, "Menschenkunde und Heilkunst bei Hildegard von Bingen," in Brück, ed., pp. 295–310.

13. Although Heinrich Schipperges may be right in arguing that Hildegard's works show no sign of being influenced by the wave of translation that brought new masses of Greek

and Arabic learning to the West, this does not preclude the possibility that she may well have come in contact with more local innovations on microcosmic themes between the time she wrote the *Scivias* and began work on the *Liber divinorum operum*. See Schipperges' "Einflüsse arabischer Medizin auf die Mikrokosmosliteratur des 12. Jahrhunderts," pp. 133–135, and my "The Eye Sees More than the Heart Knows: The Visionary Cosmology of Hildegard of Bingen," pp. 35–38, 286–295. Charles M. Czarski of the University of Kentucky has recently completed a dissertation on Hildegard's eschatology.

14. Fritz Saxl, "Macrocosm and Microcosm in Mediaeval Pictures," in his *Lectures*, vol. 1, p. 62. The lecture itself dates from the winter of 1927–28.

15. See Schrader and Führkötter, eds., p. 126. An earlier letter from Frederick to Hildegard indicates that she had once spoken with him at the imperial palace at Ingelheim; we have, however, no knowledge of what actually transpired at their meeting (pp. 127–128).

16. Ibid., p. 129.

17. *Vita* 57; *PL* 197. 129c. An account of the circumstances surrounding the interdict and German versions of the relevant letters may be found in Adelgundis Führkötter's translation of Hildegard's correspondence, *Briefwechsel: Nach den ältesten Handschriften übersetzt und nach den Quellen erläutert*, pp. 235–246. Führkötter sees in the conflict an expression of the eternal dialectics of institution and charisma within the Church (p. 245).

18. Both the new edition of the *Scivias* and the latest (1975) printing of its German translation by Maura Böckeler contain excellent reproductions of the illustrations. On the correspondence of text to illumination in the *Scivias*, see Christel Meier, "Zum Verhältnis von Text und Illustration im überlieferten Werk Hildegards von Bingen," in Brück, ed., pp. 159–169.

19. *Scivias* 3. 12, ed. Führkötter and Carlevaris, p. 606, ll. 90–99; *PL* 197. 726a.

20. In *Nature, Man, and Society in the Twelfth Century: Essays on New Theological Perspectives in the Latin West*, ed. and trans. Jerome Taylor and Lester K. Little, pp. 30–37.

21. No less distinguished a figure than Wilhelm Grimm found these puzzles intriguing; see "Wiesbader Glossen," *Zeitschrift für deutsches Altertum und deutsche Literatur* 6 (1848): 321–403. Schrader and Führkötter counter his views on the *Litterae ignotae* (pp. 52–53).

22. See n. 7 above. For a full record of Hildegard's writings and their manuscript sources, see Schrader and Führkötter, eds., especially pp. 6, 185–196.

23. See Wilhelm Preger, *Geschichte der deutschen Mystik im Mittelalter: Nach den Quellen untersucht und dargestellt*, vol. 1, pp. 29–37.

24. Peter Dronke, *Poetic Individuality in the Middle Ages: New Departures in Poetry 1000–1150*, pp. 150–192.

25. Ibid., p. 151.

26. For details, see Joseph Schmidt-Görg's comments in Hildegard's *Lieder: Nach den Handschriften herausgegeben*, ed. Pudentiana Barth, M. Immaculata Ritscher, and Joseph Schmidt-Görg, pp. 9–16; Ludwig Bronarski's *Die Lieder der hl. Hildegard: Ein Beitrag zur Geschichte der geistlichen Musik des Mittelalters*; and M. Immaculata Ritscher, "Zur Musik der heiligen Hildegard von Bingen," in Brück, ed., pp. 189–209. On the date of the *Symphonia*, see Dronke, *Poetic Individuality*, p. 151 n. 1, and his "The Composition of Hildegard of Bingen's *Symphonia*," *Sacris Erudiri* 19 (1969–1970): 381–382. Several of Hildegard's songs appear in English translation, together with an illuminating interpretative introduction, in Barbara L. Grant's "Five Liturgical Songs by Hildegard von Bingen (1098–1179)," *Signs: Journal of Women in Culture and Society* 5 (1980): 557–567.

27. On the development of the legend of Ursula from the veneration of some unnamed martyred virgins at Cologne, see W. Levison, "Das Werden der Ursula-Legende," *Bonner Jahrbücher* 132 (1927): 1–164; 139 (1934): 227–228. The artistic representation of the legend is discussed by Guy de Tervarent in *La légende de sainte Ursule dans la littérature et*

l'art du moyen âge. A lively popular account of the evolution of the legend appears in Sabine Baring-Gould's *Curious Myths of the Middle Ages.*

28. The image is entirely one of self-abnegation. Writing to her mystical contemporary, Elisabeth of Schönau, Hildegard suggests that visionaries and prophets, knowing nothing of heavenly things, "only sing forth God's secrets, like a trumpet that merely gives out sounds, and does not itself labor, but another blows into it, so that it might yield a sound" (*PL* 197. 217d). At the end of the letter she even compares her own utterances to "the weak sound of a trumpet from the living light" (*PL* 197. 217d–218a)! In other letters, she uses the trumpet as a metaphor to different ends (for example, *PL* 197. 180d, 245b, 294b).

29. On the *Ordo virtutum,* see Dronke, *Poetic Individuality,* pp. 168–179; also Bruce Hozeski, "Hildegard of Bingen's *Ordo Virtutum*: The Earliest Discovered Liturgical Morality Play," *American Benedictine Review* 26 (1975): 251–259. A comparison with an earlier woman dramatist is offered by Hozeski in "The Parallel Patterns in Hrotsvitha of Gandersheim, a Tenth Century German Playwright, and in Hildegard of Bingen, a Twelfth Century German Playwright," *Annuale Mediaevale* 18 (1977): 42–53.

30. More than one author has referred to her in just those terms. See, for example, Hermann Fischer, "Die heilige Hildegard von Bingen: Die erste deutsche Naturforscherin und Ärztin; ihr Leben und Werk," *Münchener Beiträge zur Geschichte und Literatur der Naturwissenschaften und Medizin* 7–8 (1927): 381–538, and Johannes Kohl, "Die heilige Hildegard von Bingen, die erste deutsche Naturforscherin und Ärztin," *Volk und Scholle* 7 (1929): 262–267.

31. See Schrader and Führkötter, eds., pp. 4–5, 54–59.

32. For a discussion of disease and its treatment in both the *Physica* and the *Causae et curae,* see Irmgard Müller, "Krankheit und Heilmittel im Werk Hildegards von Bingen," in Brück, ed., pp. 311–349.

33. Reeves, pp. 39, 93, 488 n. 11. Gebeno's attentions were largely responsible for the somewhat one-sided portrait later ages were to receive of Hildegard, since copies of his *Speculum futurorum temporum sive Pentachronon* (1220), in which he collected her prophecies, were to outnumber by far those of Hildegard's own works. The situation was somewhat improved after 1513, when Jacobus Faber's edition of the *Scivias* was published in Paris. For a more detailed account of the reception of Hildegard's writings, see Friedhelm Jürgenmeier, "St. Hildegard 'prophetissa teutonica,'" in Brück, ed., pp. 284–293.

34. In "Kunst und Altertum am Rhein und Main," Goethe writes, regarding his visit to Wiesbaden, "Hier ist in gedachter Rücksicht schon viel geschehen, und mehrere aus Klöstern gewonnene Bücher in guter Ordnung aufgestellt. Ein altes Manuskript, die Visionen der heiligen Hildegard enthaltend, ist merkwürdig" (*Biographische Einzelschriften,* ed. Josef Kunz, p. 532).

35. Christel Meier, "Die Bedeutung der Farben im Werk Hildegards von Bingen," *Frühmittelalterliche Studien* 6 (1972): 245–355.

36. See n. 3 above. The translations are listed in the bibliography.

37. There are indications lately that interest in Hildegard is spreading beyond the confines of the West; see Werner Lauter, "Hinweise auf Hildegard von Bingen in Japan," in Brück, ed., pp. 433–438.

38. Letter to Guibert of Gembloux; Pitra, ed., p. 332. On the various uses of mirror symbolism in Hildegard, see Margot Schmidt, "Hildegard von Bingen als Lehrerin des Glaubens: Speculum als Symbol des Transzendenten," in Brück, ed., pp. 95–157.

39. Singer, *Studies,* vol. 1, p. 53, and *From Magic to Science,* p. 232.

40. See my "The Eye Sees More than the Heart Knows," pp. 87–115. For an analysis of hallucinatory imagery, see Ronald K. Siegel and Murray E. Jarvik, "Drug-Induced Hallucinations in Animals and Man," in *Hallucinations: Behavior, Experience, and Theory,* ed. Ronald K. Siegel and Louis Jolyon West, pp. 81–161 (on migraine phenomena, see pp.

144–145). Louis Jolyon West charts the relation of memory, perception, and arousal in "A Clinical and Theoretical Overview of Hallucinatory Phenomena," in ibid., pp. 299–306.

41. For discussions of Hildegard's proficiency in Latin, see Schrader and Führkötter, eds., pp. 180–184, and Liebeschütz, pp. 156–166.

42. The problem of Hildegard's collaborators is treated by Ildefons Herwegen in "Les collaborateurs de Sainte Hildegarde," *Revue Bénédictine* 21 (1904): 192–203, 302–315, 381–403. See also Albert Derolez, "Deux notes concernant Hildegarde de Bingen," *Scriptorium* 27 (1973): 291–293, and Schrader and Führkötter, eds., pp. 180–184.

From Hildegard's Letter to Guibert of Gembloux

But from my infancy on, when my bones and nerves and veins were not yet strengthened, I have always seen this vision in my soul, up to the present time, when now I am more than seventy years old. And my soul, as God wills it, ascends in this vision to the heights of the firmament, into the changes of the varied air, and spreads itself out among various peoples, very distant from me, in faraway regions and places. Since I see these things in my soul in this fashion, I therefore observe them according to the vicissitudes of clouds and other created things. I do not hear these things, however, with my external ears, nor do I perceive them by the thoughts of my heart, nor by any combination of my five senses— but rather in my soul, with my external eyes open, so that I have never suffered the weakness of ecstasy in them, but alertly see them by day and by night. And I am constantly fettered by illness and often perplexed by severe pains that threaten to carry me off to death, but up to now God has always revived me.

So the light that I see is not bound to a place, but it is far, far brighter than a cloud that bears the sun on it. I am unable to determine its height, or its length, or its breadth, and I have been told it is called the *Shadow of the living light*. And as the sun, the moon, and the stars appear on the waters, so Scriptures, the virtues, and certain works of man shine out clearly to me in it.

Whatever I see or learn in this vision, I retain as a memory for a long time, so that when I see or hear it, I remember it, and at the same time I see, hear, and know, and as if in an instant, I learn what I know. But what I do not see, I do not know, since I am uneducated and have been taught only to read out letters in all simplicity. That which I write in the vision I see and hear, and I do not set down any words other than those that I hear. I bring them forth in unpolished Latin words just as I hear them in the vision, for in this vision I am not taught to write as the philosophers write. The words in that vision are not like the words that resound from the mouth of a man, but shine out like flames, and like clouds moving in the pure air.

In no way am I able to comprehend the form of this light, just as I cannot completely gaze upon the sphere of the sun. In this same light I once in a great while see another light, which I have been told is called the *Living light*; and when and how I am to see it I am unable to predict. But when I do see it, every sadness and every anxiety are lifted from me, so that I then feel like a simple maiden and not like an old woman.

From *Scivias* 1. 3

After this I saw a huge construction, round and shadowy, in the likeness of an egg. It was narrow on top, broad in the middle, and smaller below. All around its exterior portion there was a lucent fire that had a sort of shadowy skin beneath it. And in that fire there was a globe of shining red fire so huge that the entire construction was illumined by it, and it had three little torches placed in order up above it. By their fire they supported the globe so it wouldn't fall. And that same globe raised itself upward a little, and a great deal of fire rushed against it, so that it then extended its own flames further out. And it sank downward a little, and much cold came against it, so that it withdrew its flames quickly from it.

But indeed from that fire which surrounded the construction, a certain blast went forth with its whirlwinds, and from that skin which was below it, another blast boiled up with its whirlwinds and spread itself this way and that through the construction. In this same skin there was a certain gloomy fire so dreadful that I could not look upon it, and it shook the whole skin with its force, full of thunders, storms, and very sharp stones, large and small. And while it raised up its thunder, that lucent fire and the winds and the air were stirred up, so that the lightning preceded the thunder, since the fire first felt the agitation of the thunder in itself.

But below this skin was the purest ether, that had no skin beneath it. In it I even saw a certain globe of dazzling fire, vast in size, and it had two little torches brightly placed up above it, and they held the globe so that it would not go beyond the bounds of its course. And in this same ether many bright spheres had been placed everywhere; occasionally the globe sent out its brilliance to them, emptying itself somewhat, and so would come back beneath the fiery red globe spoken of earlier and, renewing its flames from it, would blast them out again into these same spheres. But likewise from the ether itself a certain blast poured forth with its whirlwinds, and it extended itself everywhere in the construction spoken of earlier.

But below this ether I saw watery air, which had a white skin beneath it. Spreading itself this way and that through the whole construction, it gave it moisture. And when occasionally it collected itself together suddenly, it sent forth a sudden shower with a great crash, and when it spread itself out gently, it poured out a pleasant rain with a gentle motion. But likewise from this a certain blast going out with its whirlwinds spread itself through the aforementioned construction.

And in the middle of these elements there was a certain sandy globe of vast size which these same elements so surrounded that it could slip neither this way nor that. But when these same elements and the aforementioned blasts from time to time struck each other, they made the globe move a little by their force. And between the north and the east I saw a huge mountain that had much darkness toward the north and much light toward the east, but so that the light could not reach the darkness nor could the darkness reach the light.

From the *Liber divinorum operum* 1. 1

I am the highest fiery power, who has enkindled every spark that lives and breathes out nothing mortal. I distinguish all things as they are, surrounding the circle of the world with my superior wings; that is, flying about it with wisdom, I have ordered it rightly. And I, flaming life of the divine substance, flare up above the beauty of the plains, I shine in the waters and blaze in the sun, the moon, and the stars, and with an airy wind, as if by an invisible life which sustains the whole, I arouse all things to life. For air lives in freshness and flowers, the waters flow as if they were alive. The sun, too, lives in its light, and when the moon wanes it is fired anew by the light of the sun, just as if it lived again; the stars also grow clear in their light as if it were living. . . . And so I, the fiery power, lie hidden in these things, and they themselves burn by me, as the breath unceasingly moves the man, like a windy flame in a fire. All these things live in their essence and were not devised in death, for I am Life. And I am Reason, and have the wind of the resounding Word through which every creature has been made, and I have given my breath to all these things so that none of them is mortal in its kind, for I am Life. I am Life whole and entire, not cut from stone, not sprouted from twigs, not rooted in the powers of a man's sex; rather all that is living is rooted in me. For Reason is the root, and in it blossoms the resounding Word.

From the *Ordo virtutum*

Here begins the *Ordo virtutum*.

Prologue

PATRIARCHS AND PROPHETS:
Who are these, who are as clouds?
VIRTUES:
O ancient holy ones, what makes you marvel at us?
The Word of God gleams in a human form,
and so we sparkle with it,
building the limbs of His lovely body.
PATRIARCHS AND PROPHETS:
We are the roots and you the branches,
the fruit of the living eye,
and we were a shadow within it.
THE COMPLAINT OF THE SOULS PUT IN THE FLESH:
Ah, we are wanderers,
what are we doing, straying toward sin?
We should be daughters of the King,
but have fallen into the shadow of sins.
O living sun, bear us upon your shoulders
to that most perfect legacy which we lost in Adam!
O King of Kings, in your battle we fight on.
HAPPY SOUL:
O sweet divinity, O pleasant life,
in which I shall wear a shining cloak
and receive what I lost in my first attendance,
I sigh for you and call on all the Virtues.
VIRTUES:
O happy Soul, O lovely creature of God,
formed in the boundless heights of the wisdom of God,
you love deeply.
HAPPY SOUL:
Oh, willingly would I come to you,
that you might offer me a kiss from the heart.
VIRTUES:
We should be soldiers with you, O daughter of the King.
BUT, OPPRESSED, THE SOUL COMPLAINS:
Oh, heavy labor, and hard burden

that I bear in the cloak of this life,
since it is so very hard for me to struggle against the flesh.

VIRTUES TO THE SOUL:

O Soul, fashioned by the will of God,
and O happy instrument, why are you so weak
against that which God stamped out in the virgin birth?
You should overcome the devil along with us.

THE SOUL:

Come to me, help me, that I might stand!

THE KNOWLEDGE OF GOD TO THE SOUL:

Behold in what garb you have been clothed, daughter of salvation,
be firm, and you will never fall.

THE SOUL, UNHAPPY:

Ah, I know not what to do,
or where I might flee!
Oh, woe, I cannot complete
the garb in which I am clothed.
I surely wish to cast it off.

VIRTUES:

O unhappy conscience,
O miserable Soul,
why do you hide your face in the presence of your maker?

THE KNOWLEDGE OF GOD:

You neither know nor see nor understand the one Who fashioned you.

THE SOUL:

God made the world:
I do Him no injury,
but I want to enjoy it!

THE SHOUTING OF THE DEVIL TO THE SOUL:

Fool! Fool! Where does working get you? Look to the world, and it will
   embrace you with great esteem.

VIRTUES:

Oh, this calamitous voice of utmost grief!
Ah, ah, some marvelous victory
has raised itself up in the marvelous fervent desire of God,
in which the delight of the flesh has hidden itself secretly,
alas, alas! where the will knew no defects,
and where the desire of man fled from lewdness.
Wail, wail, over these, Innocence,
you who have not lost your purity in noble modesty,
and have not swallowed the throaty avarice of the old serpent.

THE DEVIL:

What kind of command is this, that there ought to be nobody besides

God? But I say: to the one who wants me and wishes to follow my will, I shall give all things. Certainly you have nothing you can give your followers, since none of you even knows who you are!

BIBLIOGRAPHY

Primary Works

Barth, Pudentiana, M. Immaculata Ritscher, and Joseph Schmidt-Görg, eds. *Lieder: Nach den Handschriften herausgegeben.* Salzburg, 1969.

Führkötter, Adelgundis, ed. and trans. *Briefwechsel: Nach den ältesten Handschriften übersetzt und nach den Quellen erläutert.* Salzburg, 1965.

——— and Angela Carlevaris, eds. *Scivias.* Corpus Christianorum, Continuatio Mediaevalis 43. 2 vols. Turnhout, 1978.

Heilkunde: Das Buch von dem Grund und Wesen und der Heilung der Krankheiten; nach den Quellen übersetzt und erläutert. Trans. Heinrich Schipperges. Salzburg, 1957.

Kaiser, Paul, ed. *Hildegardis Causae et curae.* Leipzig, 1903.

Der Mensch in der Verantwortung: Das Buch der Lebensverdienste (Liber vitae meritorum); nach den Quellen übersetzt und erläutert. Trans. Heinrich Schipperges. Salzburg, 1972.

Migne, J.-P., ed. *S. Hildegardis abbatissae Opera omnia.* Patrologiae cursus completus, Ser. Lat. 197. Paris, 1882.

Naturkunde: Das Buch von dem inneren Wesen der verschiedenen Naturen in der Schöpfung; nach den Quellen übersetzt und erläutert. Trans. Peter Riethe. Salzburg, 1959.

Pitra, Joannes Baptista, ed. *Analecta Sanctae Hildegardis opera spicilegio Solesmensi parata.* Analecta Sacra 8. 1882. Reprint. Farnborough, Eng., 1966.

Welt und Mensch: Das Buch "De operatione Dei"; aus dem Genter Kodex übersetzt und erläutert. Trans. Heinrich Schipperges. Salzburg, 1965.

Wisse die Wege: Nach dem Originaltext des illuminierten Rupertsberger Kodex der Wiesbaden Landesbibliothek ins Deutsche übertragen und bearbeitet. Trans. Maura Böckeler. Salzburg, 1954.

Related Works

d'Alverny, Marie-Thérèse. "Le cosmos symbolique du xiie siècle." *Archives d'Histoire Doctrinale et Littéraire du Moyen Age* 28 (1953): 31–81.

Baillet, Louis. "Les miniatures du 'Scivias' de Sainte Hildegarde conservé à la bibliothèque de Wiesbaden." *Monuments et Mémoires (Fondation Eugène Piot) Publiés par l'Academie des Inscriptions et Belles-Lettres* 19 (1911): 49–149.

Baring-Gould, Sabine. *Curious Myths of the Middle Ages.* 1866. Numerous reprints.

Baumgardt, David. "The Concept of Mysticism: Analysis of a Letter Written by Hildegard of Bingen to Guibert of Gembloux." *Review of Religion* 12 (1948): 277–286.

Bernhart, Joseph. "Hildegard von Bingen." *Archiv für Kulturgeschichte* 20 (1930): 249–260.

Böckeler, Maura. "Die heilige Hildegard als Äbtissin im Rahmen des 12. Jahrhunderts." *Benediktinische Monatschrift* 11 (1929): 435–450.

Bronarski, Ludwig. *Die Lieder der hl. Hildegard: Ein Beitrag zur Geschichte der geistlichen Musik des Mittelalters.* Veröffentlichungen der Gregorianischen Akademie zu Freiburg (Schweiz) 9. 1922. Reprint. Wiesbaden, 1973.

Brück, Anton Ph., ed. *Hildegard von Bingen 1179–1979: Festschrift zum 800. Todestag der Heiligen.* Quellen und Abhandlungen zur mittelrheinischen Kirchengeschichte 33. Mainz, 1979.

Derolez, Albert. "Deux notes concernant Hildegarde de Bingen." *Scriptorium* 27 (1973): 291–295.

Dronke, Peter. "The Composition of Hildegard of Bingen's *Symphonia.*" *Sacris Erudiri* 19 (1969–70): 381–393.

———. *Fabula: Explorations into the Uses of Myth in Medieval Platonism.* Mittellateinische Studien und Texte 9. Leiden, 1974.

———. *Poetic Individuality in the Middle Ages: New Departures in Poetry 1000–1150.* Oxford, 1970.

Eltz, Monika zu. *Hildegard.* Freiburg, 1963.

Fischer, Hermann. "Die heilige Hildegard von Bingen: Die erste deutsche Naturforscherin und Ärztin; ihr Leben und Werk." *Münchener Beiträge zur Geschichte und Literatur der Naturwissenschaften und Medizin* 7–8 (1927): 381–538.

Fromm, Hans, Wolfgang Harms, and Uwe Ruberg, eds. *Verbum et signum.* 2 vols. Munich, 1975.

Führkötter, Adelgundis. "Die Gotteswerke: Vom Sinn und Aufbau des *Liber divinorum operum* der heiligen Hildegard." *Benediktinische Monatschrift* 29 (1953): 195–204, 306–314.

———. *Hildegard von Bingen.* Salzburg, 1972.

Goethe, Johann Wolfgang. *Biographische Einzelschriften.* Ed. Josef Kunz. Vol. 12 of *Gedenkausgabe der Werke, Briefe und Gespräche.* Ed. Ernst Beutler. Zurich, 1949.

Grant, Barbara L. "Five Liturgical Songs by Hildegard von Bingen (1098–1179)." *Signs: Journal of Women in Culture and Society* 5 (1980): 557–567.

Grimm, Wilhelm. "Wiesbader Glossen." *Zeitschrift für deutsches Altertum und deutsche Literatur* 6 (1848): 321–340.

Herwegen, Ildefons. "Les collaborateurs de Sainte Hildegarde." *Revue Bénédictine* 21 (1904): 192–203, 302–315, 381–403.

———. "Ein mittelalterlicher Kanon des menschlichen Körpers." *Repertorium für Kunstwissenschaft* 32 (1909): 445–456.

Hozeski, Bruce W. "Hildegard of Bingen's *Ordo Virtutum*: The Earliest Discovered Liturgical Morality Play." *American Benedictine Review* 26 (1975): 251–259.

———. "The Parallel Patterns in Hrotsvitha of Gandersheim, a Tenth Century German Playwright, and in Hildegard of Bingen, a Twelfth Century German Playwright." *Annuale Mediaevale* 8 (1977): 42–53.

Keller, Hiltgart L. *Mittelrheinische Buchmalereien in Handschriften aus dem Kreise der Hiltgart von Bingen.* Stuttgart, 1933.

Koch, Josef. "Über die Lichtsymbolik im Bereich der Philosophie und des Mystik der Mittelalters." *Studium Generale* 13 (1960): 653–670.

———. "Der heutige Stand der Hildegard-Forschung." *Historische Zeitschrift* 186 (1958): 558–572.

Kraft, Kent. "The Eye Sees More than the Heart Knows: The Visionary Cosmology of Hildegard of Bingen." Ph.D. dissertation, University of Wisconsin, 1977.

———. "Text and Illustration in Hildegard of Bingen's *Scivias.*" In *Literature and the Other Arts*, vol. 3 of *Proceedings of the IXth Congress of the International Comparative Literature Association*, ed. Zoran Konstantinović, Steven P. Scher, and Ulrich Weisstein, pp. 43–49. Innsbrucker Beiträge zur Kulturwissenschaft, Sonderheft 51. Innsbruck, 1981.

Lauter, Werner. *Hildegard-Bibliographie: Wegweiser zur Hildegard-Literatur.* Alzey, 1970.

Liebeschütz, Hans. *Das allegorische Weltbild der heiligen Hildegard von Bingen.* Studien der Bibliothek Warburg 16. 1930. Reprint. Darmstadt, 1964.

Maurmann, Renate. *Die Himmelsrichtungen im Weltbild des Mittelalters: Hildegard von Bingen, Honorius Augustodunensis und anderen Autoren.* Munich, 1976.

May, Johannes. *Die heilige Hildegard von Bingen, aus dem Orden des heiligen Benedikt (1098–1179): Ein Lebensbild.* Kempten, 1911.

Meier, Christel. "Die Bedeutung der Farben im Werk Hildegards von Bingen." *Frühmittelalterliche Studien* 6 (1972): 245–355.

Preger, Wilhelm. *Geschichte der deutschen Mystik im Mittelalter: Nach den Quellen untersucht und dargestellt.* 3 vols. Leipzig, 1874–93.

Radimersky, George W. "Magic in the Works of Hildegard von Bingen (1098–1179)." *Monatshefte* 49 (1957): 353–360.

Reeves, Marjorie. *The Influence of Prophecy in the Later Middle Ages: A Study in Joachimism.* Oxford, 1969.

Saxl, Fritz. *Lectures.* 2 vols. London, 1957.

Schipperges, Heinrich. "Einflüsse arabischer Medizin auf die mikrokosmos-literatur des 12. Jahrhunderts." In *Antike und Orient im Mittelalter: Vorträge der Kölner Mediaevistentagungen 1956–1959,* ed. Paul Wilpert, pp. 129–153. Berlin, 1962.

———. *Die Welt der Engel bei Hildegard von Bingen.* Salzburg, 1963.

Schmelzeis, J. Ph. *Das Leben und Wirken der heiligen Hildegardis nach den Quellen dargestellt: Nebst einem Anhang Hildegard'scher Lieder mit ihren Melodien.* Freiburg im Breisgau, 1879.

Schrader, Marianna, and Adelgundis Führkötter. *Die Echtheit des Schrifttums der heiligen Hildegard von Bingen: Quellenkritische Untersuchungen.* Cologne, 1956.

Siegel, Ronald K., and Louis Jolyon West, eds. *Hallucinations: Behavior, Experience, and Theory.* New York, 1975.

Singer, Charles Joseph. *From Magic to Science: Essays on the Scientific Twilight.* 1928. Reprint. New York, 1958.

———, ed. *Studies in the History and Method of Science,* 2 vols. 1917–21. Reprint. New York, 1975.

Steele, Francesca Maria. *The Life and Visions of St. Hildegarde.* London, 1914.

de Tervarent, Guy. *La légende de saint Ursule dans la littérature et l'art du moyen âge.* 2 vols. Paris, 1931.

Ungrund, Magna. *Die metaphysische Anthropologie der heiligen Hildegard von Bingen.* Beiträge zur Geschichte des alten Mönchtums und des Benediktinerorodens 20. Münster in Westfalen, 1938.

Widmer, Bertha. *Heilsordnung und Zeitgeschehen in der Mystik Hildegards von Bingen.* Basler Beiträge zur Geschichtswissenschaft 52. Basel, 1955.

THE PROVENÇAL
TROBAIRITZ

astelloza

PETER DRONKE

In medieval Europe, Provence is unique in preserving a small corpus of secular lyrical poetry composed by women. The names of twenty *trobairitz*, who flourished in the twelfth and thirteenth centuries, are still known to us; some five anonymous songs can likewise be plausibly ascribed to women poets.[1] Only two of the *trobairitz*, however, are represented in the manuscripts by more than a single composition. Four songs are well attested for the countess of Dia—though the exact dates and historical identity of this poet are still much debated.[2] I incline to follow those who see her as Beatritz, wife of a certain Count William of Poitiers in the third quarter of the twelfth century. Historical evidence is equally elusive with regard to Castelloza, of whom again four compositions survive: three are steadily ascribed to her in a group of manuscripts; but the fourth also—found alongside the others in a manuscript where all her lyrics are copied anonymously—seems to admit of no serious doubt.[3] With the melodies of the *trobairitz* we are less fortunate: music has survived for only one of the countess' songs, none remains for Castelloza's.

In the biographical note (*vida*) that in three manuscripts introduces her songs, Castelloza is said to be from the Auvergne, and her husband is named as Turc de Mairona. This Turc is also alluded to in a lyric of topical invective (*sirventes*) of 1212. Thus, if we can set Castelloza's compositions near that date, they may well be a generation later than the countess of Dia's. It seems to me likely, moreover, that Castelloza knew her predecessor's songs, though her own are keenly individual in their art; again, the songs of both *trobairitz* can be readily distinguished from those of the troubadours.

Where the countess of Dia's four songs show a Cleopatra-like variety of attitudes to love and to the man she loves, Castelloza's show intense single-mindedness. The countess celebrates her joy in the lover whom she has chosen, a joy that also emboldens her to mock the slanderers and spies who menace love affairs. She can express her physical desires without reserve, in exultant erotic provocation of her beloved; and, in her only tragic song, she reflects on his unfaithfulness with the analytic ardor of one of Ovid's Heroides, still aware of her own desirability and beauty, still hoping to persuade him back to perfect mutual love.

Castelloza's songs, by contrast, are all meditations on her own anguished love, abasing herself and knowing—even while continuing to hope—that a future of constancy and oneness is not to be hoped for. Even if she is addressing her lover, and implicitly her audience, she utters soliloquies, in a depth of solitude. Where the countess' four songs create changeable perceptions, Castelloza's are facets of one unaltering perception.

Are her songs ordered to a particular design? In the manuscripts, their order (which is unvarying) is, as Dietmar Rieger pointed out, alphabetical.[4] This might of course be coincidence, or might reflect a mechanical ordering by an earlier collector. We also have some evidence, however, that—long before Dante's *Vita Nuova*—certain troubadours ordered their songs chronologically.[5] It is admittedly risky to entertain this notion for as small a sample of lyrics as Castelloza's. Yet I cannot easily escape the sense that with her we are in the presence not just of four songs but of a brief lyrical cycle, where an inner progression can be perceived, and where reverberations from one piece to the next heighten poetic meaning, so that the group as a whole is imaginatively richer than the four pieces considered separately. This is a point that cannot be demonstrated conclusively, yet the possible interrelatedness of Castelloza's songs seems worth bearing in mind in an attempt at reading.

In Spain and Portugal many love songs (*cantigas de amigo*) are put in the mouths of women, yet the manuscript tradition ascribes these songs exclusively to men. No *trovadora* is ever named. The reason that love lyrics composed by women survive from Provence, under the *trobairitz*'s names, must be bound up with the unusual degree of personal freedom that many women (at least in the higher reaches of society, and at least for three or four generations) there enjoyed. At the same time, while this freedom made possible some women's songs of marvelous directness, it is doubtful whether any of these were in a simple sense autobiographical. They are not truly comparable to private poetry by women, such as we know from the last two centuries: by their genre, they were intended for performance, in a cultivated, worldly society. This entailed from the outset certain stylizations, certain conventions of discretion, such as the use of fictive cover names (*senhals*); it meant the creation of a dramatic persona which, even if based upon emotional realities, did not—like much of the topical poetry of the time—dwell on matters that were verifiable historically. Even the most intimate and harrowing moments of declared love in these songs are inseparable from elements of role-playing, elements of "craft" (in both senses of the term).

This is not to suggest that the content of songs such as Castelloza's should be taken lightly. There are indeed eminent scholars of troubadour poetry who see all *cansos* concerned with love in terms of a formal poetic game, a display of rhetorical and melodic skills in which content is mostly conventionalized and unimportant. It is true that in Provence (as everywhere in medieval Europe) there were many dexterous versifiers who were not poets. But for those who were poets, those whose lyrics are still worth reading and listening to as poetry today, I believe that what is said is at least as important as how it is said, and that content is fresh, not commonplace.

Castelloza, I would suggest, belongs with these poets, and does so in a way she could never have done if her lyrics were simply (as the older authorities claimed) exercises in a language of love that had been forged and refined by men. On the contrary, the singularity of her thoughts about love is grounded in what must have been a historically unusual situation. For a woman of Castelloza's time and milieu, it seems there was no insuperable social obstacle or taboo to prevent her from loving freely. And, whether it was a matter of poetic feigning or experience, or of both intermingling, Castelloza could even choose to love actively, rather than play the traditional part of waiting to be chosen. She could declare her feelings without a sense of shame or guilt: if such a frank declaration from a woman still caused surprise in her society, it did not of itself bring humiliation or moral censure. And yet, if the preconditions for a woman's loving had become relatively easy, they did not make the turmoil of the emotions easier. I am reminded of Ruth Finnegan's observations about another, externally "permissive," society, where women compose hauntingly beautiful love songs. Of the Gond women in the hill forests of central India, Finnegan writes:

> The love-songs are the more heartfelt in that, among the Gond . . . , the women enjoy much freedom and often live with two or three men before they finally choose with whom to settle down. But the corollary of this frequent changing of marriage partners . . . is a deep experience of the sorrows as well as joys of inconstancy in love: the poems abound with references to heartbreak, betrayal, and the deceitfulness of lovers . . . [6]

Among the Gond women's songs we can find moments of heady sensual invitation that have parallels particularly in the countess of Dia:

> O come, my body is alone, come laugh with me, come talk with me.
> Bring mind to mind: clasp heart to heart.
> What of the future? I care not for the past.

O come, beloved; come, laugh with me,
Come, talk with me. My body is alone.

But we can also find a rending expression of the situation that is essentially Castelloza's—a woman's realization that the man she loves loves another woman better, and that this does not lessen her love for him but only increases her wistful longing:

Rust destroys the wheat
She has destroyed your love for me
How I long to cover you
As the moon is hid by clouds
How I long to take you
All to myself
As a mother takes her child.

Castelloza's songs, like those of the Gond women, have a beauty that is bound up with a willed simplicity. The resources of language and syntax she wishes to draw on are not large: central in her four songs is the word *cor*, 'heart'; around it cluster the heart's oscillating sensations— the experience of disloyal and loyal love, sorrow and joy, dying and reviving, languishing and being healed. Against these, some rare audacious images and expressions emerge in sharp relief. Syntactically striking in the songs is the extraordinary frequency of causal connectives—especially *que* and *car*, 'for' and 'since'—which often seem to be pseudocausal, almost devoid of meaning. It is as if Castelloza were trying over and over to explain the reasons for her anguish, without ever arriving at a firm causal nexus—as if her many attempts at reasoning about her passion revealed themselves, through the syntax itself, as doomed.

The brief *vida* of Castelloza tells us, apart from her region of origin and the names of her husband and her lover, only that she was "very joyful and very well schooled and very beautiful."[7] Let us try to extend that *vida* a little, on the basis of the songs themselves—not in the hope of coming nearer to the historical Castelloza, but heuristically, so as to enter more fully into the imaginative situation she presents. We can say that the Castelloza of the lyrics, while not of lowly origin, is aware of being of lesser birth than the man she loves (let us call him Arman de Breon, as the *vida* does, even if no historical evidence about that name survives). Unlike the countess of Dia, Castelloza has not the confidence to regain confidence with reflections on her own beauty, merit, or position. She has loved Arman—it seems for a long time—and occasionally has felt her love returned by him; but of late he has abandoned her for another, more exalted woman; he has ignored her, or has responded to her signs of unabated love only with cold disdain.

What can she do? She can plead with him, provoke and challenge him,

threaten him that she will die. All these impulses form part of Castelloza's emotional world and strategy; yet these are known from other
lyrical contexts too. But there are far rarer elements in Castelloza's
thoughts: a conviction that, because she has been bold enough to give
her love so openly, she must abide by the consequences—that is, the love
is her creation, and she must find its beauty and fulfillment in herself
alone, in what she has fashioned, and in her own most beautiful memo-
ries of what had taken place. However keen the temptation for her to
subside in sorrow, the love she has created can continue to sustain her,
provided she can still hold to her belief in it. That is why, however disloyal Arman may be, Castelloza's affirmations of her own loyalty, of loving unswervingly and in perpetuity, are vital to the experience that she
portrays.

The four songs are all in *canso* form: they consist of five or six strophes,
in which the rhyme scheme of the first is maintained identically throughout the rest of the composition (*coblas unissonans*). Only the second
song has an elaborate strophic form, with verses of several different lengths,
and is followed by two four-line envois (*tornadas*), which echo the rhyme
scheme of the later part of each strophe. Like many troubadours, Castelloza chose to create her own forms—each of her four is differentiated, at
least in minor details, from all others that survive in Provençal lyric.
Since close translations can convey almost nothing of the formal aspects
of this poetry, I cite one strophe from each of her compositions in the
original in the course of my discussion below. At the same time, I would
suggest that Castelloza's forms are not among the most accomplished or
most exquisite in troubadour lyric, and that she is not among the poets
who lose most in a plain translation: what matters above all in her poetry
is the meaning, and the movements of thought and emotion. While she
has certain moments of spectacular expression, even the homeliest words
take on depth by becoming part of her brooding contemplations; in the
transitions among her griefs and fears and longings lies the essence of
Castelloza's art.

What is unusual formally in the first song is the discrepancy between
the opening line of each strophe (which has eight syllables) and the rest
(which all have ten). This gives an effect of awkwardness, that may well
have had its counterpart in the music: even though the melody does not
survive, it is clear that the melodic line of the opening could not have
been smoothly paralleled at any later point in the strophe. The poetic-
musical form, that is, suggests a deliberate asymmetry, there is something
jagged about it, that seems to mirror the protagonist's edgy hesitance—
how is she to confront the man who has scorned her?

At first (1. 1), Castelloza seems to say that, for appearances' sake, to
keep his reputation high in the world, she will accuse him only in private
and speak nothing but good of him in her songs. Yet in this opening lurks

an intrinsic irony and subterfuge, for the song, directed in the first place to Arman, is implicitly, like all troubadour lyric, directed to an audience too. The very insistence that she will present him, disloyal as he is, only in the most favorable light, undermines itself because she is already in principle proclaiming this to the world at large. The private occasion of the reproaches *is* the public one of the song. In a similar way, some two generations earlier, Heloise had written to Abelard reprehending his neglect of her, in a letter that, though initially addressed to him, was also consciously meant for posterity, to right misconceptions and present a testimony that was truthful and comprehensive.[8] Claiming that Abelard has forgotten her and fails to comfort her, Heloise writes, "If only I could make up some pretexts for excusing you!"—where the same ambivalence as Castelloza's, the same ironic disclosure that ostensibly is no disclosure but a wholly private rebuke, is at work.

In her next strophe (1. 2), Castelloza contemplates an alternative approach. Could she, who had made herself so vulnerable through giving love openly, not still gain an advantage, and recover Arman's love, by different tactics? Yet what kind of relationship would that lead to?—

> Ja mais no·us tenrai per valen,
> ni·us amarai de bon cor ni per fe,
> tro que veirei si ja·m valria re,
> s'ie·us mostrava cor felon ni enic . . .
> Non farei ja, qu'eu non vueill puscaz dir
> qu'eu anc ves vos agues cor de faillir—
> c'auriaz pois qualque razonamen
> s'ieu avia ves vos fait faillimen.

> I shall never think of you as deserving,
> or love you with all my heart, loyally,
> before I see if it might serve my turn
> were I to show you a heart hostile and rancorous . . .
> No, I shan't do it: I don't want to let you say
> that I ever had the heart to fail you—
> as then you would have some justification
> if in any of my acts indeed I failed you.

She raises the possibility of acting as a more calculating woman only to dismiss it instantly—such theatricality would be so out of character for her that he would at once perceive her weakness through it, and might take advantage of her the more coldly and selfishly.

In the third strophe and the opening of the fourth, Castelloza reflects on how unconventional she has been in asking a man for love rather than waiting to be asked. In the world's eyes, she has played her cards badly: she has frightened off the man she cares about by her domineering, sermonizing manner. And yet, she affirms, the *bienpensants* are wrong—because (and here we have the first hint of one of Castelloza's pervasive themes) her fulfillment lies far more in herself, and in her poetry, than in her man. Even if he provokes harsh thoughts (*greu pessamen*) in her, because of his failure to respond lovingly, it is her own expression of her outgoing love (*preiar*) that revives her, the poet.

Not that this sublimation is all she seeks. In the moving close of the fourth strophe, she evokes a moment of blissful love experienced with her lover: the way he solaced her then was a revelation such as the uninitiated world can never know. But Castelloza's longing for such an exultant moment to return in reality is inseparable from her conviction that "even from saying this my heart takes joy"—that an imaginative recreation, while in a sense so much less than the real experience, can be preserved untarnished in a way that the real can never be.

Even if he grants her no more happiness of love in waking life, the imaginative realm is not diminished: "through my plaints and lais I'll always have joy in you, my friend" (1. 5). To express her constancy, Castelloza uses playfully the religious turn of phrase *no·m puesc convertir*, 'I can't become a convert.' The word *convertir* had been similarly used, and given special weight by being set at the close of a composition, by Almucs (or Almueis) de Castelnau, the lady to whom Castelloza addresses the *tornada* of her next song. Almucs had said, in reply to another lady's question, if she would forgive the man who had jilted her:

> Mas si vos faitz lui pentir,
> leu podes mi convertir.

> But if you can lead him to penance,
> you can convert me easily.[9]

She would be "converted," that is, back to the role of the gracious beloved, who shows pity on her devotee. But where for Almucs "conversion" was conditional upon her lover's repenting, Castelloza affirms that she can never "convert" away from her one love, no matter what her lover's attitude may become.

The hint of a realm in which *convertir* means turning to God is taken up in the astonishing conclusion of Castelloza's song. This conclusion was so daring that it has survived intact in only one of the five manuscripts—in the rest, a tame, banal closing line has been substituted, perhaps because censorship had intervened. Alluding to the troubadour convention of sending songs to the beloved by a messenger, Castelloza declares, no, she will speak to her lover straight—as if to say, her message is too urgent and too grave to be entrusted to another. Men in love had often before Castelloza used the threat that the beloved's hardness will cause their death, and had argued that she would be responsible for that death in the sight of God. Thus, for instance, in some twelfth-century Latin verses a lover exclaims:

> If I die, how will you enter into heaven's delights—
> when the joys of heaven are barred to homicides?[10]

And in the story of Saint Basil, told in a lyrical mode in an early eleventh-century sequence in the Cambridge Songs, the infatuated daughter of Proterius threatens her father, who wanted to refuse her the marriage for which she craved:

> I'll die, father, if now
> I'm not united with that boy . . .
> If you delay,
> you'll no longer have a daughter,
> but on the day of Judgment
> you'll suffer torment
> as if you'd murdered me.[11]

Again, in Provence, Raimbaut d'Aurenga (d. 1173) had played with the conceit that God might be a rival in love, desiring his beloved and snatching her away from him.[12] But Castelloza's combination of a threat of otherworld torment for her lover with an outrageous, triumphant moment of bravado for herself—"at the Judgment I'll be the more desired"—would be hard to parallel. At the end of time, she claims, the reversal will take place: Arman will be punished for his lovelessness, while she, forsaken on earth, will be longed for supremely. She will be God's beloved—even if in life her intent had been to rouse a very different kind of desire. The song's muted lament here rises to a climax that is both irreverent and thrilling.

The next song again begins in melancholy. The self-sufficiency of the loving heart, finding its quietus in poetry, now seems a delusion—in reality this means only a resignation to disappointment and pain. As Castelloza, composing, recalls her amorous desires, she longs for a human response; while telling of her own state of feeling (2. 1), she suddenly, without a word of introduction, mentions "him": "if he does not accept me soon . . ."[13] The Provençal word, *retener*, has the specific feudal connotations of accepting as a retainer—Castelloza would gladly be in such a dependent, subservient relation to Arman, rather than be ignored by him.

The plea for his mercy, and the protestations of her own unfaltering loyalty, whatever he may do (2. 2–3), culminate in the pitiable avowal: he deserves a more exalted ladylove than me! This motif (which may well owe something, directly or indirectly, to the affirmations of Ovid's Briseis to Achilles in the *Heroides*) is made circumstantial in Castelloza's fourth song. Here she quickly reverts to a fierce recognition of how deeply—although her loving devotion had been perfect—she has been neglected.

The fifth strophe is perhaps the most difficult to interpret precisely, since none of the other lyrics by *trobairitz* offers a parallel that would help us gauge the tone. Is Castelloza's seizing her lover's glove, and then restoring it, touching, or comic, or both inseparably?—

> Si pro·i agues, be·us membrera chantan—
> aic vostre gan,
> qu'enblei ab gran tremor;
> pueis aic paor
> que·i aguesetz dampnage
> d'aicella que·us rete,
> amics—per qu'ieu dese
> l'i tornei; car ben cre
> que no·i ai podiratge!

> If it helped me, I'd remind you in my singing
> that I had your glove,
> which, all trembling, I snatched away;
> then I was afraid
> you would have trouble for that
> from her who holds you as her dependent,
> my friend—so that I afterwards
> returned the glove; for I am sure
> that I have not first claim on it!

The opening—"If it helped me, I'd remind you . . . "—confronts us with a public-private irony similar to that in the first song: even in half admitting that to recall the embarrassing episode to his mind will not help her regain his love (which should imply that she'll keep silent about it), Castelloza cannot—or pretends she cannot—prevent herself from reminding him: the song, as the conclusion makes explicit, is, after all, addressed to him. There seems to be an element of self-mockery in her account of the glove escapade; at the same time, I would see it as linking with the strophe that follows (2.6)—as a particular, involuntarily comic, instance of the woes that may befall ladies who in loving take the active part, the part that was mostly held to be the prerogative of knights. It is knightly to obtain a love token from a lady (though not to grab it from her, like the young, foolish Parzival, or to accept it and then lose it, like the troubadour Guiraut de Bornelh)[14]—but what if a lady wants a token from the man she loves? Castelloza tells how she deliberately flouted a social norm, and then suddenly felt afraid of having done so. At the close of the strophe, I have the sense that she has moved beyond comedy: the daredevil impulse, she acknowledges, was swiftly followed by humility.

Her lover is a "retainer" in the service of another lady, whom she cannot hope to rival; it would be petty for her to discountenance him in that lady's eyes (and—as her allusion to her trembling fear may imply—if she did so, she could be sure of earning his scorn forever after).

The two *tornadas* diverge in tone: in the first, Castelloza may well recall Almucs' song, already mentioned, in which she sets down conditions for relenting to the lover who has been disloyal. Castelloza, by contrast, refuses to make conditions—her love is too absolute for that. And yet a censure of her lover, comparable to those which Almucs had once made, may also lurk behind her paradoxical mode of expression: for how can a man both be the "pillar of honor" and be fickle to the woman to whom he had once promised lifelong love? In her second *tornada*, composed for him, Castelloza reaffirms that her own love can never become fickle: for her he will always be the "Fair Name" (Bels Noms— the *senhal*, in the customary way, conceals his real identity); and her power to continue living will always depend on remaining confident in the dignity of her ideal.

The third song begins, in its imaginative situation, at a later point in time. Now Castelloza looks back on the days, long since past, when Arman had promised her his unwavering faith. Her thoughts then turn to—in Juliet's words—"I should have been more strange, I must confess . . ." It was imprudent to have given her heart so candidly, to have been so palpably the seeker and not the sought, hoping to find in Arman a similar openness and refusal to be bound by conventions. The love— or is it simply longing?—becomes even more intense in disappointment: "Indeed I love you the more" (3.2). And the absence of outgoing love from him creates within herself a space in which love strives for, and at times attains, self-sufficiency: "I consider myself healed, my friend, by my own devotion, when I implore you—for this is right for me" (3. 3).

This strophe closes with an impulse of humility, another intimation that her lover would deserve a more admirable beloved than she. This again points forward to the final song, where the thought becomes most poignant in its specific application, Castelloza affirming that she is willing to take second place to the other woman, to whom her lover has become irrevocably bound. This motif is, to my knowledge, without parallel in medieval love lyric.

Despite all her attempts to make her state of loving into something inwardly complete, that can dispense with solace from the lover outside her, Castelloza is again and again overcome by a sense that this is not wholly possible for her. She does need his comfort still, even if only rarely, in order to keep alive (3. 4); with a bitter irony she admits, her attachment may be only a "minor malady"—yet this too can, if she is neglected totally, bring about her death.

The final strophe of this song is the most problematic:

Tot lo maltrach e·l dampnage
que per vos m'es escaritz
vos fai grasir mos lignage—
e sobre totz mos maritz.
E s'anc fes ves mi faillida,
perdon la·us per bona fe,
e prec que veingnaz a me
depueis que aurez ausida
ma chanson—que·us faz fiansa,
sai trobetz bella semblansa!

All the affliction and harm
that have been my lot because of you,
my birth makes me thank you for these—
and my husband above all.
And if you have ever failed me,
I forgive you, in good faith,
and I beg you to come back to me
after you shall have heard
my song—for, I give you my pledge,
you will find a fair welcome here!

René Lavaud, taking *lignage* in the third line in the concrete sense of "kinsfolk," and emending the reading *vos* of the manuscripts to *me·l*, suggested that Castelloza means, Arman's rank is so high that her relatives, and most of all her husband, welcome her passion for him and approve of her unhappy love affair. William Paden, retaining the manuscript reading *vos*, translates: "My family makes *you* welcome, and especially my husband." Yet this complaisance of family and husband does not sound psychologically convincing, nor is it borne out by any indications elsewhere in the four songs. Should one not see *lignage* as referring to Castelloza's "ancestry" or "birth," which, as her other allusions make clear, is less distinguished than Arman's? Is she not saying: "since I am of lower birth than you, it is inevitable that I should suffer through loving you, and my husband is glad that you do not bring me unalloyed happiness through extramarital love"? This would accord well, also, with the way Castelloza's thought continues—"And if you have ever failed me, I forgive you, in good faith"—leading to the ardent invitation to him to return, with its implicit sensual promise.

The fourth song I would see both as the culmination of the thoughts expressed in the other three and as Castelloza's culminating poetic achievement. Here she adds also the technical refinement of *coblas capfinadas*—the device of echoing the close of one strophe in the opening of

the next. The song begins with her melancholy acceptance that she has
been deserted, and her thought of dying, since her own love cannot be
quenched. Arman does not want to *leave* his new beloved (4. 1), so she
herself, spurned, must *leave* this world (4. 2). But then Castelloza's thoughts
turn to a very different solution of her woes, to a compromise: if he does
not want her as his "dependent," can he not still use welcoming, friendly
words to her, instead of ignoring her disdainfully? His new lady need not
be jealous if he gives Castelloza such crumbs of comfort, and Castelloza
in her turn pledges never again to reproach Arman jealously about his
new love service, never again to remind him that he had once promised
this service to her "all the days of your life" (compare 3. 1). She is now
ready to accept a subordinate share of his being:

> *Partir* m'en er, mas no·m degna,
> que morta m'an li conssir;
> e pos no·ill platz que·m retegna,
> vueilla·m d'aitant hobesir—
> c'ab sos avinens respos
> me tegna mon cor joyos;
> e ja a sidonz non tir
> s'ie·l fas d'aitan enardir,
> qu'ieu no·l prec per mi que·s tegna
> de *leis* amar ni *servir.*
>
> *Leis serva*—mas mi·n revegna,
> que no·m lais del tot morir . . .

> *Leave* I must, since he disprizes me,
> for troubling thoughts have put me to death;
> and since it does not please him to accept me,
> let him yield to me at least in this—
> that with ungrudging answers from him
> I may keep my heart lifted high;
> and let it not displease his lady
> if I encourage him so far,
> for I don't implore that for my sake he cease
> from loving or *serving her.*
>
> *Serve her* he shall—but return to me from her:
> let him not let me die entirely . . .

What alternatives could there be? Only to die, or to seek consolation
in loving another man. While in 4. 3 Castelloza seems to conjure up this
second thought, half beseeching, half threatening—"do not will me to
turn elsewhere"—in the next strophe she readily concedes it is out of the
question, since of other knights "I desire not a single one."
From this the fourth and fifth strophes rise to a climax of erotic invi-

tation, where Castelloza comes closest to some moments in the countess
of Dia's songs. Where previously (4. 2) she had hoped for ungrudging
responses (*avinens respos*) from Arman, and her assurances that his new
lady need have no jealous fears implied that such *respos* were a matter
of fair words only, now Castelloza admits that her thoughts had been
more sensual: she wants no mere courtesies, she wants to embrace him
again as a lover. The expressions in 4. 4–5 all suggest that in lovemaking,
too, hers is the passionately active part—she longs to enfold and embrace him (not to *be* enfolded and embraced)—and at last she arrives at
a candid, deeply serious affirmation of her body's hunger, and of how
she could be physically revived by his love.

These brief indications of the movements of mind and feeling in the
four songs suggest, I think, that there is a dramatic progression extending
over the four, and that they can, without forcing the texts, be perceived
as an imaginative unity. From the stinging reproaches of disloyalty at the
opening of the first song—as if she had an exclusive right to Arman—
and from her realization of how foolhardy, in social terms, she has been
in offering her love so unreservedly, without ever wondering "if thou
think'st I am too quickly won," Castelloza works her way to a resigned
recognition of the rival lady, as if to say "Let her have pride of place in
your life, but don't shut me out altogether." The unfailing loyalty to Arman, that she has proclaimed throughout her songs, reveals itself at the
last as inseparable from a never-ceasing sensual craving for him. In her
last song Castelloza in effect invites Arman to share enjoying her love
with enjoying that of the woman whom he loves more. She will not try
to win him away completely or permanently, if only she can welcome
him now and then. Here her motifs come closest to those of Briseis in
Ovid (*Heroides* 3)—Briseis who pleads with Achilles to be allowed to
remain his concubine, even if she has only the lowliest role in his life,
rather than to be parted from him entirely. Castelloza may indeed be
drawing upon Briseis' verse-epistle here, recreating it freely, though one
cannot be sure from her words alone whether she had firsthand knowledge of the *Heroides* (as seems to me probable with the countess of Dia).

The countess and Almucs de Castelnau were women who (at least in
poetry) had chosen their own style of behavior in love, rather than ac-
quiesce in the expectations of the men they loved. Castelloza also chooses,
yet with a sense that in the last resort her mode of choosing is quixotic
and fruitless. To be serenely, loyally accepted by the man she loves, on
equal terms, is something she can dream about; but in waking existence
the acceptance is only momentary, the serenity quickly changes into tormented uncertainty. Yet if on one occasion her lover solaced her in her
sorrow (1. 4), even the thought that he might do so again helps to make
existence bearable. I do not think, like the recent editor, Paden, that Cas-

telloza's attitude "borders on masochism . . . in which satisfaction comes from suffering or humiliation apart from any sexual pleasure."[15] It is the respite from misery, however brief, that counts for Castelloza, as well as the sense that, even if she has been deserted, it is better to have known joy such as hers than to have shrunk away from giving her love spontaneously. And at the close of the fourth song, it is clearly in moments of sexual pleasure that Castelloza still seeks her contentment, though she is also aware, realistically, that this contentment will always be fugitive.

At the same time, Castelloza knows a satisfaction that is not directly sexual—yet again the source of this satisfaction is not in suffering or humiliation: it is in poetry. Composing helps make abandonment livable. To create something beautiful out of loneliness, to wrest some recollections out of the anguish—this the loving woman, the projection of the poet Castelloza, sees as her reason for existence. While often, in dramatic hyperbole or in threat, she speaks of dying, she is also aware that to languish irrevocably would be an admission of failure: it would cancel once and for all what she has proclaimed to be her poetic task—the affirming of her immutable devotion. So each thought of dying for love leads back to reviving thoughts—reproachful, or pleading, or magnanimous, or erotic.

As a poet, Castelloza is no virtuoso: her language is intently, even narrowly, concentrated; she does not create dazzling forms in the way, for instance, of her somewhat older contemporary, Raimbaut de Vaqueiras. Yet she makes articulate a range of thoughts and imaginings that no man among the troubadours had expressed; she uncovers new inner landscapes of the loving mind; and her voice has a timbre that, once one has listened to her attentively, could not be mistaken for that of any other poet of the age.

In my translations, I have used as primary basis the new edition by William Paden and his collaborators. Paden has followed principally the manuscript N, which preserves some important readings unknown to the four other manuscripts and alone preserves Castelloza's fourth song. However, in the verses signaled below, I have reverted to the readings of René Lavaud (who kept chiefly to manuscript A for the first three songs), because I believe that they remain textually preferable. While Lavaud, in *Les troubadours cantaliens*, based his text of Castelloza's first three songs on Schultz' *Die provenzalischen Dichterinnen*, he added valuable corrections and a series of notes, and also gave the text of the fourth song. In my notes to the songs, where my translation is based on Lavaud's text and not Paden's, the lines in question are cited from Lavaud, with the initial L., and occasionally with a brief indication of why they have been preferred (a full textual discussion would exceed the scope of this essay). Punctuation in the strophes cited above and in the translations is my own; it does not always match either the Paden or the Lavaud edition.[16]

NOTES

1. The majority of poems by *trobairitz* can be found collected in O. Schultz, *Die provenzalischen Dichterinnen*; Jules Véran, *Les poétesses provençales*; and Meg Bogin, *The Women Troubadours*. Of these collections, only that of Véran includes the *sirventes* of Germonda (or Gormonda) of Montpellier, "Greu m'es a durar" (pp. 196–205), and the anonymous "Quan vei los praz verdesir" (pp. 64–67). None of the three collections includes Azalais d'Altier's "Tanz salutz e tantas amors," ed. V. Crescini, *Zeitschrift für romanische Philologie* 14 (1890): 128–132, or the piece "No·m posc mudar," attributed to Raimon Jordan in the unique manuscript, but more probably the work of an anonymous *trobairitz* (see the recent edition and translation by Martín de Riquer, *Los trovadores*, vol. 1, pp. 576–577). Most important in the present context is that the three collections of *trobairitz* all exclude Castelloza's fourth song, "Per joi que d'amor m'avegna."

2. There is an excellent text of the countess' songs, with notes and translation, in Riquer, vol. 2, pp. 791–802. The attribution to the countess of the anonymous woman's strophes in the *tenso* "Amics, en greu cossirier," where the partner is Raimbaut d'Aurenga, seems dubious: see most recently ibid., vol. 1, p. 452, vol. 2, pp. 791–793.

3. Compare J. Boutière and A. H. Schutz, *Biographies des troubadours*, p. 334, and the judicious discussion by Dietmar Rieger, "Die *trobairitz* in Italien: Zu den altprovenzalischen Dichterinnen," *Cultura Neolatina* 31 (1971): 210–212.

4. Rieger, "Die *trobairitz* in Italien," loc. cit.

5. Compare D'Arco Silvio Avalle in *Geschichte der Textüberlieferung der antiken und mittelalterlichen Literatur*, vol. 2, p. 292.

6. *The Penguin Book of Oral Poetry*, ed. Ruth Finnegan, p. 14 f.; the two songs are on pp. 20 and 30 respectively.

7. A fuller *vida*, published in 1701, allegedly from a manuscript of 1307, is now generally held to be a forgery: see especially the new edition of Castelloza by William D. Paden, Jr., et al., "The Poems of the *Trobairitz* Na Castelloza," *Romance Philology* 35 (1981): 158–182, at p. 159 f.

8. I have discussed this in detail in my *Women Writers of the Middle Ages: From Perpetua to Marguerite Porete*, chap. 5.

9. The complete text, with translation and discussion, is in ibid., chap. 4.

10. *Beiträge zur Kunde der lateinischen Literatur des Mittelalters*, ed. J. Werner, no. 117 ("Conpar nulla tibi"), vv. 18–19 (p. 47).

11. *Carmina Cantabrigiensia*, ed. Karl Strecker, no. 30a, st. 3a (p. 80). See Hrotsvit's *Basilius*, above.

12. W. T. Pattison, *The Life and Works of the Troubadour Raimbaut d'Orange*, no. 22 (pp. 142–143).

13. There is a comparable effect in the renowned eleventh-century Latin woman's love lament "Levis exsurgit Zephirus" (text and translation in my *The Medieval Lyric*, pp. 92 f.), where the man to whom the whole song is addressed is not mentioned before the final strophe ("Tu saltim, veris gratia . . . ").

14. Guiraut de Bornelh, *Sämtliche Lieder*, nos. 25–28.

15. Paden et al., p. 165.

16. Of the other works containing songs by Castelloza, the three collections cited in n. 1 all contain the first three songs. Both Véran and Bogin reproduce the text of Schultz. Véran's translations, however, are simply those of Lavaud, written out as continuous prose: they possess no independent value. Castelloza's second song, "Ja de chantar," is edited with a fresh translation and notes in Riquer, vol. 3, pp. 1328–1330, and in *Anthologie des troubadours*, ed. Pierre Bec, pp. 284–289.

Castelloza's Songs

I

[1]   My friend, if I found you welcoming,
modest[1] and gracious and compassionate,
I'd love you well—whilst now I call to mind
that I find you bad to me, contemptible and proud.
And yet I make songs so as to let others hear
of your good character—for I cannot bear
not to have you praised by all the world,
even when you most hurt me and make me angriest.

[2]   I shall never think of you as deserving,
or love you with all my heart, loyally,
before I see if it might serve my turn[2]
were I to show you a heart hostile and rancorous . . .
No, I shan't do it: I don't want to let you say
that I ever had the heart to fail you—
as then you would have some justification[3]
if in any of my acts indeed I failed you.

[3]   I know well this way is right for me,
even if everyone says it is unseemly
for a lady to implore a knight on her own account
and to preach at him always, at such length.
But those who say this have no means to judge—
for I want to prove, rather than surrender by dying,[4]
that in imploring I am sweetly refreshed,
when I implore the one who makes me think harsh thoughts.[5]

[4]   Whoever reproaches me for loving you
is quite mad, since it accords with me so gently—
one who speaks thus does not know how it is with me:
he's never seen you with the eyes with which I saw you
when you told me not to sorrow any more—

for, any moment, it could come about
that once again I'd have the joy of that.
Even from saying this my heart takes joy.

[5]   I set all other love at naught,
and you must know that no joy ever sustains me
except for yours, that lightens me and revives
where most anguish and most harm beset me.
And I believe through my plaints and lais I will always
have joy in you, my friend—I can't become a convert—
nor do I have joy, or expect any solace,
save insofar as I'll gain it while I sleep.

[6]   I don't know how to confront you after this,
for by fair means and by foul I have probed
your impassive heart—mine does not weary of the probing.
And I send no messenger—it is I myself who tell you,
and I *shall* die, if you will not lighten me
with any joy; and if you let me die,
you'll commit sin, and be in torment for it,
and at the Judgment I'll be the more desired!

2

[1] I ought not to have any desire to sing,
          for the more I sing
     the worse it goes with my loving,
          as in me lament
     and weeping make their lodging,
     for I have pledged my heart and myself
     to a thankless service,
     and if he does not accept me soon,
     I have waited overlong.

[2] Oh my fair friend, at least show a fair face
          to me before
     I die of sorrowing,
          for those in love
     accuse you of being barbarous,
     since no joy comes to me
     from you—though I don't recant for that
     from loving in good faith,
     at all times, heart unwavering.

[3] For you I shall never have a heart truant
         or full of wiles,
     even if I find that makes you worse to me—
         as I hold this loyally
     in great honor in my heart.
     Yet more, I reflect—when I call to mind
     the prized qualities that inform you—
     and I realize that a lady
     of higher station is right for you.

[4] Since I first saw you I have done your bidding,
         and in spite of all,
     my friend, found you none the better inclined;
         no messenger of yours
     ever implores me, or reports
     that you're turning your bridle my way.
     You do nothing at all, my friend!
     And since joy does not bear me up,
     the pain almost makes me rage.

[5] If it helped me, I'd remind you in my singing
         that I had your glove,
     which, all trembling, I snatched away;
         then I was afraid
     you would have trouble for that
     from her who holds you as her dependent,
     my friend—so that I afterwards
     returned the glove; for I am sure
     that I have not first claim on it!

[6] I realize that knights work their own undoing,
         for they beseech
     ladies, more than ladies do them—
         they have no other
     riches or sovereignty than in beseeching.
     So, when a lady decides
     to love, it is she who must beseech
     the knight, if in him she sees
     prowess and knightliness.

[7] Lady Almucs,[6] I still
     love the source of my hurt,
     for he, pillar of honor,
     has a fickle heart towards me.

[8] Fair Name, I don't recant
my loving you forever,
for in this loving I find good faith,
always, and steadiness of heart.

3

[1] A very long absence you will have made it,
my friend, since you parted from me,
and to me it seems cruel and barbarous,
for you swore to me and pledged
that all the days of your life
you would have no lady but me;
and if you are caught up with another,
you have killed me and betrayed me—
for I had my hope in you,
that you would love me without need of doubting.

[2] Handsome friend, with high longing
I loved you, since you delighted me,
and I know I committed a folly,
for you have recoiled from me the more for that,[7]
since with you I never used subterfuge—[8]
and so you render me evil for good!
Indeed I love you the more—I do not recant that—
but love has seized me so fiercely
that I believe I can never have
well-being without your loving.

[3] I shall have set a wretched precedent
for other women who love,
since it is usual that men send a message
and words that are sifted and chosen well.
As for me, I consider myself healed,
my friend, by my own devotion,
when I implore you—for this is right for me,
since even a worthier woman is enriched
if from you she wins some satisfaction
of kissing or close company.

[4] Let me be cursed if ever I had a fickle
heart towards you, or behaved flightily!
No lover, however exalted,

was ever coveted by me.
No, I am pensive and filled with pain
as you do not recall my love—
if no joy comes to me from you,
you will soon find my life is finished:
for, with a minor malady,
a lady dies, if no one frees her from it.[9]

[5] All the affliction and harm
that have been my lot because of you,
my birth makes me thank you for these—[10]
and my husband above all.
And if you have ever failed me,
I forgive you, in good faith,
and I beg you to come back to me
after you shall have heard
my song—for, I give you my pledge,
you will find a fair welcome here![11]

4

[1] From now on I'll not care to exult
in joy that comes to me from love,
for I do not believe he cherishes me,
he who never wished to hear
my fair words or my songs—
and yet there never was a season[12]
that I could do without him.
No, I fear I shall have to die of it,
since I see he lives with another woman
whom, for my sake, he does not want to *leave.*

[2] *Leave* I must, since he disprizes me,
for troubling thoughts have put me to death;
and since it does not please him to accept me,
let him yield to me at least in this—
that with ungrudging answers from him
I may keep[13] my heart lifted high;
and let it not displease his lady
if I encourage him so far,
for I don't implore that for my sake he cease
from loving or *serving her.*

[3] *Serve her* he shall—but return to me from her:
let him not let me die entirely—

for I fear it will extinguish me,
that love of him, by which he makes me languish.
Ah, my friend, valiant and good
(for you are the best that ever was),
do not will me to turn elsewhere,
since you wish to do and say nothing to me—
so that one day I steel myself
against loving or *welcoming you.*

[4] I *welcome you,* whatever may befall me—
all the affliction and cares;
and let no knight take an interest
in me, since I desire not a single one.
Fair friend, fiercely I long for you,
you on whom I keep both eyes fixed;
and it delights me to gaze on you,
for I could never single out another so fair.
I pray to God that with my arms I may enfold you,
for no other can make me *rich.*

[5] *Rich* am I, if only you bring to mind
how I could come into a place
where I would kiss you and embrace you,
for, with that, new life could come
into my body, which you make yearn
for you greatly and covetously.
My friend, do not let me die:
since I cannot withhold myself from you,
give me a loving look, to revive me
and to kill my cares!

NOTES TO THE TRANSLATIONS

1. It is also possible that *umil* is here used in the specifically courtly sense of "generous in feeling, capable of showing mercy, benign" (see the excursus "The Concept *umiltà*" in my *Medieval Latin and the Rise of European Love-Lyric,* vol. 1, pp. 158–162).

2. Tro que veirai si ja-m valria re, L.

3. Qu'auriatz pois qualque razonamen, L.

4. Qu'ieu vuoill proar, enans que-me lais morir, L.

5. Quan prec cellui don ai greu pessamen, L. (the reading *greu* is corroborated by *douz* in the previous verse).

6. The unique manuscript H of Almucs de Castelnau's song gives her name as Almucs both in the *vida* and in the song; manuscript N of Castelloza's "Ja de chantar" has Almurs. The other manuscripts have various forms; no manuscript gives the form Almueis, which is an editorial conjecture.

7. Que plus m'en etz escaritz, L. (the sense cannot support *encarzitz*, 'made dear').

8. Qu'anc non fis vas vos ganchida, L.

9. Mor dompna, s'om tot no-il lanssa, L. I am not happy about Paden's ingenious *s'om no cal lansa*, 'if no man apply a lancet'—less because of the conjecture that *lansa*, 'lance,' can also mean 'lancet' than because I know no parallel for *calar*, or *caler*, meaning 'to apply.'

10. Me-l fai grazir mos linhatge, L. (compare his notes, vol. 3, p. 88 f.), but this emendation may not be necessary—see discussion above.

11. Sai trobetz bella semblansa, L.

12. Ni anc no fon la sazos, L.

13. Grammatically, in this verse (*me tegna mon cor joyos*), *tegna* could be the first or third present subjunctive of *tener*; I prefer to take it as first person here (Lavaud and Paden take it as third).

BIBLIOGRAPHY

Primary Works

Bec, Pierre, ed. *Anthologie des troubadours*. Paris, 1979.

Bogin, Meg. *The Women Troubadours*. New York, 1976.

Lavaud, René. *Les troubadours cantaliens*. Vols. 2 and 3. Aurillac, 1910.

Paden, William D., Jr., et al., eds. "The Poems of the *Trobairitz* Na Castelloza." *Romance Philology* 35 (1981): 158–182.

Riquer, Martín de. *Los trovadores*. 3 vols. Barcelona, 1975.

Schultz, O. *Die provenzalischen Dichterinnen*. Altenburg, 1888.

Véran, Jules. *Les poétesses provençales*. Paris, 1946.

Related Works

Avalle, D'Arco Silvio. "Überlieferungsgeschichte der altprovenzalischen Literatur." In vol. 2 of *Geschichte der Textüberlieferung der antiken und mittelalterlichen Literatur*. 2 vols. Zurich, 1961–1964.

Boutière, J., and A. H. Schutz. *Biographies des troubadours*. 2nd ed. Paris, 1973.

Dronke, Peter. *Medieval Latin and the Rise of European Love-Lyric*. 2nd ed., 2 vols. Oxford, 1968.

———. *The Medieval Lyric*. 2nd ed. London and New York, 1977.

———. *Women Writers of the Middle Ages: From Perpetua to Marguerite Porete*. Cambridge, Eng., 1983.

Finnegan, Ruth, ed. *The Penguin Book of Oral Poetry*. London, 1978.

Guiraut de Bornelh. *Sämtliche Lieder*. Ed. A. Kolsen. 2 vols. Halle, 1910.

Pattison, W. T. *The Life and Works of the Troubadour Raimbaut d'Orange*. Minneapolis, 1952.

Rieger, Dietmar. "Die *trobairitz* in Italien: Zu den altprovenzalischen Dichterinnen." *Cultura Neolatina* 31 (1971): 205–223.

Strecker, Karl. *Carmina Cantabrigiensia*. Berlin, 1926.

Werner, J. *Beiträge zur Kunde der lateinischen Literatur des Mittelalters*. 2nd ed. Aarau, 1905.

THE GERMAN MYSTIC

Mechthild of Magdeburg

JOHN HOWARD

For a woman whose writings enjoyed some degree of popularity both during and shortly after her lifetime, surprisingly little is known of the life of Mechthild of Magdeburg. The only sources available on the subject are various autobiographical statements made in her sole work, *The Flowing Light of the Godhead*, a brief prologue to this work (not written by her), certain additions to the Latin translation,[1] and what one can deduce from her language, style, and frequently vague allusions to contemporary events.

Book 4. 2 is the main autobiographical section of her work, for it is here that Mechthild provides the reader with bits of information on her youth. At the age of twelve she received her first "greeting" from the Holy Spirit, which she found so overwhelming that she could "never afterward have surrendered to any great daily sin." Until this time she had been "one of the simplest people" and knew "nothing of the devil's wickedness, of the frailty of the world . . . [and] the falseness of spiritual people." She continued to have visions every day for the next thirty-one years—she was thus forty-three when book 4. 2 was composed. Since this section was written between 1250 and 1255,[2] one can place the date of her birth roughly between 1207 and 1212.[3]

Mechthild was undoubtedly born in the vicinity of Magdeburg in Lower Saxony and, to judge from her style, her references to courtly life and customs, her familiarity with the courtly love lyric (*Minnesang*), and her obvious culture and refinement, she was at the least well born. Her family, who may even have belonged to the nobility, were no doubt wealthy. Of siblings only one is known, namely, a certain Baldwin. The sole information concerning him comes from two annotations made in the Latin version of the *Flowing Light*.[4] From these we learn that he was well educated, that he entered the Dominican order (quite possibly at Mechthild's instigation), becoming subprior at Halle, and that he single-handedly made a copy of the Bible which was apparently read at table.

About 1230 Mechthild left home and went to Magdeburg, where she knew but one person, whom she assiduously avoided. Here she became a Beguine[5] and continued to have her visions for the next twenty years. During this period she testifies that with the "weapons" of her soul she "conquered the body to such an extent that . . . I was never but tired, ill, and weak" with "many a grave illness" (4. 2). Thus, by her own statement, Mechthild underwent a rather severe self-imposed regimen of asceticism for a lengthy period of time, at the conclusion of which she became seriously ill. It was at this point (approximately 1250) that "mighty Love" came and "filled me so greatly with these marvels" that she could no longer keep silent.[6] Although compelled inwardly to commit to writing what she had seen, she was beset with anxiety. So it was that seeking guidance and advice she approached her confessor, who reassured her: "he said I should go forth joyfully; God Who had called me would take good care of me" (4. 2). It is apparently also to this confessor that posterity must in some part be thankful for the *Flowing Light*, for it was he who "commanded me to do that for which I often weep in shame because my great unworthiness stands clear before my eyes—that was, that he ordered a contemptible woman to write this book out of God's heart and mouth" (4. 2).

During the next fifteen years, so we learn from the prologue, Mechthild wrote down her visions randomly on loose sheets and in her own dialect of Low German. These she in turn handed over to a certain Heinrich, most probably the very confessor who had urged her to write in the first place. Posterity has generally accepted that this was none other than Heinrich of Halle, a well-known Dominican and lector of Neuruppin, who had been a student of the illustrious Albertus Magnus.[7] This compiler organized these loose sheets into book form, parts of which most certainly circulated during Mechthild's lifetime.[8] Certain also is it that her work garnered a fair share of criticism—some have gone so far as to speculate that she was accused of heresy.[9] Be that as it may, one need but read the *Flowing Light* to understand why she could have come under attack. She does not hesitate, for example, to denounce in rather strong terms what she saw as abuses within the Church or as laxity on the part of the clergy. She speaks not infrequently of "corrupt Christianity" and "poor Christianity"; the Church she characterizes as a "maiden" whose skin is "filthy, for she is unclean and unchaste" (5. 34). Again: "God calls the cathedral clergy goats because their flesh stinks of impurity with regard to eternal truth, before His Holy Trinity . . ." (6. 3). These and similar utterances may have placed her in such disfavor that there was talk of burning her work. Mechthild certainly makes an allusion in this direction when she writes: "I was warned about this book and was told by many people that if there were no wish to preserve it, then flames could consume it." But a few lines later God reassures her: "no one may burn the truth" (2. 26).

She was accused of being unlearned and lay, which she readily admits, though she does not consider it to be cogent criticism.[10] She tells, for instance, in book 2. 4, of seeing a vision of John the Baptist saying mass for a "poor maiden" (obviously Mechthild herself). Later, she defends herself against the attack that John the Baptist could not say mass since he was a layman—the implication being that she was too unlearned to recognize this. Her critics she calls "my pharisees," and the bitterness of her counterattack bespeaks her conception of the intensity of the criticism leveled against her: "Never could a pope or bishop or priest speak the Word of God as well as did John the Baptist . . . Was this a layman? Teach me, you blind! Your lies and your hatred will not be forgiven without suffering!" (6. 36). The fact that here and elsewhere Mechthild felt the need to defend herself indeed demonstrates that parts of her work had circulated during her lifetime and that she had come under fire.[11]

In book 5. 12, Mechthild writes that Heinrich (her compiler?) had expressed surprise at the "masculine words" which appear in her book. Indeed, as one reads through this masterpiece of German mysticism, one gradually realizes that in a significantly large number of instances where Mechthild uses the masculine pronoun, she is obviously referring to herself. Her statement continues: "I wonder why that surprises you. But it grieves me more to the heart that I, a sinful woman, *must* so write."[12] Mechthild thus felt it imperative to write in the masculine, probably to head off any criticism she knew would be directed at her because she was a woman. Whether or not any such reproach was actually made we shall never know—nowhere does she defend herself against the charge. Nevertheless, there can be no doubt that the general position of women in the thirteenth century contributed to a certain extent to her difficulties. Yet, on the other hand, it must not be forgotten that few people, men or women, receive praise for being overly critical of their contemporaries. This was especially true in the Middle Ages, and Mechthild herself probably expected nothing less than rebuke from those whom she so sharply castigated.

Around 1270 Mechthild left the Beguines at Magdeburg and entered the Cistercian convent at Helfta near Eisleben in Saxony.[13] This convent had been relocated from Rodersdorf to Helfta in 1258 by its abbess, Gertrude of Hackeborn (1232–1292),[14] who exerted every effort to generate within the convent an atmosphere conducive to the contemplative life. This she approached by an insistence on rigorous study—primarily of scripture and of the liberal arts. She was so successful that during her lifetime Helfta became a center of mysticism in Germany and radiated influence in all directions. Also at Helfta at this time were Mechthild of

Hackeborn (1241–1299) and Gertrude of Helfta (1256–1302). Due to her artistry as a songstress the former had earned the epithet of Nightingale of the Lord[15] and was the author of a collection of mystical visions entitled *Liber specialis gratiae*. Gertrude (later known as the Great), who had entered the convent as a child, was a scholar of some repute; her *Legatus divinae pietatis* has been characterized as "one of the finest literary products of Christian mysticism."[16] She is credited with being one of the first exponents of devotion to the Sacred Heart, which she believed had been revealed to her in several visions.[17]

It was in this spiritual atmosphere that Mechthild spent the last dozen or so years of her life, when she composed what was to become the seventh and final book of the *Flowing Light*.[18] Little is known of these last years, although one can easily imagine that she was held in high regard and reverence by the sisters.[19] We can infer from her own statements that her health was failing and that her eyesight in particular was very poor. During the composition of book 7 she was certainly quite infirm and may have been totally blind: "You [that is, God] now clothe and feed me out of the goodness of others"; "You have taken from me the power of my eyes" and "You have taken from me the power of my hands" (7. 64).

Mechthild died at Helfta in 1282 or shortly thereafter.[20] All her life she had been apprehensive about the manner of her death. In a previous vision she had been told by God: "When that happens, I will draw My breath and you shall come to Me as to a magnet" (5. 32). If her passing was as serene and dignified as described by Gertrude (*Legatus divinae pietatis* 1. 5. 7), it was surely so.

The Flowing Light of the Godhead is an assortment of mystical visions, letters, parables, reflections, allegories, prayers, criticism, and advice. But the particular arrangement of these bits and pieces as transmitted to us is not Mechthild's doing. It is obvious to even the casual reader that she had no intention of composing a book—she simply wrote down what came to her as it came to her. Yet she frequently makes reference to her "book": "Of this book and its writer" (2. 26); "this book has . . . come . . . from God" (4. 2); "of the writing of this book" (4. 13). Mechthild was thus certainly aware that Heinrich of Halle was compiling her material into a book and that at least some of her writings were circulating in book form. Nevertheless, because Heinrich was the final editor and followed his own notions concerning organization,[21] the end result is that Mechthild's work is of no value for an investigation into her spiritual development.

Latin translations of the *Flowing Light* were apparently made shortly after Mechthild's death,[22] thereby making her work accessible to a much wider audience than could ever have been gained by the original Low

German (which has been lost to posterity). The speculation has been made that this audience extended as far south as Italy and that because of Mechthild's alleged popularity there Dante took her as the model for his Matelda (*Purgatory* 28. 40).[23] Although at one time very popular, this thesis has been well refuted.[24]

In 1344 or 1345, Mechthild's book was cast into Alemannic by Heinrich of Nördlingen at Basel. Not so much a mystic himself, this Heinrich did much to further the cause of mysticism, particularly by encouraging others to write and maintaining an active correspondence with many contemporary mystics, among them Johannes Tauler, Margareta Ebner, and Christina Ebner. From his correspondence it is clear that Heinrich made his translation directly from the Low German of the original and that his translation circulated widely in southern Germany.[25] Then, in the second half of the same century, another Heinrich (of Rumerschein) sent a copy of Heinrich of Nördlingen's translation to Margareta of the Golden Ring at the convent of Einsiedeln. After several relocations this version found its way back to the monastic library at Einsiedeln, where it remains to this day.[26]

Briefly, the surviving manuscripts of *The Flowing Light of the Godhead* are:

1. Einsiedeln, Stiftsbibliothek 277, leaves 1–166—this is the oldest German version, dating from the fourteenth century; it was first discovered in 1861 by Carl Greith[27] and published by Gall Morel in 1869.[28]

2. Würzburg, Minoritenkloster Nr. 1 110, leaves 40a–62b—German, dating from the fifteenth century.

3. Wolhusen (near Lucerne)—this version, dated 1517, is an attempt to translate from a Latin text back into German and is thus of no value for textual history.

4. Basel I, Parchment B IX 11, leaves 51–91—Latin version, dating from the fourteenth century.

5. Basel II, Paper A VIII 6, leaves 99 ff.—Latin, also dating from the fourteenth century.[29]

The styles used by Mechthild range from one end of the spectrum to the other. She employs both prose and verse, both monologue and dialogue—and she feels no qualms about mixing these at random. Often in the midst of a prose monologue she will switch abruptly to verse, or she will compose an entire dialogue in verse. Of particular interest to the student of literature is her extensive use of imagery and metaphor. Of the many such devices Mechthild employs, three are especially worthy of note.[30]

The *Flowing Light* is rich in the imagery and motifs from the culture surrounding the court—its life and customs. The images of God and Christ as emperor, king, knight, lord, and so on, which extend back to

patristic times, had by the Middle Ages become so expanded and accepted that entire works were written where the story of Christ and the
apostles was told in terms of a warlord and his retinue, complete with
all the trappings (see the Old Saxon *Heliand*, for instance). Throughout
this period God often appears as the emperor of heaven, the feudal lord.
Mary is the empress, Christ is the imperial lord, the angels are princes
and knights. Together they comprise the heavenly host (where humanity
also plays a significant role), which under the banner of the cross and
armed with divine weapons—the helmet of salvation, the sword of faith,
and the shield of love—wages battle against the prince of hell.

In book 7. 1, Mechthild describes at length the crown which Christ
will receive at the day of judgment. On this crown she sees (among much
else) the earthly imperium depicted with all its inhabitants, from the mighty
prince to the lowly peasant. Again, in 4. 3, she sees Christianity in the
symbol of a crown, this one like a fortified castle which is constantly
besieged by a huge but miserable army led by a treacherous general, the
devil.

Many other fully developed instances of this image are present
throughout Mechthild's work, but it is also found in smaller degrees—
in turns of phrase and in terminology. For example, the soul undertakes
a journey to the court of God, God sits in the heavenly palace, Christ
appears as an imperial nobleman and gives her garments "which are
worn at court" (1. 4, 4. 17, 3. 1). Christ speaks to her in "courtly language which is not understood here in this kitchen," that is, in this world
(1. 2).

The mystical dance of the soul is an image which has origins in Neo-
platonism, whence it was adopted by Dionysius the Areopagite and
transplanted into Catholic mysticism. In this image, heavenly beings move
in a circular motion about their midpoint and creator. Likewise, the soul
moves in a circular motion while continually facing inward. This image,
employed poetically and artistically throughout the Middle Ages, finds
one of its more illustrious applications in Dante.[31] In book 1.44, Mechthild unites this time-honored image with the contemporary courtly custom of the spring dance: Christ appears to her in the form of a noble
youth; he and the virtues take part in a blessed dance, which Mechthild
is invited to join.

The metaphor of the drunkenness of the soul (or the imagery of wine,
in general) is found throughout both the Old and the New Testaments,
most prominently in the Song of Songs. It is, however, not limited to the
Jewish and Christian religions—one of the more widely known roles of
wine in religion is found in the Greek cult of Dionysius. Basically, the
inebriation of the soul embodies or symbolizes the pinnacle of the marvelous and the miraculous, the highest state of the mystical union of the

soul with God.[32] It is an image which has played a significant role in Christianity throughout the centuries, not only in its literature but in its liturgy: belief in the conversion of wine into the blood of Christ in the sacrament of communion is one of the central articles of Catholic faith.

Mechthild makes ample use of the wine symbol in several passages: "Our Lord lifted in His hands two golden cups, both of which were filled with living wine. In His left hand was the red wine of suffering and in the other hand was splendid consolation. Then our Lord said: blessed are they who drink this wine, for though I offer both out of divine love, yet the white is more noble in itself, but those who drink both the white and the red are the noblest of all" (2. 7). Again: "Whenever I consider that the heavenly Father is the blessed wine-pourer, and Jesus the cup, the Holy Spirit the pure wine, and how the full cup is the entire Trinity and love is the mighty cellar . . ." (2. 24). Yet again: "I especially asked God on behalf of my wine-pourer to pour for him the heavenly wine . . ." (2. 24). Mechthild is so taken with this image that in one instance she composes an entire poem on the subject of wine (3. 3).

Of course, this does not exhaust the richness and variety of the imagery in the *Flowing Light*. Mechthild also employs, for instance, the well-known mystical metaphor of the bride-soul and the Bridegroom-Christ (for example, 1. 22), the metaphor of the hunt (1. 3), the imagery of the dog (1. 20, 2. 3, 3. 1, 4. 1, and elsewhere), and an interesting allegory of a spiritual convent (7. 36; see the translations).

Of all the personalities which the Middle Ages produced, Mechthild of Magdeburg is one of the most interesting. She has earned an eminent and well-deserved place in the history of Catholic mysticism—no one has ever disputed this. But aside from her position in the general panorama, Mechthild must be credited with two very specific original accomplishments.[33] She was the first mystic to write in her native vernacular rather than in Latin, and she was the first in the history of Christian mysticism to record a personal vision of the Sacred Heart, a cult which was to come to full flower precisely at Helfta under Gertrude the Great and Mechthild of Hackeborn. Yet these accomplishments alone would not suffice to secure for her the high regard in which she is held were it not for the freshness, the originality, and the almost childlike naïveté of her style. Mechthild is quite simply interesting to read. .

The following translations are based on the Einsiedeln manuscript edited by Gall Morel in 1869 and are cross-checked where deemed necessary with the translation into modern German by Wilhelm Oehl, who often provides valuable textual annotations. The texts here have been arranged into five major categories (plus the prologue): autobiographical texts, criticism, heaven and hell, advice, and miscellany. There is, of course, in some instances an unavoidable degree of overlap between categories.

A conscientious attempt has been made, within this limited space, to give the reader as broad a sample as possible of the entire spectrum of Mechthild's thoughts and inspirations.

NOTES

1. The earliest German version of Mechthild's work, the Einsiedeln manuscript (compare below), contains the prologue in both Latin and German. The Latin versions, however, contain this prologue only in Latin. Other marginal annotations and references of a biographical nature are found spread throughout the Latin document but are missing from the German.

2. Hans Neumann, "Beiträge zur Textgeschichte des 'Fliessenden Lichts der Gottheit' und zur Lebensgeschichte Mechthilds von Magdeburg," *Nachrichten der Akademie der Wissenschaften in Göttingen* (1954): 27–80.

3. Ibid., pp. 55–58. The prologue informs us that Mechthild began writing in 1250; of the span between 1250 and 1255, Neumann seems to prefer the earlier date. This is also true for the date of her birth.

4. There is mention in book 4. 26 of the German version of a certain Baldwin, but whether or not this is Mechthild's brother cannot be determined. Compare ibid., p. 41, especially n.43.

5. The Beguines (the feminine counterparts of the Beghards, allegedly named after Lambert le Begue—that is, "the stammerer"—a revivalist preacher at Liége who died in 1177) were organizations of sisterhoods founded in the Netherlands in the twelfth century. The members led a rather austere and semireligious communal life, but no vows of any sort were taken. They were also free to hold property, to marry, and to leave the community at will. The aim of the Beguines (and of the Beghards) was strictly philanthropic, most of their time being spent in caring for the sick and the destitute, although some time was devoted to contemplation. These organizations were long suspected of and persecuted for heresy, to the extent that by the fifteenth century they had been greatly reduced in number and were mere charitable institutions. Few remain in existence today, with most of those being in Holland or, especially, in Belgium.

6. There is probably some correlation between Mechthild's severe asceticism, with its resultant illness, and her visions. As Rufus M. Jones writes of the *Flowing Light*: "There is a large element of pathology in the story, far too much reproduction of the experiences reported in the Song of Solomon, and unwholesome dialogues which mark this type of amorous, romantic, cloistered mysticism." See *The Flowering of Mysticism: The Friends of God in the Fourteenth Century*, p. 49.

7. Wilhelm Preger was the first to propose this idea, noting that the Basel Latin version (parchment) of Mechthild's work contains, in the title of book 2. 19, "de fratro Heinrico lectore, qui hunc librum compilavit." Preger quotes further: "Frater Heinricus dictus de Hallis, lector Rupinensis, admiratus de dictis et scriptis sororis Mechthildis tale ab ipsa accepit responsum . . ." To support this assertion he then cites the work of Johann Meyer, a fifteenth-century historian of the Dominican order. In the 1466 *Liber illustrium virorum de ordine praedicatorum*, Meyer writes: "Henricus de Hallis doctor, lector, qui inter alia sua opera sororis Mechthildis de monasterio Helpeda dicta et scripta collegit et in unum volumen redegit." Compare Wilhelm Preger, "Uber das unter dem Namen der Mechthild von Magdeburg jüngst herausgegebene Werk 'das fliessende Licht der Gottheit' und dessen Verfasserin," *Sitzungsberichte der königl. bayer. Akademie der Wissenschaften zu München*

2 (1869): 158–159. However, reservations to this thesis have been expressed by Neumann, "Beiträge," p. 69.

8. Probably at least the first five books and possibly also parts of book 6 circulated while she was still at Magdeburg. While the sequence of the composition of these books is mostly unknown, only the date and place of the composition of book 7 are definitely ascertainable—namely, at Helfta between 1270 and Mechthild's death circa 1282. Compare Neumann, "Beiträge," pp. 58–59.

9. Lucy Menzies, *The Revelations of Mechthild of Magdeburg*, p. xx. Although Mechthild was definitely unlearned in theology, there is no reason to believe that she was actually accused of heresy. Compare Wilhelm Oehl, *Das fliessende Licht der Gottheit*, pp. 35–36, for a discussion of some of Mechthild's theological mistakes. See also n. 10 below. There is also the possibility that Mechthild came under attack because she was a Beguine. As mentioned in n. 5, the Beguines were frequently accused of heresy and there seems to be evidence that at least some of the houses of Beguines were connected directly with Catharism. Compare Gottfried Koch, *Frauenfrage und Ketzertum im Mittelalter*, pp. 45–48.

10. She writes in 2. 26: "O Lord, if I were a learned holy man . . ."; in 3. 1: "I am not expert in Scripture." In 2. 3 she confesses to being ignorant of Latin.

11. For example, she writes in 3. 5: ". . . my . . . enemies nip at me so constantly that I cannot conceive how it shall be at my end." In 6. 38 she speaks of herself as "a post or a mark at which people . . . throw or shoot" and of "those who have long attacked my honor with vicious cunning." In 7. 41 she sees the soul of a certain "religious" who in the past "had forgotten himself a little regarding me."

12. The italics are mine. One will notice that in this passage and in numerous others Mechthild makes ample use of the standard medieval humility formula. Here she refers to herself as a "sinful woman," whereas elsewhere she uses such phrases as "miserable wretch," "wretched woman," and "lame dog" when referring to herself.

13. Compare Neumann, "Beiträge," p. 70.

14. Gertrude of Hackeborn is to be distinguished from Saint Gertrude, the Great, who was also at Helfta at this time. The two are often confused in older works and even in the Breviary. Compare F. L. Cross, *Oxford Dictionary of the Christian Church*, p. 554.

15. Mechthild of Hackeborn was precentor and gained renown for her mastery of liturgical music.

16. Cross, p. 554.

17. Devotion to the Sacred Heart has been officially practiced only since the eighteenth century, but its roots certainly reach back to the Middle Ages. It appears to have developed from the cult of the Wound in the Side and is seen in richly developed form in Saint Gertrude's works. Mechthild of Magdeburg, however, has the distinction of being the first mystic anywhere in Christendom to have had an actual vision of the Sacred Heart directed to her (6. 24).

18. Neumann, "Beiträge," pp. 58–59, contends that Mechthild also wrote a large portion of book 6 after she had gone to Helfta.

19. Mechthild had apparently taken vows upon entering Helfta, a conclusion based on the prologue to the Latin translation of her work (made shortly after her death), where she is called *soror*. Compare ibid., pp. 35–36.

20. Neumann, ibid., p. 70, arrives at this date after a careful analysis of all available data. Many wish to place Mechthild's death much later, some as late as 1297 (for example, Menzies, *Revelations*, p. xxi). This appears to be an untenable position.

21. Compare n. 8. Oehl, *Das fliessende Licht*, pp. 18–19, believes that the sequence of parts was revised at least twice.

22. Some think the first Latin translation was made as early as circa 1290 by Heinrich of Halle himself. Compare Friedrich-Wilhelm Wentzlaff-Eggebert, *Deutsche Mystik zwischen Mittelalter und Neuzeit*, p. 292; Jeanne Ancelet-Hustache, *Mechthilde de Magdebourg:*

Etude de psychologie religieuse, p. 360; and Oehl, *Das fliessende Licht,* p. 20. Against this compare Neumann, "Beiträge," p. 70.

23. This thesis was given strong support by Ancelet-Hustache, pp. 358–369. Briefly, she makes two presuppositions: that Mechthild died in 1282 and that her work was translated into Latin very shortly thereafter. She then refers to two independently made discoveries to lend external support to the Mechthild = Matelda thesis. First, Dietrich of Apolda was obviously familiar with the Latin version of the *Flowing Light,* for in his biography of Saint Dominic (*Vita S. Dominici,* 1296–1298) he lifted entire lines from it. Compare Hubert Stierling, "Studien zu Mechthild von Magdeburg," pp. 5–15. Second, Dante bases his depiction of Saint Dominic in *Paradise* 12 on the biography of him by Dietrich. It would thus be quite conceivable that Dante read at least parts of Mechthild's book and may even have learned much about Mechthild herself.

24. Ferdinand Koenen, "Matelda," *Deutsches Dante-Jahrbuch* 10 (1928): 155–172. Koenen's arguments in favor of Matilda of Tuscany have come to be generally accepted.

25. Oehl, *Das fliessende Licht,* pp. 22–23, quotes the pertinent passages. Compare Gall Morel, *Offenbarungen der Schwester Mechthild von Magdeburg oder das fliessende Licht der Gottheit, aus der einzigen Handschrift des Stiftes Einsiedeln,* p. xx, for the original texts.

26. Oehl, *Das fliessende Licht,* p. 25. Mechthild's influence and the reception of her work seem for some curious reason to have extended toward and to have been limited to the south. This is attested by the fact that all five of the surviving manuscripts of the *Flowing Light* are from the southern part of the German-speaking area. It also appears that Mechthild and her work were forgotten and unknown from approximately the beginning of the fifteenth century until 1861, when the Einsiedeln manuscript was discovered and published by Carl Greith (see n. 27). At that time both Mechthild and the work were acclaimed as major discoveries in the history of German mysticism.

27. Carl Greith, *Die deutsche Mystik im Prediger-Orden (von 1250–1350) nach ihren Grundlehren, Liedern und Lebensbildern aus handschriftlichen Quellen,* pp. 207–277.

28. Morel, *Offenbarungen.*

29. Book 7 is missing from both Latin documents.

30. In contrast to most medieval writers, Mechthild does not avail herself too frequently of imagery from the realm of nature. One finds a reference to jasper (4. 3) and some scattered animal symbolism derived directly from the *Physiologus,* primarily in book 4. 18. Somewhat more frequent is plant symbolism—the lily of chastity, the rose of suffering, or the violets of humility (7. 30).

31. From *Dante, The Divine Comedy. 3 Paradise,* trans. Dorothy L. Sayers and Barbara Reynolds, p. 265:

> So Beatrice spoke. Those happy spirits sped,
> Whirling about fixed centres circle-wise,
> Each brightly blazing like a comet's head.
>
> As in a clock the movements synchronize
> So that the lowest wheel appears to sleep,
> To an onlooker, while the topmost flies,
>
> So did those dancers different measures keep,
> Bidding me judge how great their riches were,
> As they did swiftly whirl or slowly creep.   (*Paradise* 24. 10–18)

32. Compare Oehl, *Das fliessende Licht,* pp. 29–30, for the pertinent passages from scripture and for a brief but very cogent statement on the significance of wine symbolism in the Christian religion.

33. No less a scholar than Emil Michael wrote of Mechthild: "Mechthild of Hackeborn

and Gertrude are more refined and more mature, but Mechthild of Magdeburg is without a doubt . . . the most original personality in the history of German mysticism in the thirteenth century." See *Geschichte des deutschen Volkes*, vol. 3, p. 198 (the translation is mine).

The Flowing Light of the Godhead

Prologue

In the year of our Lord 1250, and for fifteen years afterward, this book was revealed in German by God to a sister who was a holy maiden both in body and in spirit. She served God devoutly in humble simplicity, in unheard-of poverty, and in heavenly contemplation, burdened with scorn, for more than forty years; she followed firmly and completely the light and teaching of the Order of Preachers and advanced and improved herself daily. But a brother of the same order gathered together and copied this book. Much good is in this book on many things, as is seen in the table of its contents. You should read it nine times, faithfully, humbly, and devoutly.

Autobiographical Texts

[2. 3] . . . German now fails me and I do not know Latin; so if anything good is here,[1] it is not due to me, for there was never a dog so bad, that if its master enticed it with a piece of bread, it would not come gladly.

[2. 24] Saint Lawrence! I was bound with you more than twenty years on a dreadful spit, yet God kept me unburned and released me more than seven years ago.

[2. 26] I was warned about this book
       and was told by many people
       that if there were no wish to preserve it,
       then flames could consume it.
           Then I did what I have done since childhood
       when I was saddened: I prayed.
       I bowed to my Love and spoke:
       O Lord: now I am saddened.
       In honoring You I shall receive no comfort from You.
       You have misled me
       for You Yourself told me to write it.

> Then God revealed Himself at once
> to my sad soul and held this book in His extended hand
> and said: My dear, do not be too sad:
> no one may burn the truth.
> He who would take it from My hand
> must be stronger than I!

[3. 5] ... Oh, dearest, how you speak so near to me! Yet I dare not think joyfully of these words, for my body, that dead dog, continually reeks and some of my enemies nip at me so constantly that I cannot conceive how it shall be at my end ...

[4. 2] All my life before I began this book and before a single word of it came from God into my soul, I was one of the simplest people who was ever in the spiritual life. I knew nothing of the devil's wickedness, of the frailty of the world I knew not, the falseness of spiritual people was also unknown to me. I must now speak and through the teaching in this book honor God. I, unworthy sinner, was greeted so overwhelmingly by the Holy Spirit in my twelfth year when I was alone, that I could never afterward have surrendered to any great daily sin. The loving greeting came every day and brought me both love and sorrow;[2] the sweetness and glory grew every day and this happened for thirty-one years.

I knew nothing of God except the Christian creed which I sought to follow diligently so that my heart might become pure. God Himself is my witness that I never willfully asked Him to give me the things which are written in this book. I never thought that such a thing could happen to anyone. While I was with my relatives[3] and friends, to whom I was most dear, I had no knowledge of these things. Yet I had long wished to be despised through no fault of my own. Then out of love for God I went to a town[4] where I had no friends but one. I was concerned that because of the latter I would be deprived of the disdain of the world and the pure love of God. But God never left me alone but brought me to such lovely sweetness, to such holy knowledge, to such incomprehensible marvels that I had little use for earthly things. Then for the first time my spirit was brought in my prayer between heaven and earth.[5] Then I saw with the eyes of my soul in heavenly bliss the beautiful humanity of our Lord Jesus Christ and I recognized Him by His splendid countenance[6] ... the Holy Trinity, of the Father's eternity, the Son's suffering, and the Holy Spirit's sweetness. Then I saw the angel to whom I was entrusted in baptism and my devil.

Then our Lord spoke: I will take this angel from you and give you two others in return who will care for you in these marvels. When the soul saw the two angels, oh, how she cowered in a humble faint, and prostrated herself at the feet of our Lord and thanked Him and lamented greatly her unworthiness that such great princes should be her servants. The one angel was a seraph and it was burning with love and was a holy light bearer for the favored soul. The other angel was a cherub; it is a guardian of the gifts and orders the wisdom of the loving soul.

Then our Lord let two devils come forth; they were great masters and had been taken from Lucifer's school, whence they were rarely permitted to emerge. When the soul saw these most gruesome devils, she trembled a little, rejoiced in our Lord, and gladly accepted them. The one devil is a deceiver dressed as a lovely angel. Oh, how many a false deceit he first laid before me. Once during mass he came down from the heights and said: I am very handsome. Would you worship me? The soul answered: man should worship God alone in all good things and in all distress. Then he said: will you not look up and see who I am? Then he pointed to a beautiful but false light beneath the air which had led many a heretic astray and said: on this throne and on this seat you alone will be the highest maiden and I the loveliest youth with you. But the soul said: he would not be wise who took the worst from the midst of the best. Then he said: since you will not give yourself to me, you are so holy and I so humble that I will worship you. The soul said: you will receive no grace for worshiping filth. Then he showed me marks of the five wounds on his feet and hands[7] and said: now you see who I am. If you will live as I advise, I will give you great honor. You shall tell other people of this grace, so that much good might come of it. Then the soul spoke and was depressed at this good-for-nothing tale, yet she listened gladly that she might become the wiser for it: you tell me you are God; now tell me, who is he who is now the son of the living God in the hands of the true priest? Then he wanted to go and the soul said:

In the name of Almighty God I admonish you
to listen to me.
I know your intention:
if I were to tell all people what is in my heart,
it would feel good for a while.
Then you would exert yourself most strenuously
to put a stop to the game.
You act thus
that I might fall into doubt and sadness,
into disbelief and unchastity,
and then into eternal woe.
You also do this
that I might think I am holy.
Yes, you old deceiver,

as long as God stands by me
your effort is for nothing.

Then he cried: curse your magic!—let me get away from you. I will never bother you again.

The other devil given me was a peace breaker and a master of furtive[8] impurity. But God had forbidden him to ever come near me himself. Instead he sends me as messengers perverted people who distort what is good in me and rob me of my honor as much as they can with words. He also searches for where devout people gather and if they utter any idle talk in an unseemly manner, then I, poor soul, cannot be but saddened there. That has never happened to me.

One night in the first hour of sleep when I was praying, this same devil came flying through the air and looked very closely at sinful earth. He was as large as a giant; he had a short tail and crooked nose; his head was as big as a tub; and fiery sparks engulfed in black flame[9] came flying from his mouth. Then he laughed in false rage with a terrifying voice. And the soul asked him why he was laughing, what he was seeking, and what he was up to. Then he answered and said: I rejoice. Since I cannot torment you myself, I am at least delighted to find many who look like angels and gladly torture you for me. He spoke again: I am the guardian of spiritual people and I look for two kinds of weakness in them which will separate them from God in the quickest way. The first is sanctimonious or secret impurity. When a person in the holy life seeks the comfort of the flesh when there is no true need, but only for the satisfaction of his five senses, then he becomes unchaste, that is, crude and indolent, and the true love of God grows cold within him. The second is hidden hatred in open discord; that is to me such a useful sin that whenever I find them unchanged the next day, it is my gain because this is the foundation of long-practiced evil and the loss of all holiness. Then the soul spoke: you have by nature nothing good in you; how can it be that you present this good lesson out of your evilness? But then he said: wherever I turn God holds me so firmly in His hands that I can do nothing unless He permits it.

O miserable wretch that I am! I had committed such great sins in my childhood that I would have had to stay in purgatory ten years had I remained without repentance and without confession. But now, dear Lord, when I die, I will gladly suffer there for love of You.

I do not say that with my intellect:
Love commands me to say it.
When I came to the spiritual life
and took leave of the world

I looked at my body—
it was mightily armed
against my poor soul
with much might
and with the full power of nature.
I saw that it was my enemy
and saw also that if I wished to escape eternal death
I would have to conquer myself
and that would be quite a battle.
Then I also looked at the weapons of my soul:
it was the splendid martyrdom of our Lord Jesus Christ
with which I defended myself.
I stood constantly in great fear,
and in all my youth tremendous blows
I laid upon my body.
There was sighing, weeping, confessing, fasting, watching,
whippings,[10] and constant worship.

These were the weapons of my soul with which I conquered the body to such an extent that for twenty long years I was never but tired, ill, and weak—at first because of remorse and sorrow, and afterward out of good desire and spiritual travail, as well as many a grave illness from nature.[11] Then came mighty Love and filled me so greatly with these marvels that I did not dare to keep it silent. Yet in my simplicity I regretted it. I cried: O bountiful God, what have You seen in me? Indeed, You know I am a fool, a sinner, a woman poor both in body and in soul. You should give such things to wise people so that You would be praised for them. But our Lord became very angry with me, poor wretch, and asked me to judge. Tell me, He said, are you truly Mine? Yes, Lord, I desire that from You. May I then not do with you what I will? Yes, Dearest One, gladly, even if I should be destroyed. Then our Lord said: you should follow Me and trust Me in these things. You shall be ill a long time and I will care for you Myself. And everything you need in body and in soul I will give you.

Then I, poor wretch, went trembling in humble shame to my confessor and told him this and asked his counsel. And he said I should go forth joyfully; God Who had called me would take good care of me. Then he commanded me to do that for which I often weep in shame because my great unworthiness stands clear before my eyes—that was, that he ordered a contemptible woman to write this book out of God's heart and mouth.

This book has thus come lovingly from God and is not taken from human intellect.

[5. 12] Master Heinrich! You are surprised at the masculine words which are written in this book. I wonder why that surprises you. But it grieves me more to the heart that I, a sinful woman, must so write. But I cannot describe to anyone the true knowledge and holy, magnificent revelations except with these words alone, which seem to me all too puny in comparison to the eternal truth. I asked the eternal master what He would say about this. And He answered: ask him[12] how it happened that the apostles, when they were first so weak, became so bold after they had received the Holy Spirit. Ask further where Moses was when he saw only God. Ask yet further how it was that Daniel spoke in his childhood.

[5. 33] What hinders spiritual people most of all from complete perfection is that they pay so little attention to small sins. I tell you in truth: when I hold back a smile which would harm no one, or have a sourness in my heart which I tell to no one, or feel some impatience with my own pain, then my soul becomes so dark and my senses so dull and my heart so cold that I must weep greatly and lament pitiably and yearn greatly and humbly confess all my lack of virtue—for only then can I receive the blessing of being allowed to crawl back to the kitchen like a beaten dog.

Moreover, if I have not recognized and changed a flaw in myself, there is at once an evil mark on my soul. There is no help for this. The devil who has charge of purgatory, where this sin will burn, sees at once his image. Then I begin to fear greatly for I am alone, because my soul was released from all fear when I received the gift which is called love confessed. Then I fall to the ground at once and say *miserere mei deus* or *pater noster*. Then I return at once to my sweet paradise from which the stain had driven me.

[6. 36] No one can comprehend divine gifts with human senses; therefore those persons err who do not keep their spirit open to unseen truth. What can be seen with the eyes of the flesh, heard with the ears of the flesh, and spoken with the mouth of the flesh is as different from the truth revealed to the loving soul as a candle to the bright sun.

That John the Baptist sang mass for the poor maiden—that was not of the flesh—it was so spiritual that the soul alone saw and rejoiced in it. But the body had only as much of it as it could grasp of the nobility of the soul with its human senses; therefore the words had to sound human.

My pharisee says of my tale: John the Baptist was a layman. Now the holiest of all things in the Mass is the Body of God. John the Baptist touched the Son of this same God with humble, trembling fear in such great worthiness of his holy life that he heard the voice of the heavenly Father and perceived His words and saw the Holy Spirit in them both;

John the Baptist also preached openly the holy Christian faith to all people and for the people pointed with his finger to the true Son of God, Who was present there: *ecce agnus dei.*

Never could a pope or bishop or priest speak the Word of God as well as did John the Baptist ... Was this a layman? Teach me, you blind! Your lies and your hatred will not be forgiven without suffering!

[7. 4] Not long after I came to the convent I became so painfully ill that my attendants had great pity for me. Then I spoke to our Lord: what do You want with this suffering? And our dear Lord said thus: all your paths are measured, all your footsteps counted, your life is blessed, your end will be happy, and My kingdom is very near you.—Lord, why is my life blessed, since I can do so little good? Then our Lord said: your life is sanctified because My rod has never left your back!

[7. 36] I desired of God that He let me know if it were His will that I not write anymore. Why? Because I now know I am still as despicable and unworthy as I was thirty years ago and more when I began to write ...

[7. 64] Thus speaks a beggar woman in her prayer to God:

Lord, I thank You that since with Your love You have taken from me all earthly riches, You now clothe and feed me out of the goodness of others, for all that clothes my heart in the desire of possession has become foreign to me.

Lord, I thank You that since You have taken from me the power of my eyes, You now serve me through the eyes of others.

Lord, I thank You that since You have taken from me the power of my hands ... Lord, I thank You that since You have taken from me the power of my heart, You now serve me with the hands and hearts of others.

Lord, I ask You to reward them here on earth with Your divine love so that they might beseech and serve You with all virtues until they come to a holy end.

Criticism

[3. 15] You foolish Beguines! How audacious you are that you do not tremble before our almighty judge when you so often take the Body of God out of blind habit! Now I, the least of you all, must be ashamed and blush and tremble. At a celebration[13] I was so afraid that I did not dare take it because I was ashamed of my greatest merit before His eyes. Then

I asked my Beloved to show me His will in this matter. He said: truly, if you go before Me in humble lamentation and with holy fear, then I must follow you as the river follows the mill. But if you approach Me with the flowering desire of flowing love, then I must meet you and touch you with My divine nature as My one queen. I must open myself, if I would truly receive God's goodness. But that hinders me truly no more than it hinders a hot oven to stuff it with unbaked dough.

[5. 34] . . . I, poor woman, was so bold in my prayer that I impudently took corrupt Christianity into the arms of my soul and lifted it in lamentation. Our Lord said:

Leave it! It is too heavy for you.
No, sweet Lord!
I will lift it up and carry it before Your feet,
with Your own arms
with which You bore it on the cross!
And God granted me, poor wretch, my will
that I might find rest.

When poor Christianity came before our Lord, she was like a maiden. I looked at her and saw also that our Lord looked at her.[14] And I was very ashamed. Then our Lord said: behold, is it fitting for Me to love this maid in My eternal infinite wedding bed and to draw her to Me in My imperial arms and to look at her with My divine eyes, since she is half-blind in her knowledge and crippled in her hands, which hardly do any good works? She also limps in the feet of her desire, for she rarely and then indolently thinks of Me. Her skin is also filthy, for she is unclean and unchaste. Then the poor soul spoke: what advice can one give her? And our Lord said: I will wash her in My own blood[15] and I will protect all the blessed who are truly innocent and take them intimately to Me in a blessed death . . .

[6. 3] God calls the cathedral clergy goats because their flesh stinks of impurity with regard to eternal truth, before His Holy Trinity . . .

[6. 21] Alas! Crown of holy Church, how tarnished you have become. Your precious stones have fallen from you because you are weak and you disgrace the holy Christian faith. Your gold is sullied in the filth of unchastity, for you have become destitute and do not have true love. Your purity is burned up in the ravenous fire of gluttony; your humility has sunk to the swamp of your flesh; your truth has been destroyed in the lie of this world; the flowers of all your virtues have fallen from you. Alas, crown of holy priesthood, you have disappeared, and you have nothing left but your external shape—namely, priestly power—with this you do battle against God and His chosen friends. Therefore God will humble you before you know what has happened. For our Lord speaks thus: I will touch the heart of the pope in Rome with great sadness and in this sadness I will speak to him and lament to him that My shepherds from Jerusalem have become murderers and wolves, for they slaughter the white lambs before My eyes. And the old sheep are all sickly, for they cannot eat of the healthful pasture which grows on the high mountains, that is, love and holy doctrine. Whoever does not know the way to hell, let him behold the depraved priesthood, how its path goes straight to hell with women and children and other public sins . . .

Heaven and Hell

[3. 1] . . . There I saw unheard-of things, so my confessors tell me . . . There I saw the creation and the arrangement of the house of God which He Himself built with His own mouth. In it He has placed His loved ones whom He made with His own hands. The creation of this house signifies heaven, the choirs in it signify the kingdom—therefore one speaks of them together as the kingdom of heaven. The kingdom of heaven is finite in its statutes but infinite in its essence. Heaven surrounds the choirs and between heaven and the corporeal choirs the sinners of the world are arranged almost on a plane with the choirs that they might improve themselves and be converted. The choirs are so holy and high above us that without chastity and the renunciation of all things, no one may enter them. Since all who fell from them were holy, all who enter them must also be holy. All children from baptismal age[16] to six years fill the spaces not higher than the sixth choir. From there up to the seraphim such maidens should fill the spaces as had defiled themselves in the foolishness of youth yet had done no deed and had cleansed themselves in confession. Yet since they had lost their purity they may never completely recover it. After the day of judgment holy maidens shall fill the space above the seraphim from where Lucifer and his minions had been cast. Lucifer committed at once three mortal sins: hatred, pride, and covetousness; these flung the choir down into the abyss as quickly as one might utter hallelujah. The whole kingdom was terrified and the pillars of heaven shook. Many others collapsed. This void[17] is still empty and barren; there is no one in it—yet it is light unto itself and it glitters in rapture to the glory of God. Above the void is the throne of God, vaulted by His power in bright, glowing, fiery brilliance which reaches down to the heaven of the cherubim. The throne of God and heaven form together a noble dwelling which encloses the void and the nine choirs. Above the throne of God is nothing but God, God, God, infinite, great God. Upon the throne is seen the mirror of the Godhead, the image of the humanity, the light of the Holy Spirit—and it is known that those three are one God and that they merge into one. Of this I can speak no more.

Of all these things I can speak but a brief word,
no more than as much
honey as a bee can
carry away on its foot from a full hive.
In the first choir is happiness,
the highest of all gifts,
in the second choir is meekness,
in the third choir is love,
in the fourth sweetness, in the fifth joyfulness,
in the sixth noble tranquillity,
in the seventh riches,
in the eighth worthiness,
in the ninth burning love,
and in the sweet beyond is pure holiness . . .

. . . Many people may wonder how I, a sinful person, can dare to write of such things; I say to you in truth that had not God, seven years ago, bestowed a singular grace on my heart, I would still be silent and never have done it. But due to God's kindness, no harm came to me; that comes from the reflection of my obvious wickedness, which stands openly before my soul, and from the nobility of the grace which is in the true gifts of God.

[7. 57] This I was shown and I saw how paradise was made. Of its breadth and its length there is no end. The place I came to first was between this world and the beginning of paradise; I saw there trees, leaves, and clover and grass and no weeds. Many trees bore apples but most of them had only leaves and an elegant aroma. Rushing waters flow through that place and south winds blow northward. In the waters earthly sweetness was mixed with heavenly joy. The air was sweeter than I can say. There were no animals or birds there for God had made it for man alone, that he might dwell there comfortably . . . I saw two kinds of paradise. Of the earthly part I have spoken; the heavenly part is above and protects the earthly part from all storms . . . In the highest part are the souls which did not deserve purgatory and yet had not come to God's kingdom.

They soar in joy
like the air in the sun.

Lordship and honor, reward and crowns,
they do not yet have, until they enter God's kingdom.
When the earthly paradise fades away
as God has decreed it shall,
then the heavenly paradise will also disappear.
Everyone who wishes to come to God
shall live in the same house.
There will no longer be a sick house.
Whoever comes to the kingdom of God
is rid of all illness.
Praised be Jesus Christ,
who has given us His kingdom.

[3. 21] I have seen a place—
its name is Eternal Hatred.
It is built in the deepest abyss
of the stones of mortal sin.
Pride was the first stone—
this was seen in Lucifer.

Disobedience, covetousness, gluttony, unchastity were four heavy
stones brought by Adam our father.

Anger, falseness, and murder—
Cain brought these three stones.
Lying, betrayal, despair,
those who take their own lives—

with these four stones pitiful Judas slew himself. The sins of Sodom and
false piety

are the wretched cornerstones
laid into the work.
The place was built over many years,
woe to all who helped with it!
The more help they provided,
the more harm they shall receive
when they themselves go there.

The whole place is inverted, so that the highest are relegated to the
lowest and most unworthy regions. Lucifer sits in the deepest abyss bound
by his sin and from his fiery heart and from his mouth flow endlessly all
the sin, torment, and infamy by which hell and purgatory and the earth
are so pitifully surrounded. In the deepest part of hell are fire and darkness and stench and horror and all sorts of the greatest torment—and

there Christians are arranged according to their works. In the middle part all this torment is less. There the Jews are arranged according to their works. In the highest part of hell is the least suffering, and there the heathens are arranged according to their works. They lament thus:

Alas! If we had only had a law,
such great suffering would not have come
everlastingly to us!
The Jews also lament thus:
Woe to us! Had we only followed God
according to the law of Moses,
we would not have been so severely condemned.
The Christians lament even more
since they lost by their own will
the high honor for which Christ in His love
had destined them.
They constantly gaze at Lucifer with great lamentation
and must parade before him naked in their sin.
Alas! How disgracefully they are received by him.
He greets them dreadfully and speaks bitterly:
You, who are cursed with me—
what joy do you seek here?
You have never heard any good said of me.
How then can you be so smug?

Then he seizes the arrogant first of all and crushes him under his tail and says: I have not sunk so deep that I would not be superior to you. All the Sodomites pass through his gullet and live in his belly. When he inhales they are drawn into his belly, but when he coughs they are expelled. He sets the false saints in his lap and kisses them dreadfully and says: you are my colleagues. I too was clothed in handsome falseness; thus were you all deceived. He gnaws the usurer ceaselessly and reproaches him for never being merciful. He robs the robber and then delivers him to his companions that they may hunt him and beat him and show him no mercy. The thief hangs by his feet and in hell he is a lantern, but the unblessed see no better for it. Those who were unchaste together in this world must lie bound together before Lucifer; but if one comes alone, the devil is his companion.

The unbelieving masters sit at Lucifer's feet so that they can properly behold their unclean god. He holds disputations with them and they are confounded. He devours the greedy one, for he always wanted to have more. The murderers must stand bloodied before him and be beaten by the devil with a fiery sword. Those who on earth had exercised grim hatred must there serve as his smelling salts and constantly dangle before his nose. Gluttons and drunkards must stand before Lucifer in everlasting hunger and eat red-hot stones. Their drink is sulfur and pitch. In that place bitterness is given for sweetness; we see there what we practiced here. The slothful is burdened with all sorts of torment. The wrathful are beaten with fiery whips. The miserable minstrel who with pride can arouse sinful vanity weeps more tears in hell than there is water in the sea.

Beneath Lucifer I saw the foundation of hell—it is a hard black stone which will support the structure forever. Although hell has neither foundation nor end, yet in its arrangement it has both depth and end.[18]

How hell burns and rages in itself, how the devils fight with souls, how they seethe and roast, how they swim and wade in the stench and mire and among the worms and filth, and how they bathe in sulfur and pitch—neither they nor any other creature can fully express. When I by the grace of God and without difficulty had beheld this great misery, I, poor thing, suffered so greatly from the stench and the unearthly heat that I could neither sit nor walk and all my five senses were numb for three days and I was as one struck by lightning. But my soul suffered no harm, for it had brought no infirmity with it which would there evoke eternal death. Yet if it were possible that a pure soul be among them, it would be an eternal light and a great comfort to them. For the guiltless soul must by its very nature glow and shine, since it is born from eternal light without suffering. But if it assumes the likeness of the devil, then it loses its lovely light.

I did not learn
if in this eternal hell the condemned
receive some comfort from prayer or from alms,
for they are constantly in such a dread mood
that they recoil from all good.
After the day of judgment
Lucifer will don a new robe,
which has grown of itself
from the dung heap of all despicable sins
ever conceived by men or angels,
for he is the primary vessel of all sins.
Thus he is bound,
and yet his fury and his dreadfulness
are so intermixed with all souls and all devils
that one can never be unaware of his presence.

At times he bloats himself up to such a great size and his beak expands greatly—with this he swallows Christians,[19] Jews, and heathens with one breath. Then they have their full reward and their strange festival in his belly. Woe then to soul and body! That which the tongue can speak of is as nothing compared to the unspeakable distress which happens to them there.[20] Truly, I cannot bear to think of it any longer than it takes to utter *ave Maria*. Oh, woe, how terrible it is there.

There is a head at the top of hell which is terrifying and has many horrible eyes from which flames shoot out and envelop all souls who live in the outer works[21]—from here God had taken Adam and the other patriarchs. That is now the greatest purgatory to which a sinner can go. There I saw bishops, overseers, and great lords in dire distress and indescribable pain. All who came there had narrowly been spared eternal hell by God, for I found no one there who at his death had made pure confession. Since their external senses were taken from them by the nature of death, the body lay still, nor did soul and body have a will. When they had lost earthly darkness, God sent them to the school of true knowledge. Oh, how narrow is the path to the kingdom of heaven! Then body and soul spoke in unison, for they were as yet unseparated:

True God, have mercy on me. I am truly sorry for my sins. In that short while God intimately regained many apparently lost souls. But I did not find that this happened to anyone unless he had done some good out of goodwill. The devils take the tainted souls from the body to purgatory because the pure angels may not touch them, for they are not equal in clarity to them.

But a soul may have such help from friends on earth
that the devils will be cautious
not to rage against the soul.[22]
But if the soul is very sinful, she must suffer other pain.
Yet she would rather endure all that
than have the devils snatch her
and taunt her ceaselessly.

When our holy forefathers went to hell they brought with them true hope in the Christian faith with holy love of God, many a humble virtue and loyal travail. They all went to hell, yet they were prepared for heaven. Nothing in hell could harm them. That which they brought with them they must burn there. That was love which shall burn forever in all God's children.

Should they never get to heaven,
God has calculated as follows:
what we take along with us
we must eat and drink there;
but those who squandered their lives, those who without repentance
leave this world in great sin,
must now, although not condemned, suffer nothing worse

than to stand before the mouth of hell,
where at all times
Lucifer's breath bursts forth with great torment
and so pitiably pierces them
that the poor creatures
are joined in the flames and in the manifold tortures
as the blessed were joined
in the sweet recognition of God's love.
I saw there of all women none
but the high princesses who like the princes
loved all sorts of sin in this world.
Hell also has a mouth on its summit.
It stands open at all times.
All who enter the mouth
shall never escape eternal death.

Advice

[6. 1] Power is dangerous. When someone says: you are now our prelate or our prior or our prioress, God knows, dear monk, you have been chosen for the highest . . . You should be lovingly cheerful or gently serious with your subordinates and brothers and you should be compassionate regarding all their travail and with sweet words should you send them forth, preach boldly, and piously hear confession . . .

You should go to the guesthouse
and give of God's generosity
to His young disciples all they have need of,
which is in your power to provide.
Yes, you yourself should wash their feet.
Even though you are master or mistress
you are subordinate to them.
You should not stay too long with the guests,
for you should diligently see to the convent.
The guests should not keep long watches,
for that is a sacred thing.
You should go to the infirmary every day
and anoint the sick with comforting words of God
and delight them generously with earthly things,
for God is rich above all price.
You should keep the sick clean
and in a godly way laugh sweetly with them.

You should convey their personal afflictions from them
and lovingly ask them in confidence
what their secret ailments are,
and if you stand truly by them,
God's sweetness will flow into you.
You should also go to the kitchen and see to it
that the provisions of the brothers of the house are good enough
that your thriftiness and the cook's laziness
may not rob our Lord
of sweet song in choir!
For a hungry priest never sings well
and a hungry man cannot study deeply.
Thus might God often lose the best because of the least.

In chapter you should be just with a sweet mind and judge according to the fault. You should be careful not to follow your own will against the will of the brothers or the will of the convent, for great strife comes from that. Beward also of arrogant thoughts which unfortunately come into the heart under the likeness of good and say: yes, you are prior or prioress over them all; you can indeed do what you deem good . . . When the brethren or sisters of your house offer you honor, you should fear inwardly with a sharp guard on your heart and outwardly be modest with proper behavior. You should receive all complaints with compassion and give all advice in good faith. If your brothers wish to construct tall buildings, you should turn them to holy things . . . You shall have an eagle eye and view those under you in God, lovingly and not angrily. If you find anyone who is secretly tempted, stand by him with all your love . . . Now, dear friend, there are still two things against which you must be on your guard with holy diligence, for they have never brought holy fruit. The first is that a man or woman devoted to good works and practices will do much in order to be chosen superior. This brings grief to my soul. If such persons come to power, their vices become so manifold that none of those who chose them with great desire will receive comfort. Their honors will become a reproach and their false virtues will be converted to vices.

The second thing [to guard against] is, if someone without sin is laudably chosen and then changes so much that he never wishes to give up his elected office, that is a sign of many false virtues . . .

Miscellany

[1. 4] When the poor soul comes to court, she is discreet and well mannered. She looks happily at her God. Oh, how lovingly she is received there! She is silent and wants above everything His praise. So He, with great desire, shows her His divine heart. It is like red gold burning in a great fire. And God takes the soul to His glowing heart as the high prince and the humble maiden embrace and are united as water and wine. Then the soul becomes as nothing and is so beside herself that she can do nothing. And He is sick with love for her, as He ever was, for He neither increases nor decreases. Then the soul says: Lord, You are my comfort, my desire, my flowing spring, my sun, and I am Your reflection.

This is the journey to court of the loving soul, which without God cannot exist.

[1. 27] . . . For I do it in love to the honor of God; therefore all is one. But when I sin, then I am no longer on this path.

[1. 39–43] God asks the soul what it brings.
>   You hunt much in your love,
>   tell Me, what do you bring Me, My queen?
Lord! I bring You my treasure. It is larger than the mountains, broader than the world, deeper than the sea, higher than the clouds, more lovely than the sun, more manifold than the stars; it weighs more than the whole earth. O you, image of My Godhead, made splendid with My humanity, adorned with My Holy Spirit—what is your treasure called? Lord, it is called my heart's desire! I have withdrawn it from the world, preserved it in myself, and denied it to all creatures. But I can bear it no further. Lord, where shall I lay it? You shall lay your heart's desire nowhere but in My divine heart and on My human breast. There alone will you be comforted and kissed by My spirit.

[2. 1] The soul reaches its height in love and the embellishment of the body occurs in holy Christian baptism, for there is nothing higher than love and outside of Christianity there is no embellishment.

[2. 3] There was also seen that same splendid treasure chest
>   in which Christ sat nine months
>   in soul and body,
>   as it ever shall remain
>   only without the great glory
>   which the heavenly Father on the day of judgment
>   will give to all blessed bodies.
>   Our lady must also do without this
>   as long as this earth floats on the sea.

[2. 22] But Lady Soul, you have surely seen that the angels are simple things and they do not praise or love or recognize God more than is born into them.

[3. 3] If you wish to come with me to the wine cellar,
    that will cost you much.
    If you have a thousand marks' worth
    you will spend it in an hour.
If you wish to drink the wine unmixed, you will always spend more than
you have and the host will never keep your cup filled. You will become
poor and naked and despised by all who would rather rejoice in filth
than spend their treasure in the high wine cellar.

    You must also suffer,
    that those who go with you to the wine cellar
    will envy you.
    How much they will scorn you,
    for they dare not meet such a great cost.
    They wish to have water mixed with the wine.
    Dear bride! In the tavern will I gladly
    spend all that I have
    and let myself be dragged through the fires of love
    and beaten with the brands of scorn
    so that I might often go to the blessed wine cellar.

[4. 5] Lord, my sin through which I have lost You
    stands before my eyes like the highest mountain
    and has long made darkness between me and You
    and tremendous distance between You and me.
    O Love of all love,
    take me again to You.
    But Lord, the future fall
    stands also ever before my eyes like
    the fiery mouth of a dragon
    which at all times would gladly swallow me.
    O my only Good, help me now that I
    may flow into You unblemished.

[4. 28] This book was begun in love and shall also end in love, for there
is nothing so wise, or so holy, or so beautiful, or so strong, or so perfect
as love . . .

[6. 15] . . . After that God showed me again the end of this world when
the last brothers will be martyred. Antichrist commands that they be
hung on trees by their hair, which at the special direction of God they
never cut. There they hang and die a lovely death, for their hearts burn
inwardly with the sweet fire of heaven to the degree that the body suffers

in distress. Therefore, between the comfort of the Holy Spirit and the pain of the poor flesh, their souls depart their bodies free of all horror of pain.

[7. 36] And then I saw a spiritual convent which was built with virtues.

The abbess is true love,
she has much holy sense
with which she watches over the community
in body and soul to the honor of God;
she gives them many holy teachings
as to what is the will of God.
By this her own soul becomes free.
The chaplain of love is divine humility,
which is always so subordinate to love
that pride must stand aside.
The prioress is the holy peace of God;
patience is given to her goodwill
so that she may teach the community with divine wisdom . . .
The subprioress is lovingness.
She shall gather together the small sins
and destroy them with godliness . . .
    The chapter shall have four things in it:
revelations of the holiness
in the worship of God. Her gentle travail
does much harm to enemies
but is a great honor to God:
in that she may rejoice.
She shall guard against vain honor
and be helpful to others.
If they serve diligently, then God will reward them.
    Hope is the precentor,
filled with holy, humble reverence
so that the temerity of the heart
in singing before God sounds so lovely
that God loves the notes which sing in the heart . . .
    The schoolmistress is wisdom,
who with goodwill diligently teaches the ignorant.
Thereby is the convent sanctified and honored.
    The cellarer is an outpouring of helpful gifts.
Because she does this with divine joy,
she wins divine gifts of holiness . . .
The sweet gifts of God thus flow into her heart.

Those who help her in return
shall also gain,
just as she, the sweet gifts of God.
    The steward is generosity,
who always does good in the proper measure.
She gives with goodwill what she does not have.
Because of that she will win special gifts from God.
Those to whom she gives thank God
with holy fervor, which fills their hearts
like noble drink in a pure vessel.
    The mistress of the sick is diligent compassion,
which always strives to tirelessly provide service to the sick . . .
    The portress is watchfulness,
who is always filled with holy will
to do whatever she is told:
thus her travail is never lost . . .
The disciplinarian is holy custom,
which shall always burn like a candle,
unextinguished in heavenly freedom.
The provost is divine obedience,
to whom all the virtues are subject.
Thus may the convent abide in God.
Whoever wishes to go to this convent
shall always live in divine joy,
here and in eternal life.
Blessed are they who remain there.

NOTES TO THE TRANSLATION

1. That is, in what Mechthild has written.
2. A formulaic expression very common in the courtly love lyric, that is, *liebe und leit.*
3. The text reads *tagen*, 'days,' but should obviously read *magen*, 'relatives.'
4. That is, Magdeburg.
5. The manuscript reads *lufte*, 'air' or 'atmosphere.'
6. Something is apparently missing before the next word.
7. Obviously, the hands and feet had only four wounds.
8. The manuscript reads *heiligen*, 'holy,' which is obviously incorrect. Perhaps *heim-lichen* is meant.
9. Although the German reads *flamme*, 'flame,' perhaps 'smoke' is meant.
10. Morel's text incorrectly reads *besinnen, schlege*, 'recollection, blows' (discipline). The line should read *besemen schlege = virgarum plagis.*
11. She became physically ill.
12. That is, Heinrich.
13. That is, of the Mass.

14. Morel's text reads "and saw also that she looked at our Lord," although the sense of the passage requires that "our Lord" be in the nominative. This is supported by the Latin: "etiam Dominus intuitus est eam."

15. Morel's text reads "in her own blood," although in the title to 5. 34 he gives "in His own blood." The Latin reads merely "lavabo eam in sanguine."

16. Mechthild uses *westbaren*, which refers to children of baptismal age, although here she obviously means such children who have died.

17. Mechthild uses the German *ellende*, which more accurately denotes a place of exile or banishment or a foreign or strange land; compare Neumann, "Beiträge," p. 73.

18. Compare 3. 1, where Mechthild speaks in similar terms about heaven.

19. Morel's text reads *tufel*, 'devils,' apparently a mistake, since Mechthild divides all those condemned to hell into Christians, Jews, and heathens.

20. Morel's edition has a negative here, that is, "that which the human tongue cannot describe is as nothing." Obviously, the negative is out of place.

21. The word used is *vorburg*, which refers to buildings outside a castle wall.

22. The text has "devil" but the sense of the sentence requires that one read "soul."

BIBLIOGRAPHY

Primary Works

Buber, Martin. *Ekstatische Konfessionen.* Jena, 1909.

Escherich, Mela. *Das fliessende Licht der Gottheit von Mechtild von Magdeburg: Ins Neudeutsche übertragen und erläutert.* Berlin, 1909.

Grimm, H. A. *Die Geschichte der Schwester Mechthild von Magdeburg: Aus dem fliessenden Licht der Gottheit.* Leipzig, 1918.

Langner, Ilse. "Vorläuferinnen der Emanzipation? Drei Nonnen—Drei Dichterinnen." *Neue Deutsche Hefte* 26 (1979): 497–511.

Menzies, Lucy. *The Revelations of Mechthild of Magdeburg.* New York, 1953.

Morel, Gall. *Offenbarungen der Schwester Mechthild von Magdeburg oder das fliessende Licht der Gottheit, aus der einzigen Handschrift des Stiftes Einsiedeln.* 2nd ed. Darmstadt, 1963.

Müller, J. *Leben und Offenbarungen der heiligen Mechtildis und der Schwester Mechtildis (von Magdeburg).* Vol. 2. Regensburg, 1881.

Oehl, Wilhelm. *Das fliessende Licht der Gottheit.* Munich, 1911.

———. "Neu entdeckte Mystikertexte: Elisabeth von Schönau und Mechtild von Magdeburg." *Zeitschrift für deutsches Altertum und deutsche Literatur* 64 (1927): 277–281.

Revelationes Gertrudianae ac Mechtildianae II, opus . . . editum Solesmensium O.S.B. monachorum cura. Pictavii et Parisiis, 1877.

Schleussner, Wilhelm. *Das fliessende Licht der Gottheit: Nach einer neuaufgefundenen Handschrift.* Mainz, 1929.

Simon, Sigmund. *Mechtild von Magdeburg: Das fliessende Licht der Gottheit.* Berlin, 1907.

Related Works

Ancelet-Hustache, Jeanne. *Mechthilde de Magdebourg: Etude de psychologie religieuse.* Paris, 1926.

Becker, E. "Beiträge zur lateinischen und deutschen Überlieferung des Fliessenden Lichts der Gottheit." Ph.D. dissertation, Göttingen, 1951.

Deutsch, S. M. "Mechthild von Magdeburg." In *Realenzyklopädie für protestantische Theologie und Kirche*, ed. Johann Jakob Herzog, vol. 12, pp. 483–484. Leipzig, 1903.

Greith, Carl. *Die deutsche Mystik im Prediger-Orden (von 1250–1350) nach ihren Grundlehren, Liedern und Lebensbildern aus handschriftlichen Quellen*. Freiburg, 1861.

Haas, A. M. "Die Struktur der mystischen Erfahrung nach Mechtild von Magdeburg." *Freiburger Zeitschrift für Philosophie und Theologie* 22 (1975): 3–34.

Hauck, A. *Kirchengeschichte Deutschlands*. Vol. 5. Leipzig, 1911.

———. "Kleinigkeiten I. Mechthild von Magdeburg." *Zeitschrift für Kirchengeschichte* 32 (1911): 186–198.

Hünicken, R. "Studien über Heinrich von Halle." *Thüringer Zeitschrift* 23 (1935–1936): 102–117.

Jones, Rufus M. *The Flowering of Mysticism: The Friends of God in the Fourteenth Century*. 1939. Reprint. New York, 1971.

Kemp-Welch, Alice. *Of Six Mediaeval Women*. 1913. Reprint. Williamstown, Mass., 1972.

Lüers, Grete. *Die Sprache der deutschen Mystik im Werk der Mechthild von Magdeburg*. Munich, 1926.

Menzies, Lucy. *Mirrors of the Holy: Ten Studies in Sanctity*. Milwaukee, 1928.

Michael, Emil. *Geschichte des deutschen Volkes*. Vol. 3. Freiburg, 1903.

———. "Zur Chronologie der Mystikerin Mechthild von Magdeburg." *Zeitschrift für katholische Theologie* 25 (1901): 177–180.

Mohr, Wolfgang. "Darbietungsformen der Mystik bei Mechthild von Magdeburg." In *Marchen, Mythos, Dichtung: Festschrift zum 90. Geburtstag Fr. von der Leyens*, ed. Hugo Kuhn, pp. 375–399. Munich, 1963.

Neumann, Hans. "Beiträge zur Textgeschichte des 'Fliessenden Lichts der Gottheit' und zur Lebensgeschichte Mechthilds von Magdeburg." *Nachrichten der Akademie der Wissenschaften in Göttingen, Philologisch-historische Classe* (1954): 27–80.

———. "Problemata Mechthildiana." *Zeitschrift für deutsches Altertum und deutsche Literatur* 82 (1948): 143–172.

Preger, Wilhelm. *Geschichte der deutschen Mystik im Mittelalter: Nach den Quellen untersucht und dargestellt*. Vol. 1. Leipzig, 1874.

———. "Über das unter dem Namen der Mechthild von Magdeburg jüngst herausgegebene Werk 'das fliessende Licht der Gottheit' und dessen Verfasserin." *Sitzungsberichte der königl. bayer. Akademie der Wissenschaften zu München, Historische Classe* 2 (1869): 151–162.

Ruh, Kurt. *Altdeutsche Mystik*. Bern, 1950.

Seppänen, Lauri. *Zur Liebesterminologie in mittelhochdeutschen geistlichen Texten*. Tampere, 1967.

Spiess, Emil. *Ein Zeuge mittelalterlicher Mystik in der Schweiz*. Schwyz, 1934.

Stierling, Hubert. "Studien zu Mechthild von Magdeburg." Ph.D. dissertation, Nuremberg, 1907.

Strauch, Philipp. "Kleine Beiträge zur Geschichte der deutschen Mystik." *Zeitschrift für deutsches Altertum und deutsche Literatur* 27 (1883): 368–381.

———. "Mechthild von Magdeburg." *Allgemeine Deutsche Biographie* 21 (1885): 154–156.

Tax, Petrus W. "Die grosse Himmelsschau Mechthilds von Magdeburg und ihre Höllenvision: Aspekte des Erfahrungshorizontes, der Gegenbildlichkeit und der Parodierung." *Zeitschrift für deutsches Altertum und deutsche Literatur* 108 (1979): 112–137.

Tillmann, Heinz. "Studien zum Dialog bei Mechthild von Magdeburg." Ph.D. dissertation, Marburg, 1933.

Wentzlaff-Eggebert, Friedrich-Wilhelm. *Deutsche Mystik zwischen Mittelalter und Neuzeit.* 2nd ed. Tübingen, 1947.

Zinter, Edith. "Zur mystischen Stilkunst Mechthilds von Magdeburg." Ph.D. dissertation, Jena, 1931.

THE BRABANT MYSTIC

RIA VANDERAUWERA

Of Hadewijch, we know only her name, texts (poetry and prose), and a few scattered references. Nonetheless we recognize her as one of the foremost representatives of early *minnemystiek*, a brand of mysticism to which women made an especially impressive contribution in the thirteenth century. We possess three complete manuscripts of her works, parts of her work in a recently discovered codex, and a few smaller fragments.[1] The three complete manuscripts contain thirty-one letters, forty-five stanzaic poems, fourteen visions, and twenty-nine poems mostly in rhyming couplets (one manuscript has only sixteen of them), of which thirteen were probably not by Hadewijch but by another woman of her environment. The significance of her work for Dutch literature lies in the facts that her stanzaic poetry belongs to the very few extant Middle Dutch love songs in the troubadour tradition of courtly love and that her prose, together with that of the Cistercian mystic Beatrijs of Nazareth (circa, 1200–1268), is the earliest extant prose in the vernacular.

From her writings, Hadewijch emerges as an accomplished, articulate, and sensitive woman. Although we have Latin *vitae* about other mystic women who are her predecessors or contemporaries—for example, Marie of Oignies (1177–1213) and Lutgardis of Tongeren (1228–1246)—we have no *vita* and indeed no biographical information on Hadewijch other than that contained in her writings. As a result, scholars must attempt to reconstruct the personality of this important writer from her works alone.

Modern research shows that Hadewijch lived in the first quarter of the thirteenth century and that her main literary activity took place between 1220 and 1240, if not earlier.[2] The dialect in which she wrote is Brabant. She might have lived in Antwerp, for a rather late reference (fifteenth century) speaks of her as "B[eata] Hadewigis de Antverpia." She might have lived in Brussels, where her work was read and quoted in the fourteenth century at the abbey of Groenendaal, founded by Jan van Ruus-broec.[3] Evidence is stronger for Brussels, for two manuscripts were made at the Rodeklooster, another Brussels monastery. Hadewijch must have known about or read mystic writers such as Saint Augustine, Saint Bernard, William of Saint Thierry, Hugo, and Richard of Saint Victor. Most probably she knew Latin: passages in her letters have been identified as translations of William of Saint Thierry and Richard of Saint Victor, though she might have borrowed translations. She was acquainted with the literary tradition of the age, in particular with the courtly love song and the visionary genre. Her erudition points almost certainly to a noble or aristocratic descent. Her letters suggest that though she was not a nun, she lived for some time in a small community of religious women. She has been identified with the notorious fourteenth-century heretic Heilwich Bloemaerts and the abbess of a Cistercian convent, until she was finally thought of as a laywoman, somewhat like a Beguine. But we have no conclusive proof of this, and a recent study suggests that Hadewijch was closer to the *reclusae*, more of an aristocratic artist than a leader of a Beguine community.[4]

Like so many women of her time, Hadewijch took an active part in the great spiritual revival. In the southern Netherlands, this "women's movement" led several Beguine communities to flourish in the thirteenth century. Since the late twelfth century, many women had chosen to lead a life of charity and prayer without necessarily belonging to a religious order. They lived close to monasteries or convents, accompanied traveling monks, or lived as *reclusae* or in small communities. Reformist lifestyles and alleged links with heretic movements often made these women subject to persecution. From her letters we know that, if not persecuted, Hadewijch was at least subject to criticism. Both charity and ecstasy characterized the earliest manifestations of this religious revival among women. In her letters and poems, Hadewijch encouraged her audience to help the poor and suffering, and the visions showed great exaltation. To the speculative aspect which had begun to affect the movement in the thirteenth century, she contributed the formulation of her mystic thought in the vernacular.

Apparently Hadewijch made no attempt to explain her mysticism in a systematic doctrine. But the central concept of her thinking is quite obvious: *minne*, 'love.' We have yet to establish a comprehensive understanding of *minne* in courtly love poetry and, more specifically, in relation to mystic thinking. Nevertheless, a tentative explanation is crucial to appreciating these writings. In Hadewijch scholarship, *minne* has often been identified with God or Christ, which classifies her thinking as yet another example of Christ or bridal mysticism. Yet she does not often refer to Christ, to his birth or suffering, nor does she make great use of the bridal theme. From both her letters and her poems, one gets the impression that *minne* refers more to an abstract quality than to a concrete person. This abstract concept of *minne* has been noted before; one scholar even speaks of "an amorphous entity."[5] N. de Paepe recently investigated the matter thoroughly, and for him *minne* is not God, not Christ, not even, as another suggested, the love of God for humanity but the love of a human being for God.[6]

Like the whole of the spiritual revival of the twelfth and thirteenth centuries, Hadewijch's *minnemystiek* originates in Saint Bernard, who provoked a basic shift of focus in religious life and thought from knowledge of God to experience of God. Bernard implies the equation knowledge of God = experience of God = *amor* or love or, in de Paepe's formulation, meeting-of-God-in-an-earthly-situation. Hadewijch's *minne* is precisely this *amor*, this experience of God. With Tanis Guest, who carefully considers this thesis, I tend to believe that de Paepe takes too extreme a view of the matter, neglecting instances where *minne* clearly refers to the beloved (not necessarily the bridegroom). However, the value of de Paepe's idea is that it reverses the order in which we approach Hadewijch's *minne*. He convincingly demonstrates that the guiding notion should be *minne* as *experience* rather than *minne* personified as God or Christ. On the other hand, one should be aware of other shades of meaning, especially since Hadewijch plays word games with *minne*. De Paepe further distinguishes three basic moments in Hadewijch's experience of *minne* which are helpful in reading her work: the awareness of a distance between *minne* and herself—*een ghebreken*, 'a lack'; the complete surrendering to *minne*—*een ghebruken*, 'to use and enjoy'; and, finally, restored balance. The tension between *ghebreken* and *ghebruken*, which is Hadewijch's craving for love, runs through most of her writing.

All the forty-five stanzaic poems extant are in the tradition of the courtly love song. Scholars differ on the question of Hadewijch's indebtedness to either the southern troubadours or the northern French *trouvères*. Further research will probably give more definite answers, and there may well be a number of intermediary models of which we do not know. Meanwhile, the impact of romance on her poetry or, more safely, on the type of poetry Hadewijch wrote is fairly well established, as it is on Middle Dutch literature in general. The scarcity of Middle Dutch courtly poetry complicates research in this field. The poems by van Veldeke (1140?–1190), which we know only through their German transcriptions, and those by Hadewijch betray the existence of a substantial Middle Dutch tradition of the love song. Scholars assume that many texts have been lost, probably through the vigorous reaction against courtly poetry at the end of the thirteenth century, staged by a number of didactic poets with new bourgeois ideals. That Hadewijch's work survived such an outrage might well be due to its religious, "safe" content.[7]

Hadewijch is one more link in the tradition, but establishing her exact position is difficult. Judging from her accomplishment, she was probably writing in the heyday of courtly poetry in the Netherlands. But it would contribute to our knowledge of the notions of medieval literature if we knew for certain whether she herself was acquainted with the troubadour writings or whether she relied on intermediary models in Middle Dutch. It is interesting to note that unlike van Veldeke—who acquired a reputation in German-speaking territory, where his poetical techniques became influential—Hadewijch played no such role, which might be due to the religious frame of her reference.

Tanis Guest's thorough study of the poetic form of the stanzaic poems amply illustrates how Hadewijch made use of the conventions of the courtly love song: nature opening, tripartition, tornada, rhyme scheme, concatenation, and imagery.[8] She wrote with great technical skill and in much the same way as the troubadours had composed before her; she used conventions not as rigid rules but as options, which she would sometimes take, sometimes not, and sometimes adapt to suit her own purposes or to fit the constraints of the language she was working in. Instead of using *coblas unisonas* (the same rhyme and rhyme scheme in every stanza), which is hardly possible in a Germanic language, she used *coblas singulars* (the same rhyme scheme but not the same rhyme). Her rhyme is remarkably pure. Rather than being Romance syllabic, Hadewijch's rhythm is the Germanic stress rhythm. She makes intensive use of alliteration, assonance, and repetition. On the whole, she is less interested than the troubadours in sophisticated rhyming techniques, yet sometimes she gives the impression of forcing her thoughts and emotions into the complicated stanzaic format, and her poetry is not entirely free of easy verse filling. The imagery of courtly love—the unattainable lover, the submissive service to love, the complaints, the hope and despair, the all-pervading power of love—provides the poems with a strong thematic link.

In Hadewijch, secular imagery acquired a new spiritual meaning. De Paepe points out that whereas the unattainability of the lover had become pure literary convention in the courtly love song, for Hadewijch the unattainability of *minne* was an ontological given, which time and again she attempted to transcend by striving for, and reaching, a state of union with *minne*.

In translating some of the poems, I have chosen to give precedence to sense and imagery, rather than to original rhyme and meter. The loose format of the prose poem—rhythmic and particularly able to render motions of thought—is probably today's best form to capture the riches of Hadewijch's reflections on mystic love. Indeed, this aptness of prose rather than poetry might well apply to the original text of Hadewijch as well.

Though she will remain one of the foremost representatives of the Dutch courtly love song, her prose is increasingly regarded as superior to her poetry. This is certainly true of her writings in the visionary genre, as well as of the much simpler epistolary form.

Of all Hadewijch's writings, the letters are probably the least affected by literary conventions; in fact, they are our only source of biographical data. Most scholars agree that they were written to a woman (or women) who belonged to a small religious community of which Hadewijch had also once been a member. The letters are of varying lengths. Some of the longer ones are real treatises on religious or spiritual problems. Others are more intimate communications: Hadewijch gives practical advice on living a life of charity and devotion to *minne*; she speaks about her own experience with *minne* or urges the addressee to persevere. As in the poems, she complains about love's inconstancy, and she expresses her despair. Here also she is apparently transferring motifs of courtly love to spiritual experience. Her advisory tone indicates that she must have enjoyed the high regard of whomever she wrote to; perhaps she had been the leader of the community. At the time she wrote the letters, she seems to have been wandering or living in another small community. She also appears to be the victim of enmity and jealousy.

Hadewijch's epistolary prose is rhythmic and has great clarity. As in her poetry, she uses alliteration and repetition. I have chosen to translate some of her more personal communications, as they might shed better light on her life. I have, however, also included letter 20, a long treatise on "the twelve unspeakable hours of love," which illustrates both her powerful and passionate thinking on the nature of love and her superior skill as a prose writer.

The least accessible parts of Hadewijch's writings are her visions. Nevertheless, they are often considered as one of the greatest achievements in Dutch artistic prose of the Middle Ages, by far excelling her stanzaic poems in literary importance and aesthetic value. Yet, apart from a polemical debate about her doubtful orthodoxy, based on vision 5, where she mentioned that she had once been a Lucifer, not much work on the visions has been done. She wrote the visions apparently at the request of someone; in this work, she appears reluctant and embarrassed. In her letters she refers very little to the visions; when she does so, she speaks of them as being those of a third person. The language of the visions is difficult and their composition is not logical. Usually she opens with the occasion of the vision, a church holiday. As in the prevailing tradition of visionary writing, the vision itself seems to be regarded as an actual description of her ecstatic experience. She makes use of the medieval lore of allegory and symbols as well as the obligatory angels and seraphim so typical of the genre. For the modern reader unacquainted with the conventions or the psychology of mystical experience in the twelfth and thirteenth centuries, these visions might be difficult to appreciate. However, two recent translations into modern Dutch herald a new interest. The sixteen remaining poems, mostly in rhyming couplets, are actually letters in which Hadewijch develops themes similar to those in her prose letters and gives similar advice.

After the discovery of the manuscripts in 1838, Hadewijch took her place in the present Dutch literary canon. Regarded as one of the most gifted literary geniuses of her period, she figures in every school anthology that treats Dutch literature from its beginnings. As the "discovery" of the manuscripts indicates, Hadewijch has not always been part of the canon. Not only was she pushed to the periphery; she was even lost completely. Interesting in this respect is the story of Fleribertus Rosweyde, who in the early seventeenth century intended to write a scholarly study on the lives of the saints. He had come across the inscription "B[eata] Hadewigis" and consulted a historian for more information. But the historian in his turn confirmed in at least two letters that Hadewijch was completely unknown to him.[9] However, her work might well have been known and used in smaller circles at that period. A seventeenth-century *Schala Anagogica* by a Capuchin monk contained her name plus two texts from the rhyming letters, albeit from those not attributed to Hadewijch.[10] In any case, in the seventeenth and especially eighteenth centuries, she was not or no longer part of a lively and continuous tradition of mystical literature.

We have indications that she and her writings were remembered up to the early sixteenth century—particularly letter 10, a warning against the danger of mistaking sensuous yearning for the true excitement of spiritual love, must have been widely circulated. The most important occurrence, together with excerpts from several other letters, is found in a late thirteenth- or early fourteenth-century collection of, mainly, sermons translated from German, known as the *Limburgse Sermonenen*. Interestingly, the collection also contained Beatrijs of Nazareth's small treatise *Van Seven Manieren van Minnen*. Hadewijch was known, read, and copied in the fourteenth century (all three complete manuscripts were made in this century), especially in the Brussels area. Judging from indications in catalogs, several monasteries in Brabant must have possessed work by her. Avoiding the question of direct influence, which is hardly relevant if one accepts that she belonged to a wider movement of mystic thought, we can say that, after her, Gheraert Appelmans (early fourteenth century) continued the tradition of speculative mysticism in the Netherlands and that particularly Jan van Ruusbroec (1293–1381) built his systematic doctrine on thoughts similar to those developed by Hadewijch.

Throughout the fourteenth and fifteenth centuries we find Hadewijch in *rapiaria*, collections of ideas from several writers and thinkers, in margins and annotations, and we know of a possibly fifteenth-century Latin translation of the visions. But the letters especially were widely excerpted. Their success can be attributed to a new wave in the spiritual movement, the *moderne devotie*, in which a life of charity and devotion took precedence over speculation. Hadewijch's letters give much advice precisely in this respect. Vulgarizations of religious writings became quite common in that period, and the letters were paraphrased by Hendrik Mande (circa 1360–1431), surnamed the Ruusbroec of the North and a member of the new movement. We possess at least one other fifteenth-century anthology of the letters, the so-called *Bloemlezing*. A recently discovered manuscript of part of Hadewijch's work in a codex from around 1500 indicates that her work was still copied at least up to the early sixteenth century. From then on little is known of her or her work.

Internationally, Hadewijch was known in Germany in the fourteenth century by the name of Saint Adelwip from Brabant.[11] We know at least three fourteenth-century German manuscripts containing translations from her work; in two of them letter 10 occurs once again. A comment by the Franciscan poet Lamprecht von Regenburg (circa 1250) indicates that, if not Hadewijch, at least certain mystic women from Brabant (and Bavaria) were known in thirteenth-century Germany.[12] Since the Dutch *minnemystiek* seems to precede German mysticism, scholars have tried to establish the dependence of one on the other, which is hard to prove on the strength of a limited corpus. In view of the movements of trade and the geographical situation of the Netherlands, the Low Countries might have functioned as a cultural passageway between Romance and Germanic territory. If so, early Dutch mysticism played an intermediary role in spreading eastward the spiritual revival from Cîteaux.

After the discovery of the manuscripts, modern scholars were at first preoccupied with establishing editions of reliable texts and with gathering information on Hadewijch's life. The massive editing work of Jos van Mierlo is still the chief source for all Hadewijch scholarship. Attempts to draw Hadewijch's profile, vitiated by guesswork based on personal bias, are in themselves interesting material for a metacritique of certain brands of literary study. Because we know nothing certain about her, the temptation to confuse her writings with her life is great, and it is indeed not always easy to establish what exactly is literary convention and what is not. As a woman who wrote passionately about love, Hadewijch poses much mystery. Some suggest that she was disappointed in earthly love or, as one scholar put it, that she was a "grande amoureuse" under different circumstances in a different period.[13] Too often, the emotional quality of her writing, with its exaltation and its nonsystematic exposé of her thought, is attributed to the feminine psyche. Yet those who read Hadewijch attentively cannot but be struck by the intellectual mastery of her expression. That Hadewijch wrote masterfully, belonged to a larger movement of religious women, and was for a long time regarded as a classic in the mystical tradition tells us about the position of certain women in medieval society more appropriately than any speculation on the feminine psyche ever could.

Scholars of mysticism have naturally paid much attention to Hadewijch's thought and to her affinity with other mystics, especially with William of Saint Thierry and the Victorines. Recent research focuses more on the artistic and literary aspects of her stanzaic poems and visionary prose. Modern Dutch versions of her poems, letters, and visions are available, as are translations in English, French, German, and Italian, both in anthologies and as separate volumes.

NOTES

1. Manuscripts A and B are in the Royal Library in Brussels under the numbers 2879–80 and 2877–78; manuscript C is in the University Library, Ghent, under the number 941; the recently found codex is in the Library of the Ruusbroec Genootschap, Antwerp, under the number 385 II.

2. Compare *Hadewijch, Visioenen*, ed. Jos Van Mierlo, vol. 2, pp. 127 ff.; Th. Weevers, *Poetry of the Netherlands in Its European Context: 1170–1930*, p. 28; and P. C. Boeren, *Hadewijch en Heer Hendrik van Breda*.

3. Van Mierlo, ed., *Visioenen*, pp. 127, 136.

4. Marie van der Zeyde, *Hadewijch: Een Studie over de Mens en de schrijfster*, p. 22.

5. Tanis Guest, *Some Aspects of Hadewijch's Poetic Form in the "Strofische Gedichten,"* pp. 2 ff.

6. N. de Paepe, *Hadewijch: Strofische Gedichten*.

7. Compare Weevers, pp. 24, 25–26.

8. Guest, *Aspects of Hadewijch's Poetic Form*.

9. Van Mierlo, ed., *Visioenen*, pp. 129–130.

10. K. Porteman, "Een nieuw getuigenis voor Hadewijch uit de 17de eeuw," *Spiegel der Letteren* 12 (1968–1969): 204–210.

11. Jos Van Mierlo, *Adelwip*.

12. Boeren, p. 43.

13. Van der Zeyde, p. 20.

Letters

9

May God let you know, dear child, who He is and how He uses His servants and His handmaidens in particular, and may He consume you in Him. In the depth of His wisdom he shall teach you what He is and how wondrously sweet the beloved dwells in the other beloved, and how thoroughly one dwells in the other, so that neither one nor the other knows themselves apart. But they possess and rejoice in each other mouth in mouth, heart in heart, body in body, soul in soul, and one sweet divine nature flows through them both, and both are one through themselves, yet remain themselves, and will always remain so.

11

Ah, dear child, may God give you what my heart desires for you, and may you love Him as He deserves. Still, I could never endure, dear child, that someone before me loved God as dearly as I. I believe that many loved Him as fondly and dearly, yet I could hardly bear that someone would know Him with such passion.

From the age of ten I have been overwhelmed with such passionate love that I would have died during the first two years of this experience if God had not granted me a power unknown to common people and made me recover with His own being. For He soon granted me reason, sometimes enlightened with many wonderful revelations, and I received many wonderful gifts from Him, when He let me feel His presence and showed Himself to me. I was aware of many signs that were between Him and me, as with friends who are used to concealing little and revealing much when their feelings for each other have grown most intimate, when they taste, eat, and drink and consume each other wholly. Through these many signs God, my lover, showed to me early in life, He made me gain much confidence in Him, and I often thought that no one loved Him as dearly as I. But meanwhile reason made me see that my love for Him was not the dearest, though the strong bonds of our loving had prevented me from sensing or even believing this. Such then is my present state. I do no longer believe that my love for Him is the dearest, nor do I believe that there is one alive who loves God as dearly as I. Sometimes I am so enlightened with love that I realize my failure to give my beloved what He deserves; sometimes when I am blinded with love's sweetness, when I am tasting and feeling her, I realize she is enough for me; and sometimes when I am feeling so fulfilled in her presence, I secretly admit to her that she is enough for me.

20

The nature from which true love springs has twelve hours which drive love out of herself and bring her back in herself. And when love comes back in herself she brings with her all that makes the unspeakable hours drive her out of herself: a mind that seeks to know, a heart full of desire, and a soul full of love. And when love brings these back she throws them into the abyss of the mighty nature in which she was born and nurtured. Then the unspeakable hours enter nature unknown. Then love has come to herself and rejoices in her nature, below, above, and around. And all those who stay below this knowledge shudder at those who have fallen into the abyss and work there and live and die. For such is love's command and her nature.

In the first unspeakable hour of the twelve that draw the soul into love's nature, love reveals herself and touches the soul unexpected and uninvited when her nobility leads us to least suspect it. No matter how strong-natured, the soul fails to understand, for this is truly an unspeakable hour.

In the second unspeakable hour love makes the heart taste a violent death, and the heart goes through death, but it does not die. And yet the soul has not known love for long, and has barely moved from the first to the second hour.

In the third unspeakable hour love shows how one may die and live in her, and how one cannot love without great suffering.

In the fourth unspeakable hour love makes the soul taste her hidden designs, which are deep and darker than the abyss. Then love reveals how miserable the soul is without love. But the soul does not yet partake of love's nature. This hour is truly unspeakable, for the beloved is made to accept love's designs before he possesses love.

In the fifth unspeakable hour love seduces the heart and the soul, and the soul is driven out of herself and out of love's nature and back into love's nature. The soul has then ceased to wonder about the power and darkness of love's designs, and has forgotten the pains of love. Then the soul knows love only through love herself, which may seem lower but is not. For where knowledge is most intimate the beloved knows least.

In the sixth unspeakable hour love despises reason and all that lies within reason and above it and below. Whatever belongs to reason stands against the blessed state of love. For reason cannot take away anything from love or bring anything to love, for love's true reason is a flood that rises forever and knows no peace.

In the seventh unspeakable hour nothing can dwell in love or touch her except desire. And touch is love's most secret name, and touch springs from love herself. For love is always touch and desire and feasts on herself forever. Yet love is perfect in herself.

Love cannot dwell in all things. Love can dwell in charity, but charity cannot dwell in love. Mercy and humility cannot dwell in love, nor can reason or fear, hardship or moderation, or any other thing. But love dwells in them all and gives them all sustenance, though she receives no other food than the wholeness of herself.

The eighth unspeakable hour brings bewilderment when the beloved learns that he cannot know love's nature from her face. Yet the face is held to reveal the inmost nature, and that is most hidden in love. For that she is herself in herself. Love's other limbs and her works are easier to know and understand.

The ninth unspeakable hour brings love's fiercest storm, harshest touch, and deepest desires. The face is sweetest there, at peace, and most winsome. And the deeper love wounds the one she assails, the sweeter she drowns him in herself with the soft splendor of her face. And there she shows herself in her loveliness.

The tenth unspeakable hour is that when no one judges love, but when love judges all things. From God she takes the power to judge all she loves. Love does not yield to saints or men, or angels, heaven or earth, and she enfolds the divine in her nature. To love she calls the hearts who love, in a voice that is loud and untiring. The voice has great power and it tells of things more terrible than thunder. This word is the rope love uses to bind her prisoners, this is the sword she turns on those whom she touches, it is the rod she uses to chastise her children, this is the craft she teaches her companions.

In the eleventh unspeakable hour love possesses the beloved by force. For not a moment can he stray from her, or his heart desire or his soul love. And love makes the memory shrink and the beloved cannot think of saints or men, or angels, heaven or earth, God or himself, but of love alone who has possessed him in a present ever new.

In the twelfth unspeakable hour love is the likeness of her uppermost nature. Only now she breaks out of herself and she works with herself and sinks deep in herself, utterly satisfied with her nature. She fully rejoices in herself, and even if no one loved her the name of love would give her enough loveliness in the nature of her splendid self. Her name which is her nature inside her, her name which is her works outside her, her name which is her crown above her, her name which is the soil under her.

These are the twelve unspeakable hours of love. For in none of the twelve can love be understood, except by those I mentioned, those who have been thrown into the abyss of love's mighty nature and those who belong there, and they believe in love more than they understand her.

25

Greet Sarah from me, with all I am and am not. If I could be fully for her all I want to be in my love, I would be, and indeed I shall, even though she treats me like this. She has not heeded me in my misery, yet I shall not scold or blame her. For love too leaves her in peace and does not chide her, and it is love which should press her time and again, and satiate her with love's noble being. Now that her mind is occupied with other things and my heart's misery does not touch or upset her, she may well leave me to my wandering. Yet she knows she could be a source of comfort to me in this life of misery and the other life of bliss. There indeed she will bring me comfort, who now forsakes me in dismay.

You who can obtain more from me than any living being except Sarah, both Emma and you who are equally dear to me, you too turn too little to love, while I am driven with untasted loving in her awesome embrace. My heart, my soul, my senses do not find an hour's peace by day and night; and hour upon hour the flame burns in the marrow of my soul.

Tell Margriet to beware of pride and turn to wisdom, to go to God every day and aspire to perfection, and to prepare herself to come and live with us, and not stay with those strangers. For she would be greatly disloyal if she stayed away from us, since she wants to please us so much and is really with us now, and fully so, and we too want her to be with us.

One time I heard a sermon in which Saint Augustine was mentioned; at that very moment I caught fire inside me, and it was as if the world would burn in the flames that were in me. Love is all.

26

In God I send you my greetings and my sincere affection. I urge you again and again to practice true love and to aspire to truth and perfection, that you may satisfy God, please Him, and do Him honor and justice, first in Himself and then in the good people He loves and who love Him, and may you give them all they need, whatever their state may be.

This I urge you to do unceasingly, and this I have done since I came among you, for it is the best and most becoming way to serve God that I know of, as the Scriptures say. But above all remember the one and only love, the love I love and aspire to, even though I cannot satisfy her. Understand how much I want you to try to love her as I do. See and feel how much I am grieved by our failures. We do not rejoice in love, we do not rejoice in each other. Woe is us who are deprived of love, and our despair increases. But I, unfortunate wretch, who with love require this of you all who should have brought solace to my suffering, comfort to my dismal woe, peace to my heart, and sweetness, I am wandering about, alone; I must stay far from the one I long to be with above all others, and for whom I wish to become love's fullness. And God knows He rejoices in all this, while I am deprived of all things that may lay my soul to rest in Him.

Ah, why does He allow me to serve Him with such ardor, and to find joy among His disciples, while at the same time He denies Himself and His disciples to me?

Fare well and live well.

Stanzaic Poems

8

Born is the new season as the old one that lasted so long is drawing to a close.

Those prepared to do love's service will receive her rewards: new comfort and new strength.

If they love her with the vigor of love, they will soon be one with love in love.

To be one with love is an awesome calling and those who long for it should spare no effort.

Beyond all reason they will give their all and go through all.

For love dwells so deep in the womb of the Father that her power will unfold only to those who serve her with utter devotion.

First the lover must learn charity and keep God's law.

Then he shall be blessed a hundredfold, and he shall do great things without great effort, and bear all pain without suffering.

And so his life will surpass human reason indeed.

Those who long to be one with love achieve great things, and shirk no effort.

They shall be strong and capable of any task that will win them the love of love, to help the sick or the healthy, the blind, the crippled or the wounded.

For this is what the lover owes to love.

He shall help the strangers and give to the poor and soothe the suffering whenever he can.

He shall pay loyal service to God's friends, to saints and men, with a strength that is not human, by night and by day.

And when his strength seems to falter he will still place his trust in love.

Those who trust in love with all their being shall be given all they need.

For she brings comfort to the sad and guidance to those who cannot read.

Love will be pleased with the lover if he accepts no other comfort and trusts in her alone.

Those who desire to live in love alone with all their might and heart shall so dispose all things that they shall soon possess her all.

12

Like the noble season born to bring us flowers in the fields, so the noble ones are called to bear the yoke, the bonds of love.

Faith grows forever in their deeds, and noble flowers blossom and their fruits.

The world is fathomed with faith, and the lover dwells in highest love, one with her in everlasting friendship.

"My yoke is sweet, my burden light," love's lover speaks with words conceived in love.

And outside love their truth cannot be known: to those who do not dwell in love the burden is not light but heavy, and they suffer fears unknown to love.

For the servants' law is fear but love is the law of sons.

What is this burden light in love, this yoke so sweet?

It is that noble thrust inside, that touch of love in the beloved which makes him one with her, one will, one being, one beyond revoke.

And ever deeper digs desire and all that is dug up is drunk by love, for love's demands on love surpass the mind of man.

These things are beyond the mind of man: how the lover whom love has overwhelmed with love beholds the beloved so full of love.

For he rests not an hour, before he sails with love through all that is, and looks upon her splendor with devotion.

For in love's face he reads the designs she has for him, and in truth in love's face he sees clear and undeceived so many pains so sweet.

This he clearly sees: the lover must love in truth alone.

And when in truth he sees how little he does for love, his higher nature burns with rage and pain.

But from love's face, the lover learns to live a life devoted to the love of love.

This is a design that makes pain sweet, and the lover gives his all to love's fulfillment.

Things of great wonder come to those who give their all to love.

They will be glued to love with love, and with love they will fathom love.

All their secret veins will run into that stream where love gives love away, where love's friends are made drunk with love and filled with wonder at her passion.

And all this remains concealed to strangers, but to the wise it stands revealed.

God grant that all who crave love be well prepared for love, that they may live of her wealth alone, and draw her into their love.

No cruel stranger will ever cause them grief; their life is free and undisturbed,and well may they say, "I am all of love and love is all of me."

For what will harm them when they claim the sun, the moon, and all the stars?

28

Love be praised for the birds that rejoice now and were sad in winter, and soon the proud hearts will rejoice that dwelled in pain too long.

And in the fullness of her power she shall give them a reward that will surpass the mind of man.

When the lover wants to gain love's all from highest love, he must gladly strain all his being and endure the greatest pain in the service of love.

He must be brave always and unafraid and ready to obey all love's commands.

What is the plight of the lover who obeys love's commands?

He will find no one who understands his needs, he will be met with strange eyes and cruel faces, and the pain he bears will not be known.

And this will last all the time his yearning is not fulfilled in love's burning desire.

Love's burning desire is a precious gift; the lover knows this and asks no more.

For this is love's truth: she joins two in one being, makes sweet sour, strangers neighbors, and the lowly noble.

She makes the healthy sick and the sick healthy; she cripples those who are sound of limb and heals the wounded.

To the ignorant she reveals the wide roads they must wander in weariness and teaches them all that shall be learned in the school of highest love.

Burning desire is taught in the school of highest love.

She confounds the experienced, she brings happiness to the wretched, she makes them lords of all over which love herself holds sway.

Of this I am certain beyond all doubt.

To those who can serve love no more I give this good advice.

Let them still beg for her comfort if they falter and serve her with devotion according to her highest counsel.

Let them think how great love's power is, for only those near to death cannot be healed.

They have risen high that have received love's power, and in that power they shall read her judgment over them.

35

The season is cold and dark that makes the birds grieve, and the beasts; but more grief comes to the hearts of men steeped in pride and still deprived of love.

Some rise but I must stay below, burdened forever with a heavy load, and bereft of the riches of relief.

This load is too heavy to bear; it shall not grow lighter in the greatest pain.

How can the hearts of men who know themselves unloved by love endure the taste of death so long and be deprived of all that love can give of help and pity and devotion?

Why was I born if love does not accept my love?

If love repels me so, I shall be lost without revoke; I shall moan and cry and have no peace and lose all hope of happiness, for I shall always be in want of love.

I showed my pain to love and begged her pity, but she remains without time or thought for me; nor does she heed what befalls me.

If ever she favored me, I shall dismiss that now, for she behaves in such strange ways.

And I must live by day as if by night.

Where has love gone? I cannot find her and she denies all love to me.

If love had only let me dwell one hour in her affection, I would now appeal for consolation to her loyal feelings.

But I must keep silent, and endure forever the grim designs she has for me.

It eats my soul, this grim design that I must live in want of love.

And if I strive for love's affection, I would not gain good or happiness.

For I am with grief confounded, so set against all relief that nothing can turn my heart away from my dismal fate.

Love, you were God's counsel when He made me man, but now you let me perish in misery, and I blame you for all that comes over me.

I once believed that I was loved by love, but now it seems that she has rejected me.

Therefore my faith is turned all to mourning, and my highest hopes.

From where does love's sweetest nature draw this hate so strange?

It bears me down at all hours of the day and sears with such rage the marrow of my heart.

I must wander in darkness, where light is not or sweetest comfort, and in strange fear.

Love, bring pride and love to the noble ones, and fulfill in me your first design.

Love has deceived me indeed: where shall I seek counsel now?

With faith if she receives me and guides me to love in her noble care.

Then I can give my all to love, if love will deign to look on me.

I beg her not for comfort or for counsel, but I want no more than that she may make me part of her.

Love, work your will, for your claim is my dearest consolation, to which I shall comply with all I am, in bondage or set free.

Above all other things fulfill your most precious desires, in pain, in death, or in misery.

But only make me part of love, and I shall be blessed with riches beyond all other wealth.

BIBLIOGRAPHY

Primary Works

Van Mierlo, Jos, ed. *Hadewijch, Brieven*. 2 vols. Antwerp, Brussels, Ghent, and Louvain, 1947.
――――. *Hadewijch, Mengeldichten*. Antwerp, Brussels, Ghent, and Louvain, 1952.
――――. *Hadewijch, Strophische Gedichten*. 2 vols. Antwerp, Brussels, Ghent, and Louvain, 1942.
――――. *Hadewijch, Visioenen*. 2 vols. Louvain, Ghent, and Mechlin, 1924.

Related Works

Boeren, P. C. *Hadewijch en Heer Hendrik van Breda*. Leiden, 1962.
Colledge, Eric, ed. *Mediaeval Netherlands Religious Literature*. London and New York, 1965.
De Paepe, N. *Hadewijch: Strofische Gedichten*. Ghent, 1967.
Gooday, Frances Amelia. "Mechtild von Magdeburg and Hadewijch of Antwerp: A Comparison." *Ons Geestelijk Erf* 48 (1974): 1–362.
Guest, Tanis. *Some Aspects of Hadewijch's Poetic Form in the "Strofische Gedichten."* The Hague, 1975.
Hart, Sister M. Columba. "Hadewijch of Brabant." *American Benedictine Review* 13 (1962): 1–24.
Van der Zeyde, Marie. *Hadewijch: Een Studie over de Mens en de schrijfster*. Groningen, 1934.
Van Mierlo, Jos. *Adelwip*. 1933.
Weevers, Th. *Poetry of the Netherlands in Its European Context: 1170–1930*. London, 1960.

THE FRENCH HERETIC BEGUINE

arguerite porete

GWENDOLYN BRYANT

Sometime between 1296 and 1306, in Valenciennes, Guy II, bishop of Cambrai, condemned the *Mirror of Simple Souls* as heretical and ordered it publicly burned in the presence of its author, Marguerite Porete. On June 1, 1310, Marguerite herself was burned in what Henry Charles Lea calls "the first formal auto-da-fé of which we have cognizance at Paris." [1] These two burnings mark the chronological limits of what we know of Marguerite's life, for aside from the inquisitorial account of her trial and allusions to it in fourteenth-century chronicles, no documents survive. Nevertheless, scholars agree that she came from Hainaut (a region south of Flanders and Brabant, today part of France and Belgium), since she is referred to as Margarita de Hannonia.

Marguerite escaped punishment in her first tangle with the ecclesiastical authorities; although forbidden on pain of excommunication to disseminate her ideas further, she boldly persisted, even sending her book to prominent Churchmen, some of whom actually approved it. [2] Brought before the successor of Guy II, Philip of Marigny, in 1306 or 1307, she was once again accused of heresy and of leading common folk astray. We trace her next to late 1308, in Paris, where she had fallen into the hands of William Humbert, the papal inquisitor and Dominican confessor to Philip the Fair, remembered for the part he played in the brutal trial of the Templars that same year.

Imprisoned in Paris, Marguerite refused to ask for absolution or take vows required for examination; she was left to languish for eighteen months. Since the inquisitor lacked direct testimony, he extracted a number of articles from Marguerite's book and submitted them to a commission of twenty-one theological regents of the Sorbonne for examination.

On April 11, 1310, the canon lawyers delivered their verdict, unanimously declaring at least fifteen of the articles heretical. Among them were the first—"the annihilated soul takes leave of the virtues and is no longer in their servitude, because it no longer needs them; rather the virtues obey the soul's every sign"—and the fifteenth—"such a soul no longer cares about God's consolations or His gifts; it neither should nor can because it is completely turned toward God, which prevents it from caring about them."[3]

Judged ipso facto on the evidence of her work, Marguerite was relinquished on May 31, 1310, to secular justice as a relapsed heretic, with the customary adjuration for mercy: "ut citra mortem et membrorum mutilatum secum agat misericorditer."[4] Guiart of Cressonsacq, a follower of the *vita apostolica*, apparently tried to intervene in her behalf but was also imprisoned.[5] The provost of Paris sentenced her to be burned at the stake; the following day, along with a converted Jew who had allegedly spit on an image of the Virgin, she perished in the flames in the Place de Grève. According to the continuer of the *Chronicon* of William of Nangis, her courage and devotion drew sympathetic tears from the crowd.[6]

The accounts of the proceedings of Marguerite's trial and the brief passages in contemporary chronicles provide no biographical information concerning her education, calling, or social station, except that they refer to her as a Beguine. In the *Myreur des histors* Jean des Preis described her as a "beghine en clergie mult suffissant" (a Beguine very capable in theology),[7] a judgment echoed in the *Grandes chroniques de France*, where Marguerite is called a "béguine clergesse."[8] The canon lawyers responsible for the condemnation of the *Mirror of Simple Souls* called her by the Latin term *beguina*.

What does the term "Beguine" mean, and whom did it designate? The origin of the word continues to defy the efforts of etymologists, who derive it variously from Middle English *beggar* or *beggere*, 'beggar'; from *al-BIGEN-sis*, which refers to a heresy taking its name from the French town of Albi; from the name of a twelfth-century priest, Lambert le Begue; and from Old French *beige* or *bege*, the color of the penitent rope worn by the Beguines and their male counterparts, Beghards.[9]

Although at first glance this appellation seems to define Marguerite's role and status in fourteenth-century society, certainty is out of the question, for despite the prevalence of the epithets Beghard and Beguine in the later Middle Ages, it is hard to generalize about these men and women. Roughly, however, a Beguine or a Beghard can be defined as a lay follower of the apostolic life who, in imitation of Christ, pursued a life of poverty and abstinence, like the mendicant friars. Beguines dressed in a monklike costume. Some formed self-supporting organized communities, while others led a vagabond life of beggary. Unlike members of orders recognized by the Church, they were bound by neither formal vows nor a common rule. Because of overcrowding and the high fees required to enter most convents, many unmarried women of the urban middle class associated themselves with the Beguine movement, although women from the upper classes were by no means absent from their numbers.[10] Single girls thus banded together to earn their livelihood, as "spinsters," supporting themselves by manual labor such as woolworking. Lester Little observes, "As with the poor who joined the Humiliati, the poor women of Netherlandish towns could find economic security, social stability, and a deep sense of spiritual fulfillment in the urban religious confraternity and consorority of the Beguines."[11] Many wealthy Beguines sponsored poorer ones, supplying them with housing.[12] Such arrangements as these were not an unlikely alternative in a century when the number of marriageable women far exceeded that of men.

The great variety of life-styles that the Beguine movement represented goes against E. W. McDonnell's conclusion that Marguerite "must have been an unattached beguine, with no fixed residence, regarding mendicancy as a means of livelihood, pursuing a life of moral laxity, and refusing to submit to authority."[13] The fact that her name appears on none of the registers of the occupants of organized *béguinages* is no reason to exclude other possibilities. Beguines did not necessarily live in communities or even together in the Beguine houses; some remained at home with their families. McDonnell assumes the same untenable position as did the Church in its vain attempt to distinguish between "good" and "bad" Beguines. The Church condemned the indolent life and the unregulated mendicancy of the "heretic" Beguines who lived on alms and were alleged to interpret the Bible erroneously, yet periodically it exonerated the chaste and pious Beguines who had pledged themselves to a life of charity and obedience.[14]

Actually, no such clear separation is possible; even the polyvalence of the term "Beguine" illustrates the ambiguity of their status. "Beguine" could be used to mock the ridiculously righteous or denounce those of loose morals or even expose the hypocrisy of *tartuffes*. The term was a synonym for "heretic," particularly a single female heretic; more neutrally, it could signify an unmarried secular person devoted to spiritual matters.[15] The history of the movement is marked by continuous cycles of persecution and rehabilitation, cycles that alternate between a complete condemnation of Beguine status and a conditional endorsement of the "good" Beguines, that is, of orthodox, nonmendicant laywomen.

Romana Guarnieri, whose critical introduction and transcription of a French copy of the *Mirror* remain the basic work on the subject, has done much toward reevaluating Marguerite by identifying her as the author of the "anonymous" *Miroir des simples âmes*. Guarnieri points out that the author of the *Mirror* must have been highly educated, especially in theological matters, and entirely conversant with contemporary court literature and *minnemystik*. The encouragement and protection given Marguerite by several prominent Churchmen as well as internal evidence from the *Mirror* lead Guarnieri to postulate her as a well-born, cultivated woman.[16] As Robert Lerner observes, Marguerite frequently expresses sentiments of the aristocracy and uses feudal-aristocratic metaphors as vehicles for her ideas.[17] This aura of refinement of the patrician mystic addressing herself to a clandestine feminine following contrasts sharply with the wandering promiscuity of McDonnell's beggar maiden. Whether or not one accepts Guarnieri's interpretation or Lerner's suggestion, certainly there is no evidence of Marguerite's "moral laxity"; not even Philip the Fair's inquisition leveled this favorite charge against her.

Marguerite's condemnation in 1310 must be seen against the background of growing hostility on the part of the Church toward the numerous extrareligious groups, which were resented as rivals, especially those claiming to unravel the mysteries of scripture.[18] Particularly disconcerting to the Church was the promulgation of the idea that sacred authority rested less on ordination and more on poverty, purity, and evangelism.[19] The "Clementines," decrees issued by the Council of Vienne (1311–1312), ushered in a period of official persecution which, perhaps, began with the death of Marguerite, since six of the bishops who formed her jury later served as members of this council. Although Marguerite was burned as a heretic, not as a Beguine, the decrees of Vienne rendered the words synonymous.

For example, the bull *Ad Nostrum* specifies the Beguines and Beghards as guilty of the heresy of the Free Spirit, enumerating eight errors in their beliefs: (1) humans can attain a sinless state, (2) in which sensuality is so subordinated to the soul that the body may be freely granted whatever it likes; (3) in this "spirit of liberty" individuals are not subject to human obedience (4) and can attain the same perfection of beatitude on earth as in heaven; (5) every intelligent nature is blessed in itself, (6) and the acts of virtue are necessary only for those who are imperfect, for the perfect soul no longer needs to practice them; (7) the carnal act is not a sin; (8) the perfect should not rise during the elevation of the Host, for to think of the sacrament of the Eucharist or the Passion of Christ would be a sign of imperfection, a descent from the heights of perfection.[20] While these heretical ideas are by no means novel—many of them had been refuted by Albertus Magnus' *Determinatio*, written sometime between 1262 and 1280—they do reflect the Roman papacy's urgent concern to legislate against heterodoxy. The *Ad Nostrum*, which has been called a birth certificate without a baby, asserts that the Free Spirit abounded among the Beguines and Beghards.[21]

As a mystic, Marguerite wrote of her quest of union with God. Like her contemporaries Mechthild of Magdeburg and Hadewijch, she clothed her experiences in bridal imagery. Her mysticism, deemed radical and heretic by the inquisition, differs from that of her contemporaries not so much in intensity or purpose as in method. It is her advocacy, as Lerner points out, of complete and perfect passivity of the will in attaining the divine experience—which rendered the sacramental ministry of the Church unnecessary in the final stages of the soul's ascent to perfection—that was found objectionable.[22] Her doctrinal heresy, on the other hand, adjudged by her persecutors to be of the Free Spirit, has not been unanimously established. As a Free Spirit, she was deemed guilty of pantheism and antinomianism. Pantheism she did advocate, but accusations of antinomianism seem unfounded.

Because the *Mirror of Simple Souls* contains many passages expressing ideas similar to those denounced by the Council of Vienne and attributed to the Brethren of the Free Spirit, Marguerite has been called "the first apostle in France of the German sect of the Brethren of the Free Spirit."[23] The only justification for this claim, however, lies in the fact that the *Mirror* is the only important document anterior to the Council of Vienne to assemble, in part, this heretical doctrine, but since it cannot be proved that an identifiable sect existed, it is difficult to prove her its spokeswoman. Moreover, modern theological scholars are by no means as certain of its heterodoxy as were the canonists of 1310. Neither were the accusations of heterodoxy unanimous during Marguerite's lifetime and later. The *Mirror* survived in numerous monastery copies, and it was attributed to the authorship of Ruysbroeck—two facts indicating that not everyone deemed its tenets objectionable.

Certainly two points cited as heretical by the canonists—that the soul annihilated in the love of God needs neither to pursue virtue nor perform exterior practices of devotion—are repeated often in the *Mirror*. In the third state (chapter 118) the soul is required, as a sacrifice, to give up all works in order to reach the fourth state, union with God in an ecstasy of love. A third point of contention, bearing suggestions of pantheism and antinomianism, is that the annihilated soul is free to grant nature, without remorse, all it desires.[24] While this point *is* in the text, the following sentence tempers the claim: "But such a nature is so well ordered by its transformation in the union with Love that Nature demands nothing which might be forbidden."[25] The explanation confirms the pantheistic but denies the potentially antinomian tenets of the text.

Other passages doubtless deemed improper by the canon lawyers are those that speak of the sacrament of the Church[26] as well as those that refer to the Catholic Church as "Holy Church the Little" and to the community of Free Souls as "Holy Church the Great." Holy Church the Little is governed by reason; Holy Church the Great by divine love.

Moreover, from the opening verses of the *Mirror*, Marguerite criticizes the learning of the clerics, which prevents them from understanding her mystical treatise: "Theologians or other clerics, you will not have any understanding of it [the *Mirror*], so learnèd are your minds." But the *Mirror* is a mystical treatise, not a diatribe against the clergy. A long prose tract written to be read aloud, it was dictated ostensibly to its author by Love, who appears as the major interlocutor—Love, questioned by Reason, defines the annihilated soul and the states or "beings" through which this soul must pass in order to reach the state of perfection.

Unfortunately, the *Mirror* has survived only in late manuscript copies and translations; whether or not these have been altered much cannot be determined. Of the three surviving French versions, only one is available to scholarship: Manuscript Chantilly Condé F. 14. 26 (formerly 386), written between 1450 and 1530 near Orléans. Although generally regarded as corrupt, this version is nevertheless considered closest to its prototype. There are many fifteenth-century Latin and Italian translations of the *Mirror* and three Middle English versions, one published by Marilyn Dorion in the *Archivio Italiano per la Storia della Pietà*. Another was translated into modern English in 1927 and published by the Downside Benedictines.[27]

The astonishing number of manuscripts testifies to the international popularity of the work, especially in the fifteenth century. In England, for example, it was circulated by the English charterhouses, having been introduced into the country by, perhaps, a member of the suite of Philippa of Hainaut when she arrived as the bride of Edward III in 1327. In France, the *Mirror* had at least one royal reader, Marguerite de Navarre, who praises it in her late poem "Prisons," which, like chapter 61 of the *Mirror*, tells of the Farnear.[28] But the research required to determine exactly who read the *Mirror of Simple Souls* and in what spirit remains to be done, as well as the reconstruction of the Old French archetype.

The Chantilly manuscript, transcribed by Guarnieri, has been used for the translation that follows.

NOTES

1. Henry Charles Lea, *A History of the Inquisition in the Middle Ages*, vol. 1, p. 123.

2. Romana Guarnieri, "Il movimento del Libero Spirito, testi e documenti," *Archivio Italiano per la Storia della Pietà* 4 (1965): 408.

3. Paul Frédéricq, *Corpus documentorum inquisitionis haereticae pravitatis Neerlandicae*, vol. 2, pp. 63–64.

4. Ibid., vol. 1, pp. 159–161, or Lea, vol. 2, pp. 575–577.

5. For a discussion of Guiart, see Robert E. Lerner, *The Heresy of the Free Spirit in the Later Middle Ages*, pp. 77–78. This self-possessed "Angel of Philadelphia" was the leader of a group of mendicants, the "adherents of the Lord," who wore a special habit. He insisted that even the pope himself did not have the right to strip him of his garb; however, when faced with the stake, he faltered, abjured his errors, and was sentenced to perpetual imprisonment.

6. Frédéricq, vol. 1, p. 160, or C. V. Langlois, "Marguerite Porète," *Revue Historique* 54 (1894): 295–299.

7. Guarnieri's edition of the *Mirror* in "Il movimento del Libero Spirito," p. 594, or Jean d'Outremeuse des Preis, *Myreur des histors*, vol. 6, pp. 141–142.

8. Frédéricq, vol. 2, p. 64, or *Les grandes chroniques de France*, ed. Paulin, vol. 5, p. 188.

9. Dayton Phillips, "Beguines in Medieval Strasbourg," pp. 2–6.

10. Norman Cohn, *The Pursuit of the Millennium*, p. 160.

11. Lester K. Little, *Religious Poverty and the Profit Economy in Medieval Europe*, p. 133.

12. Gordon Leff, *Heresy in the Later Middle Ages*, vol. 1, p. 320, or Phillips, p. 23.

13. E. W. McDonnell, *The Beguines and Beghards in Medieval Culture*, p. 367. See Hermann Haupt, "Zwei Traktate gegen Beginen und Begharden," *Zeitschrift für Kultur und Geschichte* 12 (1891): 85, for a similar judgment.

14. Little, pp. 130 ff., for example, discusses the bull of Gregory IX in 1233, which approved of "good" (because cloistered) Beguines (*beguinae clausae*) and disapproved of the others (*beguinae singulariter in saeculo manentes, congregationes beguinarum*).

15. See Lerner, pp. 38–40, for interesting examples.

16. Guarnieri, p. 510.

17. Lerner, p. 233.

18. See McDonnell, p. 366, for a contemporary criticism of translations and commentaries on Beguine conventicles, as well as Jean-Claude Schmitt, *Mort d'une hérésie*, p. 104. On the Church's biblical exegesis, see Bernard Hamilton, *The Medieval Inquisition*, and Malcolm Lambert, *Medieval Heresy: Popular Movements from Bogomil to Huss*.

19. See Walter L. Wakefield, *Heresy, Crusade and Inquisition in Southern France*, pp. 22–27, and Hamilton, *The Medieval Inquisition*.

20. For the *Ad Nostrum*, see E. Friedberg, *Corpus iuris canonici*, vol. 2, col. 1183, or H. Kaminsky, "The Free Spirit in the Hussite Revolution."

21. Lerner, p. 83.

22. Ibid., pp. 204–205.

23. Lea, vol. 2, p. 123.

24. This point appears only in the continuation of the *Chronicon* of William of Nangis.

25. The passage is found in chapter 8, Guarnieri, p. 527. Chapter 17, p. 537, is similar.

26. Ibid., chapter 15, p. 535.

27. See Clare Kirchberger, *The Mirror of Simple Souls*, in the bibliography.

28. See Jean Dagens, "*Le miroir des simples âmes* et Marguerite de Navarre."

The Mirror of Simple Souls

You who will read in this book,
If you want to understand it well
Think about what you will say,

For it is difficult to understand;
You must assume Humility,
Who is the treasurer of Science
And the mother of the other virtues.

Theologians or other clerics,
You will not have any understanding of it,
So learnèd are your minds,[1]
If you do not proceed humbly
And Love and Faith together,
The mistresses of the house,
Do not cause you to surmount Reason.

Reason herself witnesses to us
In the thirteenth chapter of this book,
And is not ashamed
That Love and Faith give her life
And she cannot free herself from them,
For they have dominion over her,
This is why she must humble herself.

Humble, therefore, your sciences
Which are founded in Reason,
And place all your trust
In those which are given
By Love and illuminated by Faith.
And thus you will understand this book
Which through Love gives life to the Soul.

Prologue

The Soul touched by God, and stripped of sin in the first state of grace, has risen by divine graces to the seventh state of grace, in which the Soul has the plentitude of her perfection through divine fruition in the land of life.

HERE SPEAKS LOVE: Among you actives and contemplatives[2] and you who are perhaps annihilated by true love, who will hear some of the powers of the pure love, the noble love, the high love of the Free Soul, and how the Holy Spirit put His sail in the Soul, as if in His ship, I beg of you out of love, says Love, to listen carefully with the subtle understanding within you and with great diligence, for otherwise all those if they be not so who will hear this will understand badly.

Now listen with humility to a little example of worldly love, and understand it likewise with regard to divine love.

EXAMPLE: There was once a lady, a king's daughter, of great heart and nobility and of noble courage as well, who lived in a foreign land. It happened that this lady heard tell of the great courtliness and nobility of King Alexander and at once her will loved him[3] for the great fame of his courage. But this lady was so far from this great lord in whom she had placed her love—for she could neither see nor have him—that she was often disheartened within herself, for no love except this one could content her. And when she saw that this far love, which to her was so near or within her, was so far outside of her, she thought to herself that she might ease her pain by imagining what her friend, on whose account she was so often heartbroken, looked like. So she had an image painted in the likeness of the beloved king, which resembled as nearly as possible the imagined representation that she loved with the affection of the Love which had seized her; and by means of this image and in other ways[4] she reflected upon the King himself.[5]

THE SOUL: Truly, in like manner, says the Soul who caused this book to be written, I say the same to you: I heard tell of a king of great power, who in his courtliness, his very great courtliness of nobility and generosity, was a noble Alexander; but he was so far from me, and I from him, that I could not take comfort in myself alone, and so that I might remember him he gave me this book which represents his love in several ways.[6] But although I have his image, it is not that I am not in a foreign land and far from the palace where the very noble friends of this lord dwell, who are all pure, perfect, and freed by the gifts of the king with whom they dwell.

THE AUTHOR: And therefore we shall tell you how our Lord is not at all freed from Love, but rather Love is freed from Him for our sake, in order that the little ones may hear Him through your intercession, for Love can do everything without doing harm.

AND THUS LOVE SPEAKS FOR YOU: There are seven beings of noble being, from which the creature receives her being, if the creature embraces all these beings, before she comes into perfect being; and we shall tell you how before this book ends.

2. Of the Enterprise of Love and Why She Had This Book Written

LOVE: Children of the holy Church, says Love, I have made this book for you, so that you will hearken in order to better merit the perfection of life and the being of peace to which the creature can come by the virtue of perfect charity, to whom this gift is given by the whole Trinity, this gift you shall hear explained in this book by the understanding of Love at the request of Reason.

3. Here Love Speaks of the Commandments of the Holy Church

LOVE: We shall begin here, says Love, with the commandments of the holy Church, so that each may draw sustenance from this book with the help of God, Who commands us to love Him with all our heart, with all our soul, and with all our virtue; and ourselves as we ought; and our neighbors as ourselves.

Firstly, that we love Him with all our heart. That is to say that our thoughts are always truly in Him. And with all our soul. That is to say that upon pain of death we speak only the truth. And with all our virtue. That is that we do all our works purely for Him. And ourselves as we ought. That is, we do not consider our profit, in doing this, but rather the perfect will of God. And our neighbors as ourselves. This is that we neither do, nor think, nor say to our neighbors that which we would not have them do to us. These commandments are necessary for the salvation of all: from a lesser life can no one obtain grace.

Note here the example of the young man, who said to Jesus Christ that he had kept the commandments from childhood, and Jesus Christ said to him: you must do one thing more, if you want to be perfect. This: go and sell all that you have and give it to the poor and then follow Me thus, and you shall have the treasure of the heavens. This is the counsel of all perfection of the virtues, and whoever shall keep it shall dwell in perfect charity.[7]

4. Of the Noble Virtue of Charity, and How She Obeys No One but Love

LOVE: Charity obeys no created thing except Love.

Charity has nothing of her own, and if she possesses anything, she never says that it is hers.

Charity leaves her own work and goes to do that of others.

Charity asks no return from any creature, for whatever good deed or favor she does.

Charity has neither shame, nor fear, nor sickness; she is so righteous that she cannot yield, whatever may happen.

Charity neither does nor cares for anything under the sun; all the world is her relief and her due.[8]

Charity gives to all what she has of value; she never withholds herself and often promises what she does not have, in her great generosity, hoping that for him who gives, more remains.

Charity is such a wise merchant that where others lose, she makes a profit. She escapes the bonds with which others bind themselves and therefore has a great abundance of what pleases Love.

And note that who would have perfect charity is mortified in the affections of the life of the spirit by the action of charity.

5. Of the Life Called Peace of Charity in Annihilated Life

LOVE: Now there is another life, which we call peace of charity in annihilated life. Of it, says Love, we wish to speak, asking that one find:

(1) a soul
(2) who saves herself by faith without works,
(3) who is alone in love,
(4) who does nothing for God,
(5) who leaves God nothing to do,
(6) who can be taught nothing,
(7) from whom nothing can be taken,
(8) to whom nothing can be given,
(9) who has no will.[9]

LOVE: Alas, says Love, and who will give this Soul what she needs, for it has never been given, nor shall it ever be?

LOVE: This Soul, says Love, has six wings like the seraphim. She no longer wants anything which comes by intermediary,[10] this is the seraphim being: there is no intermediary between their love and the divine love. They have constant tidings without intermediary, and this Soul also, for she does not seek the divine science among the masters of this century,[11] but by truly scorning the world and herself. O Gods, how great is the difference between the gift of a friend given by an intermediary and the gift of a friend to a friend without intermediary!

LOVE: This book spoke the truth about this Soul, when it said that she has wings like the seraphim. With two wings she covers the face of Jesus Christ, our Lord. That is to say that the more knowledge this Soul has of the divine goodness, the more perfectly she knows that she knows nothing in comparison to a single spark of His goodness, for He is not known except to Himself.

With two other wings she covers His feet. That is to say the greater her knowledge of what Jesus Christ suffered for us, the more perfectly she knows that she knows nothing in comparison to what He suffered for us, for He is not known except to Himself.

With two other wings the Soul flies, and dwells immobile and seated.[12] That is to say that all she knows and loves and praises of the divine goodness are the wings with which she flies and dwells immobile—for she is always in the sight of God—and seated, for she dwells constantly in the divine will.

Oh, and of what would such a Soul be afraid? Certainly, she neither could nor should fear or doubt anything, although she is in the world, and it is possible for the world, the flesh, and the devil and the four elements and the birds of the air and the dumb beasts to torment her, tear her to pieces, or devour her, she can lose nothing if God remains with her. For He is everywhere, all-powerful, all-wise, and all-good. He is our father, our brother, and our loyal friend. He is without beginning. He is incomprehensible except to Himself. He is without end, three persons and one single God; and such is, says this Soul, the friend of our souls.

6. How the Soul in Love with God, Living in Peace of Charity, Takes Leave of the Virtues

LOVE: This Soul of such love, says Love herself, can say to the virtues that she has been in their service for a long time and many a day.

THE SOUL: I confess it to you, Lady Love, says this Soul: there was a time that I was, but from now on it is otherwise, your courtliness[13] has removed me from their service. And because of this I am now able to say and sing to them:

Virtues, I take leave of you forevermore,
My heart will be freer and gayer for it;
Your service is too constant, well I know it.
I once placed my heart in you, without any separation;
You know that I was wholly abandoned to you;
I was then in bondage to you, now I am delivered from it.
I had placed all my heart in you, well I know it,
For which I lived a while in great fear.
I have suffered for it many a grievous torment, endured many a pain;
It is a wonder that I have escaped alive at all;
But since it is so, it does not matter: I am separated from you,
For which I thank God on high; my day is good.
I have left your dangers behind, where I had many a trouble.
Never was I free but when separated from you;
I have left your dangers, I dwell in peace.

11. How, at the Request of Reason, Love Gives Knowledge of This Soul to Contemplatives by Declaring Nine Points Which Have Been Mentioned Before

REASON: Now, Love, says Reason, I pray you, for the sake of the contemplatives who still desire to grow in divine knowledge and who are and remain in the desire of Love, to explain out of your courtliness the eleven[14] points which this Soul who wants Tender Love has, in whom Charity dwells and establishes herself by annihilated life, by which the Soul is abandoned through pure Love.

LOVE: Reason, says Love, name them.

REASON: The first point, says Reason to Love, that you said is that one cannot find such a Soul.

LOVE: This is true, says Love. This means that this Soul knows only one thing: the root of all evil and the abundance of all sin, which is without number, without weight, and without measure. And sin is nothingness, and this Soul is completely stricken and frightened by her horrible faults, which are less than nothing, and through this understanding the Soul is less than nothing, as is what is hers; therefore one may conclude that this Soul cannot be found, for such a Soul is so annihilated by humility that according to her rightful judgment if God wanted to punish her for the thousandth of one of her faults, no creature who has ever sinned would merit so great a torment or such unending confusion as she. Such humility, and no other, is true and perfect humility in the annihilated Soul.

LOVE: The second point is that this Soul saves herself by faith without works.

REASON: Oh, for God's sake! says Reason, what does this mean?

LOVE: This means, says Love, that this annihilated Soul has such a great inward knowledge by the virtue of faith that she is so occupied within herself sustaining what Faith has ministered to her of the power of the Father, and of the knowledge of the Son, and of the goodness of the Holy Spirit that no created thing, unless it passes quickly, can remain in her memory, because her other occupation has so invaded the understanding of this annihilated Soul. This Soul can work no more, and surely, she is also sufficiently pardoned and exonerated without working by believing that God is good and incomprehensible. This saves the Soul without works, for faith overcomes all work, according to Love's own witness.

LOVE: The third point is that she is alone in love.

REASON: Oh, for God's sake, Lady Love, says Reason, what does this mean?

LOVE: This means, says Love, that this Soul finds neither consolation, nor affection, nor hope in any creature created by God either in heaven or on earth, but only in the goodness of God. This creature neither begs nor asks anything of any creature. This is the phoenix,[15] who is alone; for this Soul, who satisfies herself of herself, is alone in love.

LOVE: The fourth point is that this Soul does nothing for God.

REASON: Oh, for God's sake, says Reason, what does this mean?

LOVE: This means, says Love, that God can do nothing with her work, and this Soul does nothing but that with which God can do something. She does not care about herself; let God, Who loves her more than this Soul loves herself, care about her. This Soul has so great a faith in God that she has no fear of being poor, her friend is so rich. For Faith teaches her that she will find God such as she hopes Him to be, and she hopes through faith that He is wholly rich, thus she cannot be poor.

LOVE: The fifth point is that this Soul leaves God nothing to do that she can do.

REASON: Oh, for God's sake, Love, says Reason, what does this mean?

LOVE: This means, says Love, that she can do nothing but the will of God and also cannot will anything else, and thus she leaves God nothing to do. For she lets nothing enter her thoughts which is contrary to God, and thus she leaves God nothing to do.

LOVE: The sixth point is that she can be taught nothing.

REASON: Oh, for God's sake, says Reason, what does this mean?

LOVE: This means that this Soul has such great steadfastness that if she had all the knowledge of all the creatures that ever were and are and are to come, this would seem nothing to her in comparison with what she loves which has never been known, nor shall it ever be. This Soul loves better what is in God and what has never been given, nor shall ever be given, than she loves what she has and would have, were she to have all the knowledge that all the creatures that are, and are to come, will have.

THE SOUL: And still this is nothing, says the Soul, in comparison with what is really concerned, but nothing can be said about that.

LOVE: The seventh point is that nothing can be taken from her.

REASON: Oh, for God's sake, Love, says Reason, tell what this means.

LOVE: What does this mean? says Love. And what could be taken from her? Certainly nothing could be taken from her. For though honor, riches and friends, heart and body and life were taken from this Soul, still nothing would be taken from her if God dwells with her. Thus it is apparent that no one can take anything from her, whatever his strength.

LOVE: The eighth point is that she can be given nothing.

REASON: Love, for God's sake, says Reason, what does this mean?

LOVE: What does it mean? says Love. And what could she be given? If she were given all that ever has been given and shall be given, this would be nothing in comparison with what she loves and will love: only God Himself.

AND THE SOUL SPEAKS: Lady Love loves and will love in me.[16]

LOVE: With all due respect, says Love, this I am not.

We shall say, says Love, for the sake of the auditors, that God better loves the more of this Soul in Himself than the less of her in Him.

BUT THE SOUL SPEAKS: There is no less, there is only all and this I may truly say.

LOVE: I say moreover, says Love, that if the soul had all the knowledge and the love and the praise of the divine Trinity which have ever been given or shall be given, this would be nothing in comparison with what she loves and will love; nor may this love ever be attained through knowledge.

THE SOUL SPEAKS TO LOVE: Oh, assuredly, sweet Love, says the Soul. Not even the smallest particle of it. For there is no other God than the one about Whom nothing can be perfectly known. For my God is this one alone about Whom a single word cannot be said and of Whom all those in paradise cannot understand a single point, whatever their knowledge of Him may be. And in this is implied, says the Soul, the sovereign mortification of my spirit's love, and this is all the glory of my soul's love, and will be everlastingly, and that of all those who ever understood. This point sounds small, says the Soul, in comparison to the greater one about which no one speaks. But I want to speak about it and do not know what to say. In spite of this, Lady Love, she says, my love is such that I prefer to hear you spoken ill of than that nothing be said about you. And surely, this is what I am doing; I speak ill of you, for all that I say about you is but to speak ill of your goodness. But that I speak ill of you should be pardoned by you. For Lord, says the Soul, who speaks of you constantly surely speaks ill of you, and thus never says anything of your goodness; and I myself speak similarly. I cannot stop speaking of you, either by questions or by thoughts, or listening in order to hear if someone will tell me something of your goodness; but the more I hear you spoken of, the more I am bewildered. For it would be to me a great villainy, to let me believe that something of your goodness is told me, for they who believe this are deceived, for I know with certainty that nothing can be said about it, and God grant that I never be deceived, and never want to hear your divine goodness lied about, rather that I accomplish the undertaking of this book, whose mistress, Love, told me to finish in it all my undertakings. For inasmuch as I ask anything myself from Love for herself, I will be with myself in the life of the spirit, in the shadow of the sun, where the intentions of divine love and the divine generation are seen as subtle images.[17]

But what am I saying? says the Soul. And surely, though I had all that has been told, it would still be nothing in comparison with what I love in Him, what He will give no one except Himself, what He must keep for His divine righteousness. And consequently I say, and it is true, that I can be given nothing, whatever it may be. And this complaint which you hear me voice, Lady Reason, says the Soul, is my all and my best, understand it well. Oh, what a sweet understanding! By God! Understand it wholly, for paradise is nothing other than this understanding.

LOVE: The ninth point, Lady Reason, says Love, is that this Soul has no will.

REASON: Oh, for the God of love, says Reason, what are you saying? You say that this Soul has no will?

LOVE: Oh, surely not, for all this Soul wills by consent is what God wills her to will, and this she wills in order to accomplish the will of God, not her own will; and she cannot will this by herself, rather it is the will of God which wills it in her; thus it is apparent that this Soul has no will, without the will of God, which causes her to will all that she should will.

61. Here Love Speaks of the Seven States of the Soul

LOVE: I said, says Love, that there are seven states each of higher understanding than the other, without comparison. For so great a difference as there is between a drop of water and the whole sea, which is very large, so great is the difference between the first state of grace and the second and so on for the others, without comparison. And, however, there is not so great a state of the four states that the Soul does not live there in very great servitude. But the fifth state is freed by charity, for it is disburdened of all things; and the sixth is glorious, for the opening of the sweet movement of glory, that the gentle Farnear gives, is nothing other than an apparition of His own glory which God wants the Soul to have and to have everlastingly. And therefore He gives her out of His goodness this demonstration of the seventh state in the sixth state. This demonstration is born of the seventh state, which gives the sixth being. And this demonstration is so soon given that she herself to whom it is given has no perception of her given gift.

THE SOUL: What wonder? says the Soul herself, if I could perceive it before such a gift is given, I would myself be what the gift is, through divine goodness, which would give it to me everlastingly if my soul had left my body.

THE BRIDEGROOM OF THIS SOUL: This is not within her power says the Bridegroom of this Soul herself; I sent you tokens by means of my Farnear, but let no one ask who this Farnear is, or the work he does when he reveals the glory of the Soul, for nothing can be said about him except that the Farnear is the Trinity Himself, who gives her the demonstration which we call "movement," neither because the Soul moves nor the Trinity, but because the Trinity works within this Soul to show her His glory. Of this no one can speak except the Deity Himself, for the Soul to whom the Farnear gives himself has such a great knowledge of God and of Him and of all things that she sees in God Himself, through divine knowledge, that the light of this knowledge takes from her the knowledge of herself, of God, and of all things.

THE SOUL: This is true, says the Soul; there is nothing else. And, therefore, if God wants me to have this great knowledge, then He prevents me and keeps me from knowing Him for otherwise I would have no knowledge of Him. And if He wants me to know myself, then He also keeps me from the knowledge of myself, or otherwise I cannot have any.

LOVE: What you say is true, Lady Soul, says Love. There is nothing more certain to know or more profitable to have than this work.

118. The Seven States of the Pious Soul Which Are Otherwise Called Beings

THE SOUL: I have promised, says the Soul, since Love took hold, to say something about the seven states that we call beings, for this they are. They are the degrees by which one climbs up from the valley to the summit of the mountain, which is so isolated that one sees only God there; and each degree is founded by its being.

The first state, or degree, is that of the Soul touched by God through grace and stripped of her capacity to sin, who intends to keep upon her life, that is upon pain of death, the commandments God gives in the Law. And because of this this Soul beholds with great fear that God has commanded her to love Him with all her heart, and her neighbor as herself, as well. To this Soul this seems labor enough for her—all that she can do—and it seems that though she live a thousand years, it is enough for her strength to hold and keep the commandments.

THE FREE SOUL: I was once found at this point and in this state, says the Free Soul. No one is frightened to climb the heights, certainly not if he has a valiant heart full of noble courage. But the little heart from lack of love dares neither to undertake a great thing nor to climb high. Such people are cowards; this is not astonishing, for they remain in sloth which prevents them from seeking God, Whom they will never find if they do not seek Him diligently.

THE SECOND STATE: The second state or degree is that the Soul beholds what God advises to His special friends, beyond what He commands; he who can dispense with accomplishing all that he knows pleases his friend is no friend.

And then the creature abandons herself and attempts to go beyond the advice of men by the mortification of nature, by scorning riches, delights, and honors in order to accomplish the perfection of the Gospel's counsel, of which Jesus Christ is the example. Then she fears neither losing what she has, nor the words of men, nor the weakness of the body, for her friend did not fear these things nor can the Soul who has been taken by Him.

THE THIRD STATE: The third state is that the Soul beholds herself affected by the love of works of perfection, works which her spirit, out of love's burning desire, decides to multiply within herself. And this makes known the subtlety of the understanding of her love, which can give no gift to her friend to comfort him except what he loves. For no other gift has any value in love than to give a friend the most loved thing. Therefore the will of this creature loves nothing except works of goodness, steadfastly undertaking all great labors with which it can nourish its spirit. For it rightly seems to her that she loves nothing except works of goodness and thus does not know what to give Love, unless she makes this sacrifice for him. For no death would be martyrdom for her except abstaining from the work she loves, which is the delight of her pleasure and the life of her will, which feeds on it. Therefore she abandons these works which delight her so and puts the will which led such a life to death and forces herself, for the sake of martyrdom, to obey the will of others, to abstain from her work and her will, to fulfill the will of others in order to destroy her own will. And this is harder, very much harder than the two aforementioned states, for it is harder to overcome the works of the will of the spirit than it is either to overcome the will of the body or to do the will of the spirit. Thus one must, by breaking and crushing, reduce oneself to powder in order to enlarge the place where Love will want to be and must burden oneself with several beings in order to disburden oneself and attain one's being.

THE FOURTH STATE: The fourth state is that the Soul is drawn up by highness of love through meditation into delight of thought, and abandons all outward labors and obedience to others for highness of contemplation. Then the Soul is so difficult,[18] noble, and delightful that she cannot suffer anything to touch her, except the touch of Love's pure delight which makes her singularly charming and gay,[19] which makes her proud of an abundance of love. Then she is mistress of the radiance,[20] that is to say the light of her soul, which causes her to be marvelously filled with love of great faith through the concord of union which put her in possession of her delights.

Now the Soul holds that there is no higher life than to have this of which she has lordship, for Love has so fully sated her with her delights that she does not believe that God has a greater gift to give a soul here below than this love that Love has diffused in her out of love.

Oh, it is no wonder if such a Soul is seized, for Gracious Love makes her completely drunk and so drunk that she allows her to hear nothing but Love, by the force with which Love delights her. And for this reason the Soul cannot value another being, for the great light of Love has so blinded her sight that it lets her see nothing but her love. And in this she is deceived, for there are two other beings here below given by God which are greater and more noble than this one, but Love has deceived many a soul through the sweetness of the charm of her love, which seizes the Soul as soon as she comes near. No one can withstand this force: the Soul that has Love knows this; through tender love she is raised beyond herself.[21]

THE FIFTH STATE: The fifth state is that the Soul beholds that God is what is, that of Whom all things are, and she is not, so she is not that of whom all things are. And these two considerations provoke in her a marvelous astonishment and she sees that He is all goodness who has put a free will in her who is not, but is all wickedness.

Now the divine Goodness put a free will in her out of pure divine goodness. Now as to what is not, except in wickedness, which therefore is wholly wicked, a free will has been enclosed in her by the being of God Who is being, Who wants what has no being to have being through His gift. And therefore the divine Goodness diffuses before this will a ravishing diffusion of the movement of divine light. This movement of divine light, which is diffused within the Soul by light, shows the Will. . . .[22] from the place where it is, where it ought not to be, in order to put it back there whence it came, there where it is not, there where it ought to be.

Now the Will sees by the light diffused by the divine light (this light shows itself to such a Will in order to return to God this Will, which cannot find its way back without such a light) that it cannot take advantage of itself if it is not able to depart from its own will, for its nature is evil because of its inclination toward nothingness, to which nature is inclined, and the will has itself been reduced to less than nothing.[23] Now the Soul sees this inclination and the perdition caused by the nothingness of her nature and her own will and so sees through light that the Will should will the only divine will without any other will and that this will was given for this reason. And therefore the Soul departs from this Will and the Will departs from this Soul. Then it gives itself back to God, returns, and places itself back in God where it first was, without keeping anything of its own, in order to fulfill the perfect divine will which cannot be fulfilled in the Soul without such a gift, this gift which creates in her this perfection—that the Soul has neither discord nor flaw—and thus transforms her into the nature of Love that delights her with fulfilling peace and satisfies her with divine nourishment. And therefore she has no fear of nature's discord, for her will is nakedly placed back in the place where it first was, there where it ought rightly to be; and this Soul was always in discord so much and so long as she withheld the Will within herself outside its being.

Now such a Soul is nothing, for she sees with an abundance of divine knowledge her nothingness which makes her nothing and reduces her to nothingness. And she is all, for she sees with the profundity of the knowledge of her wickedness, which is so profound and so great that she finds there neither beginning, nor measure, nor end. Who cannot reach himself cannot find himself; and the more he sees himself with such a knowledge of his wickedness, the more he truly knows that he cannot know his wickedness, not even the least particle of it. Thus this Soul is an abyss of wickedness and a gulf of such lodging and garrison—as is the flood of what is sin—that she contains in herself all perdition. This Soul sees herself such, without seeing it. And what causes her to see herself? It is profundity of humility that sits there on its throne and reigns without pride. There pride cannot push its way in since she sees herself, and thus she sees herself not; and this not seeing causes her to see herself perfectly.

Now this Soul is seated at the very bottom, there where there is no bottom and it is low; and this lowness causes her to see very clearly the true Sun of highest goodness, for she has nothing which keeps her from this sight. And this divine Goodness shows Himself to her out of goodness that draws her upward and transforms her and unites her by a bond of goodness with pure divine Goodness whose mistress is goodness. And the knowledge of these two natures, of divine Goodness and her own wickedness, of which we have spoken, is the means by which she was endowed with such goodness. And because the Bridegroom of her youth, Who is but one, wants but one, Mercy made peace with firm Justice, which transformed this Soul with goodness. Now she is all, and thus she is nothing, for her friend has made her one.

Now this Soul has fallen from love into nothingness, without this she cannot be all. This fall is so profound a fall, if she has fallen correctly, that the Soul can never raise herself from such an abyss; nor should she: on the contrary she should remain there. And there the Soul loses pride and youth, for the spirit has become an old man who lets her be charming and gay no more. The will which often made her, because of a feeling of love, haughty and proud and difficult in highness of contemplation in the fourth state has departed from her. But the fifth state, which showed this Soul herself, put her in her place. Now she sees herself and knows divine Goodness, and this knowledge of divine Goodness causes her to see herself again; and these two sights take away her will and desire and work of goodness, and for this reason she is wholly at rest and comes into possession of free being which through excellent nobility gives her rest from all things.

THE SIXTH STATE: The sixth state is that the Soul neither sees herself, whatever the abyss of humility she may have within herself, nor God, whatever high goodness He may have. But God sees Himself in her through His divine majesty that illuminates this Soul of Himself, so that she sees that no one is but God Himself Who is that of Whom all things are; and what is is God Himself. And therefore she sees but herself; for who sees what is sees only God himself Who, through His divine majesty, sees Himself in the Soul herself. And then the Soul in the sixth state is freed from all things and pure and illuminated—but not glorified, for the glorification is in the seventh state, that we will have in glory about which no one can speak. But this Soul, thus pure and illuminated, sees neither God nor herself but rather God sees Himself by Himself in her, for her, without her, Who (that is to say God) shows her that there is nothing except Himself. And for this reason this Soul knows nothing except Him, and thus loves but Him and praises but Him, for there is nothing except Him. For what is is, through His goodness, and God loves His goodness, whatever portion He may have, through goodness, given; and His given goodness is God Himself and God cannot depart from His goodness such that it no longer remains His, for He is what goodness is and goodness is what God is. And for this reason Goodness, through goodness, sees itself by divine light in the sixth state in which the Soul is illuminated. And there is no one except Him Who is, Who sees Himself in this state, with divine majesty, by the movement of love diffused and brought back to Him through goodness. And therefore He sees Himself in such a creature without giving her anything of her own; all is His own, moreover is His own self. This is the sixth state, of which we had promised to speak since the onset of Love, and Love herself, by her high nobility, has paid this debt.

And the seventh state keeps Love within the Soul to give us everlasting glory, which we will not know until our soul has left our body.

NOTES TO THE TRANSLATION

1. *Engins*, 'minds,' could also be translated as 'intelligence,' 'talent,' or even 'trick or artifice.'

2. "Actives and contemplatives" are those who live an active religious life and those given up to a reclusive life of prayer and meditation.

3. "Her will loved him": clearly this soul has not yet reached the fifth state, in which the will is annihilated.

4. *Avec ses autres usages*, 'in other ways': *usages* can be translated as 'practices'; al-

though the *Mirror* refers several times to "other practices," the word remains mysterious. See the commentary by Edmund Colledge and Romana Guarnieri on the glosses of the Middle English manuscript in Dorion, pp. 358–382.

5. This passage, in its insistence on the farness and nearness of the King, will be explained later by the author when she talks of the Farnear (*Loingprès*) in chapter 61.

6. *En aucuns usages*, 'in several ways': note the same mysterious *usages*.

7. This keeping of the commandments corresponds to the first state of the soul, but even here all the emphasis is on the commandments of love.

8. *Son relief et son demourant*, 'her relief and her due': the relief is a payment, varying in value and kind according to rank and tenure, made to the overlord by the heir of a feudal tenant on taking possession of the vacant estate. Here it may simply mean, as may *demourant*, 'what is left, the remains.'

9. These nine points are fully explained in chapter 11.

10. "Intermediary": literally, *par moyen*, 'by means.'

11. That is, the great theologians of her time.

12. *En estant et assise*, 'immobile and seated,' could also be translated as 'standing and sitting.'

13. *Courtoisie*, 'courtliness': another possible translation is 'courtesy,' but 'courtliness' renders better the origin of the word.

14. "Eleven points": copyist's error? There are only nine points, but they are discussed in chapter 11.

15. The phoenix is a mythological bird which, once burned, is reborn from its own ashes.

16. This marks the beginning of an interruption in the exposition of the nine points which illustrates that the soul cannot even be given love.

17. This is a possible allusion to Plato's allegory of the cavern.

18. *Dangereuse*, 'difficult.'

19. *Jolie*, 'gay': the Old French word had this meaning as well as its modern one of 'pretty.'

20. *Celustre*, 'radiance': see Guarnieri, p. 611.

21. *Oultre elle soubhaulciee*, 'she is raised beyond herself': *soubhaucier* can mean 'to raise up in glory, honor, or riches' or 'to exalt or praise.'

22. Lacuna in text.

23. Obscure passage.

BIBLIOGRAPHY

Primary Works

Guarnieri, Romana. "Il movimento del Libero Spirito, testi e documenti." *Archivio Italiano per la Storia della Pietà* 4 (1965): 351–708.

Related Works

Cohn, Norman. *The Pursuit of the Millennium.* 3rd ed. London, 1970.

Dagens, Jean. "*Le miroir des simples âmes* et Marguerite de Navarre." In *La mystique rhénane*, pp. 281–289. Paris, 1963.

Des Preis, Jean d' Outremeuse. *Ly myreur des histors.* Ed. S. Borman. Vol. 6.

Dorion, Marilyn. "'The Mirror of Simple Souls,' a Middle English Translation." *Archivio Italiano per la Storia della Pietà* 5 (1968): 241–382.

Frédéricq, Paul. *Corpus documentorum inquisitionis haereticae pravitatis Neerlandicae.* 5 vols. Ghent, 1889–1903.

Friedberg, E. *Corpus iuris canonici.* Vol. 2. Leipzig, 1881.

Hamilton, Bernard. *The Medieval Inquisition.* New York, 1981.

Haupt, Hermann. "Zwei Traktate gegen Beginen und Begharden." *Zeitschrift für Kultur und Geschichte* 12 (1891): 85–90.

Kaminsky, H. "The Free Spirit in the Hussite Revolution." In *Millennial Dreams in Action,* ed. Sylvia L. Thrupp. The Hague, 1962.

Kirchberger, Clare. *The Mirror of Simple Souls.* London and New York, 1927.

Lambert, Malcolm. *Medieval Heresy: Popular Movements from Bogomil to Huss.* New York, 1976.

Langlois, C. V. "Marguerite Porète." *Revue Historique* 54 (1894): 295–299.

Lea, Henry Charles. *A History of the Inquisition in the Middle Ages.* New York, 1888.

Lecler, Joseph. *Vienne.* Paris, 1964.

Leff, Gordon. *Heresy in the Later Middle Ages.* New York, 1967.

Lerner, Robert E. *The Heresy of the Free Spirit in the Later Middle Ages.* Berkeley and Los Angeles, 1972.

Little, Lester K. *Religious Poverty and the Profit Economy in Medieval Europe.* Ithaca, 1978.

McDonnell, E. W. *The Beguines and Beghards in Medieval Culture.* New Brunswick, N.J., 1954.

Müller, Ewald. *Das Konzil von Vienne, 1311–12.* Münster, 1934.

Paturier, E. "Les sources du mysticisme de Marguerite de Navarre." *Revue de la Renaissance* 5 (1904): 56.

Phillips, Dayton. "Beguines in Medieval Strasbourg." Ph.D. dissertation, 1946.

Saulnier, V. L., ed. *Marguerite de Navarre: Théâtre profane.* Paris, 1946.

Schmitt, Jean-Claude. *Mort d'une hérésie.* Paris, 1978.

Wakefield, Walter L. *Heresy, Crusade and Inquisition in Southern France.* London, 1974.

THE SWEDISH VISIONARY

aint Bridget

BARBARA OBRIST

Bridget, the fourteenth-century Swedish mystic, left a canon of revelations widely read in the vernacular at the end of the Middle Ages, especially in the fifteenth century. She was an incult lay author, meaning that she did not know Latin and thus wrote or dictated her revelations in Swedish. These were gradually translated into Latin by her confessors—Mathias, canon of Linköping cathedral; Petrus Olai of Skenninge; and Prior Petrus Olai of Alvastra. Only later were they retranslated into the vernacular. Despite these permutations, the specific features of what must have been Bridget's language seem preserved. These revelations, most very brief, consist of speeches addressed to her by Christ and Mary or by Saints Agnes and John the Baptist, and of visions such as the torments of Christ and of human souls.

Bridget was born in 1303, the seventh child of one of the richest and most powerful families in Sweden. Her father, Birger Persson, was the lawman of the province of Uppland and resided in Finsta, close to Uppsala. We know little about Bridget's education, but she probably learned to read and write from the castle chaplain. She no doubt read mainly the lives of saints.[1] At the age of thirteen, she married Ulf Gudmarsson, before long the lawman of West Gotland (Närke); she bore eight children. By no means was her life to remain domestic, for she was summoned to the court at Stockholm (circa 1336) as a mistress in the royal household of young King Magnus and his bride, Blanche de Namur. In the beginning, Bridget seemed to have a great influence on the royal couple.[2]

In 1341, accompanied by others, Bridget and her husband undertook a pilgrimage to Santiago de Compostela. On their return, Ulf retired from his legal functions; he died in 1344 at the Cistercian abbey of Alvastra. After her husband's death, Bridget had her first revelations. The *Acta et processus canonizacionis* describes the visible signs of her conversion to spiritual life: she experienced convulsions of the heart, a sign that Christ had been born into it.[3] Among the early revelations are those concerning the foundation of a new order to be located in Vadstena; consequently, in 1347, Bridget moved to the court of Stockholm in order to obtain the approbation of the king and clergy for its foundation.

In her first years of widowhood, she encouraged King Magnus in his plans for war against Finland, and she seems to have been suspected as early as 1347 of wanting to push her son Karl onto the throne. Later, from Rome, she issued at least one prophecy supporting the insurrection of Swedish nobles against the king, predicting a new regent. Not surprisingly, this prophecy corresponds to a propaganda tract of the opposing party circulating in Sweden.[4]

Until her husband's death, Bridget had led the life of a Swedish noblewoman, with its social duties. We have no undistorted view of this part of her life because of what she became as a widow: a visionary working miracles. As early as 1373, her confessors Petrus Olai of Skenninge and Petrus Olai of Alvastra supplied two *vitae* for use at the process of canonization (1377–1391).[5] Thus, her entire life was recast in the very strict forms of hagiography, since the criteria for canonization, in addition to working miracles, involve living a perfectly virtuous life. Bridget's early life was therefore stylized in the following manner. While still in the womb, she saved the ship her mother was on. At the age of seven (an important date in a saint's life), she had her first contact with Mary, who later helped her embroider a work of supernatural beauty. She entered into marriage as a duty but never forgot her spiritual goals. She frequently visited the poor and followed ascetic practices. Finally, after her husband's death, she gave away all her possessions.[6] However, there is evidence that she only complained of the burden of wealth and that as a widow she continued to be a landowner.[7] Such evidence raises problems about how we should evaluate the information that makes up the tradition of Saint Bridget.[8]

If she had not traveled to Rome, where she remained until her death in 1373, Bridget would most likely have become a saint of limited local importance in a peripheral country. But in Rome she became an influential supporter of Church politics. Her early vision of a new canonical order was realized after great difficulties in 1370. Ultimately she was canonized in 1391, for a combination of emotional, political, and even economical reasons. Less than fifty years later, grave doubts about the authenticity of her claims to sainthood diluted her importance in the official Church; but her native Sweden defended her as its patron saint (as she was named in 1396), and her revelations continued to be well known.

Bridget submitted her revelations to her confessors, who examined them for orthodoxy and who ultimately arranged them into seven books. The collection was probably completed shortly after her death in 1373. In 1391 an eighth book, the *Liber celestis imperatoris ad reges*, was added by the bishop-hermit Alfons de Jaen, who supervised the editing of Bridget's revelations during her last years. The *Extravagantes*, a collection of diverse revelations that for some reason were omitted, was added later.[9]

The division into eight books corresponds neither to a strictly chronological nor to a precisely thematic order. While books 1 and 2 contain early revelations in Sweden, marked by moral themes, books 3 and 4 depart from this locale with visions concerning the Church in Italy. Book 5 returns to the Swedish period with a dialogue on theological questions. Book 6 gathers revelations from all parts of Bridget's life and touches on a wide range of subjects. Book 7 contains the revelations from her pilgrimage to the Holy Land (1371–1373). As the title suggests, book 8 is a collection of revelations with a political content, partly drawn from the other books. Finally, the *Extravagantes* contains, among other things, revelations concerning her new order.

The first edition of Bridget's revelations appeared in Lübeck in 1492; it included prologues by her confessors and the rules of her order. A second edition followed in 1500 by Koberger in Nuremberg, at the request of Emperor Maximilian. Others followed.[10] A modern critical edition is in progress.[11]

An examination of the historical context of the midfourteenth century, along with Bridget's role in bolstering the Catholic Church—which had suffered serious blows to its authority—will permit an understanding of how such a controversial, uneducated woman attained international prominence. Because so much of her history is more fiction than fact, owing to the rudimentary state of analytical tools of studying documentation about saints,[12] these comments will be limited to information that has been carefully verified.

Bridget went to Rome in 1349 to attend the jubilee of 1350, an occasion she herself had pressed for in a delegation to Avignon which sought papal support for the new order.[13] But in a vision in 1348, between this mission and the jubilee, Christ told her to go to Rome and stay there until both emperor and pope had been to the city:

> Go to Rome where the avenues and the streets are made of gold and are
> red from the blood of saints, where a reduction [of sins] and a shortening
> of the way to heaven is made possible because of indulgences that have
> been gained by the saint pontiffs through their prayers. Stay there in
> Rome, until you have seen the highest pontiff and the emperor at the same
> time, and you will proclaim to them My words.[14]

According to the *Acta et processus canonizacionis*, people laughed at the notion of the pope's meeting with a king. Not only did the popes, who had been residing in Avignon since 1309, show no inclination to return to Rome, but the conflicts between Pope John XXII and the German Emperor Louis of Bavaria had caused unprecedented alienation. When Louis had come down to Rome in 1328 for his coronation as a Roman emperor, it was to incite insurrection and to elect a Franciscan antipope.[15] The brilliant state theoreticians who served Louis radically denied any divine origin of the pope's authority and affirmed that he could be deposed by the emperor. In truth, all of Italy was rising up against the pope. However, Bridget's revelation had some justification: it came to her two years after Charles IV's election in 1346, and it reflected the new monarch's intentions not to continue to divide the people's loyalty. He intended, on the contrary, to win the pope for the imperial side.

Actually, a short passage in one of Bridget's revelations concerning an ideal state of peace, symbolized by the reconciliation of the two swords in Rome, is repeatedly found in contemporary documents. Her prophecies expressed a yearning for a return of the glory of old Rome as well as hopes for Church reform. Thus, against the very background of a Rome reduced to a bloody battlefield, divided by the Colonna and the Orsini, and in a state of utter anarchy, Petrarch espoused the idea of reviving ancient Rome as the center of the empire.[16] His friend Cola di Rienzo dreamed equally of a unification of pope and emperor sealed in Rome and, through this unification, a restoration of the Age of Gold.[17] When Rienzo became tribune of the Roman people in 1347, the idea of ancient Rome found a new embodiment, but this hope collapsed in 1354 when the tribune, become a tyrant, was slain by the Romans in the capitol.[18]

The Church likewise envisioned a return to the golden age, with itself as the central power. As with the first jubilee in 1300, when Boniface VIII revived the cult of Constantine to show the subordination of imperial to papal power,[19] so the jubilee of 1350, permitting plenary absolution from sins, was designed to enhance the strength of the Church. Indeed, the Romans asked for such an event in 1342.[20] Thus Bridget's revelation in a way shows a synthesis of these wishes for political and religious unity. But the 1350 jubilee took place without the pope's presence in Rome; moreover, the tension between Charles IV and the Church proved to be so catastrophic that Legate Annibaldo de Ceccano barely escaped an assassination attempt during a procession. When he shortened the time for gaining indulgences, thus reducing the Romans' income, their anger rose dangerously.[21]

The Romans threatened not only the pope's representative with death but also Bridget. Her palace was almost stormed, and she thought of fleeing.[22] Although no mention of the reasons for this animosity appears in the Latin versions of the revelations, we can easily assume that Bridget favored the pope's politics too openly. They attacked her as a sorceress to be burned, probably because she had made a name for herself by curing the Romans and by uttering the darkest threats against Rome in her prophecies.[23] The Romans considered that certain tribulations she predicted had come true too readily (such as the reduction of their income)—she very likely was suspected of making these prophecies come true. However, perhaps she was spared because of other prophecies she made that could not be deflected so easily. Her apocalyptic visions of Rome, of its depravity and state of utter desolation, coincided with constant battles within the city gates, the already abundant ruins from antiquity, the Black Death of 1348 which killed thousands, and the earthquakes in 1349.[24]

The entreaties for the popes' return to Rome, found so often during the fourteenth century, were of course linked not only to the desolate state of the abandoned bride, a common contemporary metaphor for Rome, but to the idea of a general reform of the Church. This comes out very clearly in Bridget's demand for their return. The popes' residence in Avignon had become the symbol of the Church's complete failure in its spiritual duties. As Petrarch points out, the curia was the Babylonian whore, a nest of treason, a temple of heresy, and hell upon earth.[25] And the Church acted openly as a purely political power. Being the big moneylender of the time, it not only used the all-powerful weapon of excommunication (as in the case against King Magnus, who defaulted), but it would also threaten subjugation by its mercenary army (as against Florence).[26]

Thus Bridget had visions both of Rome's decay and of the decay of the Church. Again, her revelations about the Church are by no means "miraculous," for much contemporary prophecy denigrated its authority. Others who cried out for Church reform were the Joachimites and the Franciscan spirituals—for them, the contemporary Church had simply become the embodiment of evil. In fact, a stream of Italian prophecies began in the second half of the thirteenth century, in a time of great economic depression. These prophecies were formulated by the followers of Joachim de Fiore, whose interpretation of history ends in an Age of Spirit when the carnal Church is no longer necessary. The Franciscans, partly adapting Joachimite views, developed an ideal of evangelical poverty, opposing the existing ecclesiastical wealth.[27] These prophecies predicted tribulations of the Church, sometimes in the form of a chastiser belonging to the imperial party, followed by ultimate purification. Expectations for a better future projected an angelical pope, unlike John XXII, whom they declared to be the Antichrist.[28]

Although Bridget was directly influenced by Joachimite prophecy, her prophecies about the Church share only the rebel tone without developing the specific themes.[29] Bridget shares with the Joachimites and Spirituals the claim to divine inspiration, the sharply eschatological outlook, the chastising of the Church for its corruption, and the prediction of punishments, ending in a final purification. But unlike these would-be reformers, several of whom were burned at the stake by John XXII,[30] Bridget did not favor either evangelical poverty or an Age of Spirit—she did not go so far as to attack the office of the priest or deny unworthy priests authority in presiding over sacraments. Thus Bridget, who might otherwise have been persecuted as a heretic,[31] ultimately served the Church by defending its hierarchy and its spiritual power over the empire. The meeting in Rome of the pope and the emperor was clearly for the recognition of the pope, not the emperor, as supreme; thus Bridget gained the sanction of the Church and even earned political influence within it.

Bridget was congenial to papal politics, as is evident in the delegation she sent to Avignon. As an influential Swedish princess, she was important to the Church in establishing good relations between Sweden and the holy see. When she arrived in Rome, the French brother of the pope offered her his palace, which acquired the function of an embassy. In the jubilee year, important Swedish pilgrims resided there, and shortly thereafter her confessor was named the confessor to the Swedish nation in Saint Peter's. Bridget knew the highest Roman nobility; the Orsini created contacts between her and the upper Church hierarchy. In 1354 the Papazzura offered her a palace.[32] Bridget also knew the Neapolitan nobility, including Queen Giovanna.[33]

As she stayed on past the year of the jubilee, Bridget gradually became a cult object to the Romans, for she seemed to work miracles and she was liberal toward the poor. Because of her popularity, the Church could not ignore her. But Bridget was constantly surrounded by controversies, reflecting the Church's own divided attitudes about prophetic phenomena. A real distrust of prophecy arose from the constant danger that rival sects might erode authority. Economic and political crises resulted in the flowering of various dissident groups within the Church (such as the Spirituals). And more or less uncontrolled lay movements, in which women could occasionally become important, added to the expanding competition with the Church.[34]

On the whole, Bridget served Church parties that favored the popes' return to Rome, for power groups even within the Church turned to those like her for propaganda. Their opposition, of course, would attack such exploitation by rational argument, although they too used the same kind of mystification. But Bridget was an especially easy target for their venom, for she was an uneducated lay person, ignorant of Latin, and above all a woman. For example, the French cardinals accused her of everything from merely acting out what had been made up for her by her supervisors, on the one extreme, to insanity on the other.[35] In the introductions to her revelations, her confessors refute these attacks in detail. Apart from lengthy arguments claiming her revelations authentic, Bridget herself insists that Christ in any event was free to accord divine inspiration to the poor, *idiotae*, and women.[36]

One of Bridget's revelations—reflecting these struggles among influential parties—is addressed to Pope Gregory XI. Christ tells Bridget that Gregory has to go to Rome. Bridget objects that others who claim to be divinely inspired advise the pope against this trip, but Christ assures her that what he is saying is true and that the other revelations are false.[37]

Bridget's role in the Church hierarchy came later and was finally less important than her popularity among the people—this fierce defender of the Church provided a key link between lay persons and ecclesiastical authorities. What made her revelations so successful? The answer is offered by Johannes Tortsch, who, about 1424, assembled what seemed to him the most important of Bridget's revelations.[38] His explicit purpose was to collect and explain her darkest predictions concerning the fate of humanity; he entitles the collection *Onus mundi, id est prophecia de malo futuro ipsi mundo superventuro*.[39]

Bridget's emphasis on an ever-angry God who at the same time offers help touched deep chords within the people; *ira Dei* is indeed a constant theme in her revelations. Because of the sins of humankind, Christ is no longer concerned with its well-being, and God is constantly on the verge of sending severe punishments. This important theme had surfaced in one of the first revelations about the sins of the Swedish people. An irate God about to inflict either three or seven plagues upon the world is fully developed in Bridget's revelations.[40] What makes the theme of wrath specifically relevant is the correlative theme of redemption. The gap between a sinful world and an angry God having become immense, special intermediaries (saints and prophets) must reestablish a connection so that souls can be saved. At this point Bridget becomes important: Mary, traditionally an intercessor for the sinful, chooses Bridget as a representative on earth, a channel for God's will.

As Tortsch points out, this special representative had to be a woman, in keeping with a repeated tradition that the world had been lost through a woman and would be saved by one.[41] Thus, God looked down to a simple laywoman, because, as Bridget says in a revelation addressed to the pope, the Church not only failed in guiding the pious, but it increasingly led them astray.[42] Of radical importance, then, Bridget represented for the lay person a direct point of contact with heaven: she could be asked for any kind of help, whether healing of the sick or political advice, for she was authorized to transmit these appeals to heaven. Moreover, the constant desire of Christ and Mary to speak to Bridget, and through her to humanity, showed that God's anger could be appeased.

Bridget was part of the enormously increasing multitude of saints at the end of the Middle Ages. The Church took advantage of this means of deepening its authority by unifying and institutionalizing the tendency for seers and prophets to make claims on the people's faith. In her revelations, Bridget constantly recommends action for the benefit of the Church. Above all, she is an eminent propagandist for indulgences. The creation of jubilee years and the expansion of this practice in the fourteenth century established indulgence business on a large scale.[43] As the papal see grew in political power, so the need for revenues increased. Bridget's role is interesting here because she pushed for indulgences for the dead. Many of her revelations are visions of purgatory; in one, her husband appears to her, and important themes about purgatory unfold: the soul's immediate judgment after death and its consequent dwelling in purgatory, even when almost sinless, before being transferred to a definite place. Most important, the soul asks for help from the living. Although Ulf's list of sins is short, he asks for masses to be read throughout the year in honor of those who are going to deliver him from purgatory. He also wants Bridget to give the Church his precious cups so that they may be transformed into chalices.[44]

In later purgatory visions, details of judgment appear as well as details of the torture of the soul, which sometimes takes place there in front of the judge. Bridget's revelations reinforce the whole system of damnation: the categories of sins, judgments of these and of their subdivisions, the deformation of every possible part of the body symbolizing the soul's sins, the consequent series of tortures, and finally the list of indulgences by which the soul can be delivered from its tortures.[45] Several times Mary stresses the fact that indulgences are the only way to buy the soul's salvation.

Since purgatory was the place where one could still have contact with the dead, anxious relatives consulted Bridget about their fate.[46] She would present the horrible picture of what the sinful soul looked like and the manner of its torture. Her vision of the soul of Neapolitan Nicolaus de Acciolis, whose death she had not been able to prevent but whose soul she proposed to deliver with the help of Mary and Saint Lawrence, depicts Lawrence dictating a list of good works that would save Acciolis' soul: thirteen chalices, thirty masses read by thirty priests, and thirty gifts of clothes and money to the poor.[47]

These visions of purgatory show that despite traditional doctrine, which claimed that the Church's jurisdiction did not go beyond the living,[48] what clearly characterized the Renaissance Church was already practiced in the fourteenth century: everything could be bought for the sake of the soul. Unlike the *quaestuarii* (seers consulted about the fate of the dead and paid for helping them), whom the Church condemned in 1312 for similar commerce,[49] Bridget was permitted, in the name of the Church, to draw in this money. Certainly, in spite of the profits they brought, these practices concerning the dead raised questions.[50] At the Council of Basel, Bridget's revelations were attacked; Johannes Nider would speak of women's visions of purgatory as "superstitious," induced by the demon.[51] At any rate, Bridget's revelations present a condensed form of all that Luther attacked which became a tinderbox for the Reformation— the ever-angry God who constantly had to be appeased by good works, the commerce in indulgences, the absurd proliferation of saints and their superadded altars and offices.

The revelations of 1345 about the founding of a new order, the Ordo Sancti Salvatoris, and the difficulties getting support from the popes again point up the clash between lay aspirations and the Church's attempt to bring them under control. In this struggle, Bridget was less influential in realizing the terms of her visions. She seems to have wanted a double convent emphasizing the authority of women. The functions of abbess would be analogous to those of Mary toward the apostles and disciples of Christ: the thirteen priests correspond to the twelve apostles plus Saint Paul, and the sixty nuns, four deacons, and eight lay brothers correspond to the seventy-two disciples of Christ.[52]

Bridget's first demand to Pope Innocent for approbation in 1347 was blankly rejected on the grounds that since the Lateran Council of 1215, founding new orders was forbidden. Then, Pope Urban V issued a bull with the decisions of the Council of Lyons, which required that every new monastical order had to accept the rules of an existing order. Thus the Brigittine rules were declared to be a supplement to the Augustinian rules.[53] On top of that, the rules were drastically changed—the Brigittine order now included two separate convents, and in later papal bulls, the role of men was increasingly that of supervising nuns, ostensibly to check the difficulties which the Church had with female congregations, such as the Beguines.[54] Bridget could not appeal to the revelations as documents for her order. Toward amending them to conform with accepted diction, Nicolaus Orsini transformed Bridget's confessors' Latin into chancellory prose. The hallmark of her style—the direct form of speech in which Christ addressed his bride—was completely stripped; only the current formula of divine inspiration remained.[55]

Coming at a time of schism after the pope's return to Rome in 1378,

Bridget's canonization in 1391 did not end discussions about her, discussions which reflect the Church's problems. Councils that were supposed
to clarify issues instead tried to limit the pope's authority, in order to
reestablish a solid organization. A creation of this chaotic time of schism,
Bridget became a special object of controversy not only at the Council of
Constance (1414–1418) but also at the Council of Basel (1431–1439).
At the former (which faced four popes in three years), Pope John XXII
reaffirmed Bridget's canonization, brandishing her prophecies for his
purpose.[56] On the other hand, eminent Church doctors Pierre d'Ailly
and Jean Gerson fought against the increasing number who believed
themselves inspired and who were used at random to claim papal power.
Gerson goes so far as to quote the dying Gregory XI: had he not listened
so much to the prophets, both female and male, the schism would not
have occurred.[57]

Bridget's sainthood moved Gerson to write his treatise of 1415, *De
probatione spirituum*, an attempt to give theologians both a theoretical
framework and criteria for examining pretenders to inspiration. This
treatise reflects the ambiguous position of the Church regarding such
visionaries as Bridget. For Gerson, it is unworthy for the council to approve of these "false, illusionary, [and] frivolous visions," but, diplomat-
ically, he states that they cannot be condemned either and that Bridget's
canonization cannot be revoked, because the cult around her had grown
so important that this would harm the Christian faith.[58] Then, he returns
to the subject of false inspiration with biting remarks about fantasizing
women like her—religious fervor can become suspect with adolescents
and women, for it is "overheated, versatile, [and] unbridled."[59] Such
women, under pretext of confession, vision, or any other story, give free
rein to the urge of constant chat and should be scrutinized closely. "There
is hardly any other calamity more apt to do harm or that is more incur-
able. If its only consequence were the immense loss of time, this would
already be sufficient for the devil. But you must know that there is something else to it: the insatiable itch to see and to speak, not to mention . . .
the itch to touch."[60] Gerson obviously feels what Luther stated over a
hundred years later—Bridget had been crazy (*die tolle Brigit*) and had
been deceived by the devil.[61]

Gerson's authority was insufficient to settle the controversies about
Bridget. These matters, as well as problems about the Brigittine order,
were reviewed at the Council of Basel, and a list of 123 doubtful passages
in her revelations resulted.[62] The Reformation diminished the popularity
of the Brigittine monasteries, and when Sweden adopted the Reformation the cult was abolished, and the mother convent, Vadstena, was closed
toward the end of the sixteenth century.

Bridget's writings are not at all marked by speculative considerations, nor is her style full of mystical terminology. Rhetorical sophistication is absent, the short sentences sometimes approach spoken language, and her revelations are characterized by simplicity and directness. In both form and content, her revelations are more like the popular literature of this time. Christ and Mary address Bridget directly and familiarly, as if to an equal, when they speak of moral problems or give directives. Provocative and graphic depictions of judgments or scenes of torture, wherein she describes terribly deformed bodies, distinguish her works. Bridget sets forth in vivid, obsessive detail the agenda of monastic life, in accordance with the new order Christ has commanded her to found. This unique focus on the concrete in her writing is perhaps analogous to that of late medieval painting and sculpture, particularly in the northern countries. In any case, rhetorical simplicity and the sense of striking detail secured the success of her revelations.

NOTES

1. Johannes Jørgensson, *Saint Bridget of Sweden*, vol. 1, pp. 24 ff. For later readings, compare *Extravagantes 96*.

2. Jørgensson, vol. 1, pp. 78 ff.

3. *Acta et processus canonizacionis Beate Birgitte*, ed. Isac Collijn, pp. 81, 484, 500.

4. Concerning Bridget's early ambitions, see ibid., p. 514. For Bridget and King Magnus and the later propaganda tract, see Ingvar Andersson, *Källstudier till Sveriges Historia 1230–1436*, pp. 108 ff., 151 ff., and *Extravagantes 51*. See also Toni Schmid, *Birgitta och hennes Uppenbarelser*, pp. 163 ff.

5. *Acta et processus*, pp. 73–101, 614–664.

6. Ibid., pp. 75 ff., 615–617; Alfons de Jaen, prologue to book 8, especially chap. 3.

7. *Acta et processus*, p. 494; Jørgensson, vol. 1, p. 282, n. 5.

8. An attempt to analyze the cult of female saints in the later Middle Ages has been made by Ortrud Reber, *Die Gestaltung des Kultes weiblicher Heiliger im Spätmittelalter: Die Verehrung der Heiligen Elisabeth, Klara, Hedwig und Birgitta*. A more recent bibliography is *Europäisches Spätmittelalter*, ed. Willi Erzgräber, pp. 508 ff., 517 f.

9. Knut B. Westman, *Birgitta Studier* pp. 10 ff.; Jørgensson, vol. 1, p. 300 f.

10. On Maximilian's role, see Ulrich Montag, *Das Werk der heiligen Birgitta von Schweden in oberdeutscher Überlieferung*, pp. 103 ff. Early editions of Bridget's revelations are listed in Isac Collijn, *Sveriges bibliografi intill år 1600 I*, pp. 117 ff. In the present study, we are mainly using the 1500 Nuremberg edition.

11. In *Samlinger utgivna av Svenska fornskriftsällskapet*.

12. The pioneering and eminently important work of František Graus, *Volk, Herrscher und Heiliger im Reich der Merowinger: Studien zur Hagiographie der Merowingerzeit*, can be recommended as a model for an analysis of hagiography. Along with a general discussion of methodology, it offers an excellent survey of the research and includes an extensive bibliography. For a more recent bibliography, see Sofia Boesch-Gajano, *Agiografia altomedievale*.

13. Jørgensson, vol. 1, pp. 183 ff., 198 f.

14. *Acta et processus*, p. 94. Compare also *Extravagantes 8, 41*.

15. *Storia di Roma*, vol. 11: Eugenio Dupré-Theseider, *Roma dal Commune di Popolo alla Signoria Pontificia (1252–1377)*, 464 ff.

16. On Petrarch and Rome, see Dupré-Theseider, pp. 485 ff., and Karl Burdach and Paul Piur, *Briefwechsel des Cola de Rienzo*, pp. 46 ff., 118.

17. Marjorie Reeves, *The Influence of Prophecy in the Later Middle Ages: A Study in Joachism*, p. 421.

18. Dupré-Theseider, p. 652.

19. Compare Burdach and Piur, pp. 213 ff., 595 ff., 617 ff.

20. Ibid., p. 615 f.; Dupré-Theseider, pp. 527 ff.

21. Dupré-Theseider, pp. 619 ff.

22. *Extravagantes* 8; Jørgensson, vol. 2, p. 81 f.; and *Acta Sanctorum*, Octobris tomus quartus, p. 241.

23. According to Jørgensson, more information is in the Swedish *vita* of Petrus Olai of Skenninge; compare vol. 2, p. 316, n. 10. For revelations about Rome, see *Revelationes* 3. 27 and 4. 5, 10, 33, 57 and *Extravagantes* 8.

24. Ferdinando Gregorovius, *Storia della Città di Roma*, vol. 6, p. 375 f. Gregorovius cites Petrarch. Even the important church of the Lateran seems to have been roofless.

25. Petrarch, *Sonnets* 105–108.

26. On Magnus and his sins against the pope, such as going to mass despite the interdict, see *Extravagantes* 43, 80. About Florence, see Richard R. Trexler, "Economic, Political and Religious Effects of the Papal Interdict on Florence 1376–1378," p. 23 f. Also see Edmund G. Gardner, *Saint Catherine of Siena*, p. 175 f.

27. Compare Reeves, pp. 16 ff., 175 ff., 191 ff.

28. Ibid., pp. 205, 401 ff.

29. Ibid., p. 422.

30. Ibid., p. 201.

31. Compare *Revelationes* 1. 23 and 4. 41, 62, 132 ff., 136 ff.; *Acta Sanctorum*, pp. 249 ff.

32. See the index to the *Acta et processus*, p. 657: Francisca Papazzura; Jørgensson, vol. 2, p. 84; Dupré-Theseider, p. 623.

33. See *Extravagantes* 110.

34. Reeves, pp. 248 ff. Reeves says that, in 1300 in Italy, at least two women inspired by Joachimites proposed to save the world on the grounds that it was ruined by a woman and was to be saved by a woman.

35. *Acta Sanctorum* pp. 182 ff.

36. *Revelationes* 4. 113; *Acta et processus*, pp. 532, 632; compare also Alfons de Jaen's prologue to book 8, chap. 2.

37. *Revelationes* 4. 141. On the whole question of Bridget's revelations concerning the popes' return to Rome, see Eric Colledge, "*Epistola solitarii ad reges*: Alfons of Pecha as Organizer of Brigittine and Urbanist Propaganda," *Medieval Studies* 18 (1956): 19–49.

38. Montag, pp. 71 ff., 151 ff. This collection was widely circulated in the fifteenth century.

39. Johannes Tortsch's *Onus mundi* is edited by Montag, pp. 252–329; compare p. 252.

40. The revelation concerning Sweden is included in the prologue to the revelations written by Mathias. In Tortsch, ed. Montag, see particularly chaps. 7, 12, 13, and 17. In fifteenth-century woodcuts, the *Pestbilder* shows how Christ holds three arrows which he is about to hurl down.

41. Tortsch, ed. Montag, p. 260.

42. *Revelationes* 4. 141.

43. Augustin Fliche and Victor Martin, *Histoire de L'Eglise*, vol. 14, pp. 813 ff., and

Henry Charles Lea, *A History of Auricular Confession and Indulgences in the Latin Church*, vol. 3, pp. 199 ff.

44. *Extravagantes* 56.

45. *Revelationes* 4. 7 ff., 51 f., 81 and 6. 10, 31, 52 ff.

46. *Acta et processus*, p. 327.

47. *Revelationes* 4. 7–10; *Acta et processus*, p. 329 f.; Jørgensson, vol. 2, pp. 185 ff.

48. Lea, vol. 3, pp. 328, 337 ff., 346. Compare also Nikolaus Paulus, "Das Jubiläum vom Jahre 1320," *Theologie und Glaube* 5 (1913): 532–541, particularly p. 536. Paulus is a Catholic historian of indulgences.

49. Lea, vol. 3, p. 339.

50. Ibid., pp. 342 ff.

51. Johannes Nider *Praeceptuorium legis* 1. 11.

52. Tore Nyberg, *Birgittinische Klostergründungen des Mittelalters*, and *Regula sancti Salvatoris* 12.

53. Nyberg, pp. 43 ff., and *Acta et processus*, p. 230 f.

54. Montag, pp. 124 ff.

55. Ibid., p. 126.

56. Nyberg, pp. 82 ff.; *Acta Sanctorum*, p. 445; Colledge, p. 44.

57. Jean Gerson, *De examinatione doctrinarum*, in *Oeuvres complètes*, vol. 9, p. 469 f.

58. Jean Gerson, *De probatione spirituum*, in *Oeuvres complètes*, vol. 9, pp. 177 ff.; compare art. 5.

59. Ibid., art. 7.

60. Ibid., art. 11.

61. Martin Luther, *Sämtliche Schriften*, vol. 2, p. 558 f., and vol. 17, p. 1406.

62. See the *Epistola cardinalis de Turrecremata* in the Nuremberg edition of the *Revelationes*. The passages are printed in *Sacrorum conciliorum nova, et amplissima collectio . . .*, ed. Giovanni D. Mansi, vol. 30, pp. 698 ff. See also Colledge, pp. 46 ff.

Revelationes 4. 70

When the Passion of my son was about to start, tears were in His eyes and sweat over His body from fear of the Passion. And soon He was removed from my sight. I did not see Him anymore until He was led to the scourging. Then He was thrown to the earth and was torn down so cruelly that His teeth gnashed as His head hit the ground. And He was beaten so harshly on His throat and cheeks that the sound of the beating reached my ears. After that He undressed Himself upon the command of the executioner and willingly embraced the column. He was bound with a tie and flogged with a whip on which were fixed sharp rivets; and they were not pulled out in a clean way, rather they lacerated His whole body. At the first blow I lost consciousness as if my heart had been pierced. And when I awoke after some time, I saw His lacerated body, for His whole body was naked when He was being scourged. Then one of His enemies who were assisting said to the executioners: do you want to kill this man without judgment and take His death upon yourselves? While saying this he removed the bandage and at once my son was unbound from the column. The first thing that my son did was to turn to His clothes, but then they left Him no time to put them on; He put His arms into the sleeves while they dragged Him away. His footprints where He had been standing at the column were full of blood, so that I could well recognize from the signs of the blood all of His footprints. And then He wiped the streaming blood from His face with His tunic. Thereupon He was judged and, carrying the cross, He was led out; but on the way another cross was substituted for the first. When He arrived at the place of crucifixion, the hammer and the four nails were ready. And upon command He got rid of His clothes, and a small linen cloth covered His private parts. He Himself bound it around, almost comforted. The cross was fixed and His arms were lifted, so that the knot of the cross was between His shoulders and the cross offered no backing. And the plank of the title was fixed above both His arms, which were elevated over His head. Upon command, He then turned His back to the cross, and His hands were demanded; first, He extended His right hand, then his other hand. He could not reach the other horn and was stretched out. In the same way His feet were stretched out to their holes and separated beneath the tibia, and were fixed with two nails to the wood of the cross, through the solid bone; and thus were His hands also pierced. With the first blow of the hammer I fell into a stupor[1] from pain and grief; and when I returned to my senses I saw my son transfixed. I heard people say to each other: what did this one do, stealing, burglary, or lying? Some said that He was a liar; and then the crown of thorns was set very brutally upon His head. It reached down to the middle of His forehead. Many streams of blood ran down His face from the sharp thorns and filled the hair and the eyes and the beard, so that almost nothing could be seen; and He Himself could not see me though I was standing close to the cross, unless He did press out the blood by squeezing together His eyelashes. After having commended[2] me unto the care of the disciple, He raised His head, cried, and said with a voice coming from the depths of His heart: My God, my God, why have You forsaken Me? I could never forget this voice until I came to heaven. He did cry this more out of compassion for me than because of His martyrdom. Then, for lack of blood on parts of His body, the color of death could be seen. His teeth were sticking into His cheeks, His ribs that had grown thin could be counted, and His stomach, whose humors[3] had been consumed, was sticking to His back; already His nostrils had shrunk. When His heart was close to bursting, His whole body was shaken and then His head fell upon His breast. I lost consciousness and fell to the ground. As said those who could see, His mouth was open as if He had already expired; His tongue, His teeth, and the blood in His mouth were clearly visible. The half-closed eyes were cast down and the already dead body was hanging limp. The knees were bent in one part, the feet in the other part were bent over the nails as over hinges. Meanwhile, some people present said, as if scoffing: oh, Mary, your son is already dead. Others who were of a more elevated mind said: oh, lady, the martyrdom of your son is now ended in eternal glory. Shortly afterward His side was opened, and when the spear was pulled out the blood on the spear tip appeared brownish in color, so that through this it could be understood that the heart had been pierced. The piercing went through my heart; it is a miracle that it did not burst. When the others withdrew, I could not go away, but I was already almost as if comforted, for I could reach His body that had been taken down from the cross, could take it into my lap, examine the wounds, and wipe off the blood. Then my fingers closed His mouth and I also shut His eyes. But I could not bend the rigid arms in order to fold them onto His breast, but only onto His stomach; and the knees could not be stretched, but they stood out just as they had stiffened on the cross. The Mother said further: you cannot see my son the way He is in heaven, but you can know Him according to His appearance in the world. His face was so beautiful that no one remained unconsoled by the sight of it, even when that person felt a heartbreaking grief. The just were consoled by a spiritual consolation. But the evil gained relief from the sadness of the world as long as they saw Him. That is why the grieving used to say: let us go and look at Mary's son, so that we may be relieved at least during that time.

In His twentieth year He was perfect in His mien and strength. Among the mediocre men of those times, He was not fleshy, but handsome because of his muscles and bones. The hair of His eyebrows and beard was brown-yellow; the length of His beard was the breadth of the palm of a hand. His forehead was neither protruding nor engulfed, but straight. His nose was of medium size, neither too big nor too small. His eyes were so clear that even His enemies took pleasure in looking at Him. His lips were not thick, but of a clear redness. His chin was neither protruding nor too long, but pretty in its beautiful regularity. His cheeks were not too fleshy—their color was white, mixed with clear red. His stature was upright, and there was no defect on His entire body, as those testified who saw Him bound naked to the column and who scourged Him. Never came there a worm on Him; neither was there any confusion or untidiness in hair.

Revelationes 6. 52

And after this three women appeared: the mother, the daughter, and the granddaughter. The mother and the granddaughter appeared as dead, while the daughter appeared as living.[4] The above-mentioned mother seemed to be crawling out from a dark lake and from the mud. Her heart was torn out and her lips were cut off. Her chin was trembling and her teeth, shiny white and long, were gnashing together. Her nostrils were rotten and her torn-out eyes were hanging from their sockets by two nerves. Her forehead appeared as smashed in; in its place, there was a huge and dark pit. There was no skin on her head and her brains were bubbling over like lead and flew out like pitch. Her throat was turning around like wood turning in a lathe or under a plane in which the sharpest of blades has been set, scraping away without mercy. Her open chest was full of worms both long and small, winding one over the other here and there. Her arms were similar to the handles of a sculptor's tools; her hands, however, were like knotty keys and were spread wide. The vertebrae of her back were loose, so that they rose and fell in an incessant movement. A serpent, long and large, extended itself through the lower part of her stomach to the upper part and, joining head and tail, it continually revolved around her viscera like a wheel. Her legs and tibia looked like two prickly sticks; they were covered with sharp thorns. Her feet looked like those of a toad.

This dead mother spoke to her daughter and said: listen, O my snaky and poisonous daughter; woe to me that I have been your mother. It is I who laid you in the cradle of pride in which you were warmed and grew until you came of age. And you rejoiced so much in this that you wasted your life in it. Therefore, I tell you that every time you look around you with pride, just as I taught you, you pour poison that is of intolerable heat into my eyes. Every time you say proud words learned from me, I swallow the bitterest drink. Every time your ears are filled with the wind of pride, stirred up by the violent wind of presumption—that is, when you listen to compliments concerning your body and strive for worldly honors—a terrible noise comes to my ears, together with a violently blowing wind. Woe to me, poor and miserable as I am. I am poor, because I have nothing of the good, nor do I feel it; miserable, because I abound in every evil. But you, daughter, you resemble the tail of a cow as it walks in muddy places; every time the cow moves its tail, it stains and splatters those that are approaching. You, daughter, are like a cow, because you do not have divine wisdom and you function according to the workings and the movements of your body. Every time you imitate my habits, the sins that I taught you, my pains are renewed and are all the worse. Therefore, O my daughter, why are you proud of your progeny? There will never be any honor and virtue with you, for the filth of my viscera was your couch. My shameful member was your entrance into the world, and the filth of my blood your vestment when you were born. But now the belly in which you lay is completely corrupted by worms. But why do I complain about you, daughter, when there is much more reason to complain about myself? There are three things that violently afflict my heart. First, although I was born to rejoice in heavenly joy, I abused my conscience[5] and prepared myself for infernal pains. Second, God created me as beautiful as an angel, but I have deformed myself so that I am more similar to a devil than to an angel of God. Third, in the time that was accorded to me, I brought about a thoroughly evil change in myself. The rejoicing in sins was of short duration; for this I now undergo an infinite punishment, namely, the infernal recompense. And then she said to the bride: you who see me, you see me only through corporeal similitude.[6] For if you were to see me in the form I actually have, you would die from fear—for all my members are demons . . .

. . . Then also the dead granddaughter of the aforesaid dead grandmother talked to her and said: listen to me, you scorpion of a mother; woe to me, who have been misled by you. You showed me a smiling face, but in your heart you were against me. From your mouth came three counsels; three things I also learned from your doings, and you showed me three ways in which to follow you. The first counsel was to love in a carnal manner, in order to be loved according to the flesh. The second was to be lavish with money for worldly honor. And the third was to rest because of fleshly delights. These counsels cost me a lot . . .

When God's judgment came, the demons wanted my soul to be condemned to go to hell. The judge answered: I see a spark of love in her heart, and it is not to be extinguished; rather, it must remain in my presence. And therefore I judge that this soul must be purged . . .

Explanation

This she said of the three women; the third one of them entered a monastery and lived the rest of her life in great perfection.

Revelationes 6. 102

A lady from Sweden who had been sick for a long time in Rome said, as if smiling in the presence of the bride: there is a rumor that in this place can be found absolution from sin and punishment.[7] But to God nothing is impossible, for I already have suffered my punishment. Then, the following morning, the bride was spiritually rapt[8] and heard a voice that said to her: daughter, this woman is pleasing to Me, for she herself lived devoutly, and she brought her daughters up in My name. And yet she did not show as much contrition in her punishments as she had, and would have had, pleasure in her sins, had she not been held back by My love.[9] Therefore, just as I, God, foresee everything with respect to health and sickness, so I see to the facilitation of all things. Therefore, I must not be provoked with the slightest words or judged by anybody; but I ought rather to be feared and respected. Tell her also that the indulgences of the Roman Churches are better before God than they seem, that those who come to these indulgences with a pure heart will have not only remission of their sins but also eternal glory. For even if there were a human being that would kill himself a thousand times for God, he would still not be in the least worthy of the smallest amount of glory that is given to the saints. And it is not sufficient for a human being to live as many as a thousand years, for because of the infinite number of his sins, an infinite number of punishments are owed which cannot be amended and discharged during this life. Therefore, because of indulgences, many and terrible punishments are mitigated and the longest ones are transformed into the shortest possible ones. And those who receive indulgences in a state of perfect love and die in a state of real contrition are not only freed from their sins but are also exempt from punishment. I, God, do not only give to My saints and to My chosen ones[10] what they ask, but I will even increase it twofold and tenfold because of love. Therefore admonish this sick woman to be patient and steadfast, for I do for her that which is most useful for her salvation.

Explanation

Saint Bridget saw the soul of this lady as if fiery and rising upward. Several Ethiopians[11] ran up to it; at the sight of them the soul became extremely scared and started trembling. And immediately there was seen a most beautiful virgin, who came to the soul's assistance. She said to the Ethiopians: what do you want from this soul, that is of the family of my son's new bride? At once the Ethiopians fled and followed at a distance. When the soul had come to judgment, the judge said: who answers for this soul? Who is its advocate? And at once Saint James was seen and he said: it is my deed, O Lord, to answer for it, for twice it went to great pains for the sake of my memory. O Lord, have mercy on it; it intended to, but could not. The judge said to him: what is it that it wanted, but could not? James said: it wanted to serve you out of its entire heart, but it was not strong enough, for it was withheld by the sickness that broke out. The judge said to the soul: go now, for your faith and your will[12] will save you. And at once the soul vanished from the sight of the judge; it was exulting and resplendent as a star. All those who were present said:

be praised, O God, Who are and were and will be, for You do not withdraw Your mercy from those who confide in You.

Revelationes 7. 22

After this the Virgin Mary appeared again to me, in the same place, and said: it has been a long time since in Rome I promised you that I would show you here in Bethlehem how my offspring had been born. And although in Naples I showed you something of it, that is to say the way I was standing when I gave birth to my son, you still should know for sure that I stood and gave birth such as you have seen it now—my knees were bent and I was alone in the stable, praying; I gave birth to him with such exultation and joy of my soul that I had no difficulties when he got out of my body or any pain. Then I wrapped him in swaddling clothes that I had prepared long ago. When Joseph saw this he was astonished and full of joy and happiness, because I had given birth without any help.

Revelationes 7. 23

At the same place where the Virgin Mary and Joseph were adoring the boy in the cradle, I also saw the shepherds, who had been watching their flocks, coming so that they could look at the child and adore it. When they saw the child, they first wanted to find out whether it was a male or a female, for angels had announced to them that the savior of the world had been born, and they had not said that it was a savioress. Then the Virgin Mary showed to them the nature and the male sex of the child. At once they adored him with great awe and joy. Afterward they returned, praising and glorifying God for all they had heard and seen.

Extravagantes 44

The Son of God said to His bride: the one who has a ball of yarn in the middle of which is the best gold will not stop spinning until he has found the gold. The possessor of the gold that has been found uses it for his honor and profit. Thus Pope Urban[13] is gold that can be led to good, but he is hemmed in by worldly preoccupations. Therefore go and tell him on My behalf: your time is short. Get up and look at how the souls that have been entrusted to you can be saved. I have brought you the rules of the order that has to be founded and begun in Sweden, at Vadstena. It has come forth from My mouth. Now I want you not only to confirm it through a mandate,[14] but also to strengthen it through your benediction, you who are My vicar on earth. I have dictated it and endowed it with spiritual endowment, that is to say by conceding the indulgences that are in the church of Saint Peter *ad Vincula* in Rome.[15] You must approve publicly, in front of men, that which has been sanctified in the presence of my heavenly assembly. If you are asking for a sign, showing that it is I Who say this, I have already shown it to you: for when you first heard My words, your soul was spiritually consoled by the approach of My messenger. If you wish a further sign, it will be given to you, but not as it was to the prophet Jonas.

But you, My bride, to whom I have conceded the aforesaid privilege,[16] if you cannot get the pope's letter, favor, and seal for the concession of the indulgences, except by buying it beforehand, My benediction will be sufficient for you. For I will approve and confirm My word, and all the saints will be My witnesses. Let My Mother be your seal, My Father the guarantor, and the Holy Ghost the comforter of those who are coming to your monastery.[17]

Extravagantes 56

A certain dead man appeared and said: I have experienced the justice of the judge, but now the severity is diminishing little by little and mercy is drawing near. When I was alive, I transgressed most in five things of which I had not fully repented at the approach of death. The first is that I was too fond of the boy you knew; I applauded his foolishness and rejoiced in it, and I took pleasure in his nonsense. Second, out of carelessness I did not pay that widow from whom I had bought goods before my death. Therefore, so that you may know that I speak the truth, she will come to you tomorrow, and you must give back to her what she asks, for she asks not too much. The third is that I carelessly promised a certain man to stand by him in all his difficulties: this promise made him bolder, so that he rose up against the king and the law. The fourth is that I exercised myself in jousting and indulged in the vanities of the world more for idle display than because it was of any use. The fifth was that I was too unyielding and inexorable in condemning to exile a certain nobleman. Although he deserved the judgment, I showed him less mercy than I should have.

Then the Lady Bridget answered: O happy soul! What was your greatest help in gaining salvation? Or what could now be of use to you for your redemption?

He answered: there are six things that were useful to me. First, I kept my Friday confession whenever it was possible, and I had the firm intention to atone for what had been imposed on me. Second, when I sat in judgment I never judged out of love of money or favor, but tried every case carefully, ready to correct errors and to reconsider questionable judgments. Third, I followed the counsel of my father confessor in having no communion with you from the time when I knew that the embryo had gained a living soul. Fourth, I was cautious, to the best of my ability, not to be disagreeable toward the poor or to burden them when I or mine were guests; and I was eager not to borrow money without knowing how I was to pay it back. Fifth is the abstinence I practiced during the pilgrimage to Saint James. I decided not to drink on the way between meals. Through this abstinence I atoned for long stays at the table, for my loquacity and excessive eating and drinking. And I am already sure of my salvation, although I am still uncertain as to its precise moment of occurrence. Sixth, I chose through my discernment men I believed to be just to pay my debts. And because I feared to be entangled in debt, I returned to the king his provinces before I died, so that my soul might sustain the judgment of god. Now that I have been permitted to beg for help, I beg of you that for a whole year you have masses continually said in honor of our redeemer, the very holy Mary, for the angels, for all saints, and for the dead, and above all things in honor of the Passion of our savior Jesus Christ, for I hope that He will soon deliver me. Above all, have an open hand especially for the poor. Do not spare in distributing the drinking vessels and the horses and the rest, for I sinned most in taking delight in them. And if you are able, do not neglect to offer some chalices for the sacrifice to God, for they are useful in helping souls to a most speedy salvation. But leave to my sons the estates, for my conscience does not reproach me with having gained anything unjustly, or having kept, or having wished to keep.

Extravagantes 110

When Bridget was returning to Rome from her trip to the holy city of Jerusalem, a certain queen[18] sent her a sum of money at Naples for her support, out of compassion. But as the latter was doubting as to whether she should accept such a gift, Christ appeared to her and said: is friendship to be paid back with enmity? Or is evil to be given in return for good? Or is it necessary to put snow back into a cold vase, so that it becomes even colder? Therefore, although the queen gives to you out of a cold heart that which she has offered, nevertheless you must accept it with love and with reverence, and you must pray for her, so that she may succeed in reaching divine love. For so it is written: the abundance of others makes good the shortcomings of the poor, and no good works will be forgotten before God.

Acta et processus canonizacionis Beate Birgitte (p. 514)

The witness also said that he had been present and had seen it with his own eyes when, in the castle of Baghehws located in the diocese of Oslo, the younger brother of the king, Lord Haquinus, a quite mundane prince, asked one morning when he met Bridget outside of the castle whether there was going to be rain or fair weather, or will your sons be kings, and we will be deprived of the kingdom?[19] Bridget, undaunted and wholly inflamed with the Holy Ghost, said: if you do not improve your way of life, neither will you be king, nor will you live long, and you will see neither your first nor your second generation. Moreover, no mother will rejoice in you, and the memory of you will be short. Therefore, humiliate yourself publicly in the face of God, and you will find His mercy. The aforesaid was troubled and died after a short time, without progeny and without kingdom, just as had been predicted by Lady Bridget.

Regula 12

There will be sixty sisters and no more, and they will have clerics who will sing Mass and office daily at due time, as it is done in the cathedral churches of those lands in which are monasteries of this kind. These have to be completely separated from the monastery with the sisters. They shall have a court for themselves to live in and an entrance from the court to the church; the inferior choir will belong to them. The choir of the sisters will be above, under the roof, but in such a manner that they see the sacrament and hear the office. There must be thirteen priests according to the number of the thirteen apostles, among whom the thirteenth, Paul, did not suffer the least labor. And then let there be four deacons who also can act as priests if they want to do so. They are the image of the four Church doctors: Ambrose, Augustine, Gregory, and Jerome. Then, eight laymen shall handle the necessary things in the work of the clerics. Counted all together, the sixty sisters, the thirteen priests, the four deacons, and their eight servants will comprise a number of persons commensurate with that of the thirteen apostles and seventy-two disciples.

Regula 13

The abbess must be elected by the convent and must be approved by the bishop; she is the head and the mistress out of respect toward the very holy Virgin Mary, My Mother, to whom this order is dedicated. For the Virgin herself, when I ascended to heaven, became the head and the queen of the apostles and of My disciples. The abbess must also elect one of the thirteen priests as a confessor to all, in agreement with the whole congregation of sisters and brothers. Then, let the bishop appoint and confirm him. He shall secure from the bishop full power in his authority to bind and to unbind, to punish and to transform. All the priests and brothers, as well as the sisters of the abbess, must obey him in everything. They do not have the right to do anything against his orders, not even in the smallest detail. But this confessor cannot, except for the decision of the brothers and the maintenance of the order, do anything without the counsel of the abbess, for she is the head of the monastery and she shall be consulted in all that pertains to the business and to the goods of the monastery.

NOTES TO THE TRANSLATION

1. The Latin reads *in extasi fio*; that is, the spirit has become separated temporarily from the body.

2. The verb *commendare* is common in writings from feudal times; a serf, a minor, or a woman might be entrusted to the tutelage of a lord if circumstances so warranted.

3. In its general meaning, *humores* refers to the four vital fluids of the human body: yellow and black bile, phlegm, and blood.

4. According to Jørgensson, vol. 2, pt. 197, the revelation ought to be put into the Neapolitan context.

5. In this context, the word *conscientia* has the meaning of free will.

6. Bridget often stresses this point: the souls of the dead do not actually have the shape of human beings, and her descriptions are not to be understood literally.

7. In remittance from *culpa et poena*, both the soul's guilt and the punishment that would normally remain to be endured in purgatory are canceled.

8. The Latin reads *audivit in spiritu*, translated more precisely as 'she heard in her spirit.'

9. In the revelations of individual judgments by Christ, the term *charitas* is opposed to the judge's severity.

10. The *electi* are those whom God has chosen to be eternally saved; according to Saint Augustine, for example, they replace the fallen angels.

11. In Bridget's revelations, the Ethiopians are always those devils which claim a soul that is being judged. When the judgment is negative and stands as a condemnation, they lead the soul away.

12. *Voluntas*, 'will,' is to be understood here as *synderesis*, the possibility that people can work for their salvation.

13. Pope Urban V, officiating from 1362 to 1370.

14. The word *auctoritas* has here, as is frequently the case in medieval literature, the meaning of legal document.

15. The revelation concerning the securing of indulgences for Vadstena is based on the legend surrounding Saint Francis' revelation in 1223. Francis wished to obtain from the pope the promise that anyone entering the Portincula church near Assisi could obtain pardon for all sins. The Virgin and Christ selected the day for obtaining the pardon: the feast of Saint Peter *ad Vincula*.

16. The Latin reads *gratiam facere*, 'to pardon'; but as can be seen from vernacular translations, the passage was understood as a concession of privileges.

17. This passage is to be compared with Saint Francis' revelation.

18. Although the queen of Naples is alluded to in *Quaedam regina*, Giovanna, queen of Sicily (1343–1382), was well known and Bridget had been in constant contact with her. The saint reprehended the queen for her libertine life-style.

19. "... dixit Haquinus ei, utrum erit pluvia an serenum, aut filii tui erunt reges et nos privabimur regno." So reads the Latin. The prince, who must have been an eager student of logic, makes fun of Bridget's prophecies by stressing their self-fulfilling character. He opposes the prediction concerning the royal succession to a tautology (*utrum ... an*), and thus the prediction concerning the throne proves to be a logical contradiction.

BIBLIOGRAPHY

Primary Work

Opera Sante Birgitte. MS 14. 2. Nuremberg, 1500.
Samlinger utgivna av Svenska fornskriftsällskapet. Latinska skrifter. 2d ser. Uppsala, 1956–.

Related Works

Andersson, Ingvar. *Källstudier till Sveriges Historia 1230–1436.* Lund, 1928.
Boesch-Gajano, Sofia. *Agiografia altomedievale.* Bologna, 1976.
Burdach, Karl, and Paul Piur. *Briefwechsel des Cola de Rienzo.* Berlin, 1913–1928.
Colledge, Eric. "*Epistola solitarii ad reges*: Alfons of Pecha as Organizer of Brigittine and Urbanist Propaganda." *Medieval Studies* 18 (1956): 19–49.
Collijn, Isac, ed. *Acta et processus canonizacionis Beate Birgitte.* Uppsala, 1924–1931.
———. *Sveriges bibliografi intill år 1600 I.* Uppsala, 1934–1938.
Dupré-Theseider, Eugenio. *Roma dal Commune di Popolo alla Signoria Pontificia (1252–1377).* Vol. 11 of *Storia di Roma.* Bologna, 1952.
Erzgräber, Willi, ed. *Europäisches Spätmittelalter.* Wiesbaden, 1978.
Fliche, Augustin, and Victor Martin. *Histoire de L'Eglise.* Vol. 14. Paris, 1964.
Gardner, Edmund G. *Saint Catherine of Siena.* London, 1907.
Gerson, Jean. *Oeuvres complètes.* Paris, 1973.
Graus, František. *Volk, Herrscher und Heiliger im Reich der Merowinger: Studien zur Hagiographie der Merowingerzeit.* Prague, 1965.
Gregorovius, Ferdinando. *Storia della Città di Roma.* Vol. 6. Venice, 1875.
Jørgensson, Johannes. *Saint Bridget of Sweden.* 2 vols. London, New York, and Toronto, 1956.

Lea, Henry Charles. *A History of Auricular Confession and Indulgences in the Latin Church.* 3 vols. Philadelphia, 1896.

Luther, Martin. *Sämtliche Schriften.* Ed. J. G. Walsch. 23 vols. St. Louis, 1881–1910.

Mansi, Giovanni D., ed. *Sacrorum conciliorum nova, et amplissima collectio* . . . 53 vols. Paris, 1901–1927

Montag, Ulrich. *Das Werk der heiligen Birgitta von Schweden in oberdeutscher Überlieferung.* Munich, 1968.

Nyberg, Tore. *Birgittinische Klostergründungen des Mittelalters.* Lund, 1965.

Paulus, Nikolaus. "Das Jubilaum vom Jahre 1320." *Theologie und Glaube* 5 (1913): 532–541.

Reber, Ortrud. *Die Gestaltung des Kultes weiblicher Heiliger im Spätmittelalter: Die Verehrung der Heiligen Elisabeth, Klara, Hedwig und Birgitta.* Hersbruck, 1963.

Reeves, Marjorie. *The Influence of Prophecy in the Later Middle Ages: A Study in Joachism.* Oxford, 1969.

Schmid, Toni. *Birgitta och hennes Uppenbarelser.* Lund, 1940.

Trexler, Richard R. "Economic, Political and Religious Effects of the Papal Interdict on Florence 1376–1378." Thesis, Frankfurt, 1964.

Westman, Knut B. *Birgitta Studier.* Uppsala, 1911.

THE TUSCAN VISIONARY

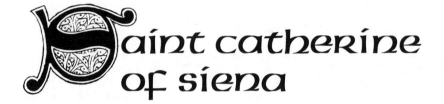

Saint catherine of siena

JOSEPH BERRIGAN

In 1970 Catherine of Siena was declared a doctor of the Church by Paul VI.[1] The only woman accorded that title, she joins the illustrious company of such men as Ambrose, Augustine, Bernard, and Aquinas. She also shares, with Francis of Assisi, the patronage of Italy; she was accorded this title by Pius XII in 1939. These twentieth-century accolades come some five centuries after her canonization by a fellow Sienese, Pius II. Her sanctity, her teaching, and her patronage of Italy are all the more remarkable when we glance at the details of her life.[2]

Born most likely in 1347, Catherine was the twenty-third child of a Sienese dyer. Early in her life she showed signs of a remarkable devotion. She refused to marry, entered the Dominican order as a tertiary around 1365, and continued to devote herself to a life of prayer and self-discipline. This spiritual activity resulted in a series of mystical experiences that would continue until the very end of her life. These included a mystical marriage with Christ and a constantly repeated endurance of his Passion. Like Saint Francis, Catherine would receive the stigmata, although in her case they were not visible.

These ecstasies and her growing reputation for sanctity caused a group of men and women to assemble around her—they included quite naturally a number of Dominicans, among whom was her future biographer, Raymond of Capua. Her influence began to expand in the 1370s as she started to compose her series of letters, which finally numbered around 350. Never able to read or write herself, Catherine dictated these epistles to a band of secretaries among her followers. Again like Saint Francis, she emerged as a powerful charismatic figure in the turbulent aftermath of the Black Death.

The inspired Catherine bombarded her correspondents with unsolicited advice. Saints with a mystical disposition tend to fuse God's will with their own, God's plan with their own, and Catherine was no different. She identified God with her calls for Church reform, for the return of the papacy to Rome, for peace within and among the cities of Italy, for a crusade against infidels, and finally for submission to Urban VI.

On occasion the written word was not enough, and Catherine would intervene personally. She traveled with her entourage to Avignon to plead the case of Florence with Gregory XI; while there she urged the pope to return to Rome. He undertook the trip shortly thereafter, with fateful consequences: he soon died there, and on April 8, 1378, the cardinals elected a native Italian, the archbishop of Bari, as Urban VI. Although this election seemed to provide a convenient way for the cardinals to choose an Italian to replace Gregory XI and thus to end the series of Avignon pontiffs, Urban's subsequent conduct so angered these same cardinals that they convened again and, on September 20 of that year, elected the cardinal of Geneva as Clement VII. The great schism had begun.

The great schism began as a protest of the college of cardinals against the high-handed conduct of Pope Urban VI. It took the cardinals several months to realize that they had erred in their selection of the archbishop of Bari—he proved to be headstrong, arrogant, and not at all respectful of their status as princes of the Church. The last straw was his creation of twenty-five new cardinals. The men who had chosen Urban now gathered in Anagni and elected one of their number, Robert of Geneva, as Clement VII. Unable to occupy Rome, he returned to Avignon. The schism had begun and would last for well over a generation, until the decisive actions of the Council of Constance in 1417.

The schism lasted as long as it did for several reasons. Both popes claimed to be legitimate; each had his own college of cardinals and the full panoply of papal apparatus, including its fiscal elements. Both Rome and Avignon—with their strong traditions of papal authority—found supporters in the turbulent politics of the late fourteenth and early fifteenth centuries. Each pope would have successors, and the first attempt to mend the schism would end in the fiasco of a third pope, elected at Pisa as Alexander V on June 26, 1409, a third college of cardinals, and so on.

This misadventure at Pisa had been the first result of a promising but slowly developing movement in the Western Church, conciliarism, which proposed to reunite and reform the Church by the intervention of the entire community of the faithful in a general council. The ecclesiastical variant of representative government, conciliarism was impeded not only by the hostility of the rival popes but by the swirling currents of late medieval international politics. Catherine intervened personally: she traveled to Rome and lent her powerful support to the beleaguered Urban, all to no avail. She died at thirty-three in 1380 in Rome. She was buried in the Dominican church of S. Maria sopra Minerva, but her head was removed from her body and returned to Siena, where it is still venerated.

Eventually the papal situation became so unbearable that conciliarism was given a second chance, this time at Constance in 1417. The three reigning popes were deposed and a new pontiff, Martin V, was elected. The new pope returned to Rome, established himself in the Vatican, and provided the basis of the Renaissance papacy, an institution that the Council of Constance had surely not intended to foster. The schism was over, but the very success of conciliarism had produced its own at least temporary eclipse. It would, however, be one of the Renaissance successors of Martin V, the Sienese Pius II, who would canonize Catherine. If Urban VI was "Christ on earth" to her, so would be Pius II, Alexander VI, Leo X, or for that matter John Paul II.

In addition to her letters, Catherine dictated a mystical treatise to her secretaries. Like the letters, the *Dialogue* or *Libro della divina dottrina* is a classic of fourteenth-century Italian literature. There is also a collection of the prayers she composed and shared with her disciples.

All her works reflect the intense personal experience she enjoyed of God in her mystical raptures. This intensity and the similarity of the Sienese dialect to that of Florence two generations earlier recall the *Divine Comedy*, as do many of her biblical references and homely similes. In both her letters and her *Dialogue* she teaches a very traditional Christianity. One is particularly reminded of Saint Augustine by her concentration upon the radical role of love. Perfect love, that is, the proper love of God, puts everything in its proper place and keeps us in our divinely intended relationship with God; all our other affections are ordered in a harmonious subordination to this love of God. Just the opposite effect results from the triumph of self-love—the true order of nature is inverted and a jumble of jangling, incoherent, competing cupidities results. The nature of perfect love (charity) is the theme of Catherine's letter to Urban VI, while the dire effects of self-love are blamed for the behavior of the three Italian cardinals in the early days of the schism.

Catherine's fiercely personal religious views were framed by her devotion to the visible Church, headed by the pope. She held an utterly nononsense attitude toward the vicar of Christ, a view that would have pleased the more extreme exponents of papal power, for example, a Boniface VIII or a Pius IX. Since the pope is "Christ on earth," union with him is essential for orthodoxy, separation from him is tantamount to heresy. This latter contention is hammered home incessantly regarding the poor Italian cardinals, while the responsibilities of the pope to exhibit and actually to possess the attributes of "Christ on earth" occupy her attention in writing to Urban VI.

This identification of the pope with Christ is all the more significant when one recalls Catherine's powerfully personal experience of Christ as the suffering Savior. He was her teacher as well as the object of her ecstasies. He was her bridegroom and she bore the invisible badges of his Passion, the stigmata. The blood he shed is ever on her mind; in her words to her correspondents, she invoked it as the most powerful reason for our loving God in Christ. Her love of God and her devotion to the Church and to Christ are sealed in her mind with his blood.

There is no critical edition of Catherine's letters, although an introductory volume by Eugenio Dupré-Theseider was published in the *Fonti per la storia d'Italia* in 1940. I have translated the first three letters that appear in a selection from her works in *Prosatori Minori del Trecento*. The *Dialogue* is available in an edition edited by Matilde Fiorilli in 1912.

NOTES

1. The designation of doctor of the Church had always been applied to men prior to 1970. The nature of the title is such that it requires a specific papal action to award it. A doctor does not have to have lived at any particular time and thus differs from a Father of the Church. Sanctity of life, soundness of doctrine, and canonization are the other prerequisites for the title. The choice of Catherine may be viewed as one of those brilliant, if underrated, gestures of Paul VI. Not only did he break the exclusive maleness of the doctors, but Catherine's high papalism would comfort the curia, sorely troubled by the Second Vatican Council. Then, too, she was an Italian.

2. The most recent biographical sketch of Catherine of Siena may be found in the *Dizionario biografico degli Italiani* 22 (1979): 361–379. The main sources of her life, including the early biography by Raymond of Capua, are in the *Acta Sanctorum*, Apr. III (1675): 853–959. The most important critical work on these sources is found in Robert Fawtier, *Sainte Catherine de Sienne: Essai de critique des sources*. Fawtier is also the coauthor, with Louis Canet, of the important study *La double expérience de Catherine Benincasa*. On the genesis of the schism see Walter Ullmann, *Origins of the Great Schism*. On conciliarism see Brian Tierney, *Foundations of Conciliar Theory*.

To Urban VI

In the name of Jesus Christ crucified and of sweet Mary.

Most holy and most dear Father[1] in sweet Jesus Christ. I, Catherine, the servant and the slave of the servants of Jesus Christ, write to you in

His precious blood, in the desire of seeing you established in true and perfect charity, so that like a good shepherd you may lay down your life for your sheep. And truly, most holy Father, he alone is established in charity who is ready to die for the love of God and the salvation of souls, since he is stripped of all self-love, of all love of himself. The man taken up with self-love is not ready to give his life. It is not simply a matter of his life; he doesn't seem willing to endure the slightest trouble. He fears for himself, for the life of his body, and for his comforts. So what he does is both imperfect and corrupt because his principal desire for which he strives is corrupt. And in every station of life he achieves little good, whether he be shepherd or subject. But the shepherd established in true charity does not behave like this; his every action is good and perfect, since his desire is joined and blended in the perfection of divine charity. He fears neither the devil nor any creature, but only his Creator. He is not bothered by the world's defamations, by slanders, derisions, or insults, by the detraction or the mutterings of his subjects. They turn to detraction and to muttering when they are rebuked by their pastor. Like a strong man, garbed in the might of charity, he pays no attention to them.

Nor thereby does the flame of his holy desire slacken and he does not lose the pearl of justice, which he bears in his breast, a pearl that is bright and united with mercy. For if justice were to exist without mercy, it would engulf us in the darkness of cruelty and would soon be injustice rather than justice. And mercy without justice would be in the subject like ointment on a sore, ointment that must be seared with fire; smearing on ointment alone and not setting it aflame would produce corruption and not a cure. But when justice and mercy are joined together they bring life in the pastor in whom they sparkle and health in the subject, so long as he is not already a member of the devil, who would in no way wish to be amended. Even if the subject is not amended, a thousand times, the pastor should not slacken his efforts to amend him, nor will his virtue be any less because the evil man does not receive any benefit.

This is the work of pure and simple charity, found in the soul that cares not for itself but for God. This soul searches after God for the glory and praise of His name insofar as it sees that He should be loved for His infinite goodness. Nor does it seek out its neighbor for itself but for God. It wishes to do for its neighbor the good it cannot do for God. It sees and knows that our God has no need for us; so it strives with great zeal to do good to its neighbor and especially to those subjects who have been entrusted to it. And it does not withdraw from pursuing the health of their body and soul by reason of the ingratitude found among them or the menaces and flatteries of man; but in truth, garbed in the wedding garment, it follows the teaching of the humble and spotless Lamb, the sweet and good Shepherd, Who, like the Beloved, for our salvation raced to the shameful death of the most holy cross. All this is the work of that ineffable love, which the soul has conceived in the object of Christ crucified.

Most holy Father, God has placed you as a shepherd above the sheep of the entire Christian Church. He has placed you as a steward to apportion the blood of Christ crucified, Whose vicar you are. He has placed you at a time when there is a greater abundance of evil among your subjects than for a long time past, both in the body of the holy Church and in the universal body of Christendom. And so there is the greatest necessity for you to be established in perfect charity, with the pearl of justice, as I have said. You must have no concern for the world or for those wretches who are sunk in evil or any of their abuse. Like a true knight and a just shepherd you must courageously amend them; you must root out vice and plant virtue and be prepared to lay down your life if need be. O sweetest Father, the world can now do no more, so great is the abundance of vices, particularly in those who are planted in the garden of the holy Church like fragrant flowers to spread abroad the pleasant aroma of virtue. We see that they abound in miserable and dreadful vices, so that they cause the whole world to reek.

Alas, where are that purity of heart and perfect integrity, whereby the incontinent became continent? Now just the opposite occurs, for often the continent and the pure taste of incontinence in their impure actions. Alas, where are that lavishness of charity, that care for souls, that giving to the poor and to the Church, even when they are in need themselves? You know that they do the opposite. O wretched me! I say it in sorrow. Their own children are fed on the means they receive through the blood of Christ. They are not ashamed to behave like barrators and to play with those sacred hands anointed by you, the vicar of Christ. I am not even mentioning the other crimes they commit. Alas, where is that profound humility, with which they confound the pride of their sensuality? In that sensual pride they indulge in great avarice as they commit sins of simony in purchasing benefices with gifts, flattery, or money, with dissolute and vain adornments; they behave not like clerics and worse than men of the world. Alas, sweet Papa, give us relief and grant refreshment to the fervent longings of the servants of God, who are dying of sorrow and yet cannot die; with great longing they are waiting for you to set your hand, like a true shepherd, to the amendment of these evils not in word but in effect, as once again there will gleam in you the pearl of justice united with mercy. Without any servile fear, amend in truth those who are feeding at the breast of your sweet Spouse; they have become ministers of blood.

But truly, most holy Father, I do not know if this can happen unless you replant, afresh, the garden of your Spouse with good and virtuous plants. You must be careful in selecting a band of holy men who are virtuous and have no fear of death. Do not look for grandeur; rather, they should be shepherds who will carefully watch over their sheep. And a band of good cardinals, who will properly be pillars for you, to aid you in bearing the weight of many labors with divine assistance. Oh, how happy will my soul then be when I see the Spouse of Christ receive what is her due, when I see fed at her breast those who have regard not for their own good but for the glory and praise of the name of God and for their nourishment, upon the table of the cross, with the food of the soul. I have no doubt that then the faithful in the world would be amended. They could not but be amended, constrained as they would be by their holy teaching and their decent life. It is no time to sleep then, but you should act courageously and attentively for the glory and praise of the name of God. Do what you can until the hour of your death.

So I pray you and constrain you by the love of Christ crucified, tend to the sheep that are outside the sheepfold (I believe that I am one of them because of my sins). I implore you by the love of that blood of which you have become the minister, receive them in mercy and with your kindness and holiness compel their harshness to yield and grant them that favor, a return to the sheepfold. If they do not request this grace in true and perfect humility, your Holiness should make whole their imperfection. Accept from the infirm what he can give you. Alas, alas, have mercy on the many souls that are perishing. And do not look upon the scandal that has occurred in this city, in which especially the devils of hell have done their best to hinder the peace and quiet of body and soul. Divine goodness has seen to it, however, that great evil would not produce great evil but your children have been pacified and even now ask of you the oil of mercy. And we suppose that you will think, most holy Father, that their request is not accompanied with the requisite peaceful deportment and with as much generous displeasure at the fault they have committed as they should display and as your Holiness would like them to display. Alas, do not weary them; they will indeed be better sons than the others. Alas, Papa, I would like not to stay here any longer. Do with me then what you will. Grant me this favor and this mercy, which I beg of you in my utter wretchedness. Father, do not deny me the little crumbs that I am asking for your children, so that, once peace comes, you may unfurl the banner of the most holy cross. You should clearly see that the infidels have come to challenge you. I hope, by the sweet goodness of God, that you will be filled with an incandescent charity; thence you shall know what harm is befalling souls and how much you are bound to love them. And thus you shall wax greater in both your hunger and concern for drawing them forth from the hands of the devil, and you shall strive to heal the mystical body of the holy Church and the entire body of Christendom, and especially to reconcile your children. You shall bring them back with kindness and with that rod of justice which they are able to bear and no more.

I am certain that none of this would happen if you were without the virtue of charity, and this is the reason I said that I yearned to see you established in true and perfect charity. It is not that I do not believe that you are in charity but that as long as we are pilgrims and wayfarers in this life, we can grow in the perfection of charity. That is the reason I said that I wanted the perfection of charity in you. You should be constantly nurturing it with the fire of holy desire and generating it, like a good pasture, among your subjects. This is how I pray you shall act, and I shall be constant and active until my death with my intercessions and with anything I can do for the honor of God, for your peace and for that of your children.

I will say nothing else to you. Remain in the holy and sweet love of God. Forgive me, most holy Father, for my presumption. May my love and my sorrow serve as my excuse in the presence of your Holiness. I humbly beg for your blessing. Jesus is sweet, Jesus is love.

To Three Italian Cardinals

In the name of Jesus Christ and of sweet Mary.

Dearest brothers and fathers[2] in sweet Jesus Christ, I, Catherine, the slave and servant of the servants of Jesus Christ, write to you in His precious blood, in the desire of seeing you return to the true and most perfect light, of seeing you leave the great darkness and blindness into which you have fallen. Then you will be fathers to me; otherwise you will not be. So I call you fathers insofar as you depart from death and return to life (since for the moment you have departed from the life of grace; you are members torn asunder from your head, from whom you received life). You will then be united in faith and obedience to the pope, Urban VI; it is in that obedience that they stand who have the light. With that light they know the truth and in knowing it they love it. What is not seen cannot be known and no man can love what he does not know. And one who does not love and fear his Creator loves himself with a sensual love and all that he loves, the delights, honors, and privileges of the world, he loves sensually. He has been created for love and cannot live without love. So he either loves God or he loves himself and the world with a love that brings him death, since it fixes the eye of the intellect, darkened by his own love of self, upon these ephemeral objects that flit away like the wind. In this way he can know neither truth nor goodness. Falsehood is all he knows, since he has no light. For in truth if he had the light, he would know that from such love he derives nothing but pain and eternal death. This love makes him have a foretaste of hell in this life: the man who disordinately loves himself and the things of this world cannot endure himself.

O human blindness! You do not see, unfortunate man, that you believe you love something firm and lasting, something delightful, good, and lovely; but they are mutable, utterly wretched, ugly, and without any goodness. This is due not to the things themselves, since they were all created by God, Who is supremely good, but to the desire of the man who disordinately possesses them. How unstable are the riches and honors of this world in him who possesses them without God, that is, without fear of Him. Today he is rich and great, tomorrow he's poor. How ugly is the life of our body; in our living we emit odors from our entire body. Quite simply, it is a bag of filth, the food of worms, the food of death. Our life and the beauty of youth pass away like the beauty of a flower once it has been cut from its plant. No one can provide a cure for this beauty or preserve it once the supreme judge decides to pick this flower of life through death, nor does anyone know when this will happen.

O wretched man, the darkness of self-love does not allow you to know this truth. If you knew it, you would prefer undergoing any suffering rather than leading your life in this way. You would dispose yourself to love and desire Him Who is. You would taste of His truth with firmness and not be moved like a leaf in the wind. You would serve your Creator and love everything in Him and nothing without Him. Oh, how great will be the reproof and rebuke of this blindness on the last day. This will be true of every creature endowed with reason but much more so of those whom God has lifted above the mire of this world and placed in the greatest possible excellence: to be the ministers of the blood of the humble and spotless Lamb. Alas, alas, where have you been brought by not following in virtue your own excellence! You were placed to nourish yourselves at the breast of the holy Church; as flowers you were sent into this garden to emit the fragrance of virtue; you were placed as columns to support this vessel and the vicar of Christ on earth; you were placed as a lamp upon a candelabrum to give light to faithful Christians and to spread the faith.

You well know if you have done what you were created to do. You certainly have not, since your self-love has not let you know it. For in truth it was only to provide strength and to give light and the example of a good and holy life that you were sent into this garden. If you had known that truth, you would have loved it and garbed yourselves in its sweetness. And where is the gratitude you should have shown to this

Bride, who has nourished you at her bosom? I see nothing but ingratitude, which dries up the fountain of piety.

What shows me that you are ingrates, boors, and hirelings? The persecution that you along with others have conducted and are still conducting against this Bride at the very time that you should have served
as shields against the blows of heresy. In this matter you know full well
that Urban VI is truly the pope, the supreme pontiff elected in an orderly
election and without any fear, truly more by divine inspiration than by
your human industry. Such was your message to us and that was the
truth. Now you have turned your backs like wretched and cowardly
knights. Your own shadow has made you afraid. You have left the truth
that strengthened you and drawn near falsehood, which weakens both
the soul and the body as it deprives you of grace, spiritual and temporal.

What is the reason for this? The prison of self-love, which has poi-
soned the world. This is what has made you, columns, worse than straw.
You are not flowers that emit a fragrance but a stench that has caused
the whole world to reek. You are not lamps placed upon a candelabrum
to spread the faith but the light which has been hidden under the bushel
of pride, and you have become not spreaders but shredders of the faith
and you shed darkness upon yourselves and others. As terrestrial angels,
you should have been in a position to save us from the infernal demons
and to play the role of angels in bringing the sheep back to the obedience
of the holy Church, but you have undertaken the mission of demons.
The evil you have within yourselves, that evil you want to give to us by
withdrawing us from our obedience to Christ on earth and inducing us
to obey the Antichrist, the devil's member. And you are together with
him, as long as you remain in this heresy.

This is not the blindness of ignorance; that is, it is not the result of
ignorance. It is not a question of your being wrongly informed about the
world. No, since you know the truth and you have told us of it, we
haven't told you. Oh, how mad you are! You gave us the truth and now
you want us to taste of falsehood through you. Now you wish to confound this truth and lead us to take the opposite view. You said that you
elected Pope Urban by reason of fear, something that is not so. Whoever
says that (I speak to you now without reverence, since you have deprived
yourselves of reverence) lies to his own damnation. You make a show of
having elected someone out of fear, but his identity was clear to anyone
who wanted to see: he was the Cardinal Tebaldeschi.

You could say to me, "Why don't you believe me? We who elected him
know the truth better than you." And I reply to you that you have yourselves shown me that you have departed from the truth in many ways
and that I should not believe your contention that Pope Urban VI is not
really the pope. If I turn my attention to the principle of your life, I do

not find there so good and holy a life that you have in conscience withdrawn from falsehood. What shows me that your life is so poorly ordered? The poison of heresy. If I turn my attention to the election ordained
by your mouths, then we have learned that you elected him canonically
and not out of fear. We have already said that the man you would have
elected out of fear was Cardinal Tebaldeschi. What shows me that the
election was a proper one in which you elected Lord Bartolommeo, the
archbishop of Bari, as true pope, the present Urban VI? This truth was
shown me in the solemnity of his coronation. That the solemnity was
carried out in truth is shown by the reverence you paid to him and by
the favors you asked of him, favors that you have enjoyed in all matters.
This truth you cannot deny, unless you resort to lies.

Ah, you fools, worthy of a thousand deaths! Like blind men, you do
not see your own evil. You have come to such confusion that you have
become liars and idolaters. For even if what you say were true (which it
is not, since Urban VI is the true pope; that I declare and do not deny),
would you not have lied to us when you said that you had elected him
pope, which he is? And would you not have falsely done him reverence
as you venerated him as Christ on earth? And would you not have been
simoniacal in ferreting out favors and then using them? Yes, you would.
Now they have elected an antipope and you have done so along with
them. Insofar as the act and the external appearances are concerned, such
is your admitted conduct, since you say that you were present when the
devils incarnate elected the devil.

You could say to me, "No, we did not elect him." I do not know whether
I believe that or not. For I do not believe that you should have allowed
yourselves to be present there, even if life itself were at stake. At least
your silence, your not exploding (since this was not in keeping with your
power), inclines me to believe you. Let us grant that perhaps you did less
evil than the others in your intention, you still did evil along with the
others. And what can I say? I can say that he who is not for the truth is
against the truth; he who was not then for Christ on this earth, Pope
Urban VI, was against him. And so I say that you have done evil along
with him, and I can say that a member of the devil was elected. If he had
been a member of Christ, he would have chosen death rather than consent to such an enormity: he knows the truth well and cannot excuse
himself on grounds of ignorance. These are the wrongs you are committing now and have committed with regard to this devil, to call him pope
(which he is not) and to do reverence to someone you should not. You
have left the light and are going into the darkness; leaving the truth, you
have associated with falsehood. On all sides I find nothing but falsehood.
You should be executed and I truly announce your execution (and so

discharge my conscience); it will fall upon you, unless you return to obedience in true humility.

O misery atop misery, O blindness atop blindness, not allowing you to see your own evil or the damnation of body and soul. If you had seen it, you would not have been so easily moved by servile fear to leave the truth; you were full of passion, like men of pride or those accustomed to having their own way in the pleasures and delights of mankind. Not only were you unable to endure any rebuke of your action, but the very word of harsh chiding made you lift your heads. And this is the reason that you were moved. Well enough does truth declare it to us: before Christ on earth began to grieve you, you honored and revered him as the vicar of Christ that he is. But the last fruit that has come forth from you shows the kind of trees you are and your tree is planted in the land of pride, produced by your self-love, which has deprived you of the light of reason.

Alas, no more of this, for the love of God! Seize the chance you have for flight. Humble yourselves beneath the powerful hand of God, in obedience to His vicar, while you still have the time. Once this time has passed, there is no further remedy. Admit your faults so that you may humble yourselves and acknowledge the infinite goodness of God, Who has not commanded the earth to swallow you or wild beasts to devour you. Rather He has granted you time to correct your soul. But if you do not acknowledge Him, what He has granted you as a grace will turn into a great judgment against you. But if you choose to return to the sheepfold and be nourished in truth at the breast of the Bride of Christ, you will be received with mercy by Christ in heaven and Christ on earth, despite the evil you have committed. I beseech you, delay no longer and do not fight against the goad of conscience that I know is constantly stinging you. Let not the confusion of your mind, of the evil you have committed, so overcome you that you abandon your salvation out of tedium and despair, as though there were no chance of finding a remedy. He does not want to act in this way. But, with lively faith, take a strong hold on hope in your Creator and with humility return to your yoke. The final offense of obstinacy and despair would be even worse and more displeasing to God and to the world. Therefore lift yourselves up with the light, since without the light you would walk in darkness, as you have walked until now.

As my soul has reflected on this, that is, that without the light we can neither know nor love the truth, I have said and still say that I yearn with the most intense yearning to see you lifted above the darkness and to unite you with the light. This yearning extends to all creatures that are endowed with reason but much more does it concern you three, about whom I have had the greatest sorrow and amazement; your sin has af-

fected me more than all the others. If everyone else abandoned their father, you should have been the sons to strengthen your father in showing
forth the truth. Even if your father had done nothing but rebuke you,
still you should not have been a Judas, denying his holiness in every way.

But now let's speak naturally (there we are all equal in our affections),
let's speak humanly: Christ on earth is an Italian and you are Italians.
The only reason I see that you are not moved by patriotism as are those
from across the Alps is your self-love. Throw it away at once and don't
wait for any other time (time is not waiting for you); crush this desire
beneath your feet, with a hatred of sin and a love of virtue.

Return, return. Do not wait for the rod of justice. We cannot escape
from the hands of God. We are in His hands, either for justice or for
mercy. It is better for us to acknowledge our faults; we shall then be in
the hands of mercy. If we remain with our faults, we shall be in the hands
of justice. Our faults do not go unpunished, especially those against the
holy Church. But I want to bind myself to bear you before God with
tears and constant prayer and along with you to undergo the prescribed
penance—as long as you wish to return to the Father, who like a true
father waits for you with the wings of mercy spread wide. Alas, alas, do
not flee it or shun it. Receive it in all humility and do not heed bad
counselors, who have given you death. Alas, sweet brothers, you will be
my sweet brothers and fathers insofar as you draw close to the truth. Do
not resist any longer the tears and the sweat that the servants of God
have shed for you; you should rather bathe yourselves in them from head
to foot. If you spurn them and the sweet concerns and sorrowful yearn-
ings offered up by them for you, your punishment will be even more
severe. Fear God and His truthful judgment. I hope that in His infinite
goodness He will accomplish in you the desires of His servants.

These words of mine that pierce you will not seem harsh, since I have
written them in my love for your salvation. I would rather indeed pierce
you with my own living voice, if God would allow it. May His will be
done. Be more deserving of deeds rather than words. I end now and say
no more; if I followed my will, I would not stop, so full of sorrow and
sadness is my soul, seeing such blindness in those who have been placed
to give light. You behave not like lambs that feed on the honor of God,
the salvation of souls, and the reformation of the holy Church, but like
thieves who steal the honor they should give to God and give it to themselves; like wolves they devour the sheep. Thus I have great bitterness.

I beg you, out of love for that precious blood that was shed with such
fiery love for you, give refreshment to my soul that is seeking your salvation. I say nothing else to you. Remain in the holy and sweet love of
God; bathe yourselves in the blood of the spotless Lamb, where you will

lose all servile fear. With the light you will abide in holy fear. Jesus is sweet, Jesus is love.

To Giovanna of Anjou. To the Queen of Naples

In the name of Jesus Christ crucified and of sweet Mary.

To you,[3] most reverend and most dear mother of mine in Christ Jesus. I, Catherine, the servant and slave of the servants of God, write and comfort you in the precious blood of the Son of God, with the desire of seeing you a true and perfect daughter of God. You know that the servant will never willingly do something wrong in the presence of the Lord, since he fears the punishment that would follow after his fault. Because of this fear he strives to serve him well and diligently. So I say that a true son would rather die than offend the father, not from any fear of punishment or any dread of him, but only out of the reverence and love he feels for his father he does not offend him. This is the son who should receive his inheritance, since he has not renounced the will of his father but has noted and followed his footsteps.

I beg you, venerable mother in Christ Jesus, to act in this fashion, like a servant, since you well know that we are always in the presence of this Lord and the eye of God sees in secrecy and is always upon us. And well does that supreme eternal truth see who serves Him and who does not. The soul should fear to offend its Creator, since He is the true Lord Who punishes every sin and rewards every good deed. And no one, whether on grounds of lordship or of wealth or of birth, can excuse himself from serving this sweet Lord Jesus. Oh, how sweet and holy is this servitude; it bridles and orders the soul. It does not allow it to undergo the perverse servitude of sin but flees from everything that could bring it to sin. It hates everything it sees that lies outside the will of the Lord, since it knows well that should it love something like that it would fall under His judgment.

Once the soul has been uplifted with fear, in its realization of itself as a servant and its understanding that it cannot hide from His eye, it begins to uproot the disordered desires and loves of this world; it begins to arrange and conform them to the will of its Lord. Otherwise it could not please Him, since, as Christ said, no one can serve two masters: if he serves one, he is opposed to the other.

After our soul has been set free by fear, it rushes along with perfect solicitude and chases away every sin and defect. This love behaves ex-

actly like the household servant who has been charged with cleaning
dirty dishes. But once the soul has become a daughter, that is, has entered
into a state of perfect charity, it behaves like a true son who loves his
own father with tenderness; he does not love with a hireling's love for
the advantage he may derive from the father and does not fear to offend
him out of dread of punishment. His only reason is the goodness of his
father, the bounty of his nature, which his father has given him with love.
It is nature and the power of love that compel him to love and to serve
him. Such a man can indeed be called a true son.

Consequently I say that our love for our Father in heaven is such that
you love Him not for any advantage you may derive from Him or from
any punishment He may impose upon us but only because He is supreme
and just, eternally good. By His infinite goodness He is worthy of being
loved. And nothing else is worthy of being loved outside God, unless in
Him and through Him we love and serve every creature. This is the love
of the Father. And as the fear I mentioned must clean the dishes, so this
love must fill the vessel of the soul with virtues and draw off all haugh-
tiness and pomp of vainglory, all impatience, injustice, vanity, and worldly
wretchedness. It draws off the memory of wrongs it has endured. All that
remains is the memory of God's grace and His goodness, along with true
and perfect humility, with patience to endure every punishment for sweet
Jesus, with a holy justice that will justly accord to each his due.

And notice that there are two ways in which you have to do justice:
first there is justice for yourself, so that you justly render glory and honor
to God, in recognizing that you have every grace from Him and through
Him. And render to yourself what is yours, that is, sin and wretchedness,
with true contrition and displeasure with sin, since the Son of God had
sin bound and nailed upon the wood of the most holy cross. The other
sort of justice is that granted over creatures. This justice you must exercise, because of your position, within your kingdom. For this reason I
pray you in Christ Jesus, turn not a blind eye to any injustice. Rather,
with justice, see that each receives his due justly, the small as well as the
great, the great as well as the small. And beware that no pleasure or fear
of creatures keeps you from doing so. Otherwise you would not be a true
daughter: if you were to keep your eyes open as justly as you should to
the honor of God, you would choose to die rather than ever fail Him.

Once the vessel of the soul is cleansed of vices and sins and filled with
virtues, one cannot keep the heart from loving, since it has discovered
that the vein of God's goodness is working in it, even in the similarity
that the creature has with its Creator, since He created it in His own
image and likeness. He did not do this because He had to or was asked
to or because He would receive any advantage from it: only the depth
and the force of love and His ineffable charity moved Him.

This was the same love that made God unite Himself with man and in so doing humble Himself. Oh, how much ashamed, sweet and venerable mother, should every creature be at its pride, no matter how great its position or majesty, when it sees its Creator so humbled and rushing with so fervent a love to the shameful death of the cross! And with this sweetest of loves my soul yearns that you be clothed, since without it you could not please God or have the life of grace.

I inform you of this good and sweet news: our sweet Christ on earth, the holy father, has sent a bull to three particular religious, to the provincial of the Dominicans, to the minister of the Franciscans, and to our brother, a servant of God. He has commanded them to be his agents in spreading information throughout Tuscany and wherever else they are able to operate. They are to determine who are eager to die for Christ across the sea and to attack the infidels. They are to write to him and apprise him of their success. He says that if he discovers that Christians possess a holy disposition and a fervent desire he wishes to give them aid and power with his might and to go against the infidels.

And so I beg you and implore you, on behalf of Christ crucified, be well disposed and kindle your desire—as often as this sweet point is reached—to give every aid and power that will be needed. That way the holy places of our sweet Savior will be taken from the hands of the infidels and their souls taken from the hands of the devils, so that they may share in the blood of the Son of God as we do. I beg you humbly, my venerable mother, do not refuse to answer me and indicate your position and your good inclination toward this holy enterprise.

I say nothing else to you. The peace and the grace of the Holy Spirit be always in your soul. Remain in the sweet love of God; pardon my presumption. Jesus is sweet, Jesus, Jesus.

NOTES TO THE TRANSLATION

1. For Catherine, only Urban VI was the rightful pope, "Christ on earth." Her attitude not only suffuses this letter but is at the root of her animosity toward the three Italian cardinals of the next letter. A classic presentation of these events may be found in Mandell Creighton, *A History of the Papacy.*

2. The three cardinals to whom this letter is directed were the surviving Italians who had participated in the election of Urban VI. Cardinal Tebaldeschi, who is alluded to later in the letter, died between the election and the disputes that led to Catherine's composing this letter. The three were Simone da Brossano of Milan, Pietro Corsini of Florence, and Giacomo Orsini of Rome. These three did indeed leave Urban VI but did not take part in the subsequent election of Clement VII. Cardinal Orsini would soon die, too, but da Brossano and Corsini would ultimately cast in their lot with Clement VII and the Avignon papacy.

3. Giovanna I was queen of Naples from 1343 to 1382. Born sometime around 1326, she was implicated in the murder of her husband, Andrew of Hungary, in 1345. His brother managed to expel her from Naples, but Louis I of Hungary could not prevent her from being restored in 1352. Finally deposed by Urban VI in 1380, she was captured and executed by her successor, Charles III of Naples. She needed but may not have been able to benefit from the spiritual advice contained in this letter. On these Angevins see Emile Leonard, *Les Angevins de Naples*.

BIBLIOGRAPHY

Primary Works

Fiorilli, Matilde, ed. *Libro della divina dottrina*. Bari, 1912.
Misciatelli, Piero, ed. *Le lettere di S. Caterina da Siena*. 6 vols. Florence, 1970.

Related Works

Creighton, Mandell. *A History of the Papacy*. London, 1897.
Dupré-Theseider, Eugenio. "Caterina da Siena." *Dizionario biografico degli Italiani* 22 (1979): 361–379.
————. *Epistolario di S. Caterina da Siena*, I. In *Fonti per la storia d'Italia* 82. Rome, 1940.
Fawtier, Robert. *Sainte Catherine de Sienne: Essai de critique des sources*. 2 vols. Paris, 1921–1930.
———— and Louis Canet. *La double expérience de Catherine Benincasa*. Paris, 1948.
Leonard, Emile. *Les Angevins de Naples*. Paris, 1954.
Tierney, Brian. *Foundations of Conciliar Theory*. Cambridge, Eng., 1955.
Ullmann, Walter. *Origins of the Great Schism*. London, 1948.

THE ENGLISH MYSTIC

Julian of norwich

CATHERINE JONES

Julian of Norwich has in recent years emerged as an outstanding theological, mystical writer of the Church. This reputation is based on the only known work attributed to her, the *Revelations of Divine Love*. Julian's revelations are extant in short and long versions which recount her sixteen visions or "showings," tracing the process whereby she experienced a detachment from self and a union with God. The short version was probably composed quite soon after she received the revelations, while the longer text, a revision of the first draft, was composed nearly twenty years later after much prayer and reflection.

Julian wrote her revelations in English, and although much of her material has its source in the numerous Latin spiritual treatises of the time, these analogues are almost always directly traceable to English vernacular translations.[1] Although Julian often demonstrates an independent quality in her form of mystical expression, she was also very much a part of an established tradition in England. As early as the twelfth century, vernacular religious prose was being written in England. This body of literature is represented by the *Ancrene Riwle* and by a collection of five related religious writings known as the Katherine Group, which consists of the lives of three saints—Katherine, Margaret, and Juliana—and two treatises, *Hali Meidenhad* and *Sawles Warde*. These writings are either for or about women, and in almost all cases they make a special point to exalt virginity.

Julian probably also had some familiarity with texts of mystical writings from the Continent which were widely circulated throughout the Middle Ages. One of the most striking similarities between English and Continental texts are the numerous extant examples of mystical writings by women. Both Julian and Margery Kempe frequently fit the pattern of their Continental counterparts while still maintaining a distinctive English quality.² Julian, therefore, was not writing in isolation but very much reflects a special need for women, in particular, to express an ever-increasing devotion toward a personal union with God.

Despite a growing interest in Julian's *Revelations*, scholars have discovered very little concerning her life; most of the biographical information available is derived either directly from the text of the *Revelations* itself or from a few external sources, such as contemporary wills. According to the *Revelations*, Julian was thirty and a half years old when she experienced a critical illness which was to end through a miraculous cure after a series of visions. This experience was granted in answer to Julian's prayer ("since her youth"), to her desire to receive the three graces of God: first, recollection of Christ's Passion; second, bodily sickness; and third, God's gift of three wounds. These visions are recorded as having taken place on May 13, 1373, and since Julian says she was over thirty at the time, her birthdate must have been sometime in January, 1343.

Other information about Julian's life appears in a number of contemporary wills. Roger Reed, rector of Saint Michael's, Coslany, in Norwich, bequeathed two shillings to "Julian anakorite" on March 20, 1393 or 1394.³ Thomas Edmund, a chantry priest of Ayslesham in Norfolk, likewise bequeathed one shilling to "Juliane anchorite apud St Juliane in Norwice" in his will of 1404.⁴ In 1415, John Plumpton of Norwich, a citizen, bequeathed forty pence to "le ankeres in ecclesia Sancti Juliani de Conesford in Norwice," along with twelve pence for her maid Alice and for a former maid as well. Finally, Isabel Ufford, whose second husband was the second earl of Suffolk, entered an Augustinian house of canonesses at Campsey Ash in Suffolk after her husband's death, and upon her own death in 1416 she made bequests to a number of religious houses and one recluse: "Item jeo devyse a Julian recluz a Norwich 20's."⁵ This kind of evidence strongly suggests that Julian was steadily gaining esteem within religious and private sectors.

Aside from these very brief references in contemporary wills, the best external evidence regarding Julian's character and personality is found in Margery Kempe's account of their meeting. Margery recounts a series of events which ultimately led her to seek the advice of Julian concerning a special grace the former had received from God. The following excerpts from Margery's account admirably depict Julian as a deeply compassionate individual:

> . . . many wonderful revelations she showed to the anchoress to learn if
> there were any deceit in them, for the anchoress was expert in such things
> and could give good counsel. The anchoress, hearing the marvellous
> goodness of Our Lord, greatly thanked God with all her heart for his
> visitation, counselling this creature to be obedient to the will of Our Lord

God and fulfill with all her power whatever he put in her soul . . . The
Holy Ghost never inspires anything against love for if he did he would be
contrary to his own self which is all love . . . and the Holy Ghost makes a
soul stable and steadfast in true faith and true belief . . . Holy Writ says
that the soul of a rightful man is the seat of God; and so, I trust, sister,
that you are such. I pray God grant you perseverance. Set all your trust in
God and fear not the language of the world; for the more despite, shame,
and reproof that you receive in the world, the more is your merit in the
sight of God. Patience is necessary for you, so that you may keep your
soul. Much was the dalliance that the anchoress and this creature had by
communing in the love of Our Lord Jesus Christ during the many days
they were together.[6]

Margery confirms that Julian was recognized for her ability to offer
sound spiritual counseling. Julian's reported speech is very much in keeping with the opinions she expresses in the *Revelations*, especially her
understanding of and insights into the workings of the Holy Spirit.[7] Margery also reports a number of scriptural allusions made by Julian, particularly from Pauline writings—such allusions are found throughout the
Revelations.[8] The tone of Julian's counsel is in keeping with that of the
Revelations: prudent, compassionate, and hopeful.

Julian and Margery's meeting probably took place sometime between
1413 and 1415,[9] and since Julian is mentioned in a will as late as 1416,
we can assume that her death took place sometime after this date. Despite Margery's account, Julian's life remains basically a mystery. Some
scholars have speculated about whether or not she was a nun. Her spiritual frame of mind at the time of her illness suggests that she might have
joined an order while in her teens or, perhaps, lived in a convent while
she was a girl—the nunnery at Carrow (outside of Norwich), for example, apparently provided board and education for young women.[10]

Edmund Colledge and James Walsh have conjectured that Julian belonged to a community of contemplative nuns for some time before her
revelations took place. In the short text she states, "Since I am a woman,
should I not therefore believe that I ought to tell you about the goodness
of God, when I saw at the same time that it was His will for it to be
known?" Colledge and Walsh point out that in the last chapter of the
long text, Julian writes, "This book was begun through God's gift and
by His grace, but to my thinking, it has not yet performed its intention."
This statement suggests that she retired to an anchor-hold to see to this
intended purpose after finishing the long text.[11] Julian demonstrates a
thorough grasp of contemporary contemplative teaching—her language
and vocabulary indicate that she must have had a good deal more contact
with the outside world than would have been possible if she had written
the *Revelations* while enclosed. Various attempts have been made to con-

nect her with the Benedictine community at Carrow, but no direct evidence has been found.[12]

Julian most probably grew up in Norwich not long after the Black Death had swept across Europe. At that time Norwich was a wealthy city with a population second only to that of London; it boasted numerous parish churches full of art objects, three colleges of secular priests, and an opulent cathedral which possessed one of the finest libraries of its time.[13] All four orders of friars had been attracted to the city—an Austin friary in Conisford opposite the lane from Julian's anchor-hold no doubt was in possession of an excellent library. Julian may have had access to this or a similar library where borrowing was permitted.[14]

Norwich housed a Franciscan *studia generalia* at this time; this was one of seven branches in England which accommodated promising students from all over Europe.[15] Undoubtedly, this contributed to the thriving intellectual and spiritual atmosphere of the city; it also attracted many famous preachers to lecture and live in Norwich. Many of the Norwich wills from that period attest the popularity of and the value placed on theological and spiritual books.[16] Along with these intellectual and spiritual pursuits, Norwich appears to have been the seat of the East Anglian school of art, which was at its height during this period. Julian's descriptions of Christ's Passion in particular have a vivid pictorial quality—accomplished through her refined expression of the mystery of divine love and its relationship to humanity. These descriptions might well be compared to the skilled modeling techniques and fine colors used so sensitively by the East Anglian artists, who characteristically excelled at endowing Passion scenes with exquisite pathos. Julian's dramatic encounter with the devil is another outstanding example of her skill at producing a poignant, spiritual effect through the employment of familiar details. Many of the masterpieces of the fourteenth-century East Anglian school achieve similar results by celebrating the spiritual life of their subjects through an abundance of material details drawn from everyday existence.[17]

Julian's environment seemed to strive toward maintaining a balance between "love of learning and a desire for God." Somehow she obtained an excellent education, and the editors of a recent critical edition have reached the "inescapable conclusion" that before she composed the short version she had a thorough knowledge of the Vulgate—especially the Pauline and Johannine epistles.[18] She often uses her own translations as references throughout the text.[19] In the long version it becomes even more evident that she was familiar with Gregory and Augustine and that—after her years of study since the short version—she had gained familiarity with the *Golden Epistle* by Saint Thierry as well as such contemporary English writings as *The Treatise of Perfection of the Sons of God*,

The Cloud of Unknowing, The Scale of Perfection, and perhaps even Chaucer's translation of Boethius' *The Consolation of Philosophy.*[20]

Julian's knowledge of scripture as well as of influential Latin and vernacular writings enabled her to interpret her visions with profundity within an orthodox framework. The personal quality of her experience is not lost because of this but greatly enhanced. As she refined her soul's progress toward a loving union with God, so did she refine her intellectual skills during the interim between composing her initial text and the long version. Part of this intellectual refinement is apparent in her skilled use of rhetoric, which enables her to transcend the limitation of her natural language and express mystical experiences in theological terms. Colledge and Walsh believe that Julian adapted numerous literary devices, anglicized them, in an effort to express the depth and potency of her visions and locutions. Few before Chaucer had attempted to stretch the semantic spectrum of the language as Julian appears to do by anglicizing and employing the rhetorician's technical vocabulary.[21] She demonstrates, even in the short text, that she is familiar with rhetoric and its *colores,* and she uses these to achieve clarity in her theological arguments.

It is, however, misleading to assume that Julian is nothing more than an able rhetorician; her style clearly reveals other literary gifts, such as a skillful use of alliteration and rhyme. Ultimately, her goal is to make sense out of her revelations—meaning and thorough explanations are never sacrificed in favor of literary conventions. The following lines, taken from chapter 15 of the short version, demonstrate Julian's technique:

> I wille make all thynge wele, I shalle make all thynge wele,
> I maye make alle thynge wele and I can make alle thynge wele . . .

This is an example of the rhetorical figure *complexio,* which consists of a repetition of both initial and final words in successive clauses; for an example outside this text, see Psalms 135:1–2.[22] The above lines were left in Middle English, as clearly there is no barrier to understanding them. Many of the more complicated rhetorical figures do not translate effectively into modern English, and the reader should be conscious of this when she or he reads a modernized version.

Both Julian and Chaucer were faced with similar problems; Chaucer was faced with the delicate task of interpreting meter and rhythm in his translation of Boethius, while Julian set out to conflate her scriptural and theological background in Latin with that of her visions.[23] It is to the credit of both that they achieved their goals in a language, Middle English, which was in most respects just beginning to establish a literary tradition. Clearly, they did not have the rich vocabulary of Latin or French, which could so easily express nuances of meaning. Julian obviously took great pains to use the language in such a way that her theological concepts would be clearly and memorably presented without fear of misinterpretation.

As previously noted, the long text resolves many of the questions left unanswered in the short version. Julian perhaps strives for and achieves greater anonymity in the long text; she strongly advises her readers to forget the wretch to whom the revelations were made and instead embrace the insights of divine truth. Her apology in Chapter 6 of the short text—"But God forbid that you should say or take me for a teacher for I don't intend that nor ever did so, for I am a woman, ignorant, weak, and frail"—is omitted from the long text. Possibly this omission was made so as not to draw attention to the fact that the author was a woman; but more likely it was made because Julian, after many years of study and continual spiritual growth, had gained an inner confidence about her work.[24]

Julian's primary goal in writing the *Revelations* is to share with others an understanding of (as far as human nature is permitted to grasp divine workings) and a belief in divine love and compassion. She painstakingly strives to reconcile God's love for us with her own age's preoccupation with God's terrible retribution for our sins. The nature of sin and its effect on our relationship with God are among her chief concerns and lead her to consider our special relationship with "God our Mother."

"God as Mother" or, more specifically, describing Christ, the second person of the Trinity, as "Mother" represents a synthesis of all Julian's reflections, especially those regarding the Incarnation and the Trinity. This understanding of the creative force of the Trinity, the *natura creatix*,[25] allows her to proceed with her meditations on the motherhood of God and the nature of the human relationship with the triune God; this relationship exists because humans possess the same substance as God. Chapter 59 in the fourteenth revelation (long text) deals poignantly with the nature of the motherhood of God—this teaching in particular stands out as an exceptional achievement in the history of Christian devotional writing. Perhaps Julian omitted this doctrine from the short text because, being a woman, she feared a hostile reception, since many of her contemporaries decried women who presumed to teach, often using scriptural authority to uphold their arguments (see, for example, 2 Tim.:12). Understandably, then, Julian gives careful and thorough explanations of every detail concerning her revelations, including her initial doubts about their authenticity—this seems to be in part an answer to or a defense against such voices. However, in spite of her initial doubts, she stands firm in accepting her duty to share her visions with her fellow Christians. She asks whether she has the right to oppose God's will and not reveal these truths simply because she happens to be a woman.

In writing about "God as Mother," in fact, Julian had a long, distinguished tradition on her side—however, her application is unique. The general concept of "God as Mother" may not have been familiar to some of her contemporaries, but a number of her immediate precursors, such as the author of the *Ancrene Riwle* and Mechthild of Hackeborn in her *Liber specialis gratiae*, incorporated the idea into their writings.[26] The doctrine may also be found in early and contemporary English homiletic literature.[27]

"God as Mother" was employed by Anselm in connection with a devotional prayer, but he does not apply the concept to the Trinity as Julian does. Anselm probably used Augustine's exegesis of Psalm 101:7 as a source.[28] Another source for the concept derives from the sapient books—wisdom is recognized as the creative female principle. There is, however, a break in the tradition of identifying Christ, the second person of the blessed Trinity, with this principle. For example, when the Apocryphal Acts of Peter were translated into Latin in the fifth century, the word "mother" used to refer to Christ was suppressed.[29] Later came the proliferation of Mariology, whereby Mary was identified as our "blessed Mother," and the concept of Christ's relationship with us as a tender and loving mother disappeared. Julian remains "the single forthright exponent of this doctrine in Western medieval tradition"; she not only reflects on Christ's relationship with us as mother, both spiritually ("substantially") and physically ("sensually"), but goes on to explain how Christ's role as mother unites us to the triune God. As the second person of the Trinity, only Christ has a sensual, that is, human, nature perfected. He assumes the role of mother toward us as part of his divine workings within the mystery of the Trinity. Julian sees Christ's motherhood as ultimately an expression of triune love—this particular understanding is what makes her interpretation of Christ as mother different from that of her contemporaries.

Perhaps Julian's most outstanding achievement is her ability to meaningfully explore the nature of the Trinity (territory which has consistently ensnared even the most gifted theologians) and its relationship with us, particularly through Christ as the mother of humankind. Her explanations are careful, generous, free of morbidity and hysteria (qualities too often characteristic of some of her contemporaries), and always consistently within an orthodox theological framework.

Many of Julian's contemporaries strove against what appeared to them to be a dry theological approach toward gaining union with God. Invariably many medieval mystics chose to relate only their emotional and subjective feelings in their works, while the theologians of that period believed that they could achieve union with God through reason. Mystics tended to believe that only a chosen few could profit from their visions, while theologians felt that all reasonable people might benefit from their findings.[30] Julian is determined to share her illuminations with all who will hear—she celebrates the unity of humankind, not its separation into various factions. She is ever hopeful that "all will be well" and is vigilant throughout the *Revelations* against the effects of Pelagianism, which could so easily cause despair. As a writer, she represents the happy combination of mysticism and theology, and although much of her life remains a mystery, we can still benefit from her remarkable work.

Perhaps it is fair to assume that the *Revelations* had limited appeal in Julian's own time, as is indicated by the meager number of texts presently extant. Additional 37790 possesses the unique copy of the short text, and Westminster is the only copy of the long text which is dated predissolution. Other contemporary spiritual classics, such as *The Cloud of Unknowing* and *The Scale of Perfection*, have survived in many more copies. It appears that Julian's work was resurrected, as it were, by Augustine Baker and his followers during the seventeenth century, and copies were made for the spiritual edification of Catholic exiles in France—especially for the English Benedictine nuns at Cambrai.[31]

Julian has now achieved equal footing with her contemporaries. Not only does she demonstrate superior literary skills and proficiency as a rhetorician, but she also expresses a restraint which serves to underline the sublimity of her feelings. Throughout her work, she employs this restraint so that she can painstakingly examine her visions and keep her account free from error. Her primary goal is spiritual progress, not just for herself alone but for all fellow Christians. Her mysticism is personal yet comprehensive. The *Revelations* continue to fulfill Julian's original intention; today her often exquisite expression and her message of optimism are both admired and esteemed. Recently the Church of England revised its calendar and appropriately chose to include "Julian of Norwich, the fourteenth-century mystic," for May 8. Julian's spirituality continues to enlighten and delight; she is of particular importance to those of us who are interested in rediscovering women's contribution to Christian devotional writing.

NOTES

1. *A Book of Showings to the Anchoress Julian of Norwich*, ed. Edmund Colledge and James Walsh, pt. 2, pp. 421–422. All passages selected from Julian's *Revelations* are based on this critical edition.

2. Wolfgang Riehle, *The Middle English Mystics*, pp. 27, 28, 165.

3. Colledge and Walsh, eds., *A Book of Showings*, pt. 1, p. 33.

4. Ibid.

5. Ibid., p. 34.

6. *The Book of Margery Kempe: A Modern Version*, ed. William Butler-Bowdon, p. 32.

7. Colledge and Walsh, eds., *A Book of Showings*, pt. 1, p. 36.

8. Ibid., pp. 36, 42. See also Edmund Colledge and James Walsh, "Editing Julian of Norwich's *Revelations*: A Progress Report," *Medieval Studies* 38 (1976): 407–410.

9. Butler-Bowdon, ed., p. 32. See also Paul Molinari, *Julian of Norwich: The Teaching of a Fourteenth-Century Mystic*, p. 11, and Colledge and Walsh, eds., *A Book of Showings*, pt. 1, p. 35.

10. Molinari, pp. 9–10.

11. Colledge and Walsh, eds., *A Book of Showings*, pt. 2, p. 418.

12. Molinari, pp. 8–9.

13. Colledge and Walsh, eds., *A Book of Showings*, pt. 1, p. 39. For further information regarding Norwich during Julian's time, consult Norman P. Tanner, "Popular Religion in Norwich with Special Reference to the Evidence of Wills, 1370–1532."

14. Colledge and Walsh, eds., *A Book of Showings*, pt. 1, p. 40.

15. Ibid.

16. Ibid., pp. 39–40.

17. Evelyn Underhill, *The Mystics of the Church*, p. 127; also Margaret Rickert, *Painting in Britain: The Middle Ages*, and Colledge and Walsh, eds., *A Book of Showings*, pt. 1, pp. 52–53.

18. Colledge and Walsh, eds., *A Book of Showings*, pt. 1, p. 43.

19. Ibid., pp. 45–46; also see Colledge and Walsh, "Editing Julian," p. 410.

20. Colledge and Walsh, eds., *A Book of Showings*, pt. 1, pp. 47–48.

21. Ibid., pp. 48–51.

22. Frances M. Nims, *Poetria Nova of Geoffrey of Vinsauf*; also see Colledge and Walsh, eds., *A Book of Showings*, pt. 2, p. 738.

23. Colledge and Walsh, eds., *A Book of Showings*, pt. 1, p. 48.

24. Ibid., p. 222 n. 40.

25. Ibid., p. 149.

26. Ibid., p. 152.

27. Ibid., p. 159.

28. Ibid., p. 153.

29. Ibid., p. 154.

30. Ibid., p. 155.

31. William A. Clebsch, *Christianity in European History*, pp. 133–175.

Revelations

1. Long Text

Here begins the first chapter. This is a revelation of love which Jesus Christ, our eternal bliss, made through sixteen showings,[1] the first of which concerns His precious crowning of thorns; this contained and specified the blessed Trinity, along with the Incarnation as well as the union between God and man's soul, along with many pleasing visions and teachings of eternal wisdom and love in which all the revelations which follow are founded and connected.

The second revelation concerns the discoloration[2] of His fair face to signify His precious Passion.

The third revelation is that our Lord God, almighty, all wisdom and all love—just as He truly made all things which exist—so does He bring about all things which are accomplished.

The fourth revelation is the scourging of His tender body along with copious shedding of His precious blood.

The fifth revelation shows that the devil is overcome by the precious Passion of Christ.

The sixth revelation is the honorable thanks given by our Lord God, by which He rewards all His blessed servants in heaven.

The seventh revelation concerns the frequent changing experiences between feelings of well-being and woe. The experience of well-being is due to the gracious touch and comfort of certain endless joy; the experience of woe comes from temptation—through the heaviness and weariness of our mortal life, with the spiritual understanding that we are preserved through love by the goodness of God in both woe and well-being.

The eighth revelation describes Christ's last sufferings and His cruel death.

The ninth revelation concerns the delight which the blessed Trinity takes in the cruel Passion of Christ, who after His sorrowful death desires that joy and delight be our solace and happiness as they are His until we come to the glory of heaven.

The tenth revelation shows how our Lord Jesus, out of love, displays His heart split in two.

The eleventh is an exalted spiritual vision concerning His dear mother.

The twelfth revelation is that our Lord God is all-sovereign life.

The thirteenth revelation is that our Lord God wants us to have a great regard for all the deeds which He has performed in the most noble act of creating all things; it deals with the excellence of man's creation, which is superior to all of God's creations, and is about the precious amends which He has made for man's sins by turning all our guilt into everlasting honor. Here He says: "Look and see, for by the same power, wisdom, and goodness by which I have done all of this, by the same power, wisdom, and goodness shall I make all things well that are not well; and you will see it." And in this He desires that we ought to preserve ourselves in the faith and truth of the holy Church, not wishing to know His mysteries, except as far as it is fitting for us in this life.

The fourteenth revelation is that our Lord God is the foundation of our petitioning. In this revelation two fair properties were evident: one is proper prayer; and the other is absolute trust—and He wishes both of them to be equally generous, and so our prayer pleases Him and out of His goodness He fulfills it.

The fifteenth revelation is that suddenly we shall be taken from all our pain and woe, and in His goodness we shall rise up to where we will have our Lord Jesus as our reward—so as to be fulfilled with joy and bliss in heaven.

The sixteenth revelation is that the blessed Trinity, our creator, eternally dwells in our souls, honorably governing and commanding all things and powerfully and wisely preserving us out of love through Jesus Christ, our Savior, in order that our enemy shall not overcome us.

2. Long Text

This revelation was made to a simple, unlettered[3] creature, living in this mortal flesh, the year of our Lord one thousand three hundred and seventy-three on the thirteenth day of May;[4] previously this creature desired three gifts by the grace of God. The first was mindfulness[5] of the Passion. The second was bodily sickness. The third was to have God's gift—the three wounds.

3. Long Text

And when I was thirty and a half years old, God sent me a bodily sickness in which I lay for three days and three nights; and on the third night I received all the rites of the holy Church and did not expect to live till day. After this, I lay two days and two nights; and on the third night I often thought that I was near death, and so did those who were with me. And yet despite this, I was reluctant to die, not that there was anything so pleasing on earth for which I would wish to live, or any pain of which I was afraid, for I trusted in God's mercy.[6]

Thus I endured till day and by then my body was dead (that is, without feeling) from the waist downward. Then, I was helped to sit upright and supported with assistance, so that my heart might be more free to await God's will—I could think of Him while my life lasted. My curate was sent for so he might be present at my death, and before he arrived my eyes became fixed upward and I could not speak. He set the cross before my face and said: "I have brought the image of your Savior; look and take comfort from it." It seemed to me that I was well, for my eyes were set upward toward heaven where I trusted by the mercy of God I might go; nevertheless I assented to set my eyes upon the face of the crucifix if I could; and so I did, for I thought I might longer endure looking straight ahead than upward. After this my sight began to fail. In the room it grew dark all about me as though it were night, except for an ordinary light which was focused upon the image of the cross. I did not know how this was accomplished. Everything surrounding the cross was ugly and terrifying to me as though all of it were occupied by devils.

After this the upper part of my body began to die to such an extent that I scarcely had any feeling in it. My greatest pain was shortness of breath and the ebbing away of my life.[7] Then, indeed, I expected to have died. And suddenly all my pain was taken from me, and I was as sound, particularly in the upper part of my body, as I had ever been before.[8] I was amazed at this sudden change, for it seemed to me that it was done by God's secret act and not because of a natural occurrence; even so in feeling this ease I still did not believe I would live, nor was the ease I felt of any comfort to me, for I thought I would be gladder to have been delivered from this world, since that was what my heart longed for. Then it suddenly came to my mind that I ought to wish for the second wound as a gift and a grace from our Lord so that my body might be completely filled with the recollection and feeling of His blessed Passion, as I had previously prayed, for I wished with compassion and longing that His pains would be my pains. Thus, I thought to myself that I might with His grace have the wound which I had desired; but in this I never wished for any bodily vision or any kind of revelation from God, but compassion which I thought that a loving soul might have for our Lord Jesus, Who for the sake of love was willing to become a mortal man. I desired, by the grace of God, to suffer with Him while living in my mortal body.

4. Long Text

And in this suddenly I saw red blood running down from under the crown, hot and flowing copiously, as though that crown of thorns were being pressed onto His blessed head. Rightly so, I perceived truly and power-fully that it was He Who was both God and man—the same Who had suffered for me—Who showed this to me without any intermediary.

And in the same revelation, suddenly the Trinity[9] filled my heart with the greatest joy, and so I understood by this that it will be so in heaven for all eternity to all who will come there. For the Trinity is God; God is the Trinity. The Trinity is our creator; the Trinity is our protector; the Trinity is our everlasting lover; the Trinity is our endless joy and bliss through our Lord Jesus Christ and in our Lord Jesus Christ.[10] And this was revealed in the first VISION and in all else, for wherever Jesus appears, the blessed Trinity is understood as I see it.

6. Short Text

Everything I say about myself, I intend to apply toward all my fellow Christians, for I am instructed that this is what our Lord intended in this spiritual revelation. Therefore I pray you for God's sake, and counsel you for your own benefit, take no notice of this wretched worm and sinful creature to whom the revelation was shown, but mightily, wisely, lovingly, and meekly contemplate God, Who out of His courteous love and endless wisdom was willing to show this vision for everyone's sake as a comfort to us all. You who hear and see this revelation and teaching, which is from Jesus Christ for the edification of your soul, it is God's will and my wish that you take it with as much joy and pleasure as if Jesus Christ had showed it to you as He did to me. I am not good because of the revelation—but only so if I love God better because of it. And so can and should every man benefit who sees and hears it with goodwill and proper intention. This is my desire—that it should be as beneficial for every man as I sought for myself from the first time I saw it, for it is common to all just as we are all one, and I am certain that I saw it for the benefit of many others. For truly, it was not shown to me because God loves me better than the humblest soul who is in a state of grace. For I am quite certain that there are very many who have never had revelations, or VISIONS, but only received the universal teaching of the holy Church, who love God better than I. If I look to myself alone, I am nothing at all; but collectively I am at one in the unity of love with all my fellow Christians. For in this unity of love stands the life of all mankind that will be saved.[11] For God is all things which are good, and God has created everything that exists, and loves it all. If any man or woman withdraws his love from his fellow Christian, he does not love anyone at all because he lacks love for one Christian. From that time on, he is in danger since he is not at peace;[12] but he who commonly loves his fellow Christian loves all else. All is comprehended for all of mankind which will be saved, that is, all created things and the Creator of all, for God is in man, and so man is part of all things. And therefore he who commonly loves all his fellow Christians loves all things, and he that loves in this way is saved. And so I will love, and so I love, and so I am love. I am but a representative of my fellow Christians—the more that I participate in this loving while I am here, the more likely I shall have eternal bliss in heaven; that is, God, out of His eternal love, desired to become our brother and suffer for us. I am certain that he who comprehends this as such will be truly taught and strongly comforted—should he need comforting.

But God forbid[13] that you should say or take me for a teacher for I don't intend that nor ever did so, for I am a woman, ignorant, weak, and frail. But I understand this well because I have it from a revelation which comes from him who is the sovereign teacher.[14] But truthfully love moves me to tell it to you, for I want God to be known, and my fellow Christians to prosper, as I would wish for myself, by hating sin more and loving God.[15] Since I am a woman, should I not therefore believe that I ought to tell you about the goodness of God, when I saw at the same time that it was His will for it to be known? You will understand this better in what follows—that is, if it be well and truly accepted. Then you will soon forget me, who am a wretch, so that I am not a hindrance to your contemplation of Jesus Who is teacher of all. I speak of those who shall be saved, for at this time God showed me no others, but in all things I believe as the holy Church teaches, for I saw the whole of the blessed revelation of our Lord as unified in God's sight, and I never understood anything within it that bewildered me or led me astray from the true doctrine of the holy Church.

7. Long Text

. . . I also saw the bodily sight of the head [of Christ] copiously bleeding. Large drops of blood dripped down from under the crown like pellets— appearing to come from the veins all brownish and red, for the blood was very thick, and as it spread the drops became bright red. When it reached the brows, the drops vanished; nevertheless the bleeding continued until many things were seen[16] and understood. The beauty and vitality, nevertheless, continued with the same loveliness and animation.[17]

This abundance was similar to drops of water falling from the eaves of a house after a heavy rainfall, which fall so profusely that no man may count them. As for the roundness of the drops—they looked like the scales of a herring as they spread over the forehead.

These three things came to mind during that time: pellets for the roundness of the blood as it poured out; the scales of a herring for the manner in which the blood spread; and the drops of water from the eaves of a house for the countless abundance. This vision was fast and vital, hideous and awesome, and pleasing and beautiful—of all that I saw during this revelation, this was the most comforting to me because of our good Lord, Who is so reverent and awesome, so familiar and so courteous—this more than anything filled my soul with pleasure and security.

10. Long Text

. . . I saw this with bodily sight in the face of the crucifix which hung before me, wherein I continually contemplated part of His Passion: the dispute, spitting,[18] soiling, scourging, and many languishing pains— changing color more often than I can tell. One time I saw how half the face, beginning at the ear, was covered over with dry blood spreading down to the middle of the face; after that the other half was covered in the same manner; meanwhile it vanished in this part in the same manner it had appeared.

This I saw bodily, fearfully, and secretly; I desired more bodily light so as to have seen it more clearly. And I was answered through my reason: if God will show you more, He shall be your light; you need nothing but Him. . . . This second vision was so modest and so humble and so simple that my spirits were greatly taxed through the contemplating, mourning, fearing, and longing of it. For some time I was fearful as to whether or not it was a vision. Then at different times our Lord gave me more insight, whereby I understood that it was indeed a vision. It was an image and a likeness of our soul, black death for which our fair blessed Lord suffered because of our sins. It made me think of the holy vernicle of Rome on which He, voluntarily accepting death, imprinted His blessed face during His painful Passion—that face often changing its color and appearance from brownness and blackness, sorrowfulness and gauntness. Many marveled how it might be so that this image portraying His blessed face, which is the fairest of heaven, flower of earth, and the fruit of a maiden's womb, could become so discolored and so plain. I want to say, as I have understood it, that this occurred by the grace of God.

32. Long Text

One time, our good Lord said: "Everything shall be well"; and another time he said: "You shall see for yourself that everything shall be well." And in these two statements the soul understood a number of things. One was that we know that He will take note of not only noble and great things but also small and humble things—and things done to one another. This is what He means when He says all kinds of things shall be well. For it is His will that we understand that the smallest thing shall not be forgotten. Another meaning is this: that we may see many evil deeds accomplished and a great wickedness about; it will seem that nothing shall ever come to a good end. Therefore, we observe, pity, and mourn these events and are unable to rest ourselves in the blissful sight of God as we ought to do. And the reason for this is that our reason is so blind, so insignificant, and so simple now that we cannot know of the high marvelous wisdom, power, and goodness of the blessed Trinity. This is what He meant when He said the following: "You shall see for yourself that all kinds of things shall be well—that is to say, do things now faithfully and truthfully and at the end you shall indeed experience the fullness of joy." [19]

50. Long Text

And in this mortal life mercy and forgiveness are the means which lead us evermore to grace;[20] the tribulations and sorrows into which we fall often seem hopeless—as far as man's judgments on earth are concerned.[21]

But in God's sight the soul that shall be saved was never dead nor ever shall be. Yet I wondered and marveled with all the diligence of my soul as to the meaning of this: God, Lord, I see that You are the very truth,[22] and I know truly that we grievously sin all day and are very much to blame; I may neither forsake the revelation of this truth nor understand the part of it concerning blame due to sin. How can this be? For I understood by the universal teaching of the holy Church and by my own faith that the blame of our sins continuously hangs upon us from the first man up till the time we come to heaven.[23] This was my wonderment as our Lord, God, revealed to us the notion of no more blame—as if we were as pure and holy as the angels in heaven. Between these two contradictions, due to my blindness, my reason was very much taxed and could not rest for fear that His blessed presence should pass from my sight, and then I would be left not knowing how He saw us with regard to our sins. Either I was moved to see in God how He viewed them—whereby I might then know how I should look upon sin and to what extent our guilt is attached to it.

My longing endured continually contemplating Him; and yet I had no patience because of great fear and perplexity, thinking that if I understand it in this way—that we are neither sinners nor guilty—it would appear as though I had erred and failed to understand this truth. And if it be true that we are sinners and guilty, good Lord! How can it be possible that I do not see the truth in You Who are my God, my Creator in Whom I desire to see all truth?[24]

54. Long Text

And for the great endless love that God has for all mankind, He makes no distinction in loving the blessed soul of Christ or the least soul that shall be saved. It is very easy to believe and trust that the dwelling of the blessed soul of Christ is very esteemed in the glorious Godhead; and truly, as I understood our Lord's meaning, where the blessed soul of Christ is, there is also the substance [spiritual essence] of all souls who shall be saved by Christ. We ought to highly enjoy that God dwells in our souls; and even more so we ought to enjoy that our souls dwell in God. Our soul is made to be God's dwelling place, and it dwells in God

Who is the first and only Creator. It is a special insight to see and know that God, Who is our Creator, dwells in our soul, and an even deeper insight to understand that our soul which is made by God shares His nature, which makes us what we are.

And I saw no difference between God and our nature[25] but that it was all God; and yet my understanding discerned that our nature is in God, that is to say, that God is God and our nature is both created and part of God. For the almighty truth of the Trinity is our Father, since He made us and keeps us in Him. And the deep wisdom of the Trinity is our Mother, in whom we are enclosed.[26] And the high goodness of the Trinity is our Lord, and in Him we are enclosed and He in us. We are enclosed in the Father, and we are enclosed in the Son, and we are enclosed in the Holy Ghost.[27] And the Father is enclosed in us, the Son is enclosed in us, and the Holy Ghost is enclosed in us, all power, all wisdom, and all goodness, one God, and one Lord. And our faith is a virtue that arises from our nature, which our soul perceives by the power of the Holy Ghost. By faith all our other virtues come to us—for without it no man may receive them, for it is nothing more than a true understanding with genuine belief and trust of our being existing in God and He in us, although we cannot see it.

And this virtue with all the others that God has granted us works great things in us, for Christ, by His mercy, is working in us, and we, by the grace of the gift and power of the Holy Ghost, are responding to Him. This working makes us Christ's children and practicing Christians.

57. Long Text

... For the same virtues that we have received from our substance given to us each by the goodness of God—the same virtues through the working of mercy are given and renewed[28] to us in grace through the Holy Ghost. These virtues and gifts are treasured by us in Jesus Christ. For at the same time that God united Himself to our body through a maiden's womb, He took our lower nature, and by so doing, He enclosed us all within Himself, uniting Himself to our nature. In this union He was a perfect man, for Christ, having united Himself to all men that shall be saved, is a perfect man.

Thus our Lady is our mother, in whom we shall all be enclosed—and Christ was born of her, and she, who is mother of our Savior, is our very mother in whom we will be endlessly borne and whom we shall never leave.

Abundantly, completely, and pleasingly was this shown; it is mentioned in the first [revelation], where it is said that "we will all be enclosed in Him and He in us." And this is spoken of in the sixteenth revelation, where it says that He sits in our soul. For it is His pleasure to reign blissfully in our understanding, and to sit restfully in our soul, and to dwell endlessly in our soul, making it all part of Himself. In this process He desires that we be His helpers, directing all our intent toward Him, learning His laws, keeping His counsels, desiring that all He does be done, truly trusting him, for truly I saw that our spirit was in God.

58. Long Text

. . . And thus in our Creation God almighty is our kindly Father, and God Who is all wisdom is our kindly Mother, with the love and the goodness of the Holy Ghost—all of Whom are one God and one Lord.[29] And in this joining and uniting, He is our true spouse and we His beloved wife and His fair maiden, with which wife He was never displeased, for He says: "I love you and you love Me, and our love shall never part in two."

I saw the working of the blessed Trinity in this vision and I saw and understood three properties: the property of fatherhood, motherhood, and lordship in one God. In our Almighty Father we have our protection and our bliss as regards the nature of our substance, which belongs to us from our Creation for eternity; and in the second person through understanding and wisdom we have our protection regarding our sensuality [physical nature] and our restoration and our salvation, for He is our Mother, Brother, and Savior; and in our good Lord, the Holy Ghost, we have our rewards and gifts from our life and work, which eternally surpass all that we desire by virtue of His marvelous courtesy and His high abundant grace. For all our life is in three parts: in the first we have our being, and in the second we have our growth, and in the third we have our fulfillment. The first is nature, the second is mercy, and the third is grace. For the first, I saw and understood that the noble strength of the Trinity is our Father, and the depth of wisdom of the Trinity is our Mother, and the great love of the Trinity is our Lord; and all these are contained in our nature and substantial making. Furthermore, I saw that the second person, who is our Mother,[30] substantially the same beloved person, is now our Mother sensual, for we have a double nature from God's making, that is to say substantial [spiritual] and sensual [physical]. Our substance is the higher part which we have in our Father, Almighty God; and the second person of the Trinity is our Mother in the nature of our substantial making, in Whom we are grounded and rooted, and He is our Mother of mercy concerning our physical needs. And so, our Mother works in us in various ways, in Whom our parts be kept undivided, for in our Mother, Christ, we profit and grow, and in mercy He reforms and restores us, and by the virtue of His Passion, His death, and His resurrection, He is united to our substance. Therefore, our Mother works mercifully toward all His beloved children who are obedient and accommodating. Grace works with mercy, namely, in two properties as it was shown—such working belongs to the third person, the Holy Ghost. He works by rewarding and giving. Rewarding is a gift of trust that the Lord rewards to them who have worked; and giving is a courteous act which He gives freely from grace, fulfilling and surpassing all that is deserved of creatures.

Thus in our Father God almighty we have our being [existence], and in our Mother of mercy we have our reforming and our restoration, in Whom our parts are united and all made into perfect men, and by the yielding and giving grace of the Holy Ghost we are fulfilled. Our nature is in our Lord God, the Holy Ghost, Who is all goodness—for our nature is whole in each person of the Trinity which is one God. Our human nature is only in the second person, Jesus Christ, in Whom the Father and the Holy Ghost is; and in Him and by Him we are mightily taken out of hell and out of wretchedness on earth, and honorably brought up to heaven, and blissfully united to our nature, increased in richness and nobility by all the virtue of Christ and by the grace and working of the Holy Ghost.

59. Long Text

We have all this bliss through mercy and grace; we might never have known this kind of bliss if that quality of goodness in God had not been opposed—whereby we have the bliss. For evil has been allowed to rise up against goodness;[31] and the goodness of mercy and grace opposed that evil and turned it into goodness and honor for all who shall be saved. For it is that quality in God which sets good against evil; thus Jesus Christ, Who engenders good against evil, is our very Mother; we have our being from Him—where the foundation of motherhood begins with all the sweet protection of love which follows endlessly. As truly as God is our Father and our Mother, He revealed that in all things—namely, with these sweet words where He says: "I am He; that is to say, I am He, the power and the goodness of fatherhood; I am He, the wisdom and the kindness of motherhood;[32] I am He, the light and the grace that is all blessed love; I am He, the Trinity; I am He, the unity; I am He, the high sovereign goodness of all kinds of things; I am He that causes you to yearn; I am He, the eternal fulfillment of all true desires." For there the soul is highest, noblest, and most honorable, yet it is most humble, meekest, and mildest. And from the substantial foundation (that is, God the Trinity), we have all our virtues in our physical being by the gift of nature, and by the help and assistance of mercy and grace, without which we may not benefit, our supreme Father, Almighty God, Who is life, has always known us and loved us. Such knowing comes out of His very marvelous and deep love through the prescient counsel of the blessed Trinity—He desired that the second person should become our Mother, Brother, and Savior. It follows, therefore, that as truly as God is our Father so too is He our Mother. Our Father wills, our Mother works, our good Lord the Holy Ghost confirms. Therefore, it is up to us to love our God in Whom we have our being by thanking Him reverently and praising Him for our Creation—fervently praying to our Mother of mercy and pity and to our Lord the Holy Ghost for help and grace. For in these three are all our life, humanity, mercy, and grace—whereof we have mildness, patience, and pity—hating sin and wickedness, for it is appropriate for virtue to hate sin and evil.[33]

And so is Jesus truly our natural Mother of Creation, and He is our Mother in grace by assuming our nature. All the fair work and the sweet, kindly offices of beloved motherhood are appropriate to the second person, for in Him we have this goodly will, whole and eternally safe, both in nature and in grace by His own proper goodness.

I understood three ways of seeing motherhood in God. The first is the foundation of our natural Creation, the second is taken from our nature, and there begins the motherhood of grace, and the third is the activity of motherhood. And within this an expansion occurs by the same grace of length, width, height, and bottomless depth—all of these are one love.

60. Long Text

Now I am moved to say a little more concerning this revelation as I understood our Lord's meaning: that is, how we would be brought again into our natural state through the motherhood of humane love—a love which will never leave us.

As our kind Mother, our gracious Mother, Christ would entirely become our Mother in all things. He began the basis of His work very humbly and meekly in a maiden's womb. He showed at first, to my mind's eye, where He took that meek maiden of humble stature—as she was when she conceived Him—that is to say our high God, the highest wisdom of all, in this humble place dressed Himself and prepared to take on our poor flesh in order to perform the service and office of motherhood in all things. The Mother's service is nearest, readiest, and surest: nearest, for it is most natural; readiest, for it is most loving; and surest, for it is most truthful. Only He alone could ever fulfill this office. We know that all our mothers bore us with pain and even death. Ah, what is that? Blessed must be He—our very Mother, Jesus, alone brings us to joy and eternal life.[34] Thus He sustains us within Himself through love and labor right up to the time when He would suffer the sharpest thorns and most grievous pains that ever were or will be and then finally die. When this was done, and He had brought us to bliss—yet all of this was not sufficient to attest His love. He expressed this by these following noble and unsurpassed words of love: "If I could suffer more I would do so." He could not suffer death again, but He would not cease working.

Wherefore it moves Him to bestow on us the honorable love of motherhood which has caused Him to take a detour to us. The mother may give her child suck of her milk,[35] but our precious Mother, Jesus, feeds us with Himself and does so very courteously and tenderly with the blessed Sacrament, which is the precious food of life itself; and He sustains us most mercifully and graciously with all the sweet sacraments—this is what He meant by these blessed words: "I am He of Whom the holy Church preaches and teaches. That is to say, all the vigor and life of the sacraments, all the virtue and grace of My word, all the goodness that is ordained in the holy Church to you, I am it."

The mother may tenderly lay her child to her breast, but our Mother, Jesus, may familiarly lead us into His blessed breast by His sweet open side and show us part of His Godhead there and the joys of heaven with the spiritual secureness of eternal bliss. He showed this in the tenth revelation, giving the same understanding in these sweet words—"See how I love you"—looking into and enjoying His blessed side.

This fair, lovely word, Mother, is so sweet and so kind in itself that it may not truly be said of anyone but Him and to Him Who is the very life of all things. To the property of motherhood belong nature, love, wisdom, and understanding, and it is God. Although our bodily birth may be insignificant, meek, and humble compared to our spiritual birth, yet it is He Who enables creatures to give birth. The loving nature of the mother, who understands and knows the needs of her child,[36] very tenderly protects the child as the nature and condition of motherhood dictate. And ever as the child grows with age and in stature,[37] she changes her duties, but not her love. And when the child grows older, she allows that child to be chastised in order to break it of vices and be ready to receive virtues and grace.

Our Lord performs this good work in all those who administer it themselves. Therefore, He is our Mother in nature by the operation of grace in the humble part [our body] for love of the higher part [our spirit]. He wants us to realize this, for He wishes all our love to be fastened onto Him. By this I understood that all debts we owe, through

God's petitioning to the Father and through His motherhood, are canceled by the true loving of God—a blessed love Christ works within us.[38] This was shown in all things—namely, by many noble words where He says: "I am He that you love."

64. Long Text

. . . And during this time, I saw a body lying on the earth—a shapeless and formless body shown as being heavy and fearful, as though it were a devouring pit of stinking mire; and suddenly out of this body sprang a very lovely creature—a little child completely shaped and formed, swift and lively and whiter than a lily, which quickly glided up to heaven.

The devouring pit of the body represents a great wretchedness of our mortal flesh; the smallness of the child represents the cleanness and purity of our soul. And I thought that neither does the loveliness of this child remain with this body, nor does the foulness of that body dwell in it. It is very blissful for man to be taken from pain rather than pain to be taken from man, for if pain is taken away from us, it may come again. Therefore it is both a great comfort and a blissful sight for a yearning soul to be freed from pain. In this promise, I saw the merciful compassion that our Lord has for us in our woe, as well as a courteous promise of pure deliverance, for He desires us to be comforted by the highest joy. He revealed this in these words: "And you shall come up above, and have Me as your reward, and be fulfilled with joy and bliss."

65. Long Text

. . . Now I have told you about fifteen revelations which God vouchsafed to minister to my mind and renewed by confirmations and divine inspirations—I hope in the same spirit in which they were all revealed. The first of these fifteen revelations began early in the morning about the hour of four[39] and it lasted, revealing by a very fair and sober process, each following the other, till it was noon or later on that day.

66. Long Text

After this the good Lord showed the sixteenth revelation on the following night—as I shall relate later; the sixteenth was both the conclusion and the confirmation of all the previous fifteen. But first I ought to tell you about my feebleness, wretchedness, and blindness. As I have said from the beginning, beginning with "and suddenly all my pain was taken from me"—pain which I suffered neither grief nor disease from during the showing of these fifteen revelations and at the end of it, all was finished, and I saw no more. Soon I felt I should live longer. Immediately my sickness recurred first in my head with a sound and noise. And suddenly my entire body was filled with the same sickness as before and I was barren and dry as I had never been—I had but little comfort, and being a wretch, I mourned greatly for the loss of feeling, for my bodily pains, and for want of spiritual and bodily comfort.

Then a religious person came to me and asked how I was, and I said I had raved that day. And he laughed aloud and inwardly. And I said that I thought the cross before my face bled copiously; with this statement the person with whom I spoke grew sad and marveled. And at once, I was deeply ashamed and stunned at my recklessness, and I thought: this man, who saw nothing of it, takes the meaning of the least word I say with sadness. When I saw that he took it so sadly and with so much reverence, I grew very ashamed and would have liked to have been confessed, but I could not tell it to any priest,[40] for I thought to myself: why should a priest believe me when by saying I raved, I showed myself as doubting our Lord, God? All this aside, I truly believed Him at the time I saw Him; and so then were my will and intention ever eternal—but like a fool I let it pass out of my mind. Oh, how wretched I was! This was a great sin and a great unkindness, because I, for the folly of fleeing a little bodily pain, so unwisely left for a time the comfort of this blessed revelation of our Lord God. Here you may see what kind of person I am, but also that our courteous Lord would not leave me. I lay still till night, trusting in her mercy, and then I began to sleep.

67. Long Text

In my sleep, it seemed to me at first, the fiend took hold of my throat, putting his face, which was similar to that of a young man—very long and extremely gaunt—very near to mine. I never saw anything like it; its color was red like a tile when it is newly fixed, with black spots like freckles—uglier than any actual tile. His hair was as red as rust, long in front with lots of hair hanging from his temples. He grinned a shrewd look at me, showing white teeth—so much so that I thought his face even uglier.[41] He had no real body or hands, but with his paws[42] he held me by the throat and would have choked and killed me, but he could not.

This horrible vision took place while I was sleeping.[43] During all this time I trusted that I would be saved and protected by the mercy of God. Our courteous Lord gave me grace to awaken—I scarcely had any life in me. The people who were around me watched and wet my temples, and my heart began to take comfort. And immediately a little smoke appeared at the door, along with a great heat and a foul stench. Then I said: "Lord, bless us! Is everything on fire here?" I believed that it was an actual fire that would have burned us all to death. I asked those who were with me if they smelled any stench. They said no, they smelled none. I said: "Blessed be God!" for then I realized very well it was the fiend that had come to tempt me only. Immediately I set my thoughts on what our Lord had revealed to me that same day with all the faith of the holy Church, for I saw it as both one and the same and fled to it as my comfort. And at once all vanished and I was brought to a great rest and peace without bodily sickness or a worried conscience.

69. Long Text

The fiend came again with his heat and stench and made me very agitated. The stench was so vile and painful, and the actual heat was fearful and exhausting. I also heard talking, as though it were from two bodies; both, to my thinking, talked at once as they held a conversation with great business, and all of it was in a soft whisper. I did not understand what they said—all this, I thought, was to steer me toward despair, it seemed to me. They scorned the bidding of beads, which they recited boisterously and lamely. We owe devotion, intention, and wise diligence to God in our prayer. And our good Lord God gave me grace to mightily trust in Him and to comfort my soul with physical speech, as I should have done for any person that had been so engaged. It seemed to me that this activity could not be compared with any other human activity.

70. Long Text

I set my bodily eye on the same cross that had comforted me before that time—my tongue with a speech of Christ's Passion and reciting the doctrine of the holy Church, and my heart directed toward unity with God with all my trust and strength. I thought to myself: you now have much to do in order to keep yourself in the faith, for that cannot be taken away from you by your enemies. Would you be so concerned from now on that you would be preserved from sin forevermore? This would be a good and noble occupation. For I thought truly that were I safe from sin, I would be completely safe from all the fiends in hell and enemies of my soul.

And in this way, he occupied me all that night and the following day until prime. Suddenly they were all gone, with nothing left but stink that lingered for a while. I scorned the devil and by doing so I was delivered from him by the nature of Christ's passion. For by His Passion was the fiend overcome, as our Lord Jesus Christ said before.

During this entire blessed revelation, our good Lord gave me an indication that the vision would pass.

86. Long Text

This book was begun through God's gift and by His grace, but to my thinking, it has not yet performed its intention.[44] For love, let us all pray together as part of God's working, thanking, trusting, enjoying, for our good Lord should be prayed to in this way, according to the understanding I gleaned from his meaning and in the sweet words where He says very joyfully: "I am the basis of your entreaty." For truly I saw and understood in our Lord's meaning that He revealed it because He would have it better known than it is. In this understanding He will give us grace to love Him and cleave to Him, for He looks upon His heavenly treasure (with so great a love on earth that He will give us more light), and happiness in heavenly joy by drawing our hearts from the sorrow and darkness which they are in.

From the time it was revealed, I often desired to know what was our Lord's intention. And after fifteen years and more, I was answered with spiritual insight, which said: "Would you like to know your Lord's meaning concerning this thing?" I knew it well, love was His meaning. "Who shows it to you? Love. What did He show you? Love. Why did He show it to you? For love. Hold this within, you will know more of the same. But you shall never understand the eternity of it."[45]

Thus I was taught that love is our Lord's meaning, and I saw most certainly in this and in all things that before God made us He loved us;[46] this love was never diminished nor shall it ever be. And in His love He has accomplished all His works; and in this love He has made all things profitable to us; and in this love our life is everlasting. In our Creation, we had a beginning, but the love out of which He made us was always within Him. In this love we have our beginning and in all this we shall see God eternally.

NOTES TO THE TRANSLATION

1. Each "showing" of the entire revelation presents an important theological viewpoint regarding Christ's relationship to humanity: his sufferings are described, contemplated, and

glorified. These sufferings reveal the operation of the triune God and its relationship and unity with humankind through Christ.

2. Possibly Julian had Isaiah 53:2 in mind.

3. "Unlettered" does not mean illiterate but is used as a rhetorical convention. See Colledge and Walsh, eds., *A Book of Showings*, pt. 1, pp. 43–52, for a detailed account of evidence which suggests that Julian was a proficient scholar.

4. According to *Revelations of Divine Love Recorded by Julian, Anchoress of Norwich A.D. 1373*, ed. Grace Warrack, p. xviii n. 1, in 1373 this was a Friday.

5. See Philippians 2:5: "For let this mind be in you which was also in Jesus Christ."

6. This thought was probably inspired by Philippians 1:21–22. Colledge and Walsh think that Julian might have been familiar with the story of Saint Martin of Tours on his deathbed.

7. See Colledge and Walsh, eds., *A Book of Showings*, pt. 1, p. ix, for a discussion of Julian's "clinical exactness" in this particular recollection.

8. Note that Julian's miraculous cure is sudden—fulfilling contemporary canonization requirements as well as completely answering the demands of later advanced medical knowledge. See ibid.

9. Julian perceives how all three persons of the Trinity participated in our redemption as they had in our Creation. The Trinitarian doctrine in this passage is a summary of Augustine's *De trinitate* 1. 8. 17–18.

10. "Through our Lord Jesus Christ and in our Lord Jesus Christ" recalls Romans 11:36.

11. This passage is inspired by Ephesians, chap. 4.

12. This passage, not found in the long text, is inspired by John 3:14–17, 23–24.

13. "But God forbid . . ." is not found in the long text. Possibly this defense of herself as a woman who teaches was deleted so as not to arouse antagonism. Julian may have also recalled the prohibition in 1 Corinthians 14:34.

14. Compare Matthew 23:8: "For one is your master."

15. Compare Psalms 96:10: "You that love the Lord, hate evil."

16. The "ghostly sights" granted to Julian in her first vision impressed her by appearing against the background of the bleeding head of Christ crucified.

17. Julian continually finds paradoxes spiritually advantageous.

18. Compare Matthew 26:67: "Then they spat in His face." Peter Comester (*Historia Scholastica*) and Pseudo-Bonaventure both place emphasis on Christ's humiliations.

19. ". . . fullness of joy": compare John 3:2 and 1 Corinthians 13:12.

20. Compare Psalms 118:132–133.

21. Compare Wisdom 3:1–5.

22. Compare John 1:14.

23. Julian speaks in the person of all who will be saved much in the same manner as does Paul.

24. Compare Psalms 24:4: ". . . direct me in Thy truth and teach me."

25. The author of *The Cloud of Unknowing* uses similar language.

26. Compare Wisdom 7:10–12, where wisdom becomes the mother of all virtues.

27. "We are enclosed in the Holy Ghost" echoes a meditative prayer of William of Saint Thierry. Compare *Meditative orationes* 6, PL 180. 224.

28. Julian is expressing the idea that the powers given to us by Christ are also given in "a new way by the spirit of Christ risen and glorified." See Colledge and Walsh, eds., *A Book of Showings*, pt. 2, p. 579 n. 39.

29. Julian is probably influenced by William of Saint Thierry here when she views the operation of the Trinity as a simple act of cooperation without diversity and complication.

30. Here Julian develops her doctrine on the motherhood of God.

31. This is a clear Pauline reference with the personifications of evil and good set up against one another. Compare Romans 5:20–21.

32. Julian once again states that the motherhood of Christ is an appropriate quality of the second person of the Trinity.

33. Julian views our own lives as Trinitarian. That is, our lives have their essence in the Godhead, with the creative powers of the Father, the restorative powers of the Son, and the grace of the Holy Ghost.

34. According to Julian, after all that has been said about pain, sin, and death, only their mystery remains.

35. Compare William of Saint Thierry, *Speculum fidei*, PL 180. 371. The image of a child at the breast of its mother was used frequently by medieval commentators, who were probably influenced by the same image in 1 Peter 2:2.

36. Compare Isaiah 66:12–13.

37. This analogy is a common one found in the *Ancrene Riwle* and *The Chastising of God's Children*. See Colledge and Walsh, eds., *A Book of Showings*, pt. 2, p. 599 n. 54, for more details.

38. The following passages of scripture commenting on the fourth commandment probably occurred to Julian: Exodus 20:12, Deuteronomy 5:16, Matthew 15:4, Ephesians 6:2, and particularly Ecclesiasticus 3:1–18.

39. Colledge and Walsh, eds., *A Book of Showings*, pt. 2, p. 631 n. 39, believe that Julian is thinking of the old Roman method which calculated the hours from sunrise.

40. Colledge and Walsh note that this passage points out an important psychological aspect of auricular confession. Not only must the confessed be truthful, but the confessors must believe in the good intent of their penitents. If the penitents should doubt this, how can they be confident of receiving absolution? Julian questions herself on presuming that someone else should believe her when she herself doubted God's credence. See ibid., pp. 633–634 n. 25.

41. Note Julian's change in style, especially in the amount of descriptive detail she includes in this passage.

42. This line represents the common medieval belief concerning the devil—if appearing in human shape, he could always be detected by some physical defect.

43. Diabolical temptations were believed to occur most often at night.

44. Julian begins with a paradox: although this chapter ends the book, the work of the book is just beginning. The seeking and finding (Luke 11:9) so prevalent in contemplative expression are very much on Julian's mind here. One is to seek a Christian relationship with Christ and find union and fulfillment with the triune God.

45. Here is an example of *ratiocinatio*, a rhetorical device which examines the original proposition—in this instance asking, "What is the meaning or purpose of this revelation?" Compare John 4:8.

46. Colledge and Walsh point out that this statement resembles Walter Hilton's doctrine on creative, redemptive, and unitive love "uniformed" in *The Scale of Perfection*.

BIBLIOGRAPHY

Primary Works

Colledge, Edmund, and James Walsh, eds. *A Book of Showings to the Anchoress Julian of Norwich*. 2 pts. Toronto, 1978.

Glasscoe, Marion, ed. *Revelations of Divine Love*. Exeter, 1976.

Hudleston, Roger, ed. *Revelations of Divine Love Showed to a Devout Ankress by the Name of Julian of Norwich*. London, 1952.

Reynolds, Sister Anna Maria, ed. *A Shewing of God's Love: The Shorter Version of Sixteen Revelations by Julian of Norwich.* London, 1958.

Walsh, James, ed. *The Revelations of Divine Love.* London, 1961.

Warrack, Grace, ed. *Revelations of Divine Love Recorded by Julian, Anchoress of Norwich* A.D. *1373.* 13th ed. London, 1949.

Wolters, C., ed. *Revelations of Divine Love.* Harmondsworth, 1966.

Works

Butler-Bowdon, William, ed. *The Book of Margery Kempe: A Modern Version.* Introduction by R. W. Chambers. New York, 1944.

Clay, Rotha Mary. *The Hermits and Anchorites of England.* London, 1914.

Clebsch, William A. *Christianity in European History.* New York, 1979.

Colledge, Edmund, and James Walsh. "Editing Julian of Norwich's *Revelations*: A Progress Report." *Medieval Studies* 38 (1976): 404–427.

Colledge, Eric. *The Mediaeval Mystics of England.* New York, 1961.

Gies, Frances, and Joseph Gies. *Women in the Middle Ages.* New York, 1978.

Knowles, David. *The English Mystical Tradition.* New York, 1961.

Meech, Sanford Brown, and Hope Emily Allen, eds. *The Book of Margery Kempe.* 1940. Reprint. London, 1961.

Molinari, Paul. *Julian of Norwich: The Teaching of a Fourteenth-Century Mystic.* London, 1958.

Nims, Frances M. *Poetria Nova of Geoffrey of Vinsauf.* Toronto, 1967.

Power, Eileen. *Medieval English Nunneries c. 1275–1535.* Cambridge, Eng., 1922.

———. *Medieval Women.* Ed. M. M. Postan. Cambridge, Eng., 1975.

Reynolds, F. "Julian of Norwich." In *Pre-Reformation English Spirituality*, ed. James Walsh, pp. 198–209. New York, 1966.

———. "Some Literary Influences in the Revelations of Julian of Norwich (c. 1342–post 1416)." *Leeds Studies in English and Kindred Languages* 7 (1952): 18–28.

Rickert, Margaret. *Painting in Britain: The Middle Ages.* London, 1954.

Riehle, Wolfgang. *The Middle English Mystics.* Trans. Bernard Standring. London, 1981.

Stone, Robert Karl. *Middle English Prose Style: Margery Kempe and Julian of Norwich.* The Hague, 1970.

Tanner, Norman P. "Popular Religion in Norwich with Special Reference to the Evidence of Wills, 1370–1532." Ph.D. dissertation, Oxford University, 1973.

Underhill, Evelyn. *The Essentials of Mysticism and Other Essays.* London, 1920.

———. *The Mystics of the Church.* London, 1925.

THE ENGLISH RELIGIOUS ENTHUSIAST

WILLIAM PROVOST

The task of introducing Margery Kempe to a twentieth-century audience is, paradoxically, simple but problematic. The simplicity is a result of the fact that Margery has in effect already done the job: her work, *The Book of Margery Kempe*, is a kind of autobiography, the first such in the English language.[1] Margery deals almost exclusively with herself in her work. Though she tells us of many of the people, great and simple, whom she encounters and describes her various journeys in some detail, her one central subject is always Margery, her thoughts, feelings, impressions, and reactions. As a result of this consistent focus, we are made privy to the workings of her mind in a manner and to a degree unusual in any age and exceptionally rare in the medieval period.[2]

But there are problems. The first is that like most of her nonclerical English contemporaries, Margery could probably neither read nor write, and her *Book* is in all likelihood the product of an amanuensis who was almost certainly a priest.[3] Margery would have dictated her thoughts and recollections to him, perhaps then having him read back to her what he had written so she could give her final approval and make any changes she wished. It is at least possible, though hardly provable one way or another, that at some stage in his transcription the amanuensis might have altered passages with an eye to toning them up, say, or to bringing them more in line with orthodox belief.[4] Other problems having to do with the reliability of the evidence stem from the fact that Margery did not begin recording her "feelings and revelations" until some twenty years after they had begun to occur. The transmission of the text to its present form, on the other hand, seems to be quite straightforward, but absolute certainty is lacking here as well.

More centrally problematic than the above, though, is Margery herself. She was a religious mystic. Many modern readers would probably prefer a term such as "fanatic" or "psychotic."[5] Christ speaks to her frequently and, though less frequently, so do God the Father, the Holy Spirit, various saints, and the devil. These conversations or "dalliances," as she likes to call those of divine origin especially, are direct—that is, there is normally no suggestion that they take place in a state of dreaming or that they have the form of anything but a literal conversation— and sometimes of extraordinary length and detail. Margery has fits of uncontrollable weeping and shrieking—what she calls her "cryings"— in response to religious experiences such as hearing a powerful sermon or seeing the consecrated Host elevated during the Mass or on particular days such as Palm Sunday.[6] On occasion she hears music (sometimes unbearably beautiful, sometimes unbearably terrifying) and smells odors of exceeding loveliness which others do not sense. Examples of several such experiences will be found in the excerpts from her *Book* which follow; the question to be dealt with here is of the reliability and usefulness of a text which is filled with reports of such events. Are we reading a work of fantasy or even fraud, rather than an early autobiography, a serious self-portrayal of a fascinating human being?

Of course any document from the Middle Ages is of at least historical interest, and any document as lively as Margery's is good reading whatever we take it to be, fact, fraud, or fantasy. The real question, then, is not whether Margery's work is worth reading but how or as what to read it. The answer to this question will also speak to the problem mentioned above, that of the extent and kind of introductory remarks necessary for prospective readers of Margery.

Let us begin with a brief summary of those biographical facts that can be established. Margery was born around 1373 in Lynn, then one of the major trade centers of Norfolk and, indeed, of England. She was the daughter of John Brunham, a prominent Lynn citizen and several times its mayor; her mother's name is not recorded in any surviving document. Margery was married in 1393 or shortly thereafter to John Kempe, another prominent Lynn businessman. She had fourteen children, though the birth of the first caused her great physical, emotional, and spiritual distress. Shortly after her first child was born, she apparently passed through an extreme version of a state that will be recognizable to many who undertake seriously the attempt to live a life of the spirit, a state often referred to as the black night of the soul. In such a "night," which may be of a few moments' or many years' duration, chronic or acute, and of greatly varying intensity, one becomes deeply aware of one's own sinfulness and inability to rectify that sinfulness. This black night can eventuate in despair or in a final joyful acceptance of divine mercy and love as the unique and sufficient rectification of sinfulness; it rarely simply goes away, leaving the person untouched or unchanged. It clearly did not do so with Margery, and *The Book of Margery Kempe* must be read as the record of her life after her dark night. Reading it thus is the essential solution to the problems mentioned above.

A few more details of the life she records should be mentioned. In 1413 Margery and her husband agreed, after her long insistence, to renounce any further sexual intercourse. She had for some time been having direct revelations from and visions of God, and shortly thereafter, perhaps in the fall of 1413, she made the first of her Continental pilgrimages, this one to various shrines in Italy and to the Holy Land. She made many such journeys and pilgrimages—sometimes with her husband but more often without him—both in Britain and on the Continent. She met the famous and the great, including Philip Repyngdon, bishop of Lincoln and later cardinal; Thomas Arundel, archbishop of Canterbury; and Dame Julian of Norwich, for whom Margery had much respect and devotion. She also met the lowly and the obscure, including a hunchbacked Irishman named Richard who guided her for a while in Rome—as she had been told previously in a vision would happen—and a poor woman, also in Rome, for whom she acted in the capacity of a menial servant for six weeks. Her fits of uncontrolled weeping began with her initial conversion experience, but what she calls her "cryings" began as a regular and continuing phenomenon after her first visit to Rome. These continued with varying frequency—once she had fourteen in a single day—for many years, perhaps to the end of her life, and brought her a great deal of notoriety. They embarrassed her fellow citizens and traveling companions to the extent that on several occasions she was threatened and/or abandoned, but they were recognized by several of the spiritual counselors with whom she discussed them as valid signs of God's working in and through her. She herself was finally able to accept them and at times even evinces a kind of pride in them.

Margery constantly called on herself and on those around her to have a simple, direct, total faith in God. She was not afraid to criticize the lack of such faith wherever she found it, even in the immediate household of an archbishop, for example. She was accused repeatedly of being a Lollard and was threatened several times with being brought to trial as a heretic.[7] The several questionings she underwent preliminary to such a trial, however, confirmed her orthodoxy in the minds of her questioners. In 1431 her husband died, and in 1433 she made another journey to the Continent, perhaps her last, with extended visits to Danzig and Aachen, returning to England in 1434. The revising and copying of the first and by far the larger part of her *Book* were begun in 1436; the writing of the second part, dealing mostly with her Danzig trip, was begun in 1438. A document from Lynn indicates that she was admitted to the Guild of the

Trinity of that town in 1438, and with this last glimpse of her—a glimpse, by the way, suggesting more local acceptance of her than she had experienced earlier—she is gone from our view. We have no date of her death and no further indications of her spiritual progress, unless the closing words of her work suggest a sort of final stage, one marked by a tone of relative peace and tranquillity: "When she came home to Lynn [after the Danzig trip] she obeyed her confessor. He gave her very sharp words, for she was under his guidance and had taken upon her such a journey without his knowledge.[8] Therefore he was very disturbed with her, but our Lord helped her so that she had as good love of him and of other friends afterward as she had had before—praised be God. Amen."

The biographical details presented above derive almost totally from Margery's *Book* itself, with a few points added from Lynn documents; the picture they present is, to say the least, sketchy. But reading Margery, even in excerpts, provides a vividness to this sketch that, if it does not exactly make up for the lack of detail, brings her powerfully to life. Margery believed totally in her calling. She was a vigorous, strong person who poured all of herself into any idea or undertaking that came to her, perhaps at times somewhat unreflectively but never hypocritically or halfheartedly. After her conversion experience in her dark night, she became a dedicated witness to and proponent of the Christian life of the spirit.

If we are to read Margery's work in a way that does it and her justice, we must accept the realness of her experience and the realness of the life she lived following it, as strange or unlikely or even grotesque as some details of that life might strike a modern sensibility. For the reader who can somehow bring such an openness and acceptance to this reading, there are great benefits. A clear, vivid picture of an immensely vital, honest, and intense human being emerges, a woman who is at times reminiscent of Saint Paul and at others of the Wife of Bath. There is little polish or refinement or subtlety in that human being, but there is much life. Such a woman might not be particularly desirable to have as an actual neighbor or traveling companion or fellow worshiper; those of us who are more timid and restrained in embracing our lives and beliefs are usually made uncomfortable by a Saint Paul or an Alisoun or a Margery when we actually come in contact with one of them. But we can safely and enjoyably read of them, and perhaps we should.

The excerpts from *The Book of Margery Kempe* which follow are translations of the text of her work as it is printed in the edition by Sanford B. Meech and Hope Emily Allen. This is the standard edition, containing complete textual and linguistic apparatus and copious notes. The line of transmission from Margery herself to the Meech and Allen text is quite direct. As has been stated, Margery was in all likelihood illiterate (though quite knowledgeable of scripture, the Church Fathers, and other writers in the English mystical tradition), and so she dictated her spiritual autobiography. Her first amanuensis, possibly her son, completed a version of what is now known as book 1 of the work, constituting about 87 percent of the whole. A second amanuensis, almost certainly a priest, revised this section under Margery's direction and completed the *Book*. The sole surviving manuscript of that work was copied by a scribe with the surname Salthows, sometime in the fifteenth century, probably in the first half of that century. This is the only authority for the text, since two early prints of short extracts from the work—one by Wynkyn de Worde around 1500 and another by Henry Pepwell in 1521—show no signs of independence from the Salthows manuscript.

The manuscript has been owned by the family of William Butler-Bowdon for many generations and was identified by Hope Emily Allen in 1934. Colonel Butler-Bowdon published a modernization of Margery's text in 1944, and brief selections from her work—some of them deriving from the de Worde and Pepwell prints before the manuscript had been identified—have appeared elsewhere. But with these exceptions, the Meech and Allen text is the only available source of Margery's work, and barring the discovery of another authority it is likely to remain so. Because of the chronological proximity of the copying of the Salthows manuscript and the completion of the writing of the *Book* by Margery's second amanuensis, it seems probable that in the Meech and Allen text we have a version of a long medieval prose work that is only two removes (and they are very close and dependable removes at that) from the author herself. This situation is indeed remarkable and perhaps unique.

In the translation I have tried to preserve as much of the flavor of Margery's prose as possible. To a very great extent, the "translations" of the passages that follow are little more than modernizations of the spelling. The English of Norfolk in the fifteenth century would no doubt have sounded very different from that of our day, but on the printed page it differs very little. I have changed words only where the one Margery uses would no longer be understandable to a modern reader or would be misleading. I have tried to follow her syntax as closely as possible, even though this results in many sentences that, by modern standards, would be considered stylistically awkward (or occasionally very awkward) or ungrammatical. I have made whatever changes seemed to me necessary to convey the basic meaning of the sentences. Ambiguities in the translation reflect, I hope, ambiguities in the original. The Meech and Allen text, following the manuscript, uses no paragraphs except at the beginning of each chapter, and I have continued this. I have punctuated quite freely, trying to use punctuation only to make the meaning as clear as possible but not following any very consistent plan. Margery's style seems to encourage this.

The reader who finds the following excerpts of interest is encouraged to explore Margery's work more fully in the Meech and Allen text. Reading that text will present very few problems because of the nature of fifteenth-century English and because of the thoroughness and helpfulness of the notes, textual apparatus, and glossary provided by Meech and Allen. Such an exploration, I can predict with confidence, will be a valuable and an enlightening experience.

NOTES

1. R. W. Chambers, introduction, *The Book of Margery Kempe: A Modern Version*, ed. William Butler-Bowdon, p. xvi.

2. Interestingly, a number of medieval fictional characters whose mental or psychological processes are shown in unusual detail and depth are also women, in particular the heroines of some of the best-known romances: for example, Criseyde of Chaucer's *Troilus and Criseyde* or Laudine of Chrétien de Troye's *Yvain*.

3. *The Book of Margery Kempe*, ed. Sanford Brown Meech and Hope Emily Allen, pp. 3, 39, 111, 143.

4. Robert Karl Stone, *Middle English Prose Style: Margery Kempe and Julian of Norwich*, pp. 19–21.

5. And so, Margery tells us several times, would some of her contemporaries, though they would, of course, have used different terms.

6. Meech and Allen, eds., pp. 138, 148–150, 185. This "gift of tears," as it is sometimes known, is a fairly common attribute of mystical experience; Saint Theresa, for example, experienced it. Margery's form seems to have been especially violent and frequent, at least during some periods of her life.

7. "Lollard" was the term used contemptuously to refer to followers or imitators of John Wycliffe (1320–1384), a famous religious reformer in England. Wycliffe stressed the personal as opposed to the institutional element in religious faith; he preached, for a while under the protection of John of Gaunt, on the need for reform of the Church, bringing religion closer to the people. After his death, persecutions and executions of confessed or alleged Lollards were frequent, especially during the first half of the fifteenth century. Margery was in real danger on several occasions as a result of her emphasis on the personal element in religion. On the other hand, she remained throughout a devout Catholic, with a deep faith and trust in the established sacraments, the efficacy and realness of which most of Wycliffe's actual adherents denied. This devotion apparently served her well.

8. On taking a spiritual adviser, one normally assents to putting oneself under that adviser's authority in any matter concerning one's spiritual life.

The Book of Margery Kempe

Chapter 1

When this creature[1] was twenty years of age or a little more, she was married to an honorable citizen of Lynn and was with child within a

short time after this, as nature would have it. And after she had conceived she was burdened with great illnesses till the child was born, and
then, what with the labor she had in childbirth added to the earlier sickness, she despaired of her life, thinking she might not live. And then she
sent for her spiritual father,[2] for she had something on her conscience
which she had never confessed before that time in all her life. For she
was always prevented by her enemy, the devil, who was constantly saying
to her while she was in good health that confession was not necessary
for her, but that she might do penance on her own, and all should be
forgiven since God is sufficiently merciful. And therefore this creature
oftentimes did great penance, fasting on bread and water only, and also
deeds of alms with devout prayers; but she would not reveal her sin in
confession. And when she was at any time sick or diseased, the devil said
in her mind that she would be damned since she was not shriven of that
failing.[3] Wherefore, after her child was born, she, uncertain of her life,
sent for her spiritual father, as said before, fully intending to be shriven
for her whole lifetime as completely as she could. And when she came to
the point of saying that thing which she had so long concealed, her confessor was a little too hasty and he did sharply reprove her before she
had fully said what she meant, and then she would say no more for
anything he might do. And at once because of the dread she had of damnation on the one side and his sharp reproving on the other side, this
creature went out of her mind and was wondrously vexed and burdened
with spirits for half a year, eight weeks, and odd days. And in this time
she saw, as it seemed to her, devils open their mouths, which were all
inflamed with burning streams of fire, as if they would have swallowed
her, sometimes lunging at her, sometimes threatening her, sometimes
pulling and calling her both night and day during this period. And also
the devils cried out on her with great threats and bade her to forsake her
Christendom and her faith and deny her God, His mother, and all the
saints in heaven, her good works and all good virtues, her father, her
mother, and all her friends. And so she did. She slandered her husband,
her friends, and her own self; she spoke many a reproachful word and
many a villainous word; she knew no virtue or goodness; she desired all
wickedness; just as the spirits tempted her to say and do, so she said and
did. She would have killed herself many a time at their instigations and
have been damned with them in hell; as a sign of this she bit her own
hand so violently that it was seen all her life afterward. And also she rent
her skin on her body over her heart despiteously with her nails, for she
had no other instruments, and worse she would have done except she
was bound and held with strength both day and night that she might not
have her will. And when she had long been tormented in these and other
temptations so that men thought she would never have escaped or lived,

then on a time as she lay alone and her keepers were away from her, our merciful Lord Jesus Christ, ever to be trusted—worshiped be His name!—never forsaking His servant in time of need, appeared to His creature who had forsaken Him, in likeness of a man most seemly, most beauteous, and most lovable that ever might be seen with man's eye, clad in a mantle of purple silk, sitting upon her bed's side, looking upon her with so blessed an appearance that she was strengthened in all her spirits, and He said to her these words: "Daughter, why hast thou forsaken Me, and I forsook thee never?" And at once, as He had said these words, she saw truly how the air opened as bright as any lightning, and He stepped up into the air, not right hastily and quickly, but fairly and easily such that she might well behold Him in the air till it was closed again. And at once the creature was settled in her wits and in her reason as well as ever she was before, and she prayed her husband as soon as he came to her that she might have the keys of the buttery[4] to take her food and drink as she had done before. Her maidens and her keepers counseled him to deliver her no keys, for, they said, she would but give away such goods as there were since she did not know what she was saying—so they thought. Nevertheless, her husband, having always tenderness and compassion for her, commanded that they should deliver to her the keys. And she took her food and drink so her bodily strength would serve her, and she knew her friends and her household and all others that came to her to see how our Lord Jesus Christ had wrought His grace in her—blessed might He be that is ever near in tribulation. Afterward this creature performed all the other duties which fell to her to do quite wisely and soberly; but she knew not truly the full force of our Lord.

And when this creature was thus by grace come again to her mind, she thought she was bound to God and that she would be His servant. Nevertheless, she would not leave her pride or her pompous array that had been her custom, neither for her husband nor at the counsel of anyone else. And yet she knew full well that men spoke very much evil of her, for she wore gold pipes on her head and the long trailing sashes of her hoods had elaborately cut patterns along their edges.[5] Her cloaks also had such patterns cut along their edges and were inlaid with diverse colors between the cuts so her appearance should be the more conspicuous to men's sight, and she herself be the more esteemed. And when her husband would speak to her about letting go her pride, she answered villainously and shortly and said that she was come of worthy kin—it was unseemly for him to have wedded her, since her father was formerly mayor of the town and afterward he was alderman of the high Guild of the Trinity in the town.[6] And therefore she would preserve the esteem of her kin whatsoever any man said. She had very great envy of her neighbors that they should be as well arrayed as she. All her desire was to be esteemed of the people. She would not take heed of any criticism or be content with the goods that God had sent her, as her husband was, but ever desired more and more. And then, because of pure covetousness and in order to maintain her pride, she began to brew and was one of the greatest[7] brewers in the town for three years or four, until she lost much wealth because she had no experience at it. For, though she had servants ever so good and clever at brewing, still it would never succeed with them. For when the ale was standing as fair under barm[8] as any man might see, suddenly the barm would fall down so that all the ale was lost, one brewing after another, so that her servants were ashamed and would not stay with her. Then this creature thought about how God had punished her before and she was not able to take heed, and now again through loss of her goods, and then she left off and brewed no more. And then she asked mercy of her husband because she was unwilling to follow his counsel before, and she said that her pride and sin were the cause of all punishing and she wanted with goodwill to amend what she had marred. But still she left not completely all worldliness, for now she bethought herself of a new sort of housewifery. She had a horse mill. She got herself two good horses and a man to grind men's grain and thus she trusted to make her living. This plan lasted not long, for a short time after on Corpus Christi Eve,[9] this marvel took place. This man—being in good health of body, and his two horses strong and dependable that had drawn well in the mill before this—he took one of these horses and put him in the mill as he had done before and this horse would draw not a bit in the mill for anything the man might do. The man was sorry and tried with all his wits how he should make this horse draw. Sometimes he led him by the head; sometimes he beat him; and sometimes he petted him; and all availed naught, for he would sooner go backward than forward. Then this man put a sharp pair of spurs on his heels and rode on the horse's back to make him draw and it was no better. When this man saw it would not work in any way, then he put up this horse again in the stable and gave him food and he ate well and freshly. And afterward he took the other horse and put him in the mill. And just as his fellow did so did he, for he would not draw for anything that the man might do. And then this man forsook his service and would no longer abide with the aforesaid creature. At once as it was noised about the town that neither man nor beast would do service for the said creature, then some said she was accursed; some said God took open vengeance upon her; some said one thing; and some said another. And some wise men, whose minds were more grounded in the love of our Lord, said it was the high mercy of our Lord Jesus Christ which summoned and called her from the pride and vanity of the wretched world. And then this creature, seeing all these adversities coming on every side, thought it to be the scourges of our

Lord that would chastise her for her sin. Then she asked God for mercy and forsook her pride, her covetousness, and the desire that she had for the esteem of the world, and did great bodily penance, and did enter the way of everlasting life, as shall be said after.

On a night, as this creature lay in her bed with her husband, she heard a sound of melody so sweet and delectable that it seemed to her as if she had been in paradise. And therewith she started out of her bed and said: "Alas that ever I did sin; it is full merry in heaven." This melody was so sweet that it surpassed all the melody that ever might be heard in this world without any comparison, and caused this creature when she heard any mirth or melody afterward to have full plenteous and abundant tears of high devotion with great sobbings and sighings for the bliss of heaven, not dreading the shames and the spites of the wretched world.[10] And ever after this drawing[11] she had in her mind the mirth and the melody that were in heaven, so much that she could not well restrain herself from the speaking thereof. For, where she was in any company, she would say oftentimes: "It is full merry in heaven." And they that knew her behavior beforetimes and now heard her speak so much of the bliss of heaven said unto her: "Why speak you so of the mirth that is in heaven; you know it not and you have not been there any more than we." And they were angry with her because she would hear no speech of worldly things as they did and as she did beforetimes. And after this time she never had desire to commune fleshly[12] with her husband, for the debt of matrimony was so abominable to her that she had rather, it seemed to her, eat or drink the slime or muck in the gutter than to consent to any fleshly communing, save only for obedience. And so she said to her husband: "I may not deny you my body, but the love of my heart and my affection are drawn from all earthly creatures and set only in God." He would have his will and she obeyed with great weeping and sorrowing that she might not live chaste. And oftentimes the creature counseled her husband to live chaste and said that they oftentimes, she knew well, had displeased God by their inordinate love and the great delectation that they had, each of them in using of the other, and now it were good that they should, by their mutual will and consenting of them both, punish and chastise themselves willfully by abstaining from their pleasure of their bodies. Her husband said it would be good to do so, but he might not yet; he should when God willed it. And so he used her as he had done before; he would not spare. And ever she prayed to God that she might live chaste, and three or four years after,[13] when it pleased our Lord, he made a vow of chastity, as shall be written after by the leave of Jesus. And also, after this creature heard this heavenly melody, she did great bodily penance. She was shriven sometimes twice or thrice in a day, and in special of that sin which she so long had concealed and covered, as it is written in the beginning of the book. She gave herself to great fasting and to great waking; she rose at two or three of the clock and went to church and was there in her prayers unto time of noon and also all the afternoon. And then she was slandered and reproved by many people because she kept so straight a living. Then she got herself a haircloth of a kiln such as men dry malt on, and placed it within her dress as carefully and secretly as she might so that her husband should not see it—nor did he, and yet she lay by him every night in his bed, and wore the haircloth every day, and bore children during this time. Then she had three years of great labor with temptations which she bore as meekly as she could, thanking our Lord for all His gifts, and was as merry when she was reproved, scorned, or ridiculed for our Lord's love, and much more merry than she was beforetimes in the esteem of the world. For she knew right well that she had sinned greatly against God and was worthy of more shame and sorrow than any man could do to her, and that despite of the world was the right way heavenward, since Christ Himself chose that way. All His apostles, martyrs, confessors, and virgins and all that ever came to heaven passed by the way of tribulation, and she desired nothing so much as heaven. Then was she glad in her conscience when she believed that she was entering the way which would lead her to the place that she most desired. And this creature had contrition and great compunction with plenteous tears and many violent sobbings for her sins and for her unnaturalness against her maker. She bethought herself of her unnaturalness from her childhood as our Lord would put it in her mind full many a time. And then beholding her own wickedness, she might only sorrow and weep and ever pray for mercy and forgiveness. Her weeping was so plenteous and so continuing that many people thought that she might weep and leave off weeping whenever she wanted, and therefore many men said she was a false hypocrite and wept before the world for support and for worldly goods. And then many forsook her that loved her before while she was in the world and would not acknowledge her, and ever she thanked God for all, desiring nothing but mercy and forgiveness of sin.

Chapter 2

And in all this time[14] she had no desire to commune[15] with her husband, but rather it was very painful and horrible unto her. In the second year of her temptations it fell so that a man whom she loved well said to her on Saint Margaret's Eve[16] before evensong that for anything he wanted to lie by her and have his pleasure of body, and she should not withstand him, for, if he might not have his will at that time, he said, he should then have it another time; she should not choose. And he did it for to test her, what she would do, but she thought he had been in full earnest at the time and said but little in answer. So they parted asunder then and went both to hear evensong, for her church was Saint Margaret's. This woman[17] was so troubled with the man's words that she was unable to hear evensong, or to say her Paternoster, or to think any other good thought, but was more troubled than ever she was before. The devil put in her mind that God had forsaken her, otherwise she should not be so tempted. She believed the devil's persuasions and did consent to them because she could think no good thought. Therefore she believed that God had forsaken her. And when evensong was done, she went to the beforesaid man so that he might have his pleasure, as she thought he had desired, but he made such pretense that she was unable to know his intent, and so they parted asunder for that night. The creature was so troubled and vexed all that night that she knew never what she might do. She lay by her husband, and to commune with him was so abominable to her that she might not endure it, and yet it was lawful for her in a lawful time, if she had wanted to. But ever she was troubled with the other man, for to sin with him inasmuch as he had spoken to her. At the last through the persistence of temptation and the lack of discretion she was overcome and consented in her mind and went to the man to know if he would consent to her. And he said he would not for all the good of this world; he would rather be cut up as small as meat for the pot. She went away all shamed and confused in herself, seeing his stableness and her own unstableness. Then she thought of the grace that God had given her beforetimes, how she had two years of great quiet in her soul, repentance of her sin with many bitter tears of compunction, a perfect will never to turn again to her sin, but rather to be dead, it seemed to her. And now she saw how she had consented in her will for to do sin. Then fell she half in despair. She thought she might have been in hell for the sorrow that she had. She thought she was worthy of no mercy since her consenting was so willfully done, nor ever worthy to do Him service since she was so false unto Him. Nevertheless she was shriven many times and often and did her penance, whatsoever her confessor would enjoin her to do, and was governed by the rules of the Church. That grace God gave this creature—blessed may He be—but He withdrew not her temptation but rather increased it as it seemed to her. And therefore she thought that He had forsaken her and dared not trust to His mercy, but was troubled with horrible temptations of lechery and of despair nearly all the next year following, except our Lord of His mercy, as she told herself, gave her each day for the most part two hours of compunction for her sins with many bitter tears. And afterward she was troubled with temptation of despair as she was before, and was as far from a feeling of grace as they that never felt any. And that she could not bear, and therefore she despaired always. Except for the time that she felt grace, her troubles were so wondrous that she could deal with them only poorly, but was ever mourning and sorrowing as though God had forsaken her.

Then on a Friday before Christmas Day, as this creature, kneeling in Saint John's chapel within the church of Saint Margaret in Lynn, wept wondrously, asking mercy and forgiveness of her sins and her trespasses, our merciful Lord Christ Jesus—blessed may He be—ravished her spirit and said unto her: "Daughter, why weepest thou so sore? I am come to thee, Jesus Christ, that died on the cross suffering bitter pains and passions for thee. I, the same God, forgive thee thy sins to the utterest point. And thou shalt never come into hell or into purgatory, but, when thou shalt pass out of this world, within the twinkling of an eye thou shalt have the bliss of heaven, for I am the same God who has brought thy sins to thy mind and made thee to be shriven thereof. And I grant thee contrition unto thy life's end. Therefore, I bid thee and command thee, boldly call Me Jesus, thy love, for I am thy love and shall be thy love without end. And daughter, thou hast a haircloth upon thy back. I will that thou put it away, and I shall give thee a haircloth in thy heart that shall please Me much better than all the haircloths in the world. Also, My most dear daughter, thou must forsake that which thou lovest best in this world, and that is the eating of meat. And instead of that flesh thou shalt eat My flesh and My blood, that is, the true Body of Christ in the Sacrament of the Altar.[18] This is My will, daughter, that thou receive My Body every Sunday, and I shall flow so much grace in thee that all the world shall marvel thereof. Thou shalt be eaten and gnawed by the people of the world as any rat gnaws the stockfish. Dread not, daughter, for thou shalt have the victory of all thy enemies. I shall give thee grace enough to answer every clerk in the love of God. I swear to thee by My majesty that I shall never forsake thee in weal or in woe. I shall help thee and keep thee that never shall any devil in hell part thee from Me, or angel in heaven, or man on earth, for devils in hell may not, nor angels in heaven will not, nor man on earth shall not. And, daughter, I will that thou leave off the praying of many beads and think such thoughts as I will put in thy mind. I shall give thee leave to pray till six of the clock to say whatever thou will. Then shall thou lie still and speak to Me in thought, and I shall give thee high meditation and true contemplation. And I bid thee go to the anchorite at the Friar Preachers[19] and make known to him My secrets and My counsels which I make known to thee, and work according to his counsel, for My spirit shall speak in him to thee." Then this creature went forth to the anchorite, as she was commanded, and made known to him the revelations such as were made known to her.

Then the anchorite with great reverence and weeping, thanking God, said: "Daughter, you suck verily on Christ's breast, and you have an earnest penny of heaven. I charge you, receive such thoughts when God will give them as meekly and as devoutly as you can and come to me and tell me what they be, and I shall, with the leave of our Lord Jesus Christ, tell you whether they be of the Holy Ghost of else of your enemy the devil."

Chapter 3

On a day long before this time,[20] while this creature was bearing children and she was newly delivered of a child, our Lord Christ Jesus said to her she should bear no more children, and therefore He bade her go to Norwich. And she said: "Ah, dear Lord, how shall I go? I am both faint and feeble." "Dread thee not, I shall make thee strong enough. I bid thee go to the vicar of Saint Stephen's[21] and say that I greet him well and that he is a high chosen soul of Mine, and tell him he pleases Me much with his preaching, and reveal to him thy secrets and My counsels such as I reveal to thee." Then she took her way Norwich-ward and came into his church on a Thursday a little before noon. And the vicar was walking up and down with another priest who was his spiritual father (who was alive when this book was made). And this creature was clad in black clothing at that time.[22] She greeted the vicar, praying him to speak with her for an hour or perhaps two hours, in the afternoon when he had eaten, about the love of God. He, lifting up his hands and blessing himself, said: "Benedicite. What might a woman know to occupy an hour or two hours about the love of our Lord? I shall never eat food till I know what you can say of our Lord God for an hour's time." Then he set himself down in the church. She, sitting a little beside, made known to him all the words which God had revealed to her in her soul. Afterward she made known to him all her manner of living from her childhood as nearly as it would come to her mind—how unnatural she had been toward our Lord Jesus Christ, how proud and vain she had been in her bearing, how obstinate against the laws of God, and how envious against her fellow Christians, and later, when it pleased our Lord Christ Jesus, how she was chastised with many tribulations and horrible temptations, and afterward how she was fed and comforted with holy meditations, and especially in thinking of our Lord's Passion. And while she conversed on the Passion of our Lord Jesus Christ, she heard so terrible a melody that she might not bear it. Then this creature fell down as if she had lost her bodily strength and lay still a great while, desiring to put it away, and

she might not. Then knew she well by her faith that there was great joy
in heaven, where the least point of bliss without any comparison passes
all the joy that ever might be thought or felt in this life. She was greatly
strengthened in her faith and more bold to tell the vicar her feelings which
she had from the revelations, both of the living and of the dead and of
his own self. She told him how sometimes the Father of heaven conversed
with her soul as plainly and as truly as a friend speaks to another through
bodily speech; sometimes the second Person in the Trinity; sometimes all
three Persons in the Trinity and one substance in Godhead conversed
with her soul and informed her in faith and in His love how she should
love Him, worship Him, and dread Him so excellently that she heard
never a book—neither Hilton's book, nor Bridget's book, nor *Stimulus
Amoris*, nor *Incendium Amoris*,[23] nor no other that ever she heard read—
that spoke so highly of the love of God but that she felt as highly in the
working of her soul, if she had known how or else had been able to have
made known how she felt. Sometimes our Lady spoke to her mind.
Sometimes Saint Peter, sometimes Saint Paul, sometimes Saint Catherine,
or whatever saint in heaven she had devotion to appeared to her soul
and taught her how she should love our Lord and how she should please
Him. Their conversation[24] was so sweet, so holy, and so devout that this
creature oftentimes could not bear it, but fell down and thrashed about
bodily and made a wondrous appearance and countenance, with violent
sobbings and a great plenty of tears, sometimes saying, "Jesu, mercy!"
sometimes "I die!" And therefore many people slandered her, believing
not that it was the work of God but that some evil spirit vexed her in her
body or else that she had some bodily sickness. Notwithstanding the
rumor and complaining of the people against her, this holy man, vicar of
Saint Stephen's church of Norwich, whom God has exalted and through
marvelous works shown and proven holy, always held with her and supported her against her enemies to the extent of his power, after the time
that she by the bidding of God had shown him her manner of behavior
and living, for he faithfully believed that she was well learned in the law
of God and endued with the grace of the Holy Ghost, to Whom it belongs to inspire where He will. And, though His voice be heard, it is not
known of the world whence it comes or whither it goes. This holy vicar
after this time was confessor to this creature always when she came to
Norwich and gave her Communion with his own hands. And when one
time she was summoned to appear before certain officers of the bishop
to answer to certain articles which should be put against her by the instigation of envious people,[25] the good vicar, preferring the love of God
before any worldly shame, went with her to hear her examination and
delivered her from the malice of her enemies. And then it was revealed

to this creature that the good vicar should live seven years after this and then he should pass hence with great grace, and he did as she [had been shown.][26]

This creature was charged and commanded in her soul that she should go to a White Friar in the same city of Norwich who was named William Southfield,[27] a good man and a holy liver, to reveal to him the grace that God wrought in her, as she had done to the good vicar before. She did as she was commanded, and came to the friar on a forenoon, and was with him in a chapel a long time, and revealed to him her meditations and such as God wrought in her soul, in order to know if she were deceived by any illusions or not. The good man, the White Friar, all the while she told her feelings, holding up his hands said: "Jesu, mercy and thanks." "Sister," he said, "dread not your manner of living, for it is the Holy Ghost working plenteously His grace in your soul. Thank Him highly of His goodness, for we all are bound to thank Him for you, that now in our days wills to inspire His grace in you to the help and comfort of us all who are supported by your prayers and by others such as you are. And we are preserved from many misfortunes and diseases[28] which we should suffer deservedly for our trespasses were not such good creatures among us. Blessed be Almighty God for His goodness. And therefore, sister, I counsel you to dispose yourself to receive the gifts of God as lowly and meekly as you can and place no obstacle or objection against the goodness of the Holy Ghost, for He may give His gifts where He will, and of unworthy He makes worthy, of sinful He makes rightful. His mercy is ever ready unto us, unless the fault be in ourself, for He dwells not in a body subject to sin. He flees all false feigning and falsehood; He asks of us a low, a meek, and a contrite heart with goodwill. Our Lord says Himself: 'My spirit shall rest upon a meek man and a contrite heart with goodwill.'[29] Sister, I trust in our Lord that you have these conditions, either in your will or in your affection or else in both,[30] and I believe not that our Lord suffers them to be deceived endlessly who set all their trust in Him and seek or desire nothing but Him only, as I hope that you do. And therefore believe fully that our Lord loves you and works His grace in you. I pray God to increase it and continue it to His everlasting worship because of His mercy." The beforesaid creature was much comforted both in body and in soul by this good man's words and greatly strengthened in her faith. And then she was bidden by our Lord for to go to an anchoress in the same city who was called Dame Julian.[31] And so she did and revealed to her the grace that God put in her soul of compunction, contrition, sweetness and devotion, compassion with holy meditation and high contemplation, and very many holy speeches and conversations[32] that our Lord spoke to her soul, and many wonderful revelations which she revealed to the anchoress in order to know if there were any deceit in them, for the anchoress was experienced in such things and good counsel could give. The anchoress, hearing the marvelous goodness of our Lord, thanked God highly with all her heart for His visitation, counseling this creature to be obedient to the will of our Lord God and to fulfill with all her might whatever He put in her soul, as long as it were not opposed to the worship of God and the profit of her fellow Christians, for, if it were, then it were not at all the moving of a good spirit but rather of an evil spirit.[33] "The Holy Ghost never moves anything in opposition to love, and if He did He would be in contradiction to His own self, for He is all love. Also He moves a soul to all chasteness, for chaste livers are called the temple of the Holy Ghost, and the Holy Ghost makes a soul stable and steadfast in the right faith and the right belief. And a man duplicitous in his soul is ever unstable and unsteadfast in all his ways. He that is evermore doubting is like the waves of the sea, moved and borne about with the wind, and that man is not likely to receive the gifts of God. Whatever creature has these tokens[34] he must steadfastly believe that the Holy Ghost dwells in his soul. And much more when God visits a creature with tears of contrition, devotion, or compassion, he may and ought to believe that the Holy Ghost is in his soul. Saint Paul says that the Holy Ghost asks for us with mournings and weepings unspeakable;[35] that is to say, He makes us ask and pray with mournings and weepings so plenteously that the tears may not be numbered. There may no evil spirit give these tokens, for Jerome says that tears torment the devil more than do the pains of hell. God and the devil are always in opposition and they shall never dwell together in one place, and the devil has no power in a man's soul. Holy Writ says that the soul of a rightful man is the seat of God,[36] and so I trust, sister, that you are. I pray God grant you perseverance. Set all your trust in God, and fear not the language of the world, for the more despite, shame, and reproof you have in the world, the more is your merit in the sight of God. Patience is necessary to you, for in that shall you keep your soul." Much was the holy conversation that the anchoress and this creature had through sharing of the love of our Lord Jesus Christ many days that they were together.

Chapter 4

Soon afterward came a man who loved her right well of goodwill, with his wife and others as well, and led her seven miles to the archbishop of York,[37] and brought her into a fair chamber, to which came a good clerk saying to the good man: "Sir, why have you and your wife brought this woman hither? She shall steal away from you and then you shall be shamed because of her." The good man said: "I dare well say she will abide and answer [to the charge] with goodwill." On the next day she was brought into the archbishop's chapel, and there came many of the archbishop's household despising her, calling her "loller"[38] and "heretic," and they swore many a horrible oath that she should be burned. And she, through the strength of Jesus, said back to them: "Sirs, I fear me that you shall be burned in hell without end unless you amend yourselves of your oath swearing, for you keep not the commandments of God. I would not swear as you do for all the good of this world." Then they moved away since they had been shamed. She then, making her prayer in her mind, asked grace to be demeaned that day as was most pleasing to God and most profit to her own soul and good example to her fellow Christians. Our Lord, answering her, said it should be right well. At the last, the aforesaid archbishop came into the chapel with his clerks and sharply he said to her: "Why dost thou go about in white?[39] Art thou a maiden?" She, kneeling on her knees before him, said: "No, sir, I am no maiden; I am a wife." He commanded those about him to bring a pair of fetters and said she should be fettered because she was a false heretic. And then she said: "I am no heretic, nor shall you prove me one." The archbishop went away and let her stand alone. Then she made her prayers to our Lord God almighty to help her and to succor her against all her enemies, of the spirit and of the body, a long while, and her flesh trembled and quaked wondrously so that she wanted to put her hands under her clothes so that it might not be seen. Then the archbishop came again into the chapel with many worthy clerks, amongst which was the same doctor who had questioned her before, and the monk that had preached against her a little time before in York. Some of the people asked whether she were a Christian woman or a Jew; some said she was a good woman and some said nay. Then the archbishop took his high seat and his clerks also, each of them in his degree, many people being present. And in the time while the people were gathering together and the archbishop was taking his seat the aforesaid creature stood all behind, making her prayers for help and succor against her enemies with high devotion so long that she melted all into tears. And at the last she cried aloud therewith, so that the archbishop and his clerks and many people had great wonder of her, for they had not heard such crying before. When her crying was passed, she came before the archbishop and fell down on her knees, the archbishop saying full violently unto her: "Why weepest thou so, woman?" She, answering, said: "Sir, you shall wish someday that you had wept as sore as I." And then at once, after the archbishop put to her the Articles of our Faith,[40] to which God gave her grace to answer well and truly and readily, without any great study, so that he might not blame her, then he said to the clerks: "She knows her Faith well enough. What shall I do with her?" The clerks said: "We know well that she knows the Articles of Faith, but we will not suffer her to dwell among us, for the people have great faith in her conversations, and perchance she might pervert some of them." Then the archbishop said unto her: "I am evilly informed concerning thee; I hear it said that thou art a right wicked woman." And she said in response: "Sir, so I hear it said that you are a wicked man. And if you be as wicked as men say, you shall never come to heaven unless you amend yourself while you are here." Then he said full violently: "Why, thou . . . What say men of me?" She answered: "Other men, sir, can tell you well enough." Then said a great clerk with a furred hood: "Peace! Speak thou of thyself and let him be." Then said the archbishop to her: "Lay thy hand on the book here before me and swear that thou shalt go out of my diocese as soon as thou might." "Nay, sir," she said, "I pray you, give me leave to go again into York to take my leave of my friends." Then he gave her leave for one day or two. She thought it too short a time, wherefore she said in response: "Sir, I may not go out of this diocese so hastily, for I must tarry and speak with my confessor, a good man, who was the good prior's confessor who is now canonized."[41] Then said the archbishop to her: "Thou shalt swear that thou shalt neither teach nor challenge the people in my diocese." "Nay, sir, I shall not swear," she said, "for I shall speak of God and reprove those that swear great oaths wheresoever I go unto the time that the pope and holy Church have ordained that no man shall be so hardy as to speak of God, for God almighty forbids not, sir, that we shall speak of Him. And also the Gospel makes mention that, when the woman had heard our Lord preach, she came before Him with a loud voice and said, 'Blessed be the womb that bore Thee and the teats that gave Thee suck.' Then our Lord said back to her, 'Truly, so are they blessed that hear the Word of God and keep it.'[42] And therefore, sir, it seems to me that the Gospel gives me leave to speak of God." "Ah, sir," said the clerks, "here we understand well that she has a devil within her, for she speaks of the Gospel." Immediately a great clerk brought forth a book and laid Saint Paul for his part against her, that no woman should preach.[43] She, answering thereto, said: "I preach not, sir; I come to no pulpit. I use but communication and good words and that will I do while I live." Then said a doctor who had questioned her beforetimes: "Sir, she told me the worst tales of priests that ever I heard." The bishop commanded her to tell that tale. "Sir, with your reverence, I spoke of but one priest by manner of example, the which, as I have learned, went astray in a wood through the sufferance of God for the profit of his soul, till night came upon him. He, destitute of lodging, found a fair arbor in which he rested that night, with a fair pear tree in the midst all flourishing and embellished with flowers and blooms full delectable to his sight; whither came

a bear, great and violent, huge to behold, shaking the pear tree and fell-
ing the flowers. Greedily this grievous beast ate and devoured those fair
flowers. And when he had eaten them, turning his tail end in the priest's
presence, he voided them out again at the hindermost part. The priest,
having great abomination of that loathsome sight, conceiving great heaviness because of doubt what it might mean, on the next day he wandered
forth on his way all heavy and pensive; to whom it fortuned to meet with
a seemly, aged man, like a palmer or a pilgrim, the which inquired of the
priest the cause of his heaviness. The priest, rehearsing the matter written
before, said he conceived great dread and heaviness when he beheld that
loathsome beast befoul and devour such fair flowers and blooms and
afterward so horribly void them before him at his tail end, and he [the
priest] not understanding what this might mean. Then the palmer, showing himself to be the messenger of God, thus advised him: 'Priest, thou
thyself art the pear tree, somewhat flourishing and flowering through thy
saying of the service and ministering of the Sacraments, though thou do
it undevoutly, for thou takest full little heed how thou sayest thy matins
and thy service, just so it gets blabbered to an end. Then goest thou to
thy Mass without devotion, and for thy sins hast thou full little contrition. Thou receivest thus the fruit of everlasting life, the Sacrament of
the Altar,[44] in full feeble disposition. Then all day after thou misspendest
thy time; thou givest thyself to buying and selling, chopping and changing, as would a man of the world. Thou sittest at thy ale, giving thyself
to gluttony and excess, to pleasure of thy body through lechery and un-
cleanness. Thou breakest the commandments of God through swearing,
lying, detractions and backbiting, and such other habitual sins. Thus, by
the misgovernance, like unto this loathsome bear, thou devourest and
destroyest the flowers and blooms of virtuous living to thy endless damnation and the hindering of many a man, unless thou have grace of repentance and amending.'" Then the archbishop liked well the tale and
commended it, saying it was a good tale. And the clerk who had questioned her beforetimes in the absence of the archbishop said: "Sir, this
tale smites me to the heart." The aforesaid creature said to the clerk:
"Ah, worshipful doctor, sir, in the place where my main dwelling is, is a
worthy clerk, a good preacher, who boldly speaks against the misgovernance of the people and will flatter no man. He says many times in the
pulpit: 'If any man be ill pleased with my preaching, note him well, for
he is guilty.' And right so, sir," said she to the clerk, "do you fare by
me—may God forgive you." The clerk knew not well what he might say
to her. Afterward, the same clerk came to her and prayed her of forgiveness because he had been so against her. And then at once the archbishop
said: "Where shall I get a man who might lead this woman from me?"
At once there leaped up many young men, and every man of them said:

"My lord, I will go with her." The Archbishop answered: "You all are too young; I will not have you." Then a good sober man of the archbishop's household asked his lord what he would give him if he should lead her. The archbishop proffered him five shillings and the man asked a noble.[45] The archbishop answering said: "I will not spend so much for her." "Yes, good sir," said the aforesaid creature, "our Lord shall reward you right well in return." Then the archbishop said to the man: "See, here is five shillings; lead her fast out of this region." She, kneeling down on her knees, asked his blessing. He, praying her to pray for him, blessed her and let her go. Then she, going again to York, was received of many people and of full worthy clerks, who rejoiced that our Lord had given her, though not lettered, wit and wisdom to answer so many learned men without villainy or blame—thanks be to God.

NOTES TO THE TRANSLATION

1. Margery almost always refers to herself in the third person, and the term "creature" is the most common form of these references. It is, perhaps, an attempt at distancing. It is also, I suspect, a true indication of Margery's attitude about herself: she thinks of herself as created by another; she is in no sense an end unto herself.

2. That is, for the priest who was her regular confessor.

3. Roman Catholic teaching stresses the efficacy and the necessity of formal, sacramental confession for all serious sins. Forgiveness is certain, but it must come through the established sacrament.

4. The keys of the household were the instrument and the symbol of a woman's authority. The action of handing them over to her is thus a dramatic indication of Margery's miraculous recovery.

5. Margery's headdress is apparently an example of the popular and costly fashion of the late fourteenth and early fifteenth centuries, in which elaborate gold or brass wire nets were used to hold the hair. Hers seem to have had ornamental projections or "pipes." The cut patterns along the edges of sashes and cloaks were known as dags. The overall effect she conveys is one of excessive vanity in dress.

6. This seems to be given as a sample of the sort of answer that Margery made to her husband during this period. She does not name the town of Lynn explicitly here, though she does so elsewhere. The Guild of the Trinity was the merchants' guild, a powerful and prestigious organization in the fifteenth century.

7. That is, in terms of the amount she brewed, not, as is obvious from the following passage, in terms of the quality of her product.

8. The barm is the yeast foam which floats on top of the fermenting liquid. It is skimmed off or the finished ale is siphoned out from under it when fermentation ceases. If it sinks down into the liquid, however, the color and taste of the ale are ruined.

9. Corpus Christi is a feast celebrating the Eucharist, or the sacrament of communion, in which bread and wine are consecrated to become the Body of Christ. It falls on the Thursday of the second week after Pentecost or Whitsunday.

10. This marks the beginning of Margery's "cryings," though she later seems to distinguish between this sort of weeping and the "cryings" proper, which began after her first journey to Rome.

11. The word Margery uses is "drawt," the past participle of the verb "to draw." She uses this word in various forms quite extensively throughout her work, especially in this section. It is intended to denote a physical drawing or pulling of great power and of divine origin.

12. That is, to have sexual intercourse.

13. The chronology of events that Margery recounts in her work is quite confusing at several points. Some of the confusion may be intentional, in order to make points more forcefully, but most of it is probably accounted for by the lapse of many years between the events and their recording.

14. That is, in the period of about two years following her initial mystical experience.

15. To have sexual intercourse.

16. Probably either the semilegendary Margaret of Antioch (feast day July 20) or, perhaps more likely, Margaret of Scotland (feast day November 16).

17. This is one of the very few times when Margery refers to herself this way.

18. The Eucharist.

19. The Dominican friars.

20. In the immediately preceding chapter, Margery has described her visit with the archbishop of Canterbury.

21. One Richard of Caister, known as a very holy man, who had at least some sympathy with the calls for clerical reform which were associated with Lollardism.

22. The reference to black clothing is significant, since several times during her career Margery dressed all in white at God's bidding (see chapter 4). This often distressed those around her greatly and was taken by many to be simply another spectacular bid for attention on her part. White clothing was also associated with some groups of religious fanatics during this period.

23. Walter Hilton's *The Scale of Perfection*, Saint Bridget's *Liber Revelationum Celestium Sancta Birgitte*, the anonymous *Stimulus Amoris*, and Richard Rolle's *Incendium Amoris* were all well-known works in the mystical tradition.

24. The word Margery uses here is "dalliance." She uses it frequently in spite of, or perhaps because of, its associations with romantic love talk. She uses it regularly to refer to talks with other holy people or with God. I have regularly translated it as 'conversation.'

25. This is one of the charges of Lollardism made against Margery frequently throughout her career.

26. The manuscript is damaged at this point, and the two or three words ending this line are conjectural.

27. William Southfield, a Carmelite friar, was a rather well known mystic. The Carmelites of Norwich in the early fifteenth century constituted a center of mystical activity.

28. In the literal, etymological sense, not only of illness but of any perturbation of mind, body, or spirit.

29. Isa. 66:2.

30. That is, in your conscious, deliberate intention, in your natural inclination, or in both.

31. Selections from Julian's writings are also to be found in this volume.

32. Here, too, Margery's word is "dalliance."

33. Somewhere along here, Margery moves from an indirect discourse reporting of Julian's words to direct discourse, but the point is not clearly marked.

34. That is, the sorts of signs that Margery has shown herself to have.

35. Rom. 8:26.

36. There is no single, specific reference intended here, though the idea is common to both the Old and New Testaments.

37. Henry Bowet, who was archbishop from 1407 to 1423. He was known as a very strong opponent of the Lollards.

38. That is, "Lollard."

39. On Margery's wearing of white, see note 22 above. I have preserved the use of the second person singular pronoun here. In conversations with God, it is used to address Margery as a sign of affection. Here, as in the common usage of the time, it is used by the archbishop probably as a sign of his contempt or, at least, of his awareness of her inferior position. Margery regularly uses the polite plural form in addressing him and, indeed, everyone else.

40. Perhaps in the form of the Apostles' Creed.

41. The prior referred to here was Saint John of Bridlington; his confessor was one William Sleightholme.

42. Luke 11:27–28.

43. 1 Cor. 14:34–35.

44. The Eucharist.

45. Ten shillings.

BIBLIOGRAPHY

Primary Works

Butler-Bowdon, William, ed. *The Book of Margery Kempe: A Modern Version*. Introduction by R. W. Chambers. New York, 1944.
Colledge, Eric. "Excerpt from *The Book of Margery Kempe*." In his *The Mediaeval Mystics of England*, pp. 283–304. New York, 1961.
Meech, Sanford Brown, and Hope Emily Allen, eds. *The Book of Margery Kempe*. 1940. Reprint. London, 1961.

Related Works

Berry, Sara Lou. "Religious Imagery in *The Book of Margery Kempe*." Thesis, University of Florida, 1962.
Collis, Louise. *The Apprentice Saint*. London, 1964.
Cross, Claire. "'Great Reasoners in Scripture': The Activities of Women Lollards 1380–1530." In *Medieval Women*, ed. Derek Baker, pp. 359–380. Oxford, 1978.
Erickson, Carolly. *The Medieval Vision: Essays in History and Perception*. New York, 1976.
Goodman, Anthony. "The Piety of John Brunham's Daughter, of Lynn." In *Medieval Women*, ed. Derek Baker, pp. 347–358. Oxford, 1978.
Knowles, David. "Margery Kempe." In his *The English Mystical Tradition*, pp. 138–150. New York, 1961.
Power, Eileen. *Medieval Women*. Ed. M. M. Postan. Cambridge, Eng., 1975.
Stone, Robert Karl. *Middle English Prose Style: Margery Kempe and Julian of Norwich*. The Hague, 1970.

THE SPANISH LOVE POET

lorencía pínar

JOSEPH SNOW

We hear of few women writers of any kind active in the Middle Ages in Spain. We are told that in Roman times, certain young women from Cádiz were famed as accomplished dancers. Evidence of chronicles and law codes confirms that women were performers of dance and song; further proof is provided in the richly illuminated manuscripts commissioned at the behest of Alfonso X of Castile and León, called El Sabio, whose court was a cultural and intellectual crossroads for Christian, Islamic, and Hebrew learning in thirteenth-century Europe. We hear naught of women authors.

But outside of court circles, in Spain as elsewhere, there was a strong and fertile folk lyric which included several forms of women's song. These were highly rhythmic, doubtless danced as well, as their parallelistic structures and recurring refrains strongly indicate. Although written by men (when there is textual evidence), these charming songs have the persona of a woman, young, winsome, and engagingly sad (for the most part), owing to the recent departure, military call-up, abandonment, deception, sailing away, and so on, of her swain. Her emotions can run the whole spectrum and are usually revealed to a confidante, who may be her friend, her sister, or her mother; they may even be directly addressed to the absent lover, as if he could hear her words. Many of the songs of this genre became popular among court poets, who imitated them in their repertoire; several—all penned by men—appear in the Galician-Portuguese *cancioneiros* or songbooks of the thirteenth and fourteenth centuries. Related early poetic forms are the Mozarabic *kharjas* and the Castilian *villancico*; the former are often favored and used by male poets while the latter, in the early centuries, are truly anonymous and—in form—genuinely flexible. Later, in the fifteenth century—at the time of Florencia Pinar—and especially in the sixteenth, these simple *villancicos* were widely popular, often glossed, set to music, and then collected and anthologized. Still, it made little difference that the persona was frequently female; the poets were male.

When all the searching that we can do is done, the women writers at the close of the Spanish Middle Ages number perhaps half a dozen, and all of these flourished in the turbulent era of the fifteenth century.[1] Leonor López de Córdoba left a series of personal reminiscences (the *Memorias*),[2] and a Spanish nun, Teresa de Cartagena, wrote two volumes of prose in which she etches a vivid picture of spiritual growth as she struggles with deafness.[3] In the area of verse composition, women's names are also scarce; there are only a scant handful from over seven hundred individual poets who figure in the frequent *cancioneros* of the period.[4] Of a certain María Sarmiento we have the initial two lines and the final stanza of a five-and-one-half-stanza poem.[5] There are two *motes*, pithy poetic mottoes developed by other poets in glosses, one each by Marina Manuel and Catalina Manrique; both survive in glosses accorded them by the poet Cartagena in Hernando de Castillo's 1511 compilation, the *Cancionero general*, alongside the poems of Florencia Pinar.[6] From the same collection comes a brief Latin poem ascribed only to "una dama" and glossed by a certain Soria; also the anonymously penned "Question to Diego Núñez by a Lady" is there. But all of these are fragments which shed very little light on the broader talents of the women poets who wrote them. The richest treasure of this kind from Castillo's florilegium is the triad of complete texts from the hand of Florencia Pinar.

From the outset it must be stated that, to date, archival reconnoiterings have not yet produced anything of value in elucidating for us the life of this unusual personality. She can, however, be safely placed in the late fifteenth century at the court of Ferdinand and Isabella, whose joint rule in Spain dates from 1479. Florencia is obviously an educated woman, which suggests a comfortably well-to-do family; the tenor of her poems suggests a clever and agile mind. Her brother is almost certainly the "Pinar" who authored many glosses in the *cancioneros*, including one of Florencia's "El amor ha tales mañas" ("Love wields so many artful ruses").[7] In fine, there is a distinctly literary aura about the content of her poems—and of the images, as we shall see—which places her at least at the edge of the fashionable court circles of her day.

However, given the general lack of female poets represented in Castillo's compilation—and we know him to have been an assiduous collector—it may well be that Florencia possessed an independent spirit that earned her a place in what was obviously a male domain: the composition of courtly lyrics. A certain amount of courage may have helped. If Alan Deyermond is correct in his belief that Florencia's verse—however subtly woven—reveals a preoccupation with sexuality, then we do begin to perceive a personality somewhat in conflict with her age. We have a rare chance to glance at a female persona, at any rate, which is created by a female, whether or not we choose to see elements of personal autobiography in the portrayal. Thus, though the evidence is proportionally small, we must be prepared to contrast Florencia's persona with other female portraits, created by men, in the *cancioneros*.

The female figure had been undergoing, since the time when Provençal poetry and its idealization of the *domna* swept through most of Europe in the twelfth century, important changes in Spain. Caught up in a trend which gradually lavished more attention on the male lover's analysis of the pains love had inflicted on him since he became subject to his lady's whim, the image of the woman as an autonomous individual tended to lose its sharper outlines.[8] She was—it is true—still the inspiration of the poem and very much a presence in the formulas of the later love lyric, but it is also true that by and large she is rarely seen close up, rarely given physical dimensions, and as a result she infrequently emerges as more than a mere abstraction. A careful reading of Florencia's poems shows that in at least two of them, but probably in all three, she is not in step with these general tendencies. While we dare not extend our discussion of her life beyond this point, I think it important to reaffirm that what little her poems have to contribute to our perception and appreciation of her life as a poet does, in fact, allow us to posit a strong personality, one which found a way—through the medium of poetry—to convey sentiments the open expression of which was forbidden by the conventions of her age.

Florencia Pinar's poems appear in three *cancioneros*. Given here are only the three which are universally attributed to her.[9] Since so little is known of this poet, who wrote so little that is extant, not much has been written about her or her poetry. The poetic texts do permit some insights into her temperament, but we must not make too much of them.[10] José Amador de los Ríos, writing in the middle of the nineteenth century, has this to say of her: "Florencia Pinar, plucking the chords of her lyre, either pretending them or really harboring the passions of love, ponders love's wounds, exaggerating their effects in the same style as did all who aspired to the name of Poet and, like them, she portrays herself impiously disdained."[11]

Noncommittal regarding the genuineness of the sentiment in the poems, Amador lumps Florencia's poetry in a semidisposable basket of not very distinguished verse. He goes on to express disappointment that she should—being privileged—have run with the common herd of poetasters. He points out the direct and sensual flavor of the poems—Florencia belongs to a circle of "erotic troubadours"—even as he dismisses their potential fine quality. There are both good and bad in Amador's evaluation: no analysis is presented for the negative marks that Florencia's poetry earns, but the erotic tone is at least not ignored.

At the turn of the century her poetry was deemed weak and insubstantial.[12] More recently, Alan Deyermond has argued the case for a reevaluation of Florencia's considerable poetic talent. His observations inform our own.[13] Manuel Alvar, who ascribes four poems to Florencia, pithily remarks that she must be accorded some esteem for her impassioned grace and innovations in thematic areas.[14] While it is always in fashion to rediscover in almost forgotten literary figures qualities which our less analytical or less perceptive critical ancestors did not see to appreciate, it is likely more accurate to say that Florencia became lost in the vast bulk of the *cancioneros* and, consequently, with no other platform from which to speak to generations much after her own, was more obscured from critical view than scorned as an artist of mediocre talent. Thus, the new positive critical appraisal of this poet may be seen as long overdue and symbolic of a healthy trend among contemporary literary historians and students of culture alike.

The first poem translated here is composed of fourteen lines of octosyllabic verse in two stanzas of five and nine lines respectively. The rhyme scheme is as follows: abbab cddc/abbab. The rhyme words of the ab lines at the end of the stanzas are the same, and the lines themselves are almost identical. The stanzaic forms are all popular ones. The first stanza is a *quintilla*, as are the last five lines of the second stanza, which are joined to a *redondilla* (cddc).

Like the first poem, the second is a *canción* and has a fairly common form, widely used in the Spanish *cancioneros*: a five-line *quintilla* introductory stanza which sets the basic theme, with a following nine-line stanza elaborating the basic theme. This second stanza is really composed of two different sections; the first four lines form a *redondilla* (four octosyllables rhyming the first and fourth against the second and third), and they are followed by another *quintilla* with the identical rhyme pattern of the initial stanza. Not only do the rhymes recall to the reader or listener the leitmotivs of the opening themesetting stanza, but the final lines repeat exactly—or almost exactly—its main idea and close the cycle. This closed form was rather popular, and I have been able to manage a fairly close rendering in my translation. The Spanish text uses full rhyme throughout, but I have had to resort to vowel rhyme at times (or ear rhyme, as in "freedom" and "receiving") to preserve the effect. The rhyme sequence is ab*aab* cddc/ab*aab* (the italicized segments show the full-line or refrain repetition) in the original, and my translation gets very close: ab*aab* ccdd/ab*aab*.

The third *canción* differs in form slightly from the previous two. Instead of an opening and closing *quintilla*, we have a *cuarteta*, four octo-syllabic lines rhyming the first and third, the second and fourth (abab). The opening lines of the second stanza remain the very popular *redon-dilla*, similar but for the rhyming in abba. As with the *quintillas* in the previous poems, the rhyme scheme of the *cuartetas* is repeated. Thus we have for the whole poem this scheme: ab*ab* cddc/ab*ab*. The italicized lines—identical but for one variant—are the theme and its poem-ending restatement. In this case, I have been able to preserve the rhyme scheme and have even—for the most part, at least—come close to an octosyl-labic line. The original text is more direct in its expression than I have been able to indicate, but I don't believe that there has been any damage inflicted on the meaning.

The three poems included here are all poems in which the attitude toward love is ambiguous: you can't live with it, and you can't live with-out it. Love is not exalted; the lover is not praised; the power of love to cause hurt through deceit seems to stand first and foremost among the plaints to which Florencia gives voice. In contrast to the bulk of *can-cionero* poetry, in which the abstractions concerning love are generally emphasized, here we have—but only in the two final poems—striking and graphic imagery involving animals whose symbolic and bestiary as-sociations are absorbed into the personal expressions of the poet as she grafts onto them her feelings about the traps and snares and lures and nets love sets for the unwary. The utilization of these graphic images makes Florencia's poetry much more palatable to modern sensibilities than most of the rest of the poetry of the *cancioneros*; it gives a sense of immediacy to the commonplace protests against love which so dominate those compilations. But for the sake of contrast we may think of Floren-cia's first poem as more typical of the abstract, complicated, and involute language characterizing the intellectual play associated with cultivated poetry at court.

This poem, with its rubric "Song by a Lady Named Florencia Pinar," [15] is difficult to begin with, dominated as it is by the presence of a homo-nymic conceit which makes it into an intellectual puzzle suitable to the age but otherwise less attractive as a lyric piece for the ages. The conceit upon which the playful lyric is constructed is the coincidence in Spanish of the interjection *ay*, which means 'woe,' 'oh,' or 'alas' but may in gen-eral be thought of as a sigh (especially in Florencia's poem), and *(h)ay* (the *h* is silent and often omitted, making even the graphic difference between the two homonyms invisible), which is the verb form 'there is' or 'there are.' This is picked up in the first line and completely dominates the entire poem; its use seems excessive. Deyermond states strongly his belief that this "is exactly the kind of thing that gets *cancionero* poetry a bad name." [16] While this may be true in many cases, I would side with Ian MacPherson that Florencia's poem has "substantial merits." [17]

Although the manuscript texts show all forms of both meanings of *ay* and *hay* in the same graphic manner, often the context is clear enough to indicate which one is meant. Still, there is considerable room for interpretation, owing to equally logical readings springing from the use of either meaning in the line and context. What I find so revealing about the poem is less the versatility and ingenuity of its use of *ay* than its close thematic union with the other two poems. Because English provides no suitable homonymic pair for the Spanish one used by Florencia, I have translated the poem for meaning, at some sacrifice to the rhyme and meter of the original. The pitiless power of love, the force of its sway over humans, and its pain—all these are placed in a poetic tension which harmonizes with the magnetic pull that love exerts against our better judgment.

A dynamic is set up and we are never quite sure whether the ensnared lover is pleased or displeased to be in this delightful-painful dilemma. "Life itself" is at risk (line 11). But the conflict between heavy hurt and great good is not resolved. Passion seems to rule in this world of antithesis and paradox, if we accept the euphemistic "glory" (Spanish *glorias*) of line 8—as I think we must—as the sexual act.[18] Passion holds complete sway over common sense, for we are made aware that countering these sighs—which translate the passion—there are unnamed others of an opposing nature which will cancel it, act as an antidote to it. The end result is the projection of a persona, of a flesh-and-blood personality, aware of the options but caught in the endless permutations of the fortunes of love and sexual attraction, who is not afraid to suggest that, for her at least, passion outweighs prudence. There is escape for some, perhaps, but not for her. She holds out to the fictive reader of the poem the lure of love's delight, if the reader should someday experience it as she certainly has done.

In the second of the poems translated here, "Another Song by the Same Lady, to Some Partridges That Were Sent to Her Live,"[19] we enter a more visual realm. Florencia identifies herself with some caged partridges; these have been snared by hunters, precisely the figures the birds have taken such pains to avoid. The link between Florencia and the birds is an emotional correspondence in their "grieving" and "grief," expressed in both instances with the Old Spanish *passion*, 'passion' or 'suffering.' Florencia's total empathy with the birds, once free but now imprisoned, comes from her own loss of freedom to passion-suffering at the hands of another hunter: love. This is clearly communicated in the refrains at lines 5 and 14. The links between their situations are joined finally in her clever wordplay on the similar sounds found in the two words at the center of the image: *perder*, 'to lose,' and *perdiz*, 'partridge.' The complete chain of associations is thus forged in concept and in sound, in word and in image.

For the sexual undercurrents of the poem, we can look to the explication offered by Deyermond. Bestiary lore, well known throughout the Middle Ages, appears directly and indirectly in many traditions: the fable, the moral-didactic tale, poetry, folklore, and so on. The behavior of the animals offered positive and negative examples and explanations for human behavior. In the particular instance of the story of the partridge, Deyermond cites the translation by T. H. White of one widely circulated medieval version: "Frequent intercourse tires them out. The males fight each other for their mate, and it is believed that the conquered male submits to venery like a female. *Desire torments the females so much that even if a wind blows toward them from the males they become pregnant by the smell.*" [20] Deyermond's acute insight is phrased thus: "It would be imprudent to assume that Pinar wrote in ignorance of the bestiary account of the partridge, especially when other Spanish writers of this period were fairly obviously aware of it. I think one must conclude that, even if the bestiary description was not primarily responsible for Pinar's choice of image, it reinforced that choice, and that she wished not only to associate her plight with that of the trapped birds, *but also to identify her instincts with those so graphically described.*" [21]

But if a difference in the two situations may be exploited, it is this: the female partridge, once captured through her own weak resistance to strong sexual drives, is then physically caged; however, a woman in the strong magnetic field of love, unable (because unwilling?) to avoid its centripetal forces, should still be free to liberate herself—through the exercise of reason, judgment, or discipline—from its strong emotional attraction. One strong implication is that Florencia's poetic persona does not seek liberation. While one part of her can perceive the sorrow of the plight of the common loss of freedom shared by the unwilling partridges (the lament contained in the refrain lines), there is no accompanying call for rescue from the passion which has led to freedom's loss. The absence of this call—in light of the sorrow expressed—seems significant; such passion will lead to the indulgence of her instincts and the satisfaction of her desire. It is, in brief, veiled eroticism, a more fervent expression of which would have been unseemly within the conventions of the courtly lyric.

Florencia's theme of suppressed sexuality is clear enough in the last poem, too. [22] Love is seen as crafty. Like a worm burrowing under the earth, so does love work its way into the inner being of one who loves. We first welcome love's presence but realize too late that once means forever. This is the strongest of the three compositions in terms of the ambiguous image of love, but I believe it is wholly consonant with the themes and the allusive sexual language of the others. The worm, that cancerous agent of nature (another ambiguous term: does it mean of the natural world or of human nature, which is weak and imperfect?), is unavoidably phallic. It degrades all that is clean. It resembles "Love . . . rightly seen." That is, love must have several guises—it wears external garb which masks its true being, and it is this deceitful being that comes under attack in Florencia's third poem. It is sex, passion, and desire that create beautiful fancies which later are exposed as subterfuges designed to enslave the lover in perpetual chains. The process is not reversible. The strength of feeling in the poem permits us to believe—especially when taken together with the partridge poem—that experience is speaking here. The vivid animal imagery underscores the sexual text that is one of the levels on which the poem must be read. It is one of the lessons of love that are learned too late.

Florencia Pinar rails against love, to be sure. Indeed, to the unskilled reader paging through the *cancioneros*, her poems will seem interchangeable with many penned by her male colleagues. Such is the density with which these kinds of poems appear there. I suggested earlier in this essay that Florencia's poetry—it is such a small sample—may have become lost in a mass of verse which, in any case, soon passed out of fashion. I meant also, in making that suggestion, that there seemed some basis for a reassessment of her qualities as a poet and image maker. If we read her few works too quickly and with little appreciation of the intelligence that shapes them (as likely happened to her poems when wedged into the *cancioneros*), we run the risk of losing their rich texture and thematic unity.

Florencia is thus not really caught—a frail victim of love's ruses—in a fate not of her own making. The pleasure compensates for the pain. Her allusive language and precise imagery allow us to perceive, through the persona of the poems—especially the last two—another dimension of the complaints against love and another, more subtle use of its accepted conventions. I think that instead of treating Florencia Pinar as a rare survival of a woman poet in competition with men at their own literary games, we need to reassess her unique contribution to the common poetic practices of her age. It is surely a keen talent which can subvert the standard conventions—while using them—to create poems which so deftly suggest a sexuality at odds with the idealized relationships those conventions were asked to portray.

NOTES

1. I recognize that such a statement appears to sidestep another issue: the possibility of lost texts. I mean here to assess only the current state of research in the area.
2. See Reinaldo Ayerbe-Chaux, "Las memorias de doña Leonor López de Córdoba,"

Journal of Hispanic Philology 2 (1977–1978): 11–33, and Alan Deyermond, "Spain's First Women Writers."

3. See Alan Deyermond, "'El convento de dolencias': The Works of Teresa de Cartagena," *Journal of Hispanic Philology* 1 (1976–1977): 19–29, in which this (her first work) is given prominence. But see also the same scholar's "Spain's First Women Writers," in which he develops, with his usual acute insight, a particularly feminist aspect of her second work, the *Admiraçion operum Dei*.

4. Although the first large collection, the *Cancionero de Baena*, dates from about the middle of the fifteenth century and possibly a few decades earlier—see A. Blecua, *Anuario de estudios medievales* 9 (1974–1979): 257–266—the evidence is that many of the poems were written in the last decades of the fourteenth century. If we assume, then, a period of about 150 years for this *cancionero* vogue, we will appreciate better the scarcity of women poets.

5. Sarmiento's poem, a sacred piece, may be consulted in *The Cancionero de Martínez de Burgos*, ed. Dorothy S. Severin, pp. xvii, 59.

6. The fragment by Catalina Manrique, "Nunca mucho costó poco" ("A Little Never Bought a Lot"), is found on fol. 143v of the *Cancionero general* of Hernando de Castillo; the one by Marina Manuel, "Esfuerce Dios el sufrir" ("Let God Encourage Suffering"), is also on fol. 143v. See the facsimile edition prepared by A. Rodríguez-Moñino.

7. The gloss, in eleven eleven-line stanzas plus a six-line envoi, is valuable because it shows how a fellow poet understood each of the lines of Florencia's poem (one line of the original poem is inserted in each of the stanzas as the penultimate verse). It can be consulted in Manuel Alvar's *Poesía española medieval*, pp. 578–579. The rubric to this poem in the *Cancionero del British Museum* reads "Glosa de Pinar, su hermano" ("gloss by Pinar, her brother").

8. For a study of this entire phenomenon, consult Mary K. Mosley, "Women in Fifteenth-Century *Cancioneros*."

9. I have taken the texts for the translations from the facsimile of the *Cancionero general*: fols. 125v, 126r, and 185v.

10. In this I heed the warning of Alan Deyermond in "The Worm and the Partridge: Reflections on the Poetry of Florencia Pinar," *Mester* 7 (1978): 7.

11. José Amador de los Ríos, *Historia crítica de la literatura española*, vol. 7, pp. 237–238. The translation is mine.

12. Manuel Serrano y Sanz, *Apuntes para una biblioteca de escritoras españolas*, vol. 2, pt. 1, p. 129.

13. See the articles mentioned above, nn. 2 and 10. I am appreciative of the fact that Professor Deyermond allowed me to consult the typescript of the long article before it was published and was, later, kind enough to examine a draft of this piece and offer helpful comments.

14. Alvar, p. 574.

15. No title is given, typically, to *cancionero* poems. Instead they are often identified by genre and author. "Cancion de una dama que se dize Florencia Pinar" is the rubric from the *Cancionero general*.

16. Deyermond, "The Worm and the Partridge," p. 3.

17. Ibid., p. 8 n. 10.

18. *Cancionero* love poetry is rife with sexual euphemism, *glorias* being one of the more used (abused?) of these ambiguous terms. For some discussion of them, consult Keith Whinnom, "Hacia una interpretación y apreciación de las canciones del *Cancionero general* de 1511," *Filología* 13 (1968–1969): 361–381.

19. The Spanish rubric is "Otra cancion de la misma senora, a vnas perdizes que le embiaron biuas."

20. T. H. White, *The Book of Beasts (Being a Translation from a Latin Bestiary of the Twelfth Century)*, p. 137. Emphasis mine.

21. Deyermond, "The Worm and the Partridge," p. 6. Emphasis mine.

22. The original rubric to this poem is simply "Cancion de Florencia Pinar."

Song by a Lady Named Florencia Pinar

A sigh! For there are some who languish[1]
because there are none who pity their sighs.
And if there is a sigh which is fearful,
there also is a sigh with which they—
unused to life without their sighs—
can counter it.

Oh, pleasure! Oh, sorrow!
Oh, glory! Oh, endless pangs![2]
There is, wherever bides Love's hurt,
great good (should you ever delight in it).
Though life itself be held captive,
if there is one who finds solace in sighs,
there is no need to ward against them;
even though there are means by which
he who does not live life without sighs
can counter them.

Another Song by the Same Lady, to Some Partridges That Were Sent to Her Live

The natural heritage[3] of these birds
is to sing with joy, in freedom;[4]
to see them caged, by huntsmen snared,[5]
grieves my heart, with feeling shared.
None knows my own heart's grieving![6]

Now they weep, who once had thought
not once of ever being caught;
instead they live deceived, decoyed
by them they sought most to avoid.
In their name my fate is heard,
my joy departs,[7] no hope receiving.

To see them caged, by huntsmen snared,
grieves my heart, with feeling shared.
None knows my own heart's grieving!

Song by Florencia Pinar

Love wields so many artful ruses[8]
that all who 'gainst them are not clever[9]
find Love's subtle subterfuges,
once in the heart,[10] are there forever.

Love, when clearly, rightly seen,
resembles most that cancerous form
of nature,[11] the snaking delving worm,
ravager of all that's whole and clean.[12]
Of his tricks and of his rages,
the storms of protest never lessen.
Lovers learn:[13] Love's subterfuges,
once in the heart, are there forever.

NOTES TO THE TRANSLATION

1. The verb form *ay* has both singular and plural meanings in Spanish ('there is' or 'there are'). Similarly, *quien* used as a subject of a verb, while grammatically singular, also has plural implications ('he who,' 'one who,' or 'they who'). Thus, throughout the poem, a singular meaning and a plural meaning run parallel, and it is important to note this. I have chosen the plural form for my translation, although I might have as easily and as legitimately used "A sigh! For there is one who languishes . . . " The first word of the line is *ay*, which I have here rendered "A sigh!" Elsewhere I use this word (singular or plural) or the representation of the sound of a sigh (lines 7–8: "Oh").

2. Here the use of *ay* is ambiguous. The ambiguity is compounded by the lack of any punctuation. I have represented the quadripartite lament exactly, leaving, however, only "pangs" in the plural since that best serves in English. The other three nouns are also Spanish plurals but seem to me to communicate better as English singulars. But the use of *ay* results in a different reading, depending on its interpretation either as interjection or as verb form. For example, the opening hemistich would read either "Oh, sorrow(s)!" or "There are sorrows." I have chosen the sigh-interjection over the verb form for what I hope are logical and poetical reasons: the poem is about sighs, and the second stanza is building emotional tension and the interjection communicates this far better than the verb form for the reader, even as the verb form—silent and subjacent—is still felt.

3. The Spanish *nacion* in context is a reference to what the whole of the partridge "nation" possesses as its destiny: to sing with joy. The English "natural heritage" is an extension of this idea.

4. "In freedom" is not justified by words in the original; rather, I have taken it as implied by the meaning of line 3.

5. The original says they are "in prison." Both "caged" and "by huntsmen snared" are logical extensions of this situation.

6. Florencia speaks only of her severe or great *passion* (passion-suffering) when seeing the birds in this confined state. My use of the word "heart" here only symbolizes the emotions felt, and the reader should be alert to the sensual, not just the sentimental, meaning that surely lies behind these lines.

7. "Their names are my life," says Florencia, "which gradually loses its joy." The play on words is visible only partly in her text, as the word for 'partridges' (*perdizes*) is not written whereas the word for 'losing' (*perdiendo*) is. It is thus that she can "hear" in their name her loss. This near homonym play seems to delight Florencia, and it is a very important device in the first poem.

8. Spanish *mañas* is a tricky word, like English "ways." The tone, I think, is maintained with "artful ruses."

9. The original literally says "guard against them." My extrapolation of "clever" for the translation is implicit in the text and suggests in what way a guard need be set against "artful ruses."

10. Somewhat free. The Spanish *entrañas* is, variously, 'innards,' 'entrails,' or 'vital organs.' I have used "heart" not only for its common symbolic usage in love poetry but also because it must be the worm's destination. It is the heart's sway over the faculty of reason which the worm strengthens (paradoxically, by corrupting or weakening its resistance to erotic love's ruses).

11. Spanish *natura*, 'nature,' may be, like *glorias*, 'glory' (in the first poem), an ambiguous word, encapsulating a euphemism for the female sex organs. I am grateful to Professor Deyermond for this information.

12. My line 8 is strongly put. The Spanish is rather more plain: "which consumes [eats] all that is sound/healthy."

13. "Lovers learn" is not in the original. I have used it to fill out the line because it seems so obviously the end of the hard lesson that gradually is impressed upon the victims of love, as they become aware of the irreversibility of their plight.

BIBLIOGRAPHY

Primary Works

Rodríguez-Moñino, A., ed. Facsimile edition of the *Cancionero general* of Hernando de Castillo. Madrid, 1958.

Related Works

Alvar, Manuel. *Poesía española medieval*. Barcelona, 1969.

Amador de los Ríos, José. *Historia crítica de la literatura española*. Vol. 7. 1865. Reprint. Madrid, 1969.

Ayerbe-Chaux, Reinaldo. "Las memorias de doña Leonor López de Córdoba." *Journal of Hispanic Philology* 2 (1977–1978): 11–33.

Deyermond, Alan. "'El convento de dolencias': The Works of Teresa de Cartagena." *Journal of Hispanic Philology* 1 (1976–1977): 19–29.

———. "Spain's First Women Writers." In *Icons and Fallen Idols: Women in Hispanic Literature*, ed. Beth Miller. Berkeley and Los Angeles, 1983.

———. "The Worm and the Partridge: Reflections on the Poetry of Florencia Pinar." *Mester* 7 (1978): 3–8.

Green, Otis H. "Courtly Love in the Spanish *Cancioneros*." *PMLA* 64 (1949): 247–301.

LeGentil, Pierre. *La poésie lyrique espagnole et portugaise à la fin du moyen âge*. 2 vols. Rennes, 1949, 1952.

Mosley, Mary K. "Women in Fifteenth-Century *Cancioneros*." Ph.D. dissertation, University of Missouri-Columbia, 1976.

Serrano y Sanz, Manuel. *Apuntes para una biblioteca de escritoras españolas*. 2 vols. 1903. Reprint. Madrid, 1975.

Severin, Dorothy S., ed. *The Cancionero de Martínez de Burgos*. Exeter, 1976.

Sponsler, Lucy A. *Women in the Medieval Spanish Epic and Lyric Traditions*. Lexington, 1975.

Whinnom, Keith. "Hacia una interpretación y apreciación de las canciones del *Cancionero general* de 1511." *Filología* 13 (1968–1969): 361–381.

———. "The Mysterious Marina Manuel ('Prologue,' *Cárcel de amor*)." In *Studia Iberica: Festschrift für Hans Flasche*, pp. 689–695. Bern, 1973.

White, T. H. *The Book of Beasts (Being a Translation from a Latin Bestiary of the Twelfth Century)*. London, 1954.

THE FRANCO-ITALIAN PROFESSIONAL WRITER

Christine de Pizan

CHARITY CANNON WILLARD

Although Christine de Pizan was one of the women invited recently to have a place at Judy Chicago's Dinner Party, she is not altogether typical of the women chosen, for her writings were far from unappreciated in her own lifetime and even during the century after her death. She was forgotten for a time because of the change in taste which threw nearly all medieval French literature into eclipse. Rediscovered toward the end of the eighteenth century, she was then alternately praised to the skies and denigrated by a prejudiced literary criticism which preferred to regard her as a woman rather than a remarkably innovative writer. She has been enthusiastically adopted by latter-day feminists, sometimes for reasons that would undoubtedly have astonished her, and she has been disdained because she was an intellectual woman, a "blue-stocking," as one nineteenth-century critic put it.[1] Both sorts of judgment were too often based on an inadequate knowledge of what Christine wrote, due in many cases to the lack of modern editions. It is only in the last half century that a serious effort has been made to improve this situation, and only recently has there been a solid basis for judging her works as a whole and her true contribution as a writer.

It is now becoming clear that Christine de Pizan should be viewed as one of the writers who marked the transition in France between the so-called late Middle Ages and the Renaissance. Her role was predestined by the circumstances of her life, for born in Venice but spending most of her years in Paris, she was able to combine her Italian heritage with her knowledge of French life and thought as she experienced them.

Christine was born around 1365 into a somewhat unusual family. Both her father and her grandfather belonged to the limited circle of university-educated men of their day, and both were public officials of the Venetian

Republic. They had originally known each other as fellow students at the University of Bologna, where Christine's father, Tommaso de Bologna, or Pizzano, received a medical degree in 1343 and held a chair of astrology from then until 1356. The study of astrology was closely allied with the practice of medicine, and in the fourteenth century the University of Bologna was one of the principal centers for such studies. Less is known of Christine's grandfather, Tommaso Mondini of Forlì, except that it was through his influence that Tommaso de Pizzano went to Venice and subsequently married his daughter.[2]

Soon after Christine's birth, her father returned to Bologna to look after some property he owned there. He was then faced with a choice between two tempting invitations, to go to Paris to the court of Charles V or to Hungary to the court of Louis I. It was an era when kings thought it advantageous to have official astrologers to advise them on medical, scientific, and even political matters, and Bologna was the obvious place to look for such men. Tommaso decided that the offer from France was more attractive, as he was especially eager to acquaint himself with the celebrated University of Paris. He agreed to go for one year, but having been persuaded by the king to remain, in 1368 he sent for his family to join him.

So it was that Christine grew to maturity in the shadow of the court of Charles V, one of the most intellectual and forward-looking monarchs of his day. Not the least of his accomplishments was the establishment of a royal library, which included translations he commissioned of the major works of Aristotle and other classical writers as well as a large collection of such scientific works as were then available in Europe. It seems possible that one of Tommaso's duties may have been to advise in the choice of these scientific works and help in their procurement, for Bologna was one of the principal centers of book production in the fourteenth century. To judge from Christine's recollections of her father, along with being an astrologer he was an accomplished mathematician with an interest in speculative natural philosophy (the ancestor of modern physics), all of which had a profound influence on her intellectual development—even though she was denied anything more than the elementary education which was then permitted to young girls.[3]

By the time she was fifteen, a husband was chosen for her—a young notary, Etienne de Castel, who must also have had a certain amount of university training, for he is often given the title of Maître de Castel in official records. In 1380, the year of their marriage, he received an appointment as royal secretary which not only opened the way to a promising career but, in his attachment to the royal chancellery, assured his contact with the young men destined to become France's first humanists. These men cultivated their Latin prose, read Petrarch and Boccaccio, and, in certain cases, exchanged letters with such Italian counterparts as Coluccio Salutati in the Florentine chancellery.[4] Therefore, if Christine herself was denied the education she longed for, she at least spent her early years in the company of educated men.

The marriage, which was a happy one, resulted in the birth of two sons and a daughter. Problems arose in the household all too soon, however, because with the untimely death of Charles V and the minority of the pleasure-loving Charles VI, the studious, middle-class courtiers of the earlier reign were no longer held in high regard. Furthermore, Tommaso's health began to fail, and he died in relative poverty around 1387. Far more devastating was the death of Etienne de Castel some three years later, for he was the victim of an epidemic in Beauvais, where he had accompanied the king on an official mission. Thus Christine, at the age of twenty-five, was left a widow with young children and an elderly mother in her care, as well as "a poor niece to marry."[5] Shortly after her father's death, her two brothers had returned to Bologna to claim a family inheritance and had remained there. Christine's sorrow was profound and nothing in her previous life had prepared her for the responsibilities she was now obliged to assume, but it was out of these misfortunes that her career as a writer developed.

Although Christine herself explains that during her early years of widowhood she turned to writing poetry in search of consolation for and distraction from the problems which beset her, this does not explain how she dealt with her serious financial problems during the ten years between the death of her husband and the beginning of her career as a writer. On the basis of manuscript copies of her works which have been identified in recent years as autographs, it now seems possible to suggest that she probably occupied herself as a copyist, employed in the book trade which was beginning to flourish in Paris at the end of the fourteenth century. This was one of the few profitable occupations open to women, and Christine's connections with the professional notaries at the royal court and with Giles Malet, the librarian of the royal library in the Louvre, as well as her subsequent close association with certain illustrators of manuscripts would all lend support to such an idea.

Among her own manuscripts, the earliest known copy of the *Epître d'Othéa* (Paris, B.N. fr. 848), the copy of the *Mutacion de fortune* presented to the duke of Burgundy (Brussels, Bibl. Roy. 9508), and the recently discovered copy of the *Avision-Christine* (formerly manuscript 128 of the Phillipps Collection), in addition to the copy of the *Epître à la reine* (B.N. fr. 580) which bears the indication *escript de ma main*, are only the most important of the manuscripts which give evidence of coming from Christine's own hand. There is also reason to believe that she may have come to know some of the sources for her later works through having made copies of them for patrons or for Paris bookdealers. This is an aspect of Christine's career which is only beginning to be understood.[6]

Eventually, as her poetry began to meet with a certain success, she wrote on other themes—mythology, events at the royal court, and so-called courtly love—for in the final years of the fourteenth century the court of Charles VI was enjoying a somewhat artificial revival of earlier chivalric customs. In her early poetry Christine favored the *balade*, the *rondeau*, and the *virelai*, forms recommended by Eustache Deschamps in his *Art de dictier*, but she experimented endlessly with these forms.[7] By 1402, the date of the first collection of her poetry, she had put together the *Cent balades* as well as cycles of the other forms. Both in the *Cent balades* and in a series of *rondeaux* she told the story of love affairs which ended in deception for the lovers, especially the woman. Disillusionment resulting from the false perceptions bred by the conventions of courtly love was to become one of her principal themes, along with the highly original theme of the sorrows of widowhood.

In the meantime, as she explained in her most autobiographical work, the *Avision-Christine*, her attention had turned to more serious matters; she read ancient history, Boethius' *The Consolation of Philosophy*, probably in Jean de Meung's French translation, and the lengthy medieval commentary on Ovid's *Metamorphoses*, the *Ovide moralisé*. The most significant result of her studies was the allegorical, mythological work entitled the *Epître d'Othea, la deesse, que elle envoya a Hector de Troye, quant il estoit en l'aage de quinze ans*. This took the form of a letter from the goddess of wisdom to a young man on the formation of a perfect knight, consisting of one hundred quatrains inspired by mythology or Trojan history, with moral and theological commentaries based on an astonishing variety of sources. Although little to the taste of modern readers, it proved to be one of her most popular works among her contemporaries.[8]

Christine's new interests were further encouraged, around 1402, by a debate over the merits of Jean de Meung's part of the *Roman de la rose* in which she became engaged with several young Parisian humanists. Christine considered the poem much overrated by certain of her contemporaries, a view in which she was seconded by at least one very important Parisian, Jean Gerson, the chancellor of the University of Paris. Her principal opponents were the provost of Lille, Jean de Montreuil, who was also a royal secretary, and two brothers, Gontier and Pierre Col, the former another royal secretary and the latter a member of the chapter of Notre Dame. Although these are the main names associated with the controversy, the text of the letters that were exchanged suggests that there were a good many others involved in the discussions.

Although it was thought for many years that Christine had stirred up the debate with some unflattering references to the poem in her 1399 poem entitled the *Epître au Dieu d'Amour*, it is now evident that Jean de Montreuil initiated the affair by writing an enthusiastic commentary on the *Roman de la rose*, which he had read during the spring of 1401, and by sending a copy of what he had written to Christine. She then saw fit to reply with an attack on several aspects of the poem, especially the slander heaped on women not only by Jean de Meung but by the whole tradition of misogynistic literature. Some of the reactions of the Parisian intellectuals were far from courteous, illustrating the attitudes about which Christine was complaining, but she did not hesitate to answer the attacks with eloquence and considerable wit. In 1402, Jean Gerson expressed his disapproval of Jean de Meung's views in *Traité contre le Roman de la rose*, and in a series of sermons preached at the end of the year. The whole discussion, in spite of the heat it apparently generated, is best understood as a sort of intellectual exercise inspired by debates among Italian humanists. Its greatest importance for Christine was that it gave her considerable publicity as a defender of her sex and encouraged her to undertake even more ambitious objectives.[9]

She next turned her attention to two more long allegorical works. The first of these was a poem entitled the *Livre du chemin de long estude*, in which she described an imaginary voyage to the celestial realms where she was advised on the affairs of France and of Europe at large by Lady Reason and was commissioned to carry a message from her back to the French rulers.[10] Her guide on this journey was the Cumaean sibyl, and the basic inspiration was undoubtedly drawn from Dante's *Divine Comedy*, which she was one of the first writers to mention in France. The second allegory, the *Mutacion de fortune*, is also a long poem (6,392 verses), although it includes a passage on universal history in prose. In addition to dwelling on her necessity of changing from a woman into a man in order to steer the ship of the family's fortunes, Christine here discussed the role of fortune in human destiny throughout the history of the world. This rather diffuse work had the merit of attracting the duke of Burgundy's attention; he immediately commissioned Christine to write an official, and humanistic, biography of his brother, the late Charles V. Unfortunately he did not live to see the completed *Livre des faits et bonnes meurs du sage Roy Charles V*, but his heir, John the Fearless, continued to interest himself in Christine's writings, procuring copies of them for the ducal library and making use of her talents for his own purposes. The court of Burgundy's marked taste for didactic literature further encouraged her interests in that direction.

Having become involved in the problem of women's role in society, Christine devoted two more long works to the subject. The first, the *Cité des dames*, described an allegorical city devoted to outstanding women.

Inspired in large measure by Saint Augustine's *Civitate Dei* and Boccaccio's *De claris mulieribus*, translated into French for the first time in 1401,[11] she described the foundation of this city under the direction of three goddesses, Justice, Reason, and Discretion, who appeared to her in a vision. The city was to be set aside for women who had made important contributions to society. Christine made use of famous women taken from Boccaccio, adapting his accounts to her own purposes; she also added examples from French history and even from contemporary society. More interesting than the biographies, however, are the discussions of women's problems in society carried on by Christine with her mentors as the city is being built.

The concept of the city once established, it seemed necessary to provide some guidelines for women who aspired to be worthy of it. This inspired Christine to write a companion volume, the *Livre des trois vertus*, dedicated to Marguerite of Burgundy on the occasion of her marriage to the French dauphin, Louis of Guienne. The book was intended, however, for women on all levels of society, suggesting how they could make the most of such opportunities as they might have. For the modern reader, it provides interesting glimpses of the life of women from different walks of life in fifteenth-century France.[12]

A treatise dedicated to the duke of Burgundy should also be mentioned. In 1405 Christine wrote her allegorical autobiography, the *Avision-Christine*. The principal source of information about her life, it also addresses the political problems of France. In spite of being a medieval dream-vision in form, the work is basically humanistic in concept—it not only provides a spiritual autobiography of the sort that Petrarch had rendered popular, but its advice to the French rulers follows the tradition already made popular by Italian humanists, who saw their role as advisers to monarchs as one of their main functions in life.

Another essentially humanistic trait is Christine's interest in the education of the young, which can already be noted in two works written early in her career for her son, Jean de Castel—the *Enseignemens moraux* and the *Proverbes moraux*, both of which enjoyed considerable popularity, the latter being printed in an English translation by William Caxton in 1477. It is probable that she also wrote the *Epître d'Othéa* with her son in mind, whereas the *Faits et bonnes meurs de Charles V* may well have been intended to provide a model of kingship for the duke of Guienne. It is certain that the *Livre du corps de policie*, a companion volume to the *Livre des trois vertus*, was intended for him, although she did not limit herself to the concept of the perfect prince, for whom she proposed an essentially Renaissance ideal, but also recommended a form of education for young men from other sections of society. The *Faits d'armes et de chevalerie* may also have been commissioned for the French dauphin by the duke of Burgundy.[13] Christine there undertook to simplify and popularize the books of Vegetius and Frontinus on Roman military art, adding a discussion of the medieval "laws of war" largely drawn from the late fourteenth-century *Arbre des batailles* by Honoré Bouvet. The treatise enjoyed a long period of success in both France and England, although in some copies all mention of Christine's authorship was suppressed.

To this group of educational treatises belongs the *Livre de la paix*, dedicated to the duke of Guienne, the official head of the French government due to Charles VI's increasing insanity. The immediate inspiration was a Parisian revolution known as the Cabochien revolt, which created a crisis in the rapidly deteriorating political situation in the country. Not only was there a mortal struggle between two French factions, the Burgundians and the Armagnacs, but an excuse was provided for English intervention, leading eventually to Henry V's overwhelming victory at Agincourt in November 1415. After the failure of the Cabochien uprising, the duke of Burgundy was exiled from Paris and the young duke died unexpectedly, leaving the Armagnacs to institute a veritable reign of terror in Paris.

It was in these troubled times that Christine wrote her *Epître de la prison de vie humaine* to console Frenchwomen who had suffered so much already; worse was in store for them all. Christine's son, Jean de Castel, was by now one of the royal secretaries attached to the new dauphin, the future Charles VII. When, in May 1418, Paris was betrayed to Burgundian troops, Jean was obliged to flee from the city. Christine likewise sought refuge outside the city, probably in the royal convent at Poissy, where her daughter had been a nun for many years. It was from behind convent walls that she wrote her last two works. In the *Heures de contemplacion sur la Passion de nostre Seigneur*, the evocation of Mary grieving for her Son at the foot of the cross suggests that the work might have been written around 1425, after her own son's death in exile.

Christine's final poem is more joyous, written to celebrate the victory of Joan of Arc at Orléans and the coronation of Charles VII at Reims. Dated July 31, 1429, it was the first poem to celebrate the events which seemed miraculously to have brought about a change in France's fortunes.[14] The fact that a young woman had brought this about seemed to crown Christine's efforts on behalf of womankind. Thus her long career ended on a note of triumph. Her voice was not heard again—a description of Paris written by Guillebert de Mets in 1434 refers to her in the past tense. Her works, however, were copied, printed, and read into the sixteenth century, especially the *Epître d'Othéa*, the *Faits d'armes et de chevalerie*, and the *Livre des trois vertus*. Several of her works were translated into English, the *Cité des dames* into Flemish, and the *Livre des trois vertus* into Portuguese.

Among those who owned and read her works were the leaders of the next generation of women, among others Marguerite of Austria and Mary of Hungary, both of them governors of the Netherlands for the Holy Roman Emperor Charles V, and Louise of Savoy, the regent of France during the minority of Francis I. Anne of Brittany, twice queen of France, encouraged the printing of the *Livre des trois vertus*, as did Queen Leonora of Portugal. The multiplicity of paper copies which exist along with the handsome illuminated manuscripts, as well as the repeated printings, attest to the fact that these works were also read by more ordinary women.[15]

From the beginning of her literary career, Christine had been preoccupied by renown, although she never seemed to doubt seriously that she would enjoy her share of it or that her name would be remembered after her death. In the *Avision* she put into the mouth of Dame Opinion the following words: "In times to come more will be said of you than during your lifetime, for . . . you have come in a bad time, when sciences are not held in high esteem."[16] Perhaps the time has finally come when she can be appreciated for her true merits and contributions, for the record she left of her evolution from sorrowful young widow to defender of the worthiness of all women, would-be reformer of France, and educator of its future rulers. All this is truly remarkable and would not be paralleled for many years to come.

At the same time, it is a mistake to expect to find too great a similarity between Christine and modern feminists, even though her thought retains a vitality which evokes a sympathetic response. It is not difficult to agree with Martin LeFranc, who said of her in 1442, "Though death may draw a curtain about her body, her name will still endure."[17]

NOTES

1. G. Lanson, *Histoire de la littérature française*, p. 163.

2. Giovanni Fantuzzi, *Notizie degli scrittori Bolognesi*, vol. 7, pp. 54–59, and Elena Nicolini, "Cristina da Pizzano, l'origine e il nome," *Cultura Neolatina* 1 (1941): 143–150.

3. See the *Avision-Christine*, ed. Sister Mary Louise Towner, pp. 161–162, where Christine comments on the lost opportunities of her youth, and the *Cité des dames* 2. 36 in the following translation.

4. Gilbert Ouy, "Paris, l'un des principaux foyers de l'humanisme en Europe au début du XVe siècle," *Bulletin de la Société de Paris et de l'Ile-de-France* (1967–1968): 72–98.

5. Towner, ed., pp. 154–156. For the sale of property in Bologna by Christine's broth-

ers in 1394, see Fantuzzi, p. 57. A gift from John the Fearless, duke of Burgundy, to marry off the poor niece is cited by G. Doutrepont, *La littérature française à la cour des ducs de Bourgogne*, p. 277.

6. The problem of Christine de Pizan's autographs, raised by my article "An Autograph Manuscript of Christine de Pizan?" *Studi Francesi* 27 (1965): 452–457, has led to further discussion in an article by Gilbert Ouy and Christine M. Reno, "Identification des autographes de Christine de Pizan," *Scriptorium* 34 (1980): 221–238. For an analysis of the writing in Brussels, Bibl. Roy. MS 9508, by Léon Gilissen, see *La librairie de Bourgogne et quelques acquisitions récentes de la Bibliothèque Royale Albert Ier*, pp. 10–11; for Christine's relations with the Parisian illustrators of her day, see Lucie Schaefer, "Die Illustrationen zu den Handschriften der Christine de Pizan," *Marburger Jahrbuch für Kunstwissenschaft* 10 (1937), and Millard Meiss, *French Painting in the Time of Jean de Berry: The Limbourgs and Their Contemporaries*. The former Phillipps MS 128 is listed and described in *The Phillipps Manuscripts: Catalogue Librorum Manuscriptorum in Bibliotheca D. Thomae Phillipps, Bt.*, p. 2; Sotheby and Company, *Bibliotheca Phillippica: Medieval Manuscripts*, pp. 61–62; and Vente Hôtel Druout, *Manuscrits, livres anciens et modernes*, no. 2, November 18 and 19, 1974. Christine Reno of Vassar College is preparing an edition of this manuscript.

7. *Oeuvres poétiques de Christine de Pisan*, ed. Maurice Roy; Pierre LeGentil, "Christine de Pisan, poète méconnu," pp. 1–10; F. Lecoy, "Note sur quelques balades de Christine de Pisan," pp. 107–114; *Christine de Pisan: Balades, Rondeaux and Virelais*, ed. Kenneth Varty; Daniel Poirion, *Le poète et le prince*, pp. 237–245; and Charity Cannon Willard, "Lovers' Dialogues in Christine de Pizan's Lyric Poetry from the *Cent Balades* to the *Cent Balades d'Amant et de Dame*," *Fifteenth Century Studies* 4 (1981): 167–180.

8. Although there is as yet no modern edition of this work, preparatory studies have been made by Gianni Mombello, "Per un'edizione critica dell'*Epistre Othea* di Christine de Pizan," *Studi Francesi* 24 (1964): 401–417; 25 (1965): 1–12; and *La tradizione manoscritta dell'Epistre Othea di Christine de Pizan*. See also P. G. C. Campbell, *L'Epître d'Othéa: Etude sur les sources de Christine de Pisan*, and editions of two early English translations: *The Epistle of Othea to Hector*, edited from the Harleian Manuscript 838 by J. D. Gordon and Stephen Scrope, and *The Epistle of Othea*, edited by Curt F. Bühler. For an illustrator known as the Epître d'Othéa Master, see Meiss, pp. 23–41; for the work's popularity, see Rosamund Tuve, *Allegorical Imagery: Some Medieval Books and Their Posterity*, pp. 33–55, and Mary Ann Ignatius, "Christine de Pizan's *Epistre Othea*: An Experiment in Literary Form," *Medievalia et Humanistica*, n.s. 9 (1979): 127–142.

9. This debate has continued to generate heat. See *Les epistres sur le Roman de la rose*, ed. Frederick Beck; A. Piaget, "Chronologie des épîtres sur le *Roman de la rose*," pp. 113–120; E. Langlois, "Le traité de Gerson contre le *Roman de la rose*," *Romania* 45 (1918–1919): 23–48; F. Ward, *The Epistles on the Romance of the Rose and Other Documents in the Debate*; A. Coville, *Gontier et Pierre Col et l'humanisme en France au temps de Charles VI*; Peter Potansky, *Der Streit um den Rosenroman*; and most recently the excellent edition of the documents *Le débat sur le Roman de la rose* by Eric Hicks and the study by Hicks and Ezio Ornato, "Jean de Montreuil et le débat sur le *Roman de la rose*," *Romania* 98 (1977): 34–64, 186–219.

10. Suzanne Solente, at the time of her death, was preparing a new edition of the *Livre du chemin de long estude*.

11. For information concerning the translation of 1401, see A. Hortis, *Studi sulle opere latine del Boccaccio*, and Carla Bozzolo, *Manuscrits des traductions françaises d'oeuvres de Boccace: XVe siècle*, pp. 23–25.

12. See Mathilde Läigle, *Le livre des trois vertus de Christine de Pisan et son milieu historique et littéraire*, and Charity Cannon Willard, "A Fifteenth-Century View of Wom-

en's Role in Medieval Society," pp. 90–120. I am preparing an edition of the text based on Boston Public Library MS 1528.

13. Ernest Nys, *Christine de Pisan et ses principales oeuvres*, pp. 56–79, and Charity Cannon Willard, "Christine de Pisan's Treatise on the Art of Medieval Warfare," pp. 179–191.

14. *Dittié de Jeanne d'Arc*, ed. Angus J. Kennedy and Kenneth Varty; Thérèse Ballet Lynn, "The Dittié de Jeanne d'Arc: Its Political, Feminist and Aesthetic Significance," *Fifteenth Century Studies* 1 (1978): 149–157; and Liliane Dulac, "Un écrit militant de Christine de Pizan: Le Dittié de Jeanne d'Arc," pp. 115–134.

15. Charity Cannon Willard, "The Manuscript Tradition of the *Livre des Trois Vertus* and Christine de Pizan's Audience," *Journal of the History of Ideas* 27 (1966): 433–444.

16. Towner, ed., p. 144.

17. Martin LeFranc, *Le champion des dames*, Brussels, Bibl. Roy. MS 9281, fol. 151.

The Debate over the Romance of the Rose

Christine to Jean de Montreuil, Provost of Lille

Now, by heaven, let us look a little further into the matter.[1] How can it be good and useful that he accuses so excessively, impetuously, and falsely, blames and defames women for several serious vices, claiming that their morals are full of perversity, and throughout so many rejoinders and by means of all of his characters he cannot seem to repeat his accusations often enough? Even if you want to tell me that the Jealous Husband does it through passion, I do not see how it is suitable to the part of Genius,[2] who recommends and even insists that women should go to bed with men without delay for the purpose he praises so highly, and then he says so many slanderous things about them because they do it. In fact, he says: "Flee! Flee! Flee from the venomous snakes."[3] And then he says that one should not cease to pursue them. This is certainly a great contradiction, to command one to flee what he is expected to pursue and pursue what one tells him to flee. As some women are so perverse, should one not rather command men not to go near them at all? Whoever is afraid of the consequences would do better to try to avoid them.

He is so insistent about not telling a secret to a woman,[4] who is so bereft of discretion, as he recalls, and I can't imagine where in the devil he found so much nonsense and so many futile words as are hurled at them throughout that long trial, but I beg all those who consider this quite authentic and put so much faith in it to tell me how many men they have known to be accused, killed, hanged, or even reproached in the street because of the denunciation of their wives; I think they will find them very thinly scattered. Although it would certainly make good sense, and also be praiseworthy, for everyone to keep a secret to himself for greater security, as there are always a certain number of evil people, and recently, as I have heard, someone was accused and even hanged for having confided in a companion he trusted, but I think that in court there are few cries or complaints of such terrible misfortunes, of such singular disloyalties or great deviltry as he claims that women are capable of perpetrating so maliciously and surreptitiously, for a secret is only a true secret when nobody knows about it! As I once said on this subject in a poem of mine called *The Letter to the God of Love*,[5] where are the countries or the realms that have been undone by women's misdeeds? Without prejudice, we would ask of what crimes even the worst of them, the most deceitful, can be accused. What can they do or how can they deceive you? If they beg you for money from your purse, if indeed they don't take it, do you give it to them if you don't want to? And if you say that they make fools of you, don't you allow yourselves to be made fools of? Do they go to your houses to seek you out, beg, or take you by force? It would be interesting to know just how they deceive you.

Moreover, the poet speaks so unnecessarily and in such an ugly way of married women who deceive their husbands, a matter of which he can scarcely know from experience and of which he speaks very categorically. Of what use is this, what good can come of it? I think it is only a hindrance to peace and well-being by making husbands who listen to such nonsense, if they pay attention to it, suspicious and mistrustful of their wives. Heavens, what an exhortation, and to what good purpose? Indeed, as he blames women in general, I am led to believe it is because he has never known or frequented any virtuous women, but through knowing a few who are dissolute and evil, as the lecherous are in the habit of doing, he believed or pretended to know what all are like, just because he never had any experience of others. If only he had blamed the dishonest ones and suggested that this sort should be shunned it would have been good and just advice. But no! Instead he accused all women without exception. But if the author took it upon himself to accuse them or judge them falsely so entirely beyond reasonable limits, they are not the ones who should be blamed, but rather him, who tells such lies that they are beyond belief, especially as the opposite can be clearly seen. For even if he and all his accomplices swear to it, let none take offense, there have nevertheless been, are now, and will always be women more valiant, more honest, better bred, and even wiser, and through whom more good has come to the world, than has ever come from him. And some are even more versed in the affairs of state and have more virtuous habits, some have been responsible for reconciling their husbands with their enemies, and have borne their affairs and their secrets and their passions gently and confidentially, even when their husbands have been disagreeable and unfaithful.[6] There are many examples of these in the Bible and other ancient histories,[7] such as Sarah, Rebecca, Esther, Judith,[8] and others, and even in our own times we have seen in France many valiant ladies, great and noble Frenchwomen: the saintly, devout Queen Jeanne,[9] Queen Blanche,[10] the duchess of Orléans who was the king of France's daughter,[11] the duchess of Anjou,[12] who is now known as the queen of Sicily, and others besides who were beautiful, chaste, honest, and wise, and also lesser noblewomen such as milady of La Ferté,[13] wife of Pierre de Craon, who are also greatly to be praised, and even others of whom it would be too long to speak here.

And do not think, dear sir, or let anyone else believe, that I am saying this or presenting this defense through favorable excuses because I am a woman, for the fact is that my motive is merely to uphold the truth as I know it by certain knowledge to be the opposite of these things I am objecting to; but as I am indeed a woman, I can bear better witness to the truth than those who have no experience of the state, but only speak through supposition or in general terms.

But after all these things, good heavens! Let us consider the end of said treatise, for as the proverb says, "All things are known by their end."[14] Let it therefore be seen and noted of what profit can possibly be the horrible and shameful end.[15] I say shameful? It is indeed so immoral that I dare say that nobody at all who loves virtue and honor could hear it without blushing for shame to find taken apart and put into shameful symbols what reason and modesty should restrain well-behaved people from even thinking. I dare say further that even the goliards[16] would be ashamed to read or hear it read in public in respectable places and before people they consider honorable. And what is so praiseworthy in reading matter which cannot be read or spoken of with propriety at the table of queens, princesses, and honorable women? If you wish to excuse it by saying that he wanted, by way of novelty, to portray the culmination of love in such images, I reply that he is not telling us anything new in this fashion! Don't we already know how men normally cohabit with women? If he were to tell us how bears or lions or birds or some other strange creatures mate, this might make amusing material for the telling of it, but he doesn't announce anything new to us. And no doubt it could have been said more agreeably and kindly and in a more courteous fashion. Would this not be more pleasing to gentle and courtly lovers, as well as to all other virtuous people?

Therefore, according to my small capacity and feeble judgment, without wasting any more words, even though there is more that could be said and surely better, I am of the opinion that all this was a great labor without any benefit. In spite of the fact that my judgment tells me that Master Jean de Meung was a very learned man and eloquent and would have been capable of writing a much better work, more profitable and with more elevated sentiments if he had tried, which is a pity, but I suppose that the great lechery which obsessed him perhaps made him more prejudiced than profitable, as by our actions our inclinations commonly reveal themselves. Nevertheless, I don't criticize all aspects of the *Romance of the Rose*, for there are certainly good things in it and well expressed, but that makes the peril all the greater, for the bad is accepted along with the good and true, and in just this way great errors have been subtly spread through being mixed and softened with truths. Just as his priest Genius says: "Flee! Flee women, the evil snakes in the grass," I say: "Flee! Flee all evil things hidden under cover of goodness and virtue."

Thus I say to you in conclusion, dear sir, and also to your allies and accomplices who praise the poem so greatly and magnify its merits to the point of diminishing the value of nearly every other book, it isn't really worthy of having such praise accorded it, and you do a great injustice to the more worthy ones, for a work without utility and beyond proper or common good—even admitting that it may be agreeable and represent a great amount of effort and labor—is not praiseworthy. As in the past the Roman triumphal entries[17] did not give praise or honor to anything which was not for the public welfare, let us consider their example to see if we should reward this *Romance*. It seems to me that I find, having considered all these things as well as a number of others, that it would be better shrouded in flames than crowned with laurel, in spite of your having called it "a mirror of the good life, an example to people of all classes in conducting themselves shrewdly and living religiously and wisely." I say, on the contrary, saving your grace, that it is rather an encouragement of vice giving comfort to a dissolute life, a doctrine full of deception, the road to perdition, public libel, a source of suspicion and disbelief, the shame of virtuous people, and perhaps even heresy.

I know very well that in excusing it you will reply that the good is there to be followed and the evil shunned. I can answer you by better reasoning that human nature, which is naturally inclined to vice, has no need to be reminded of the foot on which it limps in order to make it walk straight, and as for speaking of all the good to be found in the book, certainly more virtuous things, better said, more acceptable, and more profitable, even concerning living both a public and a private life, are to be found in other books, those written by the philosophers and the church doctors such as Aristotle, Seneca, Saint Paul, Saint Augustine, and many others (surely you know this yourself) which more worthily and fully bear witness to virtue and give instruction in following it and in avoiding vice than Master Jean de Meung would ever have known how to do, but they are not readily consulted by the lecherous and the worldly, for an ill person who is thirsty is pleased if the doctor allows him to drink a great deal, and because of his great thirst he willingly believes that it won't harm him to drink. This makes me very sure that you (may God grant you His grace) and all others led by His mercy to the light and purity of a clear conscience, without pollution of sin or the intention thereof, will be cleansed by contrition (whose sting clarifies the secrets of the conscience and as a judge of truth condemns prejudice) and may thus be led to a different opinion of the *Romance of the Rose*, and that you will perhaps wish that you had never seen it.

But let this suffice. And may it not be said that folly, arrogance, or presumption has led me, a woman, to dare to take to task and blame such a subtle author and diminish the praise of his work when he, one man alone, has dared to defame and blame without exception an entire sex.

The City of Ladies

2. 36. Against Those Who Say It Is Not Good for Women to Be Educated

After much discussion, I, Christine, said this: Lady, I can see very well that much good has come about because of women, and if a few bad ones have been the cause of some misfortune, it still appears to me that the good which has been done by the virtuous ones is far greater, especially by those who are wise and learned, notably in the sciences, as has already been mentioned here. Therefore, I am quite astonished at the opinion of some men who say that it isn't worthwhile for their daughters or wives or relatives to be educated and that their characters would indeed be the worse for it. Discretion replied: by this you can see very well that all opinions held by men are not based on reason, and that these in particular are mistaken, for it can scarcely be assumed that a knowledge of the moral sciences, which teach virtue, would affect the character adversely, as there can be little doubt that it would be improved and ennobled. How can one imagine and believe that one who learns a good lesson and doctrine will suffer from it? Such a thing should never be said or maintained. I do not say that it is desirable for either men or women to study the occult sciences,[18] or those which are forbidden, for the holy Church considers them without value and has removed them from ordinary use, but that any woman would be the worse for knowing the good ones is quite unacceptable.

Wasn't that the opinion of Quintus Hortensius,[19] the great orator and poet of Rome? He had a daughter named Hortensia, whom he loved greatly because of the subtlety of her intelligence, and he had her educated, studying especially the science of rhetoric, which she learned so well that, as Boccaccio tells it, she resembled her father not only in talent and good memory but also in every other way, in speaking well and in all sorts of speeches, so that he did not surpass her in any respect. With regard to what has been said of the benefit which comes about because of women, it resulted from that woman and her outstanding ability, for during the time when Rome was governed by a triumvirate, Hortensia undertook to defend the cause of women and to do what no man would have attempted with regard to certain taxes which were to be imposed on them for their jewels at a time when Rome was in need of money. The eloquence of that woman was so great, and as she was listened to no less respectfully than her father would have been, she won her case.

Likewise, speaking of more modern times without searching into ancient history, Giovanni Andreas,[20] the great legist at Bologna only sixty years ago, did not believe that it was bad for women to be educated when he instructed his beautiful and good daughter Novella, whom he loved greatly, so that she became so proficient in the law that when he was too occupied by some other affair to read his lectures to his classes, he sent his daughter Novella to lecture in his place. And so that her beauty would not distract her listeners, she had a little curtain placed before her, and in this manner she supplemented and sometimes lightened the work of her father, who was so fond of her that in order to have her name remembered he made one of his lectures into a legal text which he called Novella for his daughter.

Therefore not all men, and the wisest in particular, are of the opinion that it is a bad thing for women to be educated, though it is true that some who are not so wise say, because it displeases them, that women should not be allowed to know more than they. Your father, who was a great natural philosopher, did not believe that women were worth any less from studying, so that when he saw you attracted to learning, as indeed you are, he was very much pleased, but the feminine opinion of your mother, who wanted you to be occupied with girlish pursuits following the usual custom of women, was the reason that you were prevented from pursuing your studies farther and going into them more deeply. But according to the proverb already mentioned, what nature gives, none can take away, so your mother could not diminish your natural inclination to study, and you gathered up with both hands such little crumbs as were available to you, and I am sure you are none the worse for it, but rather consider it a great treasure. And certainly you are right.

And I, Christine, replied to her: certainly, Lady, what you say is as true as the Paternoster.

2. 54. After What Rectitude Has Said about Constant Wives, Christine Asks Her Why the Many Valiant Women Who Have Lived Before Have Not Contradicted the Books Written by Men Which Speak Ill of Them, and Rectitude's Reply

When Lady Rectitude had finished telling me all these things,[21] as well as a number of others which I have omitted for the sake of brevity (the case of Leontium the Greek woman,[22] for example, who never agreed, no matter how greatly she was tortured, to accuse two men that she knew even when they cut her tongue to her teeth before the judge so that there was no possibility of making her speak, and other women who were of such constant courage that they preferred to drink poison and die rather than give way before righteousness and truth), so in view of all this I said to her: Lady, you have shown me sufficiently the great constancy in woman's courage and other virtues as well, so that no more could be said of any man. Therefore, I am quite astonished at how many valiant women there have been, so wise and cultivated, who would have had the ability to write fine books, but who have suffered at such length without complaining of the many dreadful things which have been told about them by various men, when they knew very well that they weren't true.

Reply: dear friend, this question is easily enough answered. You can see, because I've already told you, how the women whose great merits I've described have been occupied in different sorts of work, and not all by the same thing. This work of building the city was reserved for you rather than for them, for enough women have been praised for their works from true understanding and appreciation without their having to write about it. As for the long time which has passed without their detractors and false witnesses being contradicted, I tell you that there is a proper moment for everything and each thing comes in its own time, just as God has suffered heresies against His holy law to exist in the world. These were rooted out with great difficulty and might still endure if they had not been contradicted and disputed. So it is with many other things which have gone on for a long time before being defeated and done away with.

Again I, Christine, said to her: Lady, you explain it very well, but I am certain that many complaints will arise among the critics of this present work, for they will say that even though some women may have been or are good, still all are not, nor even the majority.

Reply: it is not true that the majority aren't, and about this I have already said that every day one can see from experience instances of their devotion and charitable works and virtues, and it has been adequately proven that they are not the cause of the great horrors and evils which constantly beset the world. If all are not good, what a wonder! In all the city of Nineveh,[23] which was so great and so thickly inhabited, there was not one good man to be found when the prophet Jonah was sent there by our Lord to confound the city if it did not reform, nor were there any more in Sodom, it would appear, when Lot left it,[24] so that it was destroyed by heavenly fire. What is more, in the company of Jesus Christ there were only twelve men, and one of them was wicked, and yet men dare to say that all women ought to be good and that those who aren't ought to be stoned. I beg them to look at themselves, and the one without sin should cast the first stone.[25] Surely, I say, when they are perfect, women will then imitate them.

2. 55. Christine Asks Rectitude If It Is True, as Some Men Say, That There Are So Few Women Who Are Faithful in Love, with Rectitude's Reply

Continuing the conversation, I, Christine, said further: Lady, let us leave these questions, and departing a little from what we have been saying until now, I should like very much to ask you some other questions if I were sure that you wouldn't be annoyed because they are of a nature which is beyond the bounds of reason.

She replied to me: friend, say what you like, for the disciple who questions the master in order to learn should not be reproved no matter what he asks.

My lady, there exists in the world a natural law between men and women, and women and men, which was established not by human institutions but rather by the inclination of the senses, causing them to love each other with a great and unreasoning love which produces such a wild pleasure that they don't know why that love is produced in them. In that love, which is so widespread and which is known as the amorous life, men say that women, whatever they may promise, are far from constant, lacking in love, and wonderfully false and unpredictable, and that all of this comes from their natural frivolity. Among the writers who accuse them of this is Ovid in his *Book of the Art of Love*,[26] in which he makes them responsible for a great deal. When they have blamed them sufficiently for their shortcomings, Ovid and also others say that they put all these things in their books—their light morals and the tricks they play— for the common and public good in order to warn other men of their snares so that they will be able to avoid them like the snake concealed in the grass.[27] Tell me, please, dear lady, the truth about this matter.

Reply: dear friend, as for their saying that women are so deceitful, I don't know what more I can say to you, for you yourself have sufficiently treated the subject of Ovid and also others in your *Letter to the God of Love* and the *Letters on the Romance of the Rose*,[28] but as for their saying that they do it for the common good, I will show you that it is not for that at all, and here is the reason. Common or public good in a city or country or community of people exists only for the profit or general good of everyone, in which women as well as men participate and have their part. But whatever is done for the advantage of some but not for others would be called private or individual good rather than public, even less so when it is taken away from some in order to be conferred on others; such a good as this should be considered not only private or limited, but downright extortion against some in favor of others and to their detriment for the advantage of others, for they do not caution cruel women to avoid the deceptions of men, although it is certain that they deceive women by their tricks and pretenses, and there is no doubt that women are as much a part of God's people and are human beings quite as much as men, not a different species or created differently so that they should be left out of moral teachings. Thus I conclude that if it is to be for the common good, which is to say for both groups, they should also have warned women to avoid men's tricks as they have told men to beware of women. But let us leave this question and return to the other, which is that women are not so lacking in love when their hearts are engaged and that they are far more faithful than is said, as can be sufficiently proven by the examples of some of those who remained faithful until death, and first of all I will speak of the noble Dido, queen of Carthage, who has already been mentioned for her great valor, even though you yourself have already spoken of her in your own writings.[29]

The Book of Three Virtues

1. 12. The Life-Style of the Wise Princess, According to the Admonitions of Prudence

Prudence . . . will suggest to the wise princess how her life should be regulated by her teachings, so that she will follow some such regime as the following: she will rise early every morning and her first words will be addressed to God, saying: Lord, deign to keep me this day free from mortal sin, from sudden death, and from all misfortune, so may it be also with our family and our friends. Grant pardon to the dead and peace and tranquillity to all our subjects. Amen.

She will not expect to have around her any elaborate service, as was the habit of the good Queen Jeanne, formerly wife of the king of France, Charles V by name,[30] who during her lifetime arose every morning before daybreak, lit her own candle to recite her hours, and did not permit any of her servingwomen to get up and thus lose sleep. When the good princess is ready, she will go to hear mass, as often as her conscience dictates or according to the time she may have at her disposal, for there is no doubt that the lady who has been given some responsibility in the government, as certain lords have given to their ladies when they know them to be wise and good, and when they themselves are obliged to be absent and have given them charge and authority to govern their lands and to be the chief of their council, then such ladies should be excused, even by God, if they do not spend so much time in lengthy prayers as those who have greater leisure. They have no less merit for well and quietly attending to the welfare of all those in their power than if they spent more time in prayer . . . Such a lady will have arranged that as she leaves the chapel she will personally, with humility and devotion, give alms with her own hands, in recollection and as a sign that she does not despise the poor. And if there are any piteous requests to be made to her, she will listen to them kindly, always giving a gracious reply, and she will attend without delay to those requests which can be fulfilled at once. By doing this she will enhance not only the gift but her own reputation as well. If by chance she cannot hear all the requests, some virtuous man will accompany her who will be charged with listening to them, and she will see to it that he is charitable and capable of expediency, and she will above all see to it that he is honorable.

When all this has been accomplished, if the lady is charged with the government . . . she will go to the council on the days when it meets, and there she will show such presence, such bearing, and such a countenance as she sits on her high seat that she will indeed seem to be their ruler, and everyone will revere her as a wise mistress of great authority. Thus she will listen carefully to all that is proposed, and to the opinion of everyone present; she will take pains to remember the principal points of each problem and the conclusions, and she will note carefully which members speak best. Then after consideration and the best possible advice, she will make note of which seems to her the wisest and most valid opinion, but she will also give attention to the diversity of views, what causes and reasons inspire the speakers, so that she will be informed on all questions. When the time comes for her to speak or to reply, according to the circumstances, she will try to do it so wisely that she cannot be considered simple or ignorant. If she can be informed in advance as to what will be proposed in the council, and can be prepared for important matters by wise advice, it can only be to her advantage.

In addition to this, the lady will have appointed a certain number of competent gentlemen to be her advisers, those whom she knows to be good, intelligent and upright, and in no way greedy, for this is the fault which brings shame on everyone, as it has in the entourage of certain princes and princesses whose counselors are known to be greedy, for such as these encourage and advise the ones they are to counsel according to their own inclinations, and inevitably those who suffer from such a shortcoming will not give loyal and good advice for the profit of the soul or the honor of the body; therefore a prudent lady will inform herself in advance if her counselors are honorable and suitable men. She will then take counsel with them at a certain hour every day concerning the duties she must carry out.

After this morning session, she will go to the table, which on certain solemn feast days, or indeed even more frequently, will be set in the great hall, where she will seat herself among her ladies and handmaidens and other suitable people, each placed according to proper protocol. There she will be served as befits her and throughout the meal, following the fine old custom of queens and princesses, someone will be present to recite poems of ancient deeds, of virtuous ancestors, or some good morality or exemplary tale. Thus there will not be any great confusion in the hall. After the tables have been removed and the grace offered, if there are princesses or lords, knights or squires or ladies, or other strangers who have come to see her, as one well trained for such duties she will receive each one with due honor, so that everyone will be content. She will speak to everyone graciously and with a cheerful countenance, to the elderly in a more serious manner, to the young with more gaiety. And if they have come to talk, or to enjoy some entertainment, she will know how to conduct herself in such a gracious manner that all will say that she is a charming lady who bears herself well in all circumstances. After the spices have been served and the time has come to withdraw, she will go into her private apartments, where she will rest a little if need be. Then afterward, if it is a working day, and she has no more pressing occupation, in order to avoid idleness she will take up some handiwork, and she will gather her servingwomen and her ladies about her to do the same thing. In private she will allow them to indulge in all sorts of honest amusement, if they please, and will herself laugh with the others and will take pleasure in talking with them so informally that everyone will praise her great friendliness and kindness, and will love her with great devotion. She will remain thus until the hour of vespers, which she will hear in her chapel if it is a feast day and if no other occupation detains her, but she will not fail to say her prayers with her chaplain in any case, and after that, if it is summertime, she will enjoy herself in the garden until suppertime. She will wander here and there for the sake of her health. If there are some of her subjects who need her for certain causes, she will receive them and listen to them. After supper, toward her bedtime, her thoughts will return to God in prayer, and so will conclude the order of ordinary days for the prudent princess who is engaged in good and holy activity.

2. 10. How Ladies Who Live on Their Lands Should Conduct Themselves

A style of life somewhat different from that of baronesses is suitable for the simple ladies who live in fortified places or on their estates outside of the towns, but as most often knights, squires, and other gentlemen must travel to follow the wars, it befits their wives to be wise and able to manage their affairs capably, because they must spend much of their lives in their households without their husbands, who are often at court or even in distant countries. Thus it turns out that they may have the responsibility of managing their property and be placed in charge of their revenues and their lands, so it is important for any woman in such a situation, if she wants to act with good judgment, to know the yearly income of her estate. She should manage to the best of her abilities, by gentle word and good counsel addressed to her husband, to see to it that they confer together and agree to follow the course of action best suited to their revenues, so that at the year's end they do not find themselves in debt to their retainers or other creditors, for certainly there is no disgrace in leading one's life according to one's income, however small it may be, but it is rather shameful to live so extravagantly that every day creditors come to shout and bellow at the door, sometimes even raising a club in menace, or that it becomes necessary to offend one's men or tenants to the point where some sort of extortion results. It is important for such a lady to be informed about the rights of domain or fiefs, of secondary fiefs, contributions, the lord's rights of harvest, shared crops, and all such things as constitute the rights of possession according to the customs of various countries, so that she won't be misled. Because the world is full of governors of lands and of lords' jurisdictions, who are intentionally dishonest, she must also be aware of all this and be able to protect herself so that it won't turn to her disadvantage. If she is knowledgeable in accounts and often gives attention to them, she will also inform herself as to how her agents deal with her tenants or men, so that these will not be deceived or annoyed beyond reasonable bounds, for this would be against both her and her husband. In the matter of penalties against poor folk, she should be, for the love of God, more compassionate than rigorous.

With all these things, she should be a good manager, knowledgeable about farming, knowing in what weather and in what season the fields should be worked, the best way to have the furrows run according to the lay of the land, and whether it is dry or moist land, the depth of the furrows, and that they should be straight and evenly laid out and properly sown with seed suitable for the land. Likewise, she should know about the work in the vineyards, if the land should lie in a country where there are grapes, and she should see to it that she has good workers and supervisors in all such undertakings, and not hire people who change masters from season to season, for that is a bad sign, or workers who are too old, for they will be lazy and feeble, or too young, for they will be frivolous. She should also insist that they get up early, and if she is a good manager she will not depend on anyone else to see to this, but will herself arise, put on a cloak, go to the window, and watch to see them go out, for they are usually inclined to be lazy in this matter. She should often take her recreation in the fields in order to see how the work is progressing, for there are many who would willingly stop raking the ground beyond the surface if they thought nobody would notice, and there are those who are capable of sleeping in the shade of a willow tree in the field, leaving the workhorse or the oxen to graze meanwhile in a field, caring only to be able to say in the evening that they have put in their day. The good manager will keep her eye on all this. Furthermore, when the grain is ripening, even as early as the month of May, she will not wait for the season when labor is in short supply, but will engage her workers for August, taking good, strong, and diligent fellows, and she will arrange to pay them either with money or in grain. Then when the time comes for them to do this work, she will see to it, or have others verify, that they don't leave anything behind them or that they don't try any of the tricks that such people know how to practice on the unsuspecting. As with the other workers, she should get up early, for in the household where the mistress lies late abed things rarely go well. She should keep an eye on the entire household, for she will find plenty to oversee there, for usually indifference reigns where there is no supervision. She should have the sheep put out to pasture on schedule, taking note of how the shepherd looks after them and seeing to it that he knows his business and is not insolent, for shepherds feed their flocks as they want to in spite of master or mistress. She should make sure that the flocks are kept clean, protected from too much sun and from the rain, cured of the mange, so she will go herself to the roof, if she is wise, accompanied by one of her women, to observe how they are cared for. In this way the shepherd will be more careful to avoid cause for complaint. She will insist that he consider carefully when the lambs should be born, and take particular care of these lambs, for often they die from lack of care. She will give attention to raising proper food for them, will be present at the shearing, seeing to it that it is done in the proper season. And if her lands are in a warm and humid country where there are abundant meadows, she will have many horned animals, and if there is an abundance of oats which don't sell well, she will keep oxen in the manger, for they will earn her considerable money when they are fat. If she has woodlands, she will also have horses, which can be a profitable venture for anyone who knows how to make a success of it. She will take note of the time of winter when labor is cheap, and then she will have her walnut trees cut down to make stakes for the vineyards, which can be sold in the proper season, and then she will set her men to cutting wood to be stored for heating the house, or she will have them clear some field. If the weather is too cold outside, she will put them to work in the granary, and so she will never allow them to be idle, for nothing is more wasteful in a household.

Likewise, she will put her maids to looking after the animals, preparing food for the workers, taking care of the milk, weeding the gardens, hunting for herbs, even though it may muddy them up to the knees, for that is their duty. Meanwhile, she, her daughters, and her servants will undertake to make cloth, to separate the wool, sorting it and putting the fine strands aside to make cloth for her husband and herself, and to sell, if need be. The thick strands should be used for the small children, the servingwomen, and the workmen. She will make bedcovers from the large balls of wool.

She will have hemp grown on the anthills, which her servants will work and spin during the long winter evenings to make into coarse linen, and many other things which it would take too long to describe here.

In the Netherlands there is much skill in household management, and the woman who is most diligent, however important she may be, is considered the wisest and is praised for it. By following these practices the skilled housekeeper sometimes brings in greater profit than the revenue from the land itself, as was the case with that wise and prudent manager the countess of Eu, the mother of the young count who died in Hungary,[31] who was not ashamed to give herself to the honest work of her household to such an extent that the profit from it was larger than the revenue from her land. Of such a woman one can well repeat the praise concerning a wise woman from the Book of Solomon.

3. 3. The Wives of Merchants

Now we come to speak of the wives of merchants, that is to say of men who are engaged in commerce, of whom there are some very rich ones in Paris, whose wives maintain great and expensive standing. This is even more true in other cities and countries than in Paris, such as Venice, Genoa, Florence, Lucca, Avignon, and elsewhere, but in those places they are more to be excused than in France, even though extravagance is never a good thing, because there is not so much difference among the upper classes as there is in Paris and hereabout. That is to say that there are queens, duchesses, countesses, and other ladies and demoiselles among whom the differences are more marked. Therefore in France, which is the noblest realm in the world, and where everything should be most orderly, as provided for in the ancient customs of France, it is not fitting that it should be otherwise. It has been pointed out several times already that the wife of a laborer in the Low Countries has the same status as the wife of an ordinary artisan in Paris, but the wife of an ordinary artisan does not have the rank of a burgher's wife, nor does she, in turn, have the status of a demoiselle, nor the demoiselle that of a lady, nor the lady that of a countess or duchess, nor the duchess that of a queen. Each should maintain her proper place in society, and along with this the proper differences in life-style should be observed in each case. But these rules are not at all well observed in France today, nor are many of the other good customs which used to be kept. For this reason there have never been such outrageous pride and snobbery among all sorts of people from the great to the small as exist now, and one can be sure of this from the chronicles and histories of antiquity. It is for this reason we have explained that in Italy women have greater status, although it is true that it is not as costly to maintain as it is here. All are to be judged by the company they keep and the follies they commit, whereby they try to surpass one another as much as by what they wear.

And since we are speaking of merchants' wives, wasn't it truly outrageous for one of them to behave in such a fashion as this? Not at all like merchants' wives of Venice or Genoa, who travel overseas and have their representatives in other countries, buying at wholesale and conducting business on a large scale, and likewise sending merchandise to other countries in large bundles, and thus earn their wealth. Such as these are called noble merchants, but those of whom we are speaking buy at wholesale and sell at retail, for four crowns' worth of merchandise, if need be, or for more, or even less, if they are wealthy, and yet they put on airs and there are plenty of them who do it. But this particular woman made such a display of the lying-in for a child she had recently. Before one entered her own room, one passed through two others, in each of which there was a large ornamental bed, richly curtained, and in the second there was a large dresser arrayed like an altar, all covered with silver vessels. And then from that room one entered the woman's chamber, which was large and handsome and all hung with tapestries marked with her coat of arms richly worked in fine gold thread of Cyprus, the large bed well curtained with a single hanging, and the rugs surrounding the bed, on which one walked, were likewise worked in gold, the great display sheets spread wide beneath the coverlet were of such fine Reims linen that they were valued at three hundred francs, and over the coverlet, which was woven with threads of gold, there was another great coverlet of linen as fine as silk, all in one piece without seams (something newly invented and very expensive), which one might estimate to be worth two hundred francs or more, and moreover, it was so long and so wide that it covered the large bed completely, hanging over the edge of the coverlet already mentioned, covering it on all sides. In that room there was a great dresser all covered with gilded vessels. And in the bed was the woman, dressed in crimson silk, propped up against great pillows covered in the same silk and decorated with pearl buttons, and she was wearing the headdress of a lady. And God knows what other extravagances there were for celebrations, baths, and various gatherings according to Parisian customs for lyings-in, some more, some less, but in this case so much that the outrage surpassed all others, even though there are others similar, and so it is worth mentioning in this book. So the affair was reported in the queen's chamber, whereupon someone remarked that the Parisians have too much blood, which sometimes brings on certain maladies, which is to say that great wealth is capable of leading them astray, and for this reason it would be better if the king were to put some tax, loan, or tithe on them so that their wives would not be tempted to try to rival the queen of France, who could scarcely do more.[32] So such things are out of proportion, and they come from presumption rather than good judgment, for those who practice them gain scorn rather than merit because of them, for although they take on the status of great ladies or princesses, that is by no means what they really are, and they are not called such, for they do not lose the name of merchant's wife. Indeed, in Lombardy they don't even call such as these merchants, but rather retailers, as they sell in small lots. So it is a great folly to dress up in somebody else's costume when everyone knows who she really is, which is to say to take on the estate which belongs to somebody else rather than to be content with one's own . . . Such people must be considered disguised, and we do not say this to diminish their honor, for as we have already said, the merchant's place is excellent and good for anyone who fills it properly. We say this with good intent in order to offer counsel and advice to the wives to whom we speak, that they should avoid such extravagances, for such things are good for neither the body nor the soul, and can indeed be the cause of new taxes for their husbands. So it is better for them to wear suitable clothes, properly adapted to their lives, which can be handsome, rich, and honest without any pretensions to being something other than what they are, no matter how rich they may be . . .

NOTES TO THE TRANSLATION

1. This passage is taken from Christine's first letter in the debate, written during the summer of 1401 (Hicks, ed. pp. 15–22). I am most indebted to Professor Hicks for the valuable advice he has given me with regard to this translation.

2. Christine is referring to the extraordinary misogyny of Nature's confession to Genius, in vv. 16293–16676 of the *Romance of the Rose*. The references here are to the Harry W. Robbins translation, pp. 347 ff. The discourse of the Jealous Husband is to be found in vv. 8437–9330, pp. 171–188.

3. This is an allusion to ibid., vv. 16548–16586, p. 354, which includes these lines:

Beware! Beware! Beware! Beware! Beware!
Good fellows, flee, I charge and counsel you,
Without deceit or guile, from such a beast!
Note Vergil's words, and plant them in your hearts
So that they never can be rooted out:
"O children, who pluck strawberries and flowers
So clean and fresh, flee from the serpent cold
That's lying in the grass."

The reference is to Virgil's *Bucolics* 3. 92–93. Jean Gerson will refer to the same passage in one of his sermons at the end of 1402 (*Oeuvres complètes*, ed. P. Glorieux, vol. 7, p. 826, and Hicks, ed., p. 201). Christine will also cite this passage again in the *Cité des dames*.

4. This is an allusion to advice given by Genius, vv. 16347–16706, p. 349:

A man who trusts his secrets to his wife
Makes her his mistress. None of women born,
Unless he's drunk or crazy, will reveal
To women anything that should be hid,
Unless he wants to hear it coming back
To him from others. Better 'twere to flee
From out the land than tell his wife to keep
A secret, though she meek and loyal be.
Nor will he any secret act perform
In presence of a woman, for she'll tell
About it soon or late, though it involve
For him a mortal peril.

5. Roy, ed., vol. 2, pp. 1–27.

6. Christine returns to this same theme in both the *Cité des dames* and the *Livre des trois vertus*.

7. One of Christine's favorite sources was the *Histoire ancienne jusqu'à César*. See Campbell, *L'Epître d'Othéa*, pp. 87–89; *Livre de la mutacion de fortune*, ed. Suzanne Solente, vol. 1, pp. lxiii–xcii; and Towner, ed., p. 163.

8. For Sarah, see Genesis 17–22; for Rebecca, see Genesis 24–28. These are to be found

in the *Histoire ancienne*. See the *Mutacion de fortune*, ed. Solente, vol. 1, pp. lxvii–lxix, lxxi. The same examples are used again in the *Cité des dames* 2. 38–39; Judith is mentioned in the *Cité des dames* 2. 31, the *Livre de la paix*, and the *Dittié de Jeanne d'Arc*, Esther in the *Lettre à Isabeau de Bavière* and the *Cité des dames* 2. 32.

9. Although Hicks sees here a reference to Jeanne d'Evreux, third wife of Charles IV, it seems more likely that Christine was referring to Charles V's queen, Jeanne de Bourbon (1338–1377), who was undoubtedly her model for the virtuous queen described in the *Livre des trois vertus* 1. 12.

10. Blanche of Navarre (1331–1398), second wife of Philip VI of France. She is also mentioned in the *Livre de faits et bonnes meurs du sage Roy Charles V*, ed. Suzanne Solente, vol. 1, p. 55, the *Cité des dames* 1. 12, and the *Livre des trois vertus* 1. 11.

11. Blanche of France, duchess of Orléans (1328–1393), daughter of Charles IV and Jeanne d'Evreux, likewise mentioned in the *Faits et bonnes meurs de Charles V*, ed. Solente, vol. 2, p. 122, the *Cité des dames* 1. 12, and the *Livre des trois vertus* 1. 23.

12. Jeanne of Anjou—better known as the queen of Sicily—who was assassinated in 1382 after having made Louis of Anjou, Charles V's younger brother, her heir. This prince undertook a military expedition to Italy in the same year against her third husband, Charles of Durazzo. Christine speaks of her, and her murder, in the *Livre du chemin de long estude*, ed. Robert Püschel, p. 157; the *Faits et bonnes meurs de Charles V*, ed. Solente, vol. 1, pp. 138–139, vol. 2, pp. 204–205; and the *Mutacion de fortune*, ed. Solente, vol. 4, pp. 72–73.

13. Jeanne de Chastillon (died 1433), lady of Rosay en Thiérarche, wife of the Breton nobleman Pierre de Craon, whose lands, after his attack on Constable Olivier de Clisson, were confiscated by the crown and given to the king's brother, Louis of Orléans.

14. A common proverb listed by both Le Roux de Lancy, *Le livre des proverbes*, vol. 2, p. 324, and J. Morawski, *Proverbes français antérieurs au XVᵉ siècle*, no. 44.

15. The conclusion of the *Romance of the Rose*, pp. 454–461. To judge from such a copy as the early fifteenth-century Valencia MS 387, the illustrations must have added to the scandal in certain cases. See J. V. Flemming, *The Roman de la Rose: A Study in Allegory and Iconography*, especially the illustrations at the end.

16. Goliards were wandering students who wrote satiric Latin verses and who often served as minstrels or buffoons. Christine usually spoke of them with scorn.

17. Christine describes this Roman custom of triumphal entries in the *Livre du corps de policie*, ed. Robert H. Lucas, pp. 33–34, 73, 89, 111. The probable source of her knowledge was the translation of Valerius Maximus made at the end of the fourteenth century by Simon of Hesdin and Nicolas of Gonesse.

18. See, for instance, T. O. Wedel, *The Medieval Attitude toward Astrology, Particularly in England*.

19. The story of Quintus Hortensius and his daughter is taken from Boccaccio's *De claris mulieribus* 82.

20. Giovanni Andreas would have been at the University of Bologna while Christine's father was there, so she is probably telling this tale on his authority. Professor Oskar Kristeller accepts it with some hesitation, however. See his "Learned Women of Early Modern Italy: Humanists and University Scholars," pp. 102–114.

21. This selection follows Christine's recounting of the examples of Florence of Rome, based on a thirteenth-century combination epic and adventure tale; of Bernabo of Genoa's wife, inspired by Boccaccio's *Decameron*; and of Griselda, whose story Christine undoubtedly knew through Petrarch's version of the tale, although it is not certain whether she knew it directly or through the French translation of Philippe de Mézières. For these last two women, see Carla Bozzolo, "Il *Decameron* come fonte del *Livre de la Cité des Dames* di Christine de Pisan," pp. 3–24.

22. The case of Leontium is told in Boccaccio's *De Casibus* 58.

23. The story of Jonah's warning, recounted after the Old Testament book of Jonah 3, is also mentioned by Christine in the *Mutacion de fortune*, vv. 4246–4272.

24. Lot and Sodom are also mentioned in the *Mutacion de fortune*, vv. 4223–4230.

25. This is an allusion to a passage from the story of the woman taken in adultery, John 8:7.

26. Christine paid her disrespect to Ovid's *Ars Amatoria* in her *Letter from the God of Love*; she thought it would be better named the *Art of Great Deception* (v. 377). She could have known it through a French translation, a copy of which is known to have been included in the duke of Berry's library. See Meiss, p. 288.

27. See n. 3.

28. See n. 5 and the first section of the translation.

29. Christine had already recounted Dido's part in the foundation of Carthage in book 7 of the *Mutacion de fortune* and included a chapter on her in the first part of the *Cité des dames*—"Of the Prudence of Queen Dido."

30. See n. 9.

31. Philip of Artois, count of Eu (1387–1397) and constable of France (1392–1397), was an enthusiastic crusader against the Turks. One of the survivors of the French disaster at Nicopolis in 1396, he died in Turkish captivity the following year, shortly before the duke of Burgundy was able to ransom his son, Jean of Nevers, and his companions. His mother was Isabelle of Melun.

32. The accounts for the lying-in of the duke of Burgundy's daughter-in-law, Jeanne of Saint-Pol, countess of Rethel, in 1403 are no more elaborate. See E. Petit, *Itinéraires de Philippe le Hardi et de Jean sans Peur*, pp. 568–573.

BIBLIOGRAPHY

Primary Works

The Book of the City of Ladies. Trans. Earl Jeffrey Richards. Foreword by Marina Warner. New York, 1982.

Bühler, Curt F., ed. *The Epistle of Othea*. London, 1970.

Byles, A. T. P., ed. *The Book of Fayttes of Armes and of Chyvalerye*. London, 1937.

du Castel (de Pisan), Christine. *The Morale Proverbes of Christyne*. New York, 1970.

Cerquilini, Jacqueline, ed. *Cent ballades d'amant et de dame*. Paris, 1982.

Gollancz, Israel, ed. "Letter of Cupid." In his *Hoccleve's Works: The Minor Poems*. London, 1925.

Hicks, Eric, ed. *Le débat sur le Roman de la rose*. Paris, 1977.

Kennedy, Angus J., ed. *Lamentacion sur les maux de la France*. In *Mélanges de langue et littéraire françaises du Moyen Age et de la Renaissance offerts à Charles Foulon*, vol. 1, pp. 177–185. Rennes, 1980.

―――― and Kenneth Varty, eds. *Dittié de Jeanne d'Arc*. Oxford, 1977.

Legge, M. Dominica, ed. *Anglo-Norman Letters and Petitions from All Souls MS 182*. Oxford, 1971.

Lucas, Robert H., ed. *Livre du corps de policie*. Geneva, 1967.

Püschel, Robert, ed. *Livre du chemin de long estude*. 1881. Reprint. Geneva, 1974.

Rains, Ruth Ringland, ed. *Sept psaumes allegorisés*. Washington, D.C., 1965.

Roy, Maurice, ed. *Oeuvres poétiques de Christine de Pisan*. 3 vols. Paris, 1886–1896.

Solente, Suzanne, ed. *L'Epistre de la prison de vie humaine.* In "Un traité inédit de Christine de Pisan," *Bibliothèque de l'Ecole des Chartes* 85 (1924): 263–301.
———, ed. *Livre de la mutacion de fortune.* 4 vols. Paris, 1959–1966.
———, ed. *Livre des faits et bonnes meurs du sage Roy Charles V.* 2 vols. Paris, 1936–1941.
Towner, Sister Mary Louise, ed. *L'Avision-Christine.* Washington, D.C., 1932.
Varty, Kenneth, ed. *Christine de Pisan: Balades, Rondeaux and Virelais.* Leicester, 1965.
Willard, Charity Cannon, ed. *Livre de la paix.* The Hague, 1958.

Related Works

Beck, Frederick, ed. *Les epistres sur le Roman de la rose.* Neuburg, 1888.
Bornstein, Diane. "Humanism in Christine de Pisan's *Livre du Corps de Policie.*" *Les Bonnes Feuilles* 3 (1974): 100–115.
———, ed. *Ideals for Women in the Works of Christine de Pizan.* [Detroit?], 1981.
Bozzolo, Carla. "Il *Decameron* come fonte del *Livre de la Cité des Dames* di Christine de Pisan." In *Miscellanea di studi e ricerche sul Quattrocento Francese,* ed. Franco Simone, pp. 3–24. Turin, 1967.
———. *Manuscrits des traductions françaises d'oeuvres de Boccace: XVᵉ siècle.* Padua, 1973.
Campbell, P. G. C. "Christine de Pisan en Angleterre." *Revue de Littérature Comparée* 5 (1925): 659–670.
———. *L'Epître d'Othéa: Etude sur les sources de Christine de Pisan.* Paris, 1924.
Coville, A. *Gontier et Pierre Col et l'humanisme en France au temps de Charles VI.* Paris, 1934.
Curnow, Maureen Cheney. "*The Boke of the Cyte of Ladyes,* an English Translation of Christine de Pisan's *Le Livre de la Cité des Dames.*" *Les Bonnes Feuilles* 3 (1974): 116–137.
Doutrepont, G. *La littérature française à la cour des ducs de Bourgogne.* Paris, 1909.
Du Castel, Françoise. *Damoiselle Christine de Pisan, veuve de M. Etienne de Castel.* Paris, 1972.
Dulac, Liliane. "Un écrit militant de Christine de Pisan: Le Dittié de Jeanne d'Arc." In *Aspects of Female Existence,* pp. 115–134. Gyldendal, 1980.
———. "Un mythe didactique chez Christine de Pisan: Sémiramis ou la Veuve Héroïque, du *De Claris Mulieribus* de Boccace à la *Cité des Dames.*" In *Mélanges de philologie romane offerts à Charles Camproux,* vol. 1, pp. 315–343. Montpellier, 1978.
Fantuzzi, Giovanni. *Notizie degli scrittori Bolognesi.* Vol. 7. Bologna, 1789.
Finkel, Helen Ruth. "The Portrait of the Woman in the Works of Christine de Pisan." *Les Bonnes Feuilles* 3 (1974): 138–151.
Flemming, J. V. *The Roman de la Rose: A Study in Allegory and Iconography.* Princeton, 1969.
Hicks, Eric, and Ezio Ornato. "Jean de Montreuil et le débat sur le *Roman de la rose.*" *Romania* 98 (1977): 34–64, 186–219.
Hortis, A. *Studi sulle opere latine del Boccaccio.* Trieste, 1879.
Ignatius, Mary Ann. "Christine de Pizan's *Epistre Othea:* An Experiment in Literary Form." *Medievalia et Humanistica,* n.s. 9 (1979): 127–142.
———. "A Look at the Feminism of Christine de Pizan." *Proceedings of the Pacific Northwest Conference on Foreign Languages* 29 (1978): 18–21.

Jeanroy, A. "Boccace et Christine de Pisan: Le 'De Claris Mulieribus,' principale source du 'Livre de la Cité des Dames.'" *Romania* 48 (1922): 92–105.

Kemp-Welch, Alice. *Of Six Medieval Women.* 1913. Reprint. Williamstown, Mass., 1972.

Kristeller, Oskar. "Learned Women of Early Modern Italy: Humanists and University Scholars." In *Beyond Their Sex: Learned Women of the European Past,* ed. Patricia H. Labalme, pp. 102–114. New York, 1980.

Läigle, Mathilde. *Le livre des trois vertus de Christine de Pisan et son milieu historique et littéraire.* Paris, 1912.

Lancy, Le Roux de. *Le livre des proverbes.* 2 vols. Paris, 1842.

Langlois, E. "Le traité de Gerson contre le Roman de la rose." *Romania* 45 (1918–1919): 23–48.

Lanson, G. *Histoire de la littérature française.* Paris, 1895.

Lecoy, F. "Note sur quelques balades de Christine de Pisan." In *Fin du Moyen Age et Renaissance: Mélanges de philologie offerts à Robert Guiette,* pp. 107–114. Antwerp, 1961.

LeGentil, Pierre. "Christine de Pisan, poète méconnu." In *Mélanges d'histoire littéraire offerts à Daniel Mornet,* pp. 1–10. Paris, 1951.

Lynn, Thérèse Ballet. "The Dittié de Jeanne d'Arc: Its Political, Feminist and Aesthetic Significance." *Fifteenth Century Studies* 1 (1978): 149–157.

McCleod, Enid. *The Order of the Rose: The Life and Ideas of Christine de Pizan.* London, 1976.

Meiss, Millard. *French Painting in the Time of Jean de Berry: The Limbourgs and Their Contemporaries.* New York, 1974.

Mombello, Gianni. "Per un'edizione critica dell'*Epistre Othea* di Christine de Pizan." *Studi Francesi* 24 (1964): 401–417; 25 (1965): 1–12.

———. "Quelques aspects de la pensée politique de Christine de Pizan d'après ses oeuvres publiées." In *Culture et politique en France à l'époque de l'humanisme et de la Renaissance,* ed. Franco Simone, pp. 43–153. Turin, 1974.

———. "Recherches sur l'origine du nom de la Déesse Othea." *Atti della Accademia delle Scienze di Torino* 103 (1968–1969): 1–33.

———. *La tradizione manoscritta dell'Epistre Othea di Christine de Pizan.* Turin, 1967.

Morawski, J. *Proverbes français antérieurs au XVe siècle.* Paris, 1925.

Nicolini, Elena. "Cristina da Pizzano, l'origine e il nome." *Cultura Neolatina* 1 (1941): 143–150.

Nys, Ernest. *Christine de Pisan et ses principales oeuvres.* Brussels, 1914.

Ouy, Gilbert. "Paris, l'un des principaux foyers de l'humanisme en Europe au début du XVe siècle." *Bulletin de la Société de Paris et de l'Ile-de-France* (1967–1968): 72–98.

——— and Christine M. Reno. "Identification des autographes de Christine de Pizan." *Scriptorium.* Forthcoming.

Petit, E. *Itinéraires de Philippe le Hardi et de Jean sans Peur.* Paris, 1888.

Piaget, A. "Chronologie des épîtres sur le *Roman de la rose.*" In *Etudes romanes dediées à Gaston Paris,* pp. 113–120. Paris, 1891.

Pinet, Marie-Josèphe. *Christine de Pisan, 1364–1430: Etude biographique et littéraire.* Paris, 1927.

Poirion, Daniel. *Le poète et le prince: L'Evolution du lyrisme courtois de Guillaume de Machaut à Charles d'Orléans.* Paris, 1965.

Potansky, Peter. *Der Streit um den Rosenroman.* Munich, 1972.

Richardson, Lula McDowell. *The Forerunners of Feminism in French Literature of the Renaissance.* Baltimore, 1929.

Robbins, Harry W., ed. and trans. *The Romance of the Rose.* New York, 1962.

Schaefer, Lucie. "Die Illustrationen zu den Handschriften der Christine de Pizan." *Marburger Jahrbuch für Kunstwissenschaft* 10 (1937).

Solente, Suzanne. "Christine de Pisan." *L'Histoire Littéraire de la France* 40 (1969).

Tuve, Rosamund. *Allegorical Imagery: Some Medieval Books and Their Posterity.* Princeton, 1966.

Ward, F. *The Epistles on the Romance of the Rose and Other Documents in the Debate.* Chicago, 1911.

Wedel, T. O. *The Medieval Attitude toward Astrology, Particularly in England.* New Haven, 1920.

Willard, Charity Cannon. "An Autograph Manuscript of Christine de Pisan?" *Studi Francesi* 27 (1965): 452–457.

———. "Christine de Pisan's Treatise on the Art of Medieval Warfare." In *Essays in Honor of Louis Francis Solano*, ed. R. J. Cormier and U. T. Holmes, pp. 179–191. Chapel Hill, 1970.

———. "A Fifteenth-Century View of Women's Role in Medieval Society." In *The Role of Women in the Middle Ages*, ed. R. T. Morewedge, pp. 90–120. Albany, 1975.

———. "Lovers' Dialogues in Christine de Pizan's Lyric Poetry from the *Cent Balades* to the *Cent Balades d'Amant et de Dame*." *Fifteenth Century Studies* 4 (1981): 167–180.

———. "The Manuscript Tradition of the *Livre des Trois Vertus* and Christine de Pizan's Audience." *Journal of the History of Ideas* 27 (1966): 433–444.

———. "A Re-Examination of *Le Débat de Deux Amants*." *Les Bonnes Feuilles* 3 (1974): 73–88.

———. "An Unknown Manuscript of Christine de Pizan's *Livre de la Paix*." *Studi Francesi* 64 (1978): 90–97.

notes on contributors

JOSEPH BERRIGAN is professor of history and director of the Medieval Studies Program at the University of Georgia.

GWENDOLYN BRYANT is an instructor at the American Institute at Lugano.

PETER DRONKE is professor of medieval languages and literatures at the University of Cambridge, England.

JOAN M. FERRANTE is professor of comparative literature and Romance languages at Columbia University.

JOHN HOWARD is associate professor of Germanic languages at the University of Georgia.

CATHERINE JONES is completing her dissertation for the University of York, England.

KENT KRAFT is assistant professor of comparative literature at the University of Georgia.

JAMES MARCHAND is professor of Germanic literature at the University of Illinois.

BARBARA OBRIST is professor at the Gymnasium am Kohlenberg, Basel.

WILLIAM PROVOST is assistant professor of English at the University of Georgia.

BETTY RADICE is editor of the Penguin Classical Series.

JOSEPH SNOW is associate professor of Romance languages at the University of Georgia.

RIA VANDERAUWERA is fellow of the Dutch Academy of Sciences.

CHARITY CANNON WILLARD is professor emerita of Ladycliff College.

KATHARINA M. WILSON is assistant professor of comparative literature at the University of Georgia.